Writing

POST-CONTEMPORARY INTERVENTIONS

Series Editors • Stanley Fish and Fredric Jameson

Writing

The Political Test

CLAUDE LEFORT   *David Ames Curtis, Translator*

Duke University Press   Durham and London 2000

© 2000 Duke University Press

All rights reserved

Printed in the United States of America on acid-free paper ∞

Typeset in Minion by Tseng Information Systems, Inc.

Library of Congress Cataloging-in-Publication Data appear
on the last printed page of this book.

The translation presents selections from Claude Lefort's
Écrire. À l'épreuve du politique, © 1992 Fondation
Saint-Simon/Calmann-Lévy.

Assistance for the translation was provided by the
French Ministry of Culture.

Contents

Translator's Foreword

S o, you, the reader, have found yourself here, which is perhaps as good a place to start, or to end, as anywhere else. Perhaps you are
looking for words of explanation as to what the author I have chosen to
translate has wanted to say, or—the height of embarrassment for a translator, whose role is eminently self-effacing (though, as I have written before,[1] there is also on the translator's part a civic duty of *presentation* of a
translated author, as well as of *self-presentation,* in the transnational Republic of Letters)—what I myself have to say. Perhaps you have come across this
sentence by pure accident. Or, perhaps—a greater (?) embarrassment—you
have been assigned these lines as a textbook example of how not to begin a
translator's foreword. In any case, you, the reader of the published version
of the present text, are someone I probably do not know, from a millen-
nium in which I have not (yet) lived. Almost everything I have to say to you
to whom I address these lines is enveloped in the precarious indeterminacy
of our only now commencing dialogue—your personality, your experience,
your motivations remain in suspense as I write these lines which I am constantly going back over to revise, not sure, beyond a vague outline and a
general sense of both form and content, what it is I have to say or what you
might be expecting, and yet I write them to you and you, somehow, are
reading them and trying to discern what purpose, if any, may lie behind the
generalities I have recorded so far. Even the physical basis by which these
words come to you has been opened to question: recently, I myself read (on
newsprint) a piece about the advent of the e-book, and the day thereafter I
read (again on newsprint) that DNA, apparently an excellent electrical con-
ductor, could replace silicon chips (which I am now using to write to you),
so that that former support for ink, dead trees ground to pulp, might one
day be supplanted by some kind of engaged symbiotic encounter with an

organic machine (a twentieth-century writer takes this last phrase to be an oxymoron),[2] thus making possible in a new and unforeseeable way what is already (still?) being described as a discreet and unique "event" conjured up in hypercyberspace.

What, in order to go on, can be retained from the foregoing? I take the word *encounter*—more specifically, an open-ended, vulnerable, never fully assured and always to be recommended improvisatory experience whereby the subjective and objective elements in both reading and writing do not so much "meet" as arise together within a temporally diffuse and divided space, one surrounded on all sides by question marks—therefore bounded, but in an abeyant, interrogative mode. This choice of word, and my other word choices so far, it may already be obvious, have been made in response to some of the themes raised in the book I have chosen to translate, which includes extensive and wide-ranging reflections on the arts of reading and writing.

I could thus cite here some general reflections the author Claude Lefort shares with us while discussing "Machiavelli's writing art":

> If one wants to know the intentions of a writer, it seems worthwhile to ask oneself who are his privileged interlocutors, what are the opinions he targets, what are the circumstances that summon up his desire to speak. Let us note in passing that, in order to account for his thinking, it doesn't suffice to answer these questions, supposing that one could, for it is equally true that he writes for no one, that he becomes intimate with a reader who has no definite identity. The reader's place will be occupied, in a future he could not imagine, by unknown people. And again it is true that he draws on circumstances for an ability to think that transcends the contingency of his situation.

A multifaceted sense of uncertainty would therefore seem essential to the writer's situation and to his relationship to his reader. In order to look at the other half of this variable equation and to see if it has any solution, we could turn to Lefort's thoughts on "the art of reading," inspired by his examination of the Marquis de Sade's combination of his writing art with an "art of *jouissance*":

> What I mean to say, in short, is that every reading of a text implies, for the one who reads it, some manner of saying it to oneself—and, always already, some manner of interpreting it, simply by the inflection one gives to the words, the rhythm to the phrase, by a modulation of speech that in oneself remains unpronounced. One does not read Molière as one reads Racine or Descartes. But the difference is not dic-

tated entirely by the text; it also arises from the operations performed by the reader. Indeed, what would be the point of learning to read if not to decipher and to communicate what are called "messages"? The thing is well known, but usually everything happens as if this knowledge served no purpose. Ordinarily, we are reluctant to admit that the interpretation based on one's understanding, the learned interpretation, is inseparable from this first sensible interpretation of which every reading is made. And there is an indefinable shuttling back and forth between them. It is one's manner of reading that leads to understanding, and it is also one's understanding that leads to rereading, to rearticulating, to scanning the text in another way. Of course, the distance between the actor-performer [*l'interprète-acteur*] on stage and the scholar-interpreter may be unbridgeable, but there is still a sort of mediation: the art of reading, which is impossible to define.

In this latter case, writing and its art seem to come partially to the rescue, when faced with the avowed impossibility of providing any reliable definition for this art of reading; for, Lefort continues: "Since I have just advanced the idea that the manner of reading is not dictated entirely by the text, I must qualify this statement by adding that it is nevertheless from the power of a piece of writing that a reading draws its power. For, the reader knows that there has to be a proper reading." And yet this comforting talk about a "proper reading" suggested by the power of writing proves to be only a prelude to his introduction of the disturbing idea that there is an inherent "insecurity of reading" and to his assertion that, furthermore, Sade's own writing is of a sort to "throw us into a state of the greatest insecurity." Speaking, in another chapter — "Philosopher?" — of philosophy's potential relationship to nonphilosophical writing (we are reminded here of Maurice Merleau-Ponty's "Philosophy and Non-Philosophy since Hegel," a posthumous text Lefort himself edited),[3] he goes on to ask himself: "What remains, then, of the exigency of philosophy . . . that prompts one indeed to declare that it can manifest itself in writings that do not know that they are philosophical?" and he admits: "I still couldn't find an answer to a question like that. But it doesn't seem to me to be a futile one because it leaves me disarmed." An interesting response indeed, one that indicates that the uncertainty, and the danger, of any true thought by which writing and reading might attempt to advance are not only ineluctable but, as far as he is concerned, also in some way welcome.

In providing you with these quotations, I am, however, getting ahead of, or perhaps behind, myself. For, I have offered the reader a series of English words that Lefort himself has never spoken or written: all the words chosen in this translation have been chosen by me[4] — a crushingly banal point, except if we reflect upon the strange situation of the translator, who, in performing his daunting and nearly absurd job, imagines himself over an extended and exhausting period of time to be someone who not only isn't himself but also doesn't exist — in this case, a native English-speaking "Claude Lefort" — while at the same time endeavoring in some creative and indefinable way to "retain" within the translated text a sufficiently alien presence, so that the translation can also honestly fulfill its eminent, though implicit, civic purpose — that is, the introduction of foreign ideas into what we think of as a determinate yet evolving literary community or "body politic," so as to open that body to the possibility of a considered assimilation of something that is not (yet) itself. It is in emerging from this experience of speaking (writing through translating) in an imaginary voice that is not my own — that is, strictly, no one's and that will now somehow live on, in its own right and closely associated with Lefort and, to a lesser extent, with myself — that I, changed forever by this disconcerting and destabilizing experience, try to find again my own voice in order to indicate to you in writing some provisional guidelines for reading what I have, and yet have not, written in this translation.

It will perhaps not be surprising if I now say that another word I could retain from the first paragraph, besides *encounter,* is *embarrassment.* The discomfort built into the constant insecurity of the translation encounter is an experience every translator knows unmistakably, in his constant hesitations as well as in his ultimate choices. That old adage, *traduttore, traditore* (the translator as traitor), is manifestly true, yet it speaks to the translator's experience only to the extent that the translator has also adopted the apparently contradictory, yet truly complementary, project of rendering a "faithful" translation — which is an infinite and impossible yet unavoidably necessary as well as positively desirable task.

I could begin my endless list of embarrassments with the problems surrounding my translation of the book's subtitle. Whereas the title, *Écrire,* is fairly straightforward — "writing" or "to write" (though the entire book is an extended meditation on what it means to write!) — this subtitle, *À l'épreuve du politique,* has posed fairly insurmountable problems. An *épreuve* is a "test," a "trial," even an "ordeal" — or, to use another French word also found in English, a "travail." I have called upon or called attention to all of these options in the present translation — though the first may sound too scientific or academic, the second too tentative or legalistic, the third overly harsh or downright medieval, and the last merely a melodramatic literary flourish — in order to capture the term's sense of a challenging experience that involves a confrontation with reality. Compounding the inevitable polysemy of *épreuve* is the appearance, almost right after it, of the curious masculine noun of recent vintage,[5] *le politique*—"the political" or "the political sphere," as is sometimes said now in English—which contrasts in French with the more straightforward, concrete, and familiar feminine noun *la politique*—"politics" or "policy," depending upon the context—and which derives from *das politische,* a neuter German word popularized by the Nazi-era German constitutional scholar and political thinker Carl Schmitt and then by his American emigrant former student Leo Strauss (to whom, moreover, Lefort devotes three extensive and critical Notes). "The political" has been associated, too, with the writings of Hannah Arendt (wrongly, according to one young political scientist, who claims that "this term, developed by the right-wing jurist Carl Schmitt, has been ascribed to her by Marxist thinkers more influenced by Schmitt than she is"),[6] and *le politique* is employed today by a wide variety of other French-speaking writers besides Lefort, including the late emigrant Greek political and social thinker Cornelius Castoriadis, whose usage of the *le/la politique* distinction differs markedly from his,[7] and leading French classicist Jean-Pierre Vernant, who, in insisting that "the political," like "politics," has a datable birth and origin in the *poleis* of Ancient Greece, differs from both Castoriadis and Lefort on this score.[8] Yet, "the political," as substantive noun, still reads rather inelegantly on the cover of an English-language book[9]—even if we note the existence of *Reinterpreting the Political,* a recently published American anthology of "Continental" political theory that borrows its title directly from a (questionably translated) passage in Lefort's influential 1985 essay, "The Question of Democracy."[10] After considering, and then rejecting, the nearly literal *Writing: The Test* [or *the Ordeal*] *of the Political* and the simpler *Writing the Political,* I searched, without much success, for more satisfactory alternatives, ones that somewhat deceptively transform this unusual noun, however, back into an adjective: *Writing: The Political Test* ultimately survived only because it seemed mildly less dissatisfactory than *Writing and the Ordeal of Politics* and marginally less deceptive than such precious (though not entirely misleading) options as *The Literature of Politics and the Politics of Literature* or such trendy ones as *Writing/Politics,* which employ the alternative noun, *politics,* and without incorporating *épreuve.*[11]

Adding to the humiliation of not finding, for the first time in my fourteen years as a professional translator, a book title with which I could feel reasonably satisfied was the disquiet I felt before what might appear to be a widely disparate collection of essays—a quick glance at the table of contents begins to reveal part of the wide range of Lefort's "privileged interlocutors," both living and dead: George Orwell, Salman Rushdie, Alexis de

Tocqueville, the Marquis de Sade, François Guizot, Niccolò Machiavelli, Leo Strauss, Pierre Clastres.[12] I purchased the book shortly following its publication in 1992 by Calmann-Lévy and a while after I had attended some lectures on the fall of Communism given by Lefort here in Paris, because it contained some "reflections" on that topic and with the idea of translating it eventually. (Lefort cofounded the now-legendary postwar left-wing anti-Communist group Socialisme ou Barbarie with Castoriadis, of whose vast writings I have now translated and edited about a million words.[13]) I quickly realized that what seemed to be a bunch of occasional pieces preceding those "Reflections on the Present" had a much greater depth and a much tighter thematic organization than I had first suspected, but my enthusiasm, which increased considerably as I read through the volume, was of no avail with publishers, who, one after another, rejected my translation proposals on the basis of their initial negative impression of its apparently eclectic contents.

It was, however, precisely Lefort's linkage of political reflection with a literary concern to investigate the arts of reading and writing that tied these chapters together thematically and offered, I came to think, an excellent opportunity to introduce English-speaking readers to his work—which, despite the publication in English of two previous collections more than a decade ago,[14] and notwithstanding the occasional appearance in English translation of writings by his former teacher, Maurice Merleau-Ponty, edited and prefaced by Lefort himself,[15] has not gained the recognition in the English-speaking world that that work undoubtedly deserves.[16] A first opening came by chance, when Vassilis Lambropoulos was seeking contributions for a 1996 special issue of Duke University Press's literary journal *South Atlantic Quarterly* on "Ethical Politics." Lefort's article on Sade, subtitled "The Boudoir and the City," fit perfectly Lambropoulos's goal of encouraging "nomoscopic analysis," that is, a critical examination of laws and ethical norms as explored in literary texts. The fact that this chapter from *Écrire* looked at Sade's *Philosophie dans le boudoir*—a hybrid[17] work hovering somewhere between the genres of the novel, the dialogue, the political tract (i.e., the performative reading of the celebrated and fabled "Français, encore un effort" pamphlet embedded in the text), and the theatrical play—was also propitious, for "nomoscopy," in Lambropoulos's view,[18] would privilege criticism of more public forms of literary engagement, such as drama, which have taken a back seat to the novel in recent times. Subsequent interest from Duke University Press editor J. Reynolds Smith and a grant from the French Ministry of Culture and Communication have made this translation a reality.[19] The Sade gig also provided me with an unprecedented and very welcome opportunity to challenge myself as a translator while trying to capture the extraordinary richness and subtlety of Lefort's literary-philosophical investigations and descriptions.[20]

Georges André Claude Lefort was born April 21, 1924, in Paris to an artisan painter, Maurice-Alphonse Lefort, and his wife Rose, née Cohen, a fashion designer. His high school years under the Occupation were spent at the Lycée Carnot, where he had the extraordinary experience of taking a young Maurice Merleau-Ponty's course in philosophy, and then at the Lycée Henri IV, where, upon joining with French Trotskyism, he became a politically active radical with a considerable following. After encountering Castoriadis (1922–1997) at a postwar Trotskyist meeting, the two joined forces to build an oppositional tendency that eventually transformed itself into the independent group of workers and intellectuals Socialisme ou Barbarie, which published a review by the same name. Lefort attended the University of the Sorbonne, receiving there his doctorate in literature and human sciences, and passed the *agrégation* to teach high school philosophy courses himself, first in Nîmes (1949) and then in Reims (1950). He was employed from 1951 to 1953 as a scholarly researcher at the Centre National de la Recherche Scientifique, returning to work at the CNRS from 1956 to 1965 and again from 1971 to 1976, with teaching stints in between at the University of São Paolo in Brazil (1953–1954), the Sorbonne (1954–1956), and the University of Caen (1966–1971). In 1976, he was elected as a Director of Studies at the École des Hautes Études en Sciences Sociales, teaching there until his retirement in 1989. Since Merleau-Ponty's death in 1961, Lefort has also acted as the French philosopher's literary executor.

What, then, are "the intentions of the writer" Claude Lefort, who has set out to scrutinize the political aspects of literary texts and the literary aspects of political ones? We have already mentioned some of his "privileged interlocutors," but a few more words are still in order on that score. There is, especially, the Italian political thinker Machiavelli, "to whom I devoted a work that occupied me for so long that I dare not tell the amount of time," he tells us quite humbly about this monumental 778-page work in his autobiographical piece on philosophical reading and writing, "Philosopher?"[21] Tocqueville, the thinker of the advent and significance of modern democracy, is an author Lefort has already investigated prior to the two Notes he devotes to him here.[22] What is particularly interesting in these Notes is how he explores not only the contradictions and complexity of Tocqueville's thought in *Democracy in America* and *The Old Regime and the Revolution* but its underlying meaning: Tocqueville himself, Lefort argues in sum, became caught up in, and ended up expressing in his own writing, the improvisatory and open-ended character of the democratic experience. Not only Tocqueville, alongside Sade and Guizot, but also a number of other revolutionary-era and nineteenth-century French thinkers including the historians Jules Michelet and Edgar Quinet (who pop up several times in *Écrire*) have been central to his work for the past two decades.[23] Turning to German eighteenth- and nineteenth-century thinkers, we note that one chapter of *Écrire* is devoted to Kant's *Perpetual Peace* and broaches the question of the difficult and halting genesis of an international community dedicated to the values of human rights and peace (a theme addressed in his Rushdie text, as well). While Hegel is mentioned several times, it is usually only in quite cursory historical or critical terms that Lefort discusses the latter's work.[24] Marx, of course, loomed large for the former cofounder of Socialisme ou Barbarie. In *Écrire*, however, Lefort, who no longer identifies himself as a Marxist, makes no more than passing references to the founder of "scientific socialism," even though Marx remains a focal point for his reflections in other writings.[25]

Weber's influence, by way of contrast, may be felt throughout the present volume, yet without his ever being especially highlighted in any one chapter.[26] One of the distinctive contributions of Socialisme ou Barbarie, and specifically of Lefort and Castoriadis, is to have extended and eventually to have gone beyond Marxism, doing so by introducing the question of *bureaucracy* into the heart of Marxian discourse and by bringing this Weberian category of analysis to bear on the bureaucratization of the socialist movement in general and of Bolshevism in particular, as well as of Western capitalist societies.[27] In this way, S. ou B. went far beyond the analyses Leon Trotsky formulated merely as warnings in his very last writings. It was with an in-depth critique of the "Soviet" bureaucracy and a militant advocacy, in contrast, of workers' management that S. ou B. broke from the Parti Communiste Internationaliste (PCI), the French section of the Trotskyist Fourth International, in 1948 and set itself up as a separate organization the following year.[28] Paired with Weber, and also not the object of a separate chapter but turning up on several crucial occasions, is Friedrich Nietzsche, whose thinking on democracy and modernity, Lefort reminds us, played such a key role in informing Weber's thought.

The name of Leo Strauss, another thinker influenced by Nietzsche, has already been mentioned, but it should be noted that the presence of this distinctive thinker, who did so much to revive the study of classical political philosophy, can be felt throughout *Écrire* and that Lefort is now generally recognized as himself the person who has done the most to revive political philosophy in modern France. Significantly, Lefort examines at length Strauss's practice of "reading between the lines" of political-philosophical texts. In this case, not "paired" with Strauss but accompanying Lefort along his own path of political thought is another political philosopher, Hannah Arendt, whose mid-century analysis of *The Origins of Totalitarianism* and whose championing of the workers' councils during the 1956 anti-Communist Hungarian Revolution remarkably parallel positions taken by S. ou B.[29] Lefort, in fact, was recently awarded the Arendt Prize from a German foundation. Nevertheless, in the present volume her overt presence is minimal. Another thinker of democracy and totalitarianism, more sociologist than political philosopher, is Raymond Aron, who appears in a rather critical light during Lefort's discussion of the collapse of Communism at the end of the book. It was under Aron's direction that Lefort wrote his thesis on Machiavelli. Also, Alexander Solzhenitsyn is discussed briefly in this last chapter. *Un homme en trop* was Lefort's 1976 book that helped bring attention in France to the analyses of the author of *The Gulag Archipelago*.[30]

The sixteenth-century French author La Boétie makes several appearances, especially in the chapter Lefort devotes to his late friend and colleague, the anthropologist Pierre Clastres, whose remarkable work analyzing tribes of South American Indians, and "primitive" peoples in general, as instances of a *Society against the State* is given a fresh, in-depth examination there.[31] One can sense the poignant significance of a friendship lost due to the premature death of one of the parties — which doesn't stop Lefort from offering a critical appreciation of his friend's substantial, if incomplete, body of work, applying to it his own idea of the political as the *mise en forme* ("setting into form") of a human society. He joined Clastres in contributing original texts to a 1976 scholarly edition of La Boétie's famous essay on voluntary servitude.[32] Both of them, we may also note, collaborated with Castoriadis, Miguel Abensour, Marcel Gauchet, and a number of other uncommon French intellectuals at the journal *Libre* from 1977 to 1980. This was Lefort's and Castoriadis's second and last attempt to work together on a journal after their final S. ou B. split in 1958. A dispute over the contemporary significance of totalitarianism, occasioned by the Russian intervention in Afghanistan, put a definitive end to one of the most remarkable and fecund political-intellectual collaborations in postwar times.[33]

Almost last, but certainly not least, is the phenomenologist Maurice Merleau-Ponty, who taught Lefort's 1941–42 high school philosophy class and who first suggested to Lefort that his youthful political views might receive concrete expression in French Trotskyism, which is where Lefort met Castoriadis and formed a tendency that became Socialisme ou Barbarie.[34] Merleau-Ponty's proximity is palpable throughout the book, and not just when Lefort speaks of Tocqueville's exploration of the "flesh of the social" or talks personally and explicitly in "Philosopher?" about the great influence his former teacher continues to exercise over himself and his thought.

Edmund Husserl, the father of phenomenology, makes a few appearances, too, but Husserl's student, Martin Heidegger, who maintained a long personal relationship with Arendt and with whom Merleau-Ponty entertained an enduring but ambiguous intellectual affinity, only appears once, and then in quite negative terms. "Nothing," Lefort says decisively,

> better instructs one about the phantasm of a world entirely ruled by technology than the argument advanced by Heidegger, who shows his disdain for any attempt to distinguish its centers, its uses, and its effects, and who, in order to respond to what he calls its "challenge," joins with Nazism, that is, a totalitarian formation that wanted to rivet everyone to his particular post and to destroy every sign of independence in society—to achieve, in short, under cover of a moral revolution, that strict integration of men and things that was being imputed to the artificialist philosophy of the West.

Evidently, Lefort is *not* to be classified among the French Heideggerians, who have exerted such a baleful influence over large portions of America's academic "Left." In "The Question of Democracy," Lefort had already expressed surprise and dissatisfaction in his criticism of many of his contemporaries in the philosophical profession. "How," he asked, "can they handle ontological difference with such subtlety, vie with one another in exploiting the combined resources of Heidegger, Lacan, Jakobson, and Lévi-Strauss, and then fall back upon such crass realism when the question of politics arises?"[35]

Lefort also counsels us, when examining a writer, to inquire as to "what are the opinions he targets." As far as recurring themes found in *Écrire* are concerned, relativism as well as absolutism and a universalism divorced from actual experience, along with sociologism, culturalism, historicism, and positivism are repeated targets of his criticism. The challenging idea of an interminable and unresolvable "war of the gods" introduced by Weber has led today, regrettably, to a rather slack and slippery response—for example, in the uncritical affirmation of a generalized and undifferentiated "right to difference"—on the part of many who are unmindful of the methodological and indeed philosophical problems this idea raised for Weber himself, problems that retain a political as well as a philosophical urgency for Lefort:

> Now, just as much as respect for the other's identity or the critique of egocentrism, of ethnocentrism—and particularly of Eurocentrism— can be fully justified, and tolerance, consequently, can be erected into a principle, so an unbridled relativism turns out to confer a legiti-

macy upon all sorts of impostures and, more precisely, upon all systems of oppression that, under cover of an ethic placed in the service of the purity of a race, of the integrity of a nation, or of the instauration of a classless society, goes about hounding individuals and groups whose characteristics are judged not to be in conformity with the right model.

Likewise, the recent claims concerning "the end of philosophy" leave him cold. Continuing his positive evaluation of questions that challenge him, that leave him "disarmed," he adds:

> As I have already said, it is the discourse about the disappearance of philosophy that I deem to be futile. But that very discourse isn't devoid of motives. Its only error is to convert an interrogation into an affirmation — that is to say, in the present circumstance, into a negation.

The fashionable discourse on the "death of man" (or of "the subject") is, in his view, no less vain. Without taking a stand in favor of a warmed-over "humanism" — as a younger generation of French intellectuals has done in reaction against Louis Althusser's ridiculous idea that a still-extant humanism explains Stalin's errors and against Jacques Derrida's reprehensible attribution of Heidegger's Nazism to a residual "metaphysical" humanism — Lefort explores, upon several occasions, the complex, sometimes complementary, sometimes contradictory components that go to make up "man" in society and that give "human rights" a force and a value today that, he argues, go beyond any ideological defense of "bourgeois democracy."

Democracy and totalitarianism, the dual theme that served as a title for a book by Aron, one that Lefort discusses in the last chapter of the present volume, have long been at the center of Lefort's concerns, and increasingly so as time goes on, even after the progressive decomposition, collapse, and ultimate disappearance of "Soviet" Communism.[36] Here, Merleau-Ponty's idea of the body and of perception as central and privileged phenomenological categories of existence is given a unique political-philosophical twist in Lefort's study not only of the "flesh of the social" in Tocqueville's exploration of democracy but also in his study of totalitarianism's attempt, in the wake of the rise of democracy, to "revitalize" the "body politic"[37] from both above and below.[38] This leads us to mention Ernst Kantorowicz — another of Lefort's "privileged interlocutors," in fact — whose *The King's Two Bodies* Lefort returns to again and again in order to comprehend the distinctiveness, by contrast, of modern democracy[39] — where power, law, and knowledge are, so to speak, disincorporated and can no longer be embodied unambiguously in a distinct sovereign entity, the king (who once doubled as Christ's earthly representative but whose head has since been severed)—as well as of totalitarianism—which endeavors, in its hatred of democracy's characteristic dissolution and disentanglement of these three spheres, to effect a total reunification of them in "an impossible swallowing up of the body in the head," which also entails "an impossible swallowing up of the head in the body."[40] We are evidently quite far from Michel Foucault's "power/knowledge" rhetoric—which would have us believe that there is an inescapable identity between power and knowledge and which so many of his American followers have confused with being a radical posture of contestation and defiance.[41] Lefort receives inspiration, rather, from Freud, when conducting his fine literary-political study of "the interposed body" in Orwell's antitotalitarian novel *1984*.

In trying to revive political philosophy—as the effort to think the constituting political element in the formation of a society and not simply as some kind of historical-interpretative undertaking or an empirically based policy-making endeavor—Lefort also targets "political science" in general: "Interpreting the political means breaking with the viewpoint of political science, because political science emerges from the suppression of this question," he had said in "The Question of Democracy."[42] The debt owed to Strauss here as well as in his criticisms of relativism, sociologism, culturalism, historicism, and positivism is obvious, but their mutual affinity on this score has in no way prevented him from criticizing Strauss's formulations or from questioning whether Strauss himself, in his most extreme formulations (i.e., when our reading between the lines of Strauss's own exoteric texts yields what we think we can glimpse to be his own esoteric doctrine), doesn't end up, contrary to Strauss's own intentions, putting into question the very possibility of our continuing to do political philosophy today. Instead of making the supposed shortcomings of democracy his ultimate target, as Strauss had done (while also confounding democracy with a mass society still riddled with the ever-transmuting destructive contradictions of capitalism), Lefort argues for a nuanced point of view:

> There is nothing to hide about the ambiguities of democracy. Criticism is healthy. Still, such criticism must not sink to the ridiculous level of putting reason or unreason on trial. It must know how to denounce relativism without abandoning the sense of relativity that the totalitarian system sought to destroy.

The reflection on the legacy of totalitarianism, modern democracy's historically contemporaneous and contiguous Other, again proves to be crucial to his revaluation of democracy and to his reevaluation of its inherent problems.

Lefort advises us, finally, to look at "what are the circumstances that summon up [a writer's] desire to speak." We might recall here that one of Lefort's very first published texts—written in 1948, as he and the Socialisme ou Barbarie tendency were withdrawing from the PCI—brought out "The Contradiction of Trotsky" by attacking head-on the myths Trotsky himself had propagated that concealed his longtime hesitations with regard to Stalin before he was excluded from the Party and sent into internal and then foreign exile.[43] This article proved controversial both in "revolutionary" circles—because it appeared in the nonrevolutionary press, that is, in Jean-Paul Sartre's *Les Temps Modernes*—and at *Les Temps Modernes* itself—where Merleau-Ponty, the review's political editor, had to serve as Lefort's protector within an otherwise hostile environment.[44] A few years later, in response to Sartre's long serialized *Les Temps Modernes* article, "The Communists and the Peace,"[45] which heralded Sartre's closer ties with the French Communist Party (PCF) in the aftermath of the 1952 anti-Ridgway demonstrations (PCF-led protests against the visit of an American army general), Lefort published in the same review a strongly-worded assault on Sartre's nascent fellow-traveling. "Marxism and Sartre" elicited an equally strong "Response to Claude Lefort" on Sartre's part, Castoriadis entering the fray in Lefort's defense with an *S. ou B.* text, "Sartre, Stalinism, and the Workers."[46] All this proved to be a historically significant prelude to Merleau-Ponty's departure from *Les Temps Modernes* and the publication of his *Adventures of the Dialectic* (1955), which included a long penultimate chapter on "Sartre and Ultrabolshevism."[47] Lefort returned to the offensive in a 1958 *S. ou B.* article, "The Method of 'Progressivist' Intellectuals," criticizing there "the 'critical' thinkers of *Les Temps Modernes, L'observateur, L'express,* or *L'étincelle*" who were unable to come to terms in a forthright and creative way with the upheavals then taking place in Eastern Europe and Russia—Khrushchev's secret report, the Hungarian and Polish Revolutions, the "Soviet" invasion of Hungary—upheavals that S. ou B. had not only understood clearly (a rarity on the French Left at the time) but could be said to have anticipated.[48] These texts, of an unmistakable polemical bent, are still worth reading today to remind us of the historical circumstances surrounding the heyday of totalitarian Communism, especially since the collapse of the "Soviet Union" and the ensuing chaos (fostered by IMF-tutelage, in a Russia run by apparatchiks turned rapacious capitalists and Mafia-like thugs, and a very weak democratic tradition there) might now lead some on the Left to wax nostalgic for the era of French intellectuals' fellow traveling.

As Lefort's understanding of totalitarianism, informed by his growing interest in political philosophy, deepened, another approach, often still quite sharp in tone but no longer so polemical, began to take shape. He was still, in the tradition of Socialisme ou Barbarie and of a few other radical French workers and intellectuals, willing and eager to challenge not only the orthodoxy of the PCF but also the heterodoxy of those who gravitated around the PCF merely as its internal or external oppositions. Nevertheless, in order to engage his readers in a more transformative sort of way he sought to find the words, the ideas, and the themes that would move them beyond their settled positions. "Now," he asks in "Philosopher?", offering a retrospective account of his changing orientation as a writer:

> how could I have tried to gauge, to take the measure of what was meant by totalitarianism's denial of social division — denial of the division between the State and civil society, of class division, of the division of sectors of activity — its denial, too, of the difference between the order of power, the order of law, and the order of knowledge (a difference that is constitutive of democracy) without seeming to legitimate, without fearing to see myself legitimate, the de facto divisions that characterize the established democratic regimes in which we live? How was I to provide a glimpse of the deadly finality of totalitarianism without justifying the conditions of oppression and inequality belonging to our own regimes? How, too, was I to carry out a critique of Marxism, which reveals everything that has fed the phantasm of totalitarianism, without erasing what constituted the truth of Marx's critique of the society of his time?

It was through a revaluation of democracy, as an open-ended political form of society — as "savage democracy," he has said on occasion[49] — and not merely as a set political system of established procedures, that questions and problems associated with the arts of reading and writing came ever more clearly to the fore and eventually became his own questions and problems.[50] "To give readers a feeling for the dynamic of democracy, the experience of an ultimate indetermination at the bases of the social order and of an unending debate over right and law," he goes on to say,

> I had to try to shake up not only their convictions but their intimate relationship with knowledge; I had to try to reawaken in them a sense of the kind of questioning that would induce them to undertake the necessary mourning of "the good society" and, at the same time, I had to escape from the illusion that what seems real here and now is to be confused with the rational. Is this undertaking philosophical or political? I wouldn't know how to answer. What is certain is that this task, which little by little had taken shape inside me, had driven me to a

method of reading that I had never decided to adopt. It is one that merges with my way of being and that is not normally associated with philosophy.

Lefort's revaluation of political philosophy and "the political" in general and of democracy as an unprecedented political form of society in particular doesn't entail, however, a denigration of "politics" or the adoption of an ostensibly a- or antipolitical perspective that is characteristic of much contemporary liberal discourse (the term *liberal* being taken here and elsewhere in its Continental acceptation as a generally conservative ideological defense of supposedly unrestricted "free-market" policies). In his chapter on Machiavelli, for example, Lefort takes time to explain that "Reflection on the political and reflection on politics are at once distinct and intertwined. Everything happens, nevertheless, as if for many people the political was noble and politics trivial." Nor does he champion "civil society" at the expense of everything else. In the first of his two Notes on Tocqueville, he comments that Tocqueville "is always keeping an eye on adversaries in his own country who seek only to reinforce state power and do not understand the new character of civil society"; but, in bringing out Tocqueville's contradictions and thus not adopting an uncritical Tocquevillean outlook himself, as some other French intellectuals have done recently, he also asks:

> In our time, don't we still need to denounce the illusion of those who would wish to protect the state administration from the effects of all kinds of associations, since their demands hinder its action and don't easily lend themselves to projects crafted by experts? And don't we likewise still need to denounce the inverse illusion of those who place their only hopes in strictly civil associations and who hold "politics" in contempt?

A simplistic, smug, and celebratory liberal attitude is by no means being endorsed here by this political philosopher for whom questions count at least as much as any provisional "answers" that might be obtained. This is evident in his chapter on Kant: "The critique of all forms of totalitarianism would be futile if it were reduced to the statement of a de facto preference for a regime based on liberties. The meaning of the relative does not erase, but rather carries within it, a universal exigency." This "universal exigency," or overriding moral requirement, which is not to be confused with any sort of blind or automatic universalism and that is expressed, he believes, in a foundational and generative democratic "right to have rights," means that no convenient formula can be found that would allow one to limit in advance what becomes in fact an unending and ever-expanding search for truth and justice in the social sphere. In his "Reflections on the Present," Lefort adds:

> Furthermore, is it not true that the search for democracy is by its nature tied to the desire for an improvement in the material conditions of existence? And isn't it true that this desire in no way obliterates the value of political freedoms? How would one remove from democracy the social question and therefore that of economic organization, if not by joining up with the most reactionary form of free-market liberalism?

Lefort no longer speaks in terms of "workers' management" or of a "republic of Councils,"[51] but this does not necessarily put him in the camp of the present, heavily ideological status quo, the minimalist and difficult-to-challenge "invisible ideology" of "the Western democracies of our time."[52] Indeed, as he goes on to ask in his early 1990s "Reflections on the Present":

> In response to the aspirations now dawning in the East and to the kinds of resistance to which these aspirations are giving rise, are we doomed to fall back on a cramped position, limiting ourselves to Isaiah Berlin's notion of "negative liberties"? Isn't the task before us to conceive democracy as a form of political society, a regime in which we have an experience of our humanity, rid of the myths that conceal the complexity of History?

If we thus begin to understand "what are the circumstances that summon up" Lefort's own "desire to speak," and to speak in such a way that he can be heard amid the clamorous and repetitive rhetoric of outdated Marxist and Liberal dogmas, we still need to try to understand that "way of being" of which he spoke that is his both as a person and as a writer. I was struck by the prefatory remarks Lefort made at a Paris dance concert/colloquium I helped to organize recently. The object was to relate the main ideas of his life's work in an extemporaneous way to the themes of the multimedia choreographic event, *Corpsensus,* which was intended to "explore the connections that unite the Body—lived as field of the sensual experience of a flesh that is an already socialized tissue—and the City—considered as the space of political experience, the weaving together [*tissage*] of acting and reflecting bodies."[53] Before presenting a lucid and succinct exposition of his political-intellectual itinerary and connecting that itinerary with the democratic and improvisatory themes of the evening's performance (which included the European premiere of a solo violin piece written by jazz musician and classical composer Ornette Coleman), Lefort first told the audience with candor, and in a hushed voice, that he felt rather "embarrassed" and "intimidated." Lefort is not someone who launches into a topic directly, with a clearly defined thesis to be "defended." He approaches the themes he wishes to discuss via a process that develops in close and ongoing contact with the subject matter itself. That is why one finds it so hard to extract a concrete "lesson" from his writings and also why he may easily be misunderstood, for his process-oriented exploration of a line of thought may be (mis)taken as conclusive, whereas in fact it is one side of a continuing exploration that "concludes" only with new questions, not ready-made answers or a full-blown doctrine. "For [the practitioner of political philosophy], quite particularly," he says in his preface, clearly thinking of himself as well,

> writing is therefore facing up to a risk [*l'épreuve d'un risque*]; and the risky test he faces offers him the resources for a singular form of speech that is set in motion by the exigency that he spring the traps of belief and escape from the grips of ideology, bringing himself always beyond the place where one expects him via a series of zigzag movements that disappoint by turns the various sections of his public. No doubt, it is toward the true that he tends, otherwise he wouldn't be a philosopher; but he must, via a winding path, clear a *passage* within the agitated world of passions. Such an undertaking always fails by half, moreover, as shown by the welcome he most often receives from his contemporaries and, still more, by the stupidity of readers who will later press upon him a vulgar or scholarly discourse in order to celebrate or condemn his "theory" or to discover his "contradictions." Think only of the fate that awaited Machiavelli or Rousseau.

Characteristically, he adds that "he therefore is not, cannot be the master of the effects of his speech."

The broad but winding path Lefort has chosen has led him away from the straight and narrow one of spotting and exposing the "contradictions" and errors of a Trotsky or of another political or literary writer, whether Marxist or Liberal. He thereby invites the reader, too, to face the "risky test" of thinking (reading thoughtfully) through a text's implicit political *mise en scène* (its "staging") as well as its explicit political positions and implications. The ties between philosophy and literature become both apparent and themes for further literary-philosophical reflections and investigations. The "result" is not a grammatology, a unilateral—and shaky—assertion that the text is everything and the author and/or reader nothing, or a proclamation of the end of philosophy and/or its dissolution in the element of the literary—the sorts of "high-altitude thinking" Merleau-Ponty had denounced for having lost contact with our experience, which is aesthetic, political, and philosophical, as well. It brings out the difficulties associated with reading and writing and makes the "arts" of reading and writing central to the problem of philosophical reflection today, which is now also unavoidably caught up in the enterprise of reading and writing about texts both philosophical and nonphilosophical. And for Lefort it is their *political* meaning that continues to be of crucial importance, even as their literary character is being foregrounded—in the first place because they continually remake the social bond in their very act of being written and being read. Thus you, the reader, are potentially one of Lefort's privileged interlocutors, upon the condition that you are ready to have the opinions you hold most dear become on occasion his targets for criticism, that you have been able to summon up a desire to listen to him, as part of a precarious mutual relationship only you can activate—and, finally, upon the condition that you, too, will summon up a desire to speak, to talk back to him, to question him and his questions.

Ever since I was first faced with the task of writing a foreword to a book I had translated, I found myself placed before a series of quandaries. If I had done my work well in the translation, it seemed superfluous, I thought, to tell the reader, in a separate introduction, what it is that he would be reading or had already read in the body of the text. Since the principal authors I have chosen to translate—Castoriadis, the historian Pierre Vidal-Naquet, now Lefort—are themselves quite articulate in their own right and historically associated with a libertarian socialist outlook, it also seemed to me presumptuous as well as premature on my part to tell the reader in advance what he should think of work only now becoming available for the first time in the English language. Yet it also seemed to me that the translator has a *civic duty,* in the transnational Republic of Letters, to present an author to his foreign reading public—and to make a self-presentation, an explanation of reasons for making this choice of author and an exposition of the problems encountered and solutions discovered in the course of translation. And this entailed a challenging self-reflection on my part in my work as a translator and, more broadly, as a go-between who introduces an author to his new public.

What seemed most appropriate, I thought, would be to provide some background knowledge the reader might not otherwise have. I have done this knowing that it involved choices of emphasis and subject matter for which only I could take responsibility and which others would handle differently. Yet the last thing I wanted to do was just to *repeat* the same format each time, for I would thereby be avoiding the challenge of the specific work I had translated and the inspiration to new ways of thinking that work contains. (And we now know Lefort's own stated opinion that knowledge of such background information does not suffice for the reader to gain an adequate understanding of a writer.) Thus, the problem of the literary *form* of the translator's foreword was posed for me in a radical way from the very outset and continues to be so for each new one I write. Since the writers I have consciously chosen to translate have been ones who do not try to impose some doctrine or other but who seek, rather, to raise philosophical, political, and/or historiographical questions, it also was clear that my forewords should include improvisatory, experimental, or otherwise openended features not necessarily associated with a traditional introduction written by a translator. If I, as first reader in English of a foreign author's writings, had indeed been moved by his work (and what would my translation be worth if I hadn't been?), I should also be able to express in my introductory remarks some of that moving experience, to face up to that risky *épreuve,* as Lefort himself might say. I constantly wonder to what extent, if at all, I ever succeed in conveying this enterprise, which is both emulative and, I hope, somewhat creative on my own part.[54] And I continually worry that what I say and how I say it will remain too repetitive and derivative of the ways in which the author I have translated has already expressed himself (now through me, in translation) or that, on the contrary, I might be going too far afield, thereby losing the connection with the author whom I am supposed to be introducing. I thus find myself placed in new quandaries (ones reminiscent, however, of my initial translation encounters with the author), never settled down upon any solid and secure ground. And that is perhaps not a bad thing.

Musical metaphors, and specifically the democratic experience that is *jazz,* have been foremost in my mind when I composed these essays. It was not a matter of mere "variations on a theme" or an "accompaniment" in the sense of a strict subordination to the author as main instrument but, rather, of riffing and improvising on a given theme that remains open to further interpretations. Here "accompaniment" is expressing oneself in a voice of one's own that has *something else* to say but that also speaks in response to the living work at hand. I have been inspired especially by Ornette Coleman's musical theory in this regard.[55] In Coleman's democratic conception of "Harmolodics," harmony, motion (or rhythm), and melody are treated as equal elements of improvisatory composition and performance, so that any instrument (or voice) can intervene at any moment to help move the music in new and unprecedented directions. Everyone "solos" at once,[56] and yet the result of such a collective improvisation is not mere cacophony if there is a general and genuine "participation in a value-idea," to borrow his phrase.[57] Coleman, I note, has never conceived "Harmolodics" as a strictly musical concept but one applicable, rather, to all aspects of life and at the same time specific to democratic societies.

What I have gained from translating *Écrire. À l'épreuve du politique* and from writing about *Writing: The Political Test* is a heightened sense of a simultaneously self-reflective and political challenge to encounter the work —and my translation work on the work—in such a way that the arts of writing and reading now come ever more clearly to the fore, and yet without that occulting *what* the work has to say, even as one examines and endeavors to express *how* it is said.[58] If I have been able to impart to the reader a small bit of the adventure this experience has inspired in me, then this foreword will not have been written, and perhaps read, totally in vain.

—Paris, April–May 1999

Notes

1 In the unpublished version of what became the Translator's Note to my 1996 Pierre Vidal-Naquet translation: *The Jews: History, Memory, and the Present* (New York: Columbia University Press).

2 Or science fiction within science fiction: I just attended a showing of David Cronenberg's film *Existenz*.

3 See the "Présentation," for Maurice Merleau-Ponty, "Philosophie et non-philosophie depuis Hegel. Notes de cours," ed. Claude Lefort, *Textures* 8–9 (1974): 83–87. This text appeared in *Telos* 29 (fall 1976): 43–105, with Lefort's introductory remarks ("Presenting Merleau-Ponty," ibid., 39–42). Lefort is himself the author of a text called "Philosophie et non-philosophie" (*Esprit* [June 1982]: 101–12). Here and elsewhere, I am relying on Hugues Poltier's excellent and very extensive (as well as generally accurate) "Bibliographie chronologique des publications de Claude Lefort," a first version of which was published at the end of Claude Habib and Claude Mouchard's valuable Lefort Festschrift, *La démocratie à l'œuvre* (Paris: Éditions Esprit, 1993), 369–81, and which appeared in its updated form in Poltier's *La passion du politique. La pensée de Claude Lefort* (Geneva: Labor et Fides/Le Champs Éthique, 1998), 285–94, followed by a bibliography of "Études sur Claude Lefort" (secondary source material), 294–96, which I have also consulted. Poltier previously published another book on Lefort entitled *Claude Lefort. La découverte du politique* (Paris: Michalon, 1997).

4 I should note that Lefort kindly made himself available to answer my translation questions and also helped me to track down various bibliographic references. I, of course, take final responsibility for the translation and for any shortcomings it may include.

5 The masculine French noun *le politique* can also mean, in its older acceptation, merely a "statesman."

6 John Ely, "The Polis and 'the Political': Civic and Territorial Views of Association," *Thesis Eleven* 46 (August 1996): 33–65; see 33.

7 Lefort calls "the political" the "form" of a society. In "Power, Politics, Autonomy" (1988), Castoriadis defines "the political" as "a dimension of the institution of society pertaining to *explicit power,* that is, to the existence of *instances capable of formulating explicitly sanctionable injunctions*" (*Philosophy, Politics, Autonomy,* ed. David Ames Curtis [New York:

Oxford University Press, 1991], 156). As such, it does and must pertain to *any* society. By way of contrast, "Greek politics, and politics properly conceived, can be defined as the explicit collective activity which aims at being lucid (reflective and deliberate) and whose object is the institution of society as such" (ibid., 160). "Politics" thus appertains, for Castoriadis, only to those societies in which the "project of autonomy" has already emerged and become operative.

8 See my forthcoming Jean-Pierre Vernant translation, "The Birth of the Political," in the Australia-based social theory journal *Thesis Eleven*. Like Lefort, and despite their differing definitions of *le* and *la politique* (see preceding note), Castoriadis, too, considers "the political" to be an essential and inescapable element of any human society. Vernant's argument could be summarized by saying that it makes no sense to speak of either "the political" or "politics" before the advent of the *polis* as an effective social-historical institution. That raises the question whether both of these terms might be datable (and thereby *historical* in character), instead of one or another or both being a "form" or "dimension" of *all* societies. But what would one then call this element, in pre-polis times, whereby a society gives itself its "form" through social division (Lefort) or organizes its "explicit power" (Castoriadis)?

9 Upon seeing Dick Howard's book title, *Defining the Political*, my ever pragmatic father exclaimed, in confusion and disgust, "Defining the political *what?*" Clearly, "the political" does not necessarily go without saying in an English-language book title. Fred Dallmayr's "Postmetaphysics and Democracy," *Political Theory*, 21 (February 1993): 101–27, the second section of which reviews the 1988 English-language Lefort translation *Democracy and Political Theory*, offers "polity" and "policy" as provisional translations of *le politique* and *la politique*, respectively. I have not adopted these intriguing suggestions, but they are worth keeping in mind. In addition, Dallmayr suggests "staging" for *mise en scène* (which I use already), but also "shaping" for *mise en forme* (I prefer "setting into form," since mere "shaping" assumes work on a preexistent material) and "meaning assignment" for *mise en sens* (a phrase that doesn't appear in *Écrire*, but that I translate elsewhere, for similar reasons, as "putting into meaning"). Two more tangential comments to conclude the present note: (1) Lefort's terms *mise en scène* and *mise en sens* were developed in the 1970s by Castoriadis's wife at the time, Piera Aulagnier (author of the important post-Lacanian metapsychological treatise *La violence de l'interprétation* [Paris: Presses Universitaires de France, 1975], which I one day hope to translate), and (2) the *Telos* issue in which Hugh J. Silverman's translation of Lefort's edited version of Merleau-Ponty's "Philosophy and Non-Philosophy since Hegel" appeared (see note 3 above) also includes Dallmayr's "Marxism and Truth" (ibid., 130–59) and Silverman's "Re-Reading Merleau-Ponty" (ibid., 106–29).

10 "The Question of Democracy," *Democracy and Political Theory*, trans. David Macey (Minneapolis: University of Minnesota Press, and Cambridge, England: Polity Press, 1988), 10. Cf. *Reinterpreting the Political: Continental Philosophy and Political Theory*, ed. Lenore Langsdorf and Stephen H. Watson, with Karen A. Smith (Albany: SUNY, 1998), vii. This book retains the rather artificial "Continental philosophy/Anglo-American philosophy" distinction that creates so many misleading oppositions (despite their mutual incomprehension, both the Logical Positivists and Heideggerians in reality shared, for example, a ferocious and somewhat scattershot antipathy to all things "metaphysical"). There is in this volume a text by Steven Hendley, "Reconsidering the Limits of Democracy with Castoriadis and Lefort" (ibid., 171–82), that treats Lefort's and Castoriadis's views only in very

general terms and presents a harmonizing reading that fails to bring out the considerable and probably unbridgeable differences between the two. I also note the existence in this volume of an excellent article on Castoriadis by the gifted young Italian philosopher Fabio Ciaramelli: "The Circle of the Origin," 127–40.

11 *Épreuve* can also mean "proof," as in *mettre quelque chose à l'épreuve* (to prove something or to put it to the test), *à l'épreuve du feu* (fireproof), and *les épreuves* (galley proofs). I haven't opted for "proof" in the present translation, but one shouldn't forget this alternative meaning, either. *Épreuve* has the meaning of "experience," as well, but it seemed that this choice of word might confuse the reader, since *expérience* is also a term Lefort uses on occasion.

12 For reasons of space and because of financial considerations, it was agreed that the English-language translation of *Écrire* would not include the seventh and eighth chapters of the original volume: "Foyers du républicanisme" and "Formation et autorité. L'éducation humaniste."

13 Cornelius Castoriadis, *Political and Social Writings*, 3 vols. (Minneapolis: University of Minnesota Press, 1988, 1988, 1993); *Philosophy, Politics, Autonomy* (New York: Oxford University Press, 1991); *The Castoriadis Reader* (Malden, Mass. and Oxford, England: Blackwell, 1997); *World in Fragments* (Stanford, Calif.: Stanford University Press, 1997). For a more extensive Castoriadis bibliography in nearly a dozen languages, one may consult <http://aleph.lib.ohio-state.edu/~bcase/Castoriadis>, the Cornelius Castoriadis/ Agora International Website.

14 *The Political Forms of Modern Society: Bureaucracy, Democracy, Totalitarianism,* ed. and intro. John B. Thompson (Cambridge, Mass.: MIT Press and Cambridge, England: Polity Press, 1986), and *Democracy and Political Theory* (1988). *Telos* published a number of Lefort texts in the 1970s, including: "What Is Bureaucracy?" (see also note 27 below), *Telos* 22 (winter 1974–75): 31–65; "The Age of Novelty," *Telos* 29 (fall 1976): 23–38; "Then and Now" (translation of the introductory statement for the first issue of *Libre*), *Telos* 36 (summer 1978): 29–42; and "French-Style Socialism," *Telos* 55 (spring 1983): 189–92. See also note 3 above and 28 below.

15 Maurice Merleau-Ponty, *The Visible and the Invisible,* followed by *Working Notes* (both published posthumously in 1964), ed. Claude Lefort, trans. Alphonso Lingis (Evanston, Ill.: Northwestern University Press, 1968), with Editor's Foreword, xi–xxxiii, and Editorial Note, xxxiv–xxxix; and *The Prose of the World* (published posthumously in 1969), ed. Claude Lefort, trans. John O'Neill (Evanston, Ill.: Northwestern University Press, 1973), with Editor's Foreword, xi–xxi, and Editor's Note, xxiii–xxiv. Lefort also contributed a *préface* to Merleau-Ponty's posthumous *L'œil et l'esprit* (Paris: Gallimard, 1964): I–VIII (published, without Lefort's *préface*, as "Eye and Mind" in *The Primacy of Perception and Other Essays*, ed. James M. Edie [Evanston, Ill.: Northwestern University Press, 1964]); an introduction to the 1980 Gallimard reprint of his 1947 book *Humanisme et terreur. Essais sur le problème communiste,* 11–38; and a *préface* to his *Notes de cours au Collège de France 1958–1959 et 1960–1961* (Paris: Gallimard, 1996), 7–30. A nonexhaustive collection of Lefort's writings on Merleau-Ponty was published as *Sur une colonne absente. Écrits autour de Merleau-Ponty* (Paris: Gallimard, 1978). See also note 3 above.

16 The American political philosopher Dick Howard deserves credit for having been the first person (after George Lichtheim and his brief discussion of S. ou B., "Bureaucracy and Totalitarianism," in *Marxism in Modern France* [New York: Columbia University Press, 1966], 182–92) to have presented Lefort's work to the English-speaking world, in his "Introduction to Lefort," *Telos* 22 (winter 1974–75): 2–30. This Introduction was re-

worked and reprinted (minus the characteristic "constitutive editing" to which it had been subjected by Paul Piccone's *Telos*) as "Bureaucratic Society and Traditional Rationality: Claude Lefort," in Howard's book, *The Marxian Legacy* (New York: Urizen Books and London: Macmillan, 1977), 222–61 (the 1988 second edition [Minneapolis: University of Minnesota Press and London: Macmillan] includes an afterword with a section entitled "Claude Lefort: History as Political," 306–20). Shortly thereafter, Mark Poster's *"Socialisme ou Barbarie"* section appeared in the "Stalinism and the Existentialists" chapter of his *Existential Marxism in Postwar France* (Princeton: Princeton University Press, 1975), 202–5, as did a translation of Richard Gombin's 1971 book on *gauchisme: The Origins of Modern Leftism,* trans. Michael K. Perl (London: Penguin, 1975), which examines Lefort (pseudonym Montal), Castoriadis (pseudonyms Chaulieu and Cardan), as well as their groups Socialisme ou Barbarie and Informations et Liaisons Ouvrières. John B. Thompson published "Ideology and the Social Imaginary," on Lefort and Castoriadis, in *Theory and Society* 1982: 659–81, a revised version appearing in his *Studies in the Theory of Ideology* (Cambridge, England: Polity Press, 1984). Also of note, in English, is Bernard Flynn, "Lefort: The Flesh of the Political," *Political Philosophy at the Closure of Metaphysics* (Atlantic Highlands, N.J.: Humanities, 1992), 164–202. Flynn has written a forthcoming book on Lefort that is tentatively titled *The Political Philosophy of Claude Lefort.*

17   In "Philosopher?" Lefort makes clear that works of a "hybrid" character attract him the most.

18   See Lambropoulos's "Introduction: Approaches to Ethical Politics" and his "Nomoscopic Analysis," in the special "Ethical Politics" issue of the *South Atlantic Quarterly* 95 (fall 1996): 849–54 and 855–79, respectively.

19   *SAQ* Managing Editor Candice Ward should be thanked for her role as instigatrix in introducing the book to her journal's publisher, Duke University Press. I am also very appreciative of the letters of support Benjamin R. Barber and Henry Louis Gates Jr. sent to the Press on my behalf. My Paris study group with Warren Breckman, Max Blechman, and Fabien Doyennel has been of immense help in furthering my understanding and appreciation of Lefort's œuvre.

20   The text is bursting, so to speak, with sexual double-entendres. For example, the French word *culbuter*—from *cul,* "ass," and *buter,* to "butt against" or "to knock over"—could have been rendered by "tumble" to convey both the idea of knocking someone over on his ass and that of "laying" a person sexually (its more "impolite" meaning, as dictionaries say; cf. *Hamlet,* act 4, scene 5, line 60, regarding "tumble"). I ultimately settled upon "upend" to heighten the sexual overtones in this article on Sade, whose obsession with anal sodomy is very deep-seated.

21   See the published version of Lefort's thesis, *Le travail de l'œuvre, Machiavel* (Paris: Gallimard, 1972), which includes parts of a 1960 text, "Réflexions sociologiques sur Machiavel et Marx," *Cahiers internationaux de sociologie* 28 (1960): 113–35, and a 1971 text, "La guerre, le discours sur la guerre et la politique," *Textures* 2–3 (1971): 79–129. A year prior to the publication of this book, he contributed "Machiavel et les jeunes" to an Aron Festschrift, *Science et conscience de la société. Mélanges en l'honneur de Raymond Aron,* ed. Jean-Claude Casanova, vol. 1 (Paris: Calmann-Lévy, 1971), 191–208. Lefort's 1974 Toronto lecture, "Machiavel: la dimension économique du politique," appeared in his *Formes de l'histoire* (Paris: Gallimard, 1978), 127–40, and he wrote a *préface* to a new edition of Machiavelli's *Discours sur la première décade de Tite-Live* (Paris: Berger-Levrault, 1980), 9–19. We might note that Merleau-Ponty's "A Note on Machiavelli," published in *Signs* (1960), trans. Richard C. McCleary (Evanston, Ill.: Northwestern University Press, 1964),

211-13, was originally written as a "paper sent to the Umanesimo et scienza politica Congress, Rome-Florence, September 1949" (ibid., 211).

22 Among Lefort's other essays dealing with Tocqueville, see, in English, "Reversibility: Political Freedom and the Freedom of the Individual" (1982) and "From Equality to Freedom: Fragments of an Interpretation of *Democracy in America,*" in *Democracy and Political Theory,* 165-82 and 183-209, respectively.

23 Among Lefort's essays in English translation on the French Revolution, on historians of the French Revolution such as Jules Michelet and Edgar Quinet, and on certain other nineteenth-century French authors, see, in English, "The Revolutionary Terror," "Interpreting the Revolution within the French Revolution," "Edgar Quinet: The Revolution That Failed," "The Revolution as Principle and as Individual," "Permanence of the Theologico-Political?", and "The Death of Immortality?" in ibid., 59-88, 89-114, 115-34, 135-48, 213-55, and 256-82, respectively.

24 Dante is also examined here briefly, and in a more favorable way than Hegel. Dante may thus be considered another of Lefort's "privileged interlocutors." A year after the publication of *Écrire,* Lefort wrote an introduction, "La Modernité de Dante," for a Dante volume in French translation: *La monarchie* (Paris: Belin, 1993): 6-75.

25 Among Lefort's essays on Marx, see, in English, "Rereading *The Communist Manifesto,*" *Democracy and Political Theory,* 149-62, as well as "Marx: From One Vision of History to Another" and "Outline of the Genesis of Ideology in Modern Times," *The Political Forms of Modern Society,* 139-80 and 181-236.

26 Lefort's first article on Weber, "Capitalisme et religion au XVIe siècle," *Les Temps Modernes* 78 (April 1952): 1892-1906, appeared three years before Merleau-Ponty published his chapter on "The Crisis of Understanding" in *The Adventures of the Dialectic* (1955), trans. Joseph Bien (Evanston, Ill.: Northwestern University Press, 1973), 9-29; that chapter concludes: "It is only by beginning with Weber, and with this Weberian Marxism, that the adventures of the dialectic of the past thirty-five years can be understood."

27 Lefort published a synthetic article on bureaucracy, "Qu'est-ce que la bureaucratie?" in *Arguments* 17 (1960): 64-81 (reprinted in *Éléments d'une critique de la bureaucratie,* 2nd ed. [Paris: Gallimard, 1979], 271-307, and translated as "What Is Bureaucracy?" in *The Political Forms of Modern Society,* 89-121). *Arguments* was the review of dissidents led by Edgar Morin who had left or been expelled from the French Communist Party by or before 1956, the time of the Khrushchev's secret report and the Russian repression of the Hungarian Revolution. It was Lefort who, speaking for the Socialisme ou Barbarie group, had replied to Morin's mocking attack ("Solecisme ou barbarisme," *Arguments* 3 [April 1957]: 13-19) against S. ou B.'s revolutionary conception of Russia as a form of "bureaucratic capitalism" in "Sur l'article de Morin" (ibid., 19-21). Later, Arguments and Socialisme ou Barbarie cooperated rather closely, the two groups quietly sharing subscription lists and Morin speaking publicly at S. ou B.-organized events in the early 1960s (after Lefort's departure from the group); and Lefort coauthored with Morin a 1964 volume, *Marxisme et sociologie* (Paris: EDI, 1964). Morin and Castoriadis later teamed up with Lefort to publish the first book on the May '68 student-worker rebellion, *Mai 1968: La brèche. Premières réflexions sur les événements* (Paris: Fayard, 1968). Lefort's contribution, "Le désordre nouveau" (The new disorder) was reprinted in the second edition (*Mai 1968: La brèche suivi de Vingt ans après* [Brussels: Complexe, 1988], 35-62), along with his 1988 retrospective "Relecture" (Rereading, ibid., 199-212). Only Castoriadis's contributions— "The Anticipated Revolution" (*Political and Social Writings,* 3:124-56) and "The Movements of the Sixties" (*World in Fragments,* 47-57) — exist in English. For Morin's recollec-

tions of his various collaborations with Lefort, now definitively ended, see "Mes années Lefort" (*Démocratie à l'œuvre*, 359-67). In relation to the Socialisme ou Barbarie theme of bureaucratization, it should also be pointed out that Castoriadis was himself the first to translate Weber into Greek, during his wartime years in Athens.

28 The journal *Socialisme ou Barbarie* was published between 1949 and 1965, the group itself disbanding in 1967. Its history was punctuated by a number of breaks, or "scissions," principally those of 1952 and 1958, when Lefort and Castoriadis found themselves as spokesmen for opposite sides in disputes over the organizational question. See Lefort, "Le prolétariat et le problème de la direction révolutionnaire," *Socialisme ou Barbarie* 10 (July-August 1952): 18-27 (reprinted as "Le prolétariat et sa direction," *Éléments*, 59-70), and "Organisation et parti. Contribution à une discussion," *S. ou B.* 26 (November-December 1958): 120-34 (reprinted in *Éléments*, 98-113). Castoriadis's *S. ou B.* texts on organization-in addition to "Le parti révolutionnaire (résolution)," *S. ou B.* 2 (May-June 1949): 99-107 (reprinted as "Le parti révolutionnaire," *L'expérience du mouvement ouvrier*, vol. 1: *Comment lutter* [Paris: Union Générale d'Éditions, 1974], 121-43, and followed by "Postface au *Parti révolutionnaire* et à *La direction prolétarienne*," ibid., 163-78), which testifies to a first dispute on this organizational question—are "Proletarian Leadership" (1952), *Political and Social Writings*, 1:198-205, with a postface, ibid., 1:205-6, and "Proletariat and Organization" (1959), *Political and Social Writings*, 2:193-222. The second part, "Prolétariat et organisation (suite et fin)," appeared in *S. ou B.* 28 (July-August 1959): 41-72 and was reprinted as "Prolétariat et organisation, II," *L'expérience du mouvement ouvrier*, vol. 2: *Prolétariat et organisation* (Paris: Union Générale d'Éditions, 1974), 189-248; an English translation exists only in typescript form. With Henri Simon and other members, Lefort left *S. ou B.* definitively in 1958 to form Informations et Liaisons Ouvrières (ILO), which later became Informations et Correspondances Ouvrières (ICO) after Lefort's departure. For background information on both *S. ou B.* and ILO/ICO, see Lefort's "An Interview with Claude Lefort" (originally conducted 19 April 1975 in French as a pamphlet for *Anti-Mythes* 14 [November 1975]), trans. Dorothy Gehrke and Brian Singer, *Telos* 30 (winter 1976-77): 173-92, and Castoriadis's 26 January 1974 interview conducted by the precursor to *Anti-Mythes* (now available in English as " 'The Only Way to Find Out If You Can Swim Is to Get into the Water': An Introductory Interview," *The Castoriadis Reader*, 1-34), as well as Simon's 7 September 1974 interview, "De la scission avec Socialisme ou Barbarie à la rupture avec ICO (entretien avec H. Simon)," *Anti-Mythes* 6 (December 1974), and his *I.C.O., un point de vue* (available c/o Échanges, B. P. 241, 75866 Paris Cedex 18 France). A final internal conflict developed in the early 1960s, after Lefort's ultimate departure from *S. ou B.*; that conflict culminated in the break of 1964, when a group including Alberto Véga, Pierre Souyri, and Jean-François Lyotard left, taking *S. ou B.*'s monthly militant newspaper, *Pouvoir Ouvrier*, with it. Of the *Libidinal Economy*-era Lyotard, Lefort says: "It is really hilarious how Lyotard, who then strapped himself into a Bolshevik uniform and who played Trotsky to Castoriadis's Lenin, is the same Lyotard who now plays with madness . . ." ("An Interview with Claude Lefort," 177). See Castoriadis's "An Introductory Interview" (*Castoriadis Reader*, 14-15), his "Postface to 'Recommencing the Revolution' " (*Political and Social Writings*, 3:80-85), and my own discussion of this last split in ibid., 3:85-87n1, which provides further references.

29 See also Lefort's two-part article "Une interprétation politique de l'antisémitisme: Hannah Arendt," *Commentaire* 20 (winter 1982-83): 654-60, and 21 (spring 1983): 21-28, as well as "Hannah Arendt and the Question of the Political" (1985), in *Democracy and Political Theory*, 45-55. On the Hungarian Revolution and the effervescence of Eastern Euro-

pean contestation during the mid-1950s, Lefort's key texts are "L'insurrection hongroise," *S. ou B.* 20 (December 1956–February 1957): 87–116 (reprinted in *L'invention démocratique. Les limites de la domination totalitaire* [Paris: Fayard, 1981], 202–46); "Retour de Pologne," *S. ou B.* 21 (March–May 1957): 15–58 (reprinted in the first edition of *Éléments* [Geneva: Droz, 1971], 221–59, and then in *L'invention démocratique*, 273–332); "La situation en Pologne," *S. ou B.* 22 (July–September 1957): 163–65; and "Pologne: La Kadarisation froide," *S. ou B.* 24 (May–June 1958): 107–10. Regarding these texts, Lefort notes his close collaboration with Castoriadis, which contrasts with their ongoing disagreements over organizational and philosophical matters: "In the face of major events (French politics, East Berlin, de-Stalinization, Poland, Hungary and Algeria), Castoriadis and I found ourselves so close that the texts published by either of us were also in large part the product of the other" ("An Interview with Lefort," 177). And to return to Arendt, Castoriadis stated, in his 1996 interview with *Drunken Boat's* Max Blechman, which is to accompany my translation of Castoriadis's 1994 interview, "The Rising Tide of Insignificancy. An Interview with Cornelius Castoriadis": "There is little difference between [Hannah Arendt's political] thinking at the time and what S. ou B. was saying."

30 Claude Lefort, *Un homme en trop. Réflexions sur "l'Archipel du Goulag"* (Paris: Éditions du Seuil, 1976). This volume incorporates a previously published commentary on *The Gulag Archipelago,* "Soljénitsyne," *Textures* 10–11 (1975): 3–38.

31 See also "An Interview with Claude Lefort," 186–87.

32 See, in *Le Discours de la servitude volontaire suivi de La Boétie et la question du politique,* ed. Miguel Abensour (Paris: Payot, 1976; 5th ed., 1993), Clastres's text ("Liberté, Malencontre, Innommable," 229–46) and Lefort's contribution ("Le nom d'Un," 247–307). Of note is my as yet unpublished translation of Fabio Ciaramelli's recent essay on La Boétie, "Friendship and Desire," which draws upon Lefort and Castoriadis as well as upon Freud.

33 For Lefort's writings on totalitarianism, see notes 29 and 30 above and notes 36 and 37 below. Castoriadis published the first installment of what later became his book *Devant la guerre* (Paris: Fayard, 1981; 2nd ed., 1983) in the last issue of *Libre* 8 (1980): 217–50, arguing there that Russia had become a "stratocracy" and was no longer a classic totalitarian State. The other journal Lefort and Castoriadis collaborated on in the 1970s, before *Libre,* was *Textures* (1971–75). There was also a period of collaboration within the "Cercle Saint-Just," later renamed the Cercle de Recherches et d'Études Sociales et Politiques (CRESP). See Lefort's comments on CRESP in his *Anti-Mythes* interview, 21–22 (this response was not translated for "An Interview with Claude Lefort"), Pierre Vidal-Naquet's description in "Souvenirs à bâtons rompus sur Cornelius Castoriadis et 'Socialisme ou Barbarie' " (*Revue Européenne des Sciences Sociales* 86 [December 1989]: 19–20; this journal issue was reprinted as *Autonomie et autotransformation de la société. La philosophie militante de Cornelius Castoriadis* [Geneva: Droz, 1989], with the same pagination), and Philippe Gottraux's section in his (often informative but deeply flawed) Bordieu-inspired sociology of the Socialisme ou Barbarie group, *"Socialisme ou Barbarie". Un engagement politique et intellectuel dans la France de l'après-guerre* (Lausanne: Payot, 1997), 309–12.

34 In "An Interview with Claude Lefort" (173), Lefort explains: "I owe my political orientation to much more than a chance encounter. In 1941–42, I was in Merleau-Ponty's class at the Lycée Carnot. He was able to establish a personal rapport with some of his students, so that one day, toward the end of the school year, he asked me if I were interested in politics and then, more precisely, what I thought of the French Communist Party. Astonished by my answers, he then asked if I were familiar with Trotsky. I replied that I wasn't, and

he made a remark I won't ever forget: 'It seems to me that if you knew him, you would be a Trotskyist.' . . . Although I cannot say when my 'ideas' were formed, at least in one sense they certainly were formed prior to my philosophy class. But in another, decisive sense, they were formed during that year under Merleau-Ponty's influence. His course in psychology was a condensed version of *The Structure of Behavior,* which he was about to publish, and his course on ethics dealt largely with sociology and Marxism. This influence is extremely important, for when I became a Trotskyist in 1943, I immediately discovered that my inclinations diverged from those of my elders and companions." Lefort was soon running a "clandestine group" at the Lycée Henri IV, holding weekly meetings that drew, on average, one hundred people, and he eventually "created a network of work groups" before Castoriadis came from Greece on a student scholarship at the end of 1945. Lefort adds: "I don't know what would have become of this faction, however, if Castoriadis had not arrived in France at that time. As I recall, I first heard him lecture to the Party on the USSR in preparation for the Third Congress. His analysis overwhelmed me. I was convinced by him even before he reached his conclusion" (ibid., 174). And yet a "first conflict" arose, even "before the birth of *Socialisme ou Barbarie,*" over the organizational question of how and when to leave the PCI, Castoriadis looking for an open and public break, well timed to bring along as many sympathizers as possible, Lefort opting for an earlier and quieter exit: "A handful of us were convinced that this delayed departure was harmful; our faction would only be corrupted by staying in the Party any longer. We thought it essential to regroup independently, with the dramatization of the break being of minor importance" (174–75). In this little episode, we see, perhaps more than the differing articulated principles (Lefort considers them revelatory), the essence of two opposing characters, their quite contrary "ways of being" (see below, in the text of the present Translator's Foreword). For Castoriadis's account of the transition from PCI to S. ou B., see "An Introductory Interview," 1–4. It must be added that sometimes Lefort is just plain mistaken about his differences with Castoriadis. Later in "An Interview with Claude Lefort" (177), he says that Castoriadis's close association with a "vaguely Hegelian" Raya Dunayevskaya, "who used the pen name Rya Stone," was the first of the three principal reasons for him to "intensify [his] opposition" to S. ou B. and its "rigidity." However, Lefort has confused Ria Stone (pseudonym for the Chinese American Grace Lee Boggs, who greatly influenced Castoriadis's thinking by opening him up to nonworkerist issues of women's liberation, civil rights, etc., in the early 1960s—traces of which can be found in the crucial 1962 internal S. ou B. document, "For a New Orientation," *Political and Social Writings,* 3:7–26) and the Hegelian-Marxist Raya Dunayevskaya (Trotsky's former secretary in Mexico and, along with C. L. R. James's "Johnson," "Freddie Forest" of the Johnson-Forest Tendency, which broke from Trotskyism in America about the same time S. ou B. did so in France). Castoriadis vividly told me one day how he couldn't stand Dunayevskaya when he met her in Paris in 1947; for her account of their meeting— "we are in the process of serious discussions, and I have hopes of winning him"—and of her discovery of the Chaulieu-Montal group—"this is the biggest thing since my arrival here"—see her letter to James in *C. L. R. James: His Intellectual Legacies,* ed. Selwyn R. Cudjoe and William E. Cain (Amherst: University of Massachusetts Press, 1995), 298–300. In fact, Stone/Boggs, who also was a member of Johnson-Forest, later broke with that group's continuators, opting for a less Hegelian-Marxist orientation that would be able to talk revolution in the American vernacular; for example, in her 1985 talk "I Must Love the Questions Themselves" (from the privately printed pamphlet *Grace: Selected Speeches by Grace Lee Boggs,* 26), she speaks of "tongue-tied U.S. Marxists." Misunderstandings as well as personality differences, we see here clearly, play an important role in history. (Thanks here to the meticulous Johnson-Forest scholar Scott McLemee and to Grace L. Bogg's recently published *Living for Change: An Autobiography,* foreword by Ossie Davis [Minneapolis: University of Minnesota Press, 1998], which has helped to clear up some of my own misconceptions.)

35 *Democracy and Political Theory,* 10.

36 Lefort has just published a critique of François Furet's 1995 book, *Le passé d'une illusion. Essai sur l'idée communiste au XXe siècle*—just translated into English (with a title that, unless I am mistaken, slightly misses Furet's clever allusion to Freud's *The Future of an Illusion*) as *The Passing of an Illusion: The Idea of Communism in the Twentieth Century,* trans. Deborah Furet (Chicago: University of Chicago Press, 1999)—and of Martin E. Malia's *The Soviet Tragedy: A History of Socialism in Russia, 1917–1991* (New York: Free Press, 1994). This new Lefort book, *La complication. Retour sur le communisme* (Paris: Calmann-Lévy, 1999), develops his critique of totalitarianism and brings it up to date.

37 "The Image of the Body and Totalitarianism," *The Political Forms of Modern Society,* 305. Lefort's other writings in English on totalitarianism include: "Totalitarianism without Stalin" (originally published as "Totalitarisme sans Staline—L'U.R.S.S. dans une nouvelle phase," *S. ou B.* 19 [1956]: 1–72; reprinted in *Éléments,* 155–235), "The Logic of Totalitarianism" (1980), and "Pushing Back the Limits of the Possible" (1981), ibid., 52–88, 273–91, and 307–19, respectively.

38 I say "from both above and below," for, according to Lefort, the totalitarian "Egocrat" ("or . . . his substitutes, the bureaucratic leaders") "coincides with himself, as society is supposed to coincide with itself" (ibid., 306). My perspective being close to that of Castoriadis while also being informed by Lefort's skeptical attitude toward "above" and "below" formulations (which still owe a great deal to political theology, he believes), I have highlighted, instead, some possibilities for *the democratic self-transformation of society* in my Translator's Foreword to Pierre Lévêque and Pierre Vidal-Naquet's *Cleisthenes the Athenian: An Essay on the Representation of Space and Time in Greek Political Thought from the End of the Sixth Century to the Death of Plato* (Atlantic Highlands, N.J.: Humanities, 1996), ix–xxvii. Lévêque and Vidal-Naquet's book, which is not a traditional intellectual history, contrasts the Pythagoreans' failed efforts to effect political change in society from without—i.e., via the formation of a separate group possessing an allegedly scientific knowledge (based in numbers mysticism)—from Cleisthenes' successful radical reorganization of civic space and time, which simultaneously associated the masses with his political grouping and provided a mathematically based formula and framework designed to enable greater citizen participation. I thus challenged in this foreword the ostensible "history from below" perspective of classical historian Joshua Ober, who neglects the important connections between political thought and mass action and who thereby reestablishes such false dichotomies as "organization" versus "spontaneity."

39 Ernst Kantorowicz, *The King's Two Bodies: A Study in Medieval Political Theology* (Princeton: Princeton University Press, 1957).

40 "The Image of the Body and Totalitarianism," *The Political Forms of Modern Society,* 306.

41 Ibid. (see the chapter's final paragraph). We may note that the Foucauldian power/knowledge dyad doesn't adequately account for what is Lefort's third term: *law.* The Nietzschean "vitalism" characteristic of Foucault, as well as of Lyotard during his post-*S. ou B.* days, here reveals its limits; both these authors found themselves belatedly (though not very convincingly) obliged to return to questions of *justice* that they had previously overlooked.

42 *Democracy and Political Theory*, 11.

43 "The Contradiction of Trotsky," *The Political Forms of Modern Society*, 31–51. "La contradiction de Trotsky et le problème révolutionnaire," *Les Temps Modernes* 39 (December 1948–January 1949): 48–69, was reprinted as "La Contradiction de Trotsky" in *Éléments*, 33–58.

44 On the controversial nature of the publication of this article in a nonrevolutionary journal, see Gottraux's book, 206–10. An article, "Les mains sales" (Dirty hands), which appeared in the Trotskyist organ, *La Vérité* 228 (15–28 February 1949): 5, and which was signed "P. F." (i.e., the Trotskyist leader Pierre Frank), violently attacked the young upstart Lefort for his critique of Trotsky. (Gottraux reminds us that David Rousset had just split off from the "right wing" of the PCI to form, with Sartre, the short-lived Rassemblement Démocratique Révolutionnaire; we may note, moreover, that *Les mains sales* was a 1948 play written by Sartre.) Under his pen name Pierre Chaulieu, Castoriadis responded even more violently in Lefort's defense with "Les Bouches inutiles" (Useless mouthings) in the inaugural issue of *S. ou B.* 1 (March 1949): 104–11. *Internationalisme*, the organ of the non-Trotskyist ultra-left organization of Bordigists, the Groupe Communiste de France, picked up on this controversy in "Salut à *Socialisme ou Barbarie*," *Internationalisme* 43 (June–July 1949): 36–43. Twenty-five years later (see "An Interview with Claude Lefort," 177), Lefort still retained a negative recollection of the Bordigists (followers of the Italian left-wing Communist Amadeo Bordiga), whom he calls "blundering comrades" and some of whom, in the meantime, had joined S. ou B.

45 "Les Communistes et la paix" was originally published in *Les Temps Modernes* 81 (July 1952): 1–50; 84–85 (November 1952): 695–763; and 101 (April 1954): 1729–1819; reprinted in *Situations* (Paris: Gallimard, 1964), 6:80–384, and translated by Martha H. Fletcher in *The Communists and the Peace* (New York: George Braziller, 1968), 3–231.

46 Claude Lefort, "Le Marxisme et Sartre," *Les Temps Modernes* 89 (April 1953): 1541–70; Jean-Paul Sartre, "Réponse à Claude Lefort," ibid., 1571–1629 (reprinted in *Situations* [Paris: Gallimard, 1965], 7:7–93, and translated by Philip R. Berk as "Response to Claude Lefort," *The Communists and the Peace*, 233–96); Pierre Chaulieu (Castoriadis), "Sartre, le stalinisme et les ouvriers," *S. ou B.* 12 (August 1953): 63–88 (reprinted in *L'expérience du mouvement ouvrier*, 1:179–248, and translated as "Sartre, Stalinism, and the Workers," *Political and Social Writings*, 1:207–41). Lefort's response to Sartre, "De la réponse à la question," finally appeared a year later in *Les Temps Modernes* 104 (July 1954): 157–84. Lefort's earliest published article, "L'analyse marxiste et le fascisme" (a review of a new edition of Daniel Guérin's *Fascisme et grand capital*), was, according to the Poltier bibliography, printed in the second issue of *Les Temps Modernes*, 1 November 1945, 357–62; it is the first of the dozen *Les Temps Modernes* texts Lefort penned between 1945 and 1954.

47 *The Adventures of the Dialectic*, 95–201. Interestingly, near the conclusion of his epilogue Merleau-Ponty writes: "One of my Marxist friends says that Bolshevism has already ruined the revolution and that it must be replaced by the masses' unpredictable ingenuity" (ibid., 232). One would think that this "Marxist friend" would have been Lefort, but the "masses' unpredictable ingenuity" formula is more likely Castoriadis's (see the opening paragraphs of his "Proletarian Leadership" text), and Castoriadis himself, in conversations with me, claimed paternity for this Merleau-Pontean reference (see the "1973" reference in Appendix F to Castoriadis's *Political and Social Writings*, 3:347).

48 "La Méthode des intellectuels dits 'progressistes': Échantillons," *S. ou B.* 23 (January–February 1958): 126–53, was reprinted as "La Méthode des intellectuels progressistes" in *Éléments*, 236–68. This article discusses, among other texts, Marcel Péju's "Retour de

Pologne," *Les Temps Modernes* 137–38 (July–August 1957): 37–56, which is also the title of a March 1957 *S. ou B.* article by Lefort (mentioned in note 29 above). See note 14 on page 55 of Péju's article for pejorative references to S. ou B.

49 See Miguel Abensour's "Savage Democracy and the Principle of Anarchy," trans. Max Blechman, *Philosophy and Social Criticism* (forthcoming).

50 In fact, Lefort's interest in the possible connections between phenomenological philosophy, radical politics, and literary theory extends back quite far. "For me," he says, speaking in retrospect about the influence his high school philosophy professor Merleau-Ponty exercised over him, "Marx's thought found its true expression in the language of phenomenology and phenomenology, in turn, found its basis and teleology in Marx" ("An Interview with Claude Lefort," 173). One early text especially worth highlighting is "L'Expérience prolétarienne," his unsigned editorial for *S. ou B.* 11 (November–December 1952): 1–19, the first issue published after his short-lived 1952 split (see note 28 above). The historian of the group, Stephen Hastings-King, devotes an entire chapter to this Lefort text in his laudable 1999 Cornell University History dissertation, *Fordism and the Marxist Revolutionary Project: A History of Socialisme ou Barbarie, Part I.* Elements of Hastings-King's discussion of this editorial statement regarding workers' writing (*témoinages* — eyewitness accounts or testimony — Lefort calls them) may also be found in his article for the special Castoriadis issue of *Thesis Eleven* 49 (May 1997): 69–84, "On the Marxist Imaginary and the Problem of Practice, Socialisme ou Barbarie, 1952–6." Hastings-King has also written in this dissertation the first serious treatment of the working-class writing of S. ou B. member Daniel Mothé (Jacques Gautrat), a former automobile worker at Renault's Billancourt factory who became a workplace sociologist in the 1970s. On the S. ou B. group, including comments on Lefort, see Mothé's own 8 June 1976 interview for *Anti-Mythes* 18 (1976).

51 "L'insurrection hongroise," 91; reprinted in *L'invention démocratique*, 210.

52 "The Invisible Ideology" is a section of Lefort's "Outline of the Genesis of Ideology in Modern Societies," *The Political Forms of Modern Society*, 224–36; see page 224 for the phrases quoted in the text.

53 *Corpsensus* was conceived and performed by the Paris-based American choreographer Clara Gibson Maxwell, who is also my life partner, in collaboration with the dancer Isabelle Pierre, the musicians Roman Garioud, Paul Susen, and Pierre Trocellier, and the painter Daniel Chompré. The mention of weaving refers to a text by Jean-Pierre Vernant, "Tisser l'amitié," which I have translated as "Weaving Friendship" for a forthcoming issue of *Salmagundi*; in French, *tissu* means both (human) *tissue* and *fabric* (either "cloth" or "the fabric, e.g., of society").

54 Such efforts have had varying degrees of success, from Castoriadis praising my *World in Fragments* foreword as one of the best things ever written about his work, to my having my forewords cut down — a little (a few paragraphs in my foreword to *Philosophy, Politics, Autonomy* were removed without my being informed of this editorial decision, thus creating an imbalance still found in the published version; the editor also added a subtitle, *Essays in Political Philosophy,* which neither Castoriadis nor I had approved: in contrast to [in response to?] Lefort, Castoriadis has nothing but contempt for political philosophy, a term that he almost invariably places within quotation marks before denigrating it) or a lot (see the reference regarding my Translator's Note to Pierre Vidal-Naquet's *The Jews,* above, note 1; Vidal-Naquet had told me that I "shouldn't change a word" right before the bulk of my essay was eliminated by the publisher) — or to my feeling compelled to abandon writing any introductory remarks at all, because of the publisher's objections to the

untraditional format I had adopted as most suited to a particular book (my Dick Howard translation, *The Birth of American Political Thought, 1763–87* [London: Macmillan Press, 1990], contains no translator's foreword).

55 Even before meeting Coleman and encountering his theory of "Harmolodics" in 1990, I made jazz the central metaphor for my discussion of Castoriadis's work in the foreword to my translation of the first volume of his *Political and Social Writings* (see xvii–xx). Coleman, moreover, provided the cover art for my last two Castoriadis translations: *The Castoriadis Reader* and *World in Fragments.*

56 Jacques Derrida was invited to "solo" in a duet with Coleman during the July 1997 Festival de la Villette in Paris, at which Coleman was the featured performer. *Grammatologie oblige,* Derrida stumbled through his reading of a prepared text—a "lesson," as he called it!—and was promptly booed off stage by most of the six hundred jazz fans in attendance. We may conclude that there is not only poetic but also musical justice in the world. A privately-printed account of this event is available by writing to my E-mail address: <curtis@msh-paris.fr>.

57 Coleman employed this phrase to describe the choreographic process of Clara Gibson Maxwell, the creator of *Corpsensus* (see note 53 above). Her interview with Coleman on friendship and collaboration in the face of commercial vicissitudes appears in the November 1999 issue of the jazz magazine *Cadence.*

58 Lefort's combination of literary with philosophical concerns should in no way be confused with the much-touted "linguistic turn" of some other philosophers.

Author's Preface

I HAVE BROUGHT together in this volume a series of articles published over the course of the past few years, adding to them a small number of previously unpublished texts. I have chosen these over other ones because, despite their variety, they testify to a certain kinship. Without having conceived them (need it be specified?) with the express purpose of directing them toward the same goal, I have followed the same slant and have found myself again and again, by one path or another, at grips with the same task: to scrutinize a specific mode of writing and to understand how it tallies with a certain mode of knowing, guided by a concern to decipher the political [*le politique*] or certain aspects of the political.

For me, the propensity to interpret is, dare I say it, natural, and similarly so is the attraction I feel for the questions that are at the heart of political life. Nevertheless, over the course of time I have become better aware of the peculiar connection between literature and political philosophy, or the movement of thought and the movement of writing, when they are subjected to the test of the political. The study of certain literary works reveals this connection. I regret that I haven't made greater room for such works. At least my exploration of Orwell's work *Nineteen Eighty-Four*—so famous and yet so misunderstood by those who completely separate the novel itself from its critique of the totalitarian universe—indicates one direction. But as different as it might be, this connection is revealed to be no less close when one considers a political work. To go straight to the things themselves, let us say that the novelist refuses to take the detour of argumentation, while the author of a political work rejects the detour of fiction. Nonetheless, it is a fact that the first can awaken our thought and that the second can provoke in us a troubled feeling.

Political science (inasmuch as it is concerned with works of the past) and the history of political philosophy share a common disposition, to ascertain and to analyze doctrines or theories. As I have emphasized elsewhere upon various occasions, there may be a difference between the two, the second challenging the principles of scientific neutrality and objectivity and preserving some traces of philosophy's own intention, but that difference isn't of consequence for our present purpose. I am simply drawing the reader's attention to an approach used to discover principles or key ideas that would allow one to identify certain "species," such as Platonism, Aristotelianism, Thomism, the theory of natural right, that of the social contract, or, closer to us, liberalism and socialism, and even, in the best of cases, the wide variations in these species. As each doctrine or theory originates in the work of one thinker or of a few eminent thinkers, this approach requires that one detect the "ideas" those thinkers have introduced as well as their connection, and it leads one to compare "systems of ideas."

Of course, I am far from believing that one might dispense with spotting currents of thought or the distinctive traits of a political philosophy. Still, one mustn't confuse what is of the order of *noting the particulars* [*signalement*] and what is on the order of *knowledge*. As soon as we read an individual [*singulière*] work, we are drawn into an adventure that makes us forget the boundaries set by political science and the history of political philosophy. This is an adventure that is always rich in new surprises. Indeed, however little we may refer to a text, once we believe we have finally understood it, we often discover, upon a second or third reading, that we have been blind to what was nevertheless there before our eyes. Now, the experience of reading teaches that the ideas are not detached from the language and that it is always by a process of incorporation of the other's writing that we gain the ability to think what is itself seeking to be thought.

Without doubt, this observation doesn't apply only to the political thinker. A long time ago already, in the wake of Maurice Merleau-Ponty's reflections and in contact with his own writings, I was connecting philosophy with literature. I was astonished to learn that philosophy had for so long been haunted by the "phantom of pure thought," to the point of not knowing what it was *doing*, not knowing what was being engendered in its writing and what bore the trace of its singularity, at the moment when it was attempting to attain universal truths. I am therefore not forgetting that *the philosopher is a writer-thinker*. I will add that this judgment applies equally to every great historian or sociologist. Michelet (or Weber) still exerts the same attraction upon us, even after one or another of his theses, which was no doubt dear to him, has been contested; we remain responsive [*sensibles*] to the inventiveness of his thought, which is delivered to us in the mobility of his writing.

Nevertheless, political philosophy establishes a peculiar connection with writing. Someone who practices it cannot yield entirely to the illusion that he is removed from his own time, from the society he inhabits, from the situation in which he thus finds himself, from the events that touch him, from the sense of a future that eludes his knowledge and that both excites his imagination and brings him back to an awareness of his limits. He knows, at least tacitly, that his work will fall into the hands of readers who will be affected by his remarks because he raises questions that directly or indirectly concern them and strike a blow against their prejudices. He doesn't wish to furnish arguments to persons whom he holds to be adversaries, imbeciles, or devotees of a doctrine, nor does he wish to seduce others who are in a rush to grasp one or another of his formulas and, without understanding him, hasten to make themselves his supporters while making him the hero of a cause.

For him, quite particularly, writing is therefore facing up to a risk [*l'épreuve d'un risque*]; and the risky test he faces offers him the resources for a singular form of speech that is set in motion by the exigency that he spring the traps of belief and escape from the grips of ideology, bringing himself always beyond the place where one expects him via a series of zig-zag movements that disappoint by turns the various sections of his public. No doubt, it is toward the true that he tends, otherwise he wouldn't be a philosopher; but he must, via a winding path, clear a *passage* within the agitated world of passions. Such an undertaking always fails by half, moreover, as shown by the welcome he most often receives from his contemporaries and, still more, by the stupidity of readers who will later press upon him a vulgar or scholarly discourse in order to celebrate or condemn his "theory" or to discover his "contradictions." Think only of the fate that awaited Machiavelli or Rousseau. He therefore is not, cannot be the master of the effects of his speech.

But it suffices that that speech be rigorous in order for some readers, at a remote distance, to be capable of hearing him and of placing him within the horizons of their time. His writing, which bears the mark of a resolve not to allow itself to be swallowed up in the ocean of opinions, nor to be blinded by the shock of events, sets his readers in motion even when they don't know the details of the controversies that mattered to him so much. His is therefore a very controlled [*concertée*] form of writing, not so much because it obeys the imperative of consistency but because it endeavors to bypass those places where each has settled so as to find shelter for his certitudes.

On the art of writing that political philosophy requires, Leo Strauss has cast vivid light, examining works of some thinkers from Antiquity and of some Jewish and Arab thinkers from the Middle Ages, who, he shows, endeavored to escape the dangers of persecution. (As will be seen, I devote several *Notes* to him.) Strauss suggests that there is in modern society another peril besides that of being a victim of political or religious authority: someone who wants to put into question the principles the majority holds to be self-evident exposes himself, Strauss says, to social ostracism. It may be that Strauss is neglecting how diverse are the invisible forms of censorship that menace independent thought.

Whatever the case may be, one would be mistaken to want to retain from political writing only the mark of mastery, of a learned expression placed in the service of some *design*. Such writing, in part so well governed, is, for another part, ungovernable, no less so than in the case of the *depth psychologist*. Someone who has agreed to move around in the "cavern" and to explore it patiently, the very same person who has imagined himself climbing back down into it after having glimpsed the things themselves in the light of the sun, has gained but the power to *advance* in the darkness. As Nietzsche said, under the cavern there is another one, then still another. In endeavoring to decipher what is closest to him, the political thinker allows himself to be carried away along several channels; he can wish not to soar over [*survoler*] times and spaces but rather to traverse them, the better to grasp the configuration of his own space-time, in order at least to detect the ultimate questions.

But even in his best attempt, these questions seem so general that, however confident at some point he might be that he has discovered *the principles whence are deduced all consequences,* they only bring him back into contact with the singular enigma the present poses for him. Thinking the political goes beyond the bounds of every doctrine or theory. Through writing, it sustains the tension inhabiting it; it submits to the exigency that one take on the questions that are at the heart of every human establishment and the exigency to face up to what arises. Furthermore, the reader cannot just seek to understand what the writer-thinker meant to say; that reader must still hear what makes him speak.

I thought it worthwhile to include in the very last part of this collection a few "interventions" in the debate that has been prompted by the decomposition of totalitarianism. These articles expose me to the event and to the uncertainty of the future.

Note

This "préface" was originally published in *Écrire. À l'épreuve du politique,* 9–13.

The Interposed Body:
George Orwell's *Nineteen Eighty-Four*

AS I WRITE this essay on *Nineteen Eighty-Four* in 1984, I am beginning to doubt that the book now being celebrated is the same or completely the same as the one that inhabits my memory. I am pleased with the homage being paid to it. What is said is generally well said. But everything is happening as if, by virtue of some operation I cannot explain, the book we are being presented with today had somehow shrunk. I cannot help but mention this operation, for Orwell himself speaks to us of it: under the reign of Big Brother, language itself was shrinking. As it became *Newspeak,* specialists were assigned to carve unsparingly into its flesh. "Useless" words were pared away bit by bit, so that they might not abet "thought crimes."

What is this operation? Let's give it another name: censorship. *Nineteen-Eighty-Four* became the object of an initial censorship that had nothing mysterious about it. Some people allowed themselves to ignore the fact that the book's theme was modeled on Stalinism, and others, inversely, didn't notice that the plot was situated in Oceana, and quite specifically in London. That kind of censorship, it seems to me, has by and large been lifted by now. But another kind persists. It is of a more surprising nature, since it is the work of politically aware commentators who say that they set a high value upon the lucidity of this writer. Yet this last word coming from my pen is ill chosen, and its imprecision leads me to get ahead of what I want to say. A short time ago, I heard three competent men assert on television that Orwell was not a "great writer" (the power of the epithet . . .). What it seems to me is therefore being censored is quite simply Orwell's artistry, this artistry that gives *Nineteen Eighty-Four* its terrifying charm and carries its enigma into our very depths. This phenomenon, moreover, doesn't date from yesterday. I find in the preface to the 1960 Gallimard edition of Orwell's *Essais choisis* these words from his French translator and editor, Philip Thody: "*Nineteen Eighty-Four* is less a novel than a mixture of political essay and science fiction. The love between Winston and Julia, as touching as it is, takes a back seat to the ideas in the novel's plot."[1]

Nineteen-Eighty-Four—to borrow an expression the author applies first to language, then to Winston at the end of his interrogation—has been "cut down . . . to the bone" (54), "strip[ped] to the bones" (298).

Here, then, is its skeleton. Everyone moves under the watchful eye [*regard*] of Big Brother. Private life has been destroyed. Every home has its own telescreen that spies on its inhabitants. Rules and regulations extend to all aspects of life, even to sexual practices. Basic values are turned upside down by means of such slogans as "War is peace," "Freedom is slavery," and "Ignorance is strength." Conspiracies are concocted by the regime, which keeps them going forever as a condition for its legitimacy. The country fights a foreign power whose very existence remains in doubt, and the identity of the adversary changes, even though the propaganda machine proclaims that the enemy was always the same. Truth—the truth of the understanding or factual truth—is abolished. By order, two plus two equals five, and the tortured individual sees five fingers when four are held up before him. The physicality of past facts vanishes. Mastery of time becomes total, as the slogan "Who controls the past controls the future: who controls the present controls the past" testifies (37 and 260). Thinking must constantly be doubled (*doublethink*), which implies the coexistence of the act of knowing with the act of not knowing. Through its purge of language, *Newspeak* seeks to reach that state of perfection where the stock of available words will one day render heretical thought impossible.

Let us halt here an inventory that we could continue beyond what is reported to us in the usual commentaries. Everything that has just been mentioned certainly brings out Orwell's political intelligence. If we were to continue the exploration, we would bring to light other, more subtle articulations in this skeleton of a theory. Orwell, it seems to me, formulated a number of themes that were being treated during the same period by Hannah Arendt, notably in the penultimate chapter of her work on *The Origins of Totalitarianism*.[2]

And yet, were one to stick to them, an essential part of *Nineteen Eighty-Four* would remain unknown. Its very design would escape our notice. In fact, in order to say what he was endeavoring to say, in order to put into words and to share his experience of the totalitarian universe, it really was a novel that Orwell wanted to compose, a *literary investigation* that he undertook. He is presented as someone who was overcome with timidity before his theory and who preferred to take the detour of a fictional account. Is it not, rather, that he was advancing into a region that he knew eluded the glaring light of the concept and that he felt capable of venturing into through characters and a "story"? What region would that be? Psychology? But wouldn't psychology lend itself just as well to a theoretical exposition? It is, I would say, that region where the boundaries between the "internal" and the "external," between personal existence and the political, break down.

So far as I know, the story hardly seems to have attracted the critics' attention. One would think that it is a simple setup conceived merely to facilitate the exercise of the proof. Let us summarize it.

Winston Smith is an employee of the Ministry of Truth. He works in the Records Department. His role is to reshape, as a function of the decisions of the day, those documents bearing a trace of a past that is to be erased. Nagged for some time by a doubt, he resolves to keep a diary. A personal diary if there ever was one, for its discovery would mean his downfall. Chance places him upon several occasions in the presence of an Inner Party member in whom he believes, without any proof, to have found an ally and, soon, an agent of the grand conspiracy known as the Brotherhood. This man, O'Brien, enters into contact with him, introduces himself, indeed, as an agent of Goldstein, and sends to him by a supposedly clandestine emissary the Book, a secret and sacred document in which the Brotherhood's analyses are written down.

He has been fooled completely. Arrested and sent to prison, Winston sees O'Brien enter his cell at the head of a group of policemen. He learns that O'Brien has kept him under constant surveillance and is himself the author or one of the authors of the Book. O'Brien becomes his tormentor; by turns relentless and kind, he embodies omnipotence. He imagines for Winston a torture specially adapted to the latter's personality. Winston will have to betray the only being he loves and, once broken psychically, he will have to submit to Big Brother.

His downfall thus seems to be brought on by the unconditional confidence he had placed in a false conspirator. But it also seems to be heralded by a need for love that arose from his encounter with a young woman. Julia had at first inspired in him feelings of distrust and hostility, inasmuch as she appeared to embody the very type of the hardy militant who is devoted to the Party. Literally accosted by her, he finds her to be independent-minded, more lucid than he ever was about the regime, and politically cynical. His passion leads him to find a love nest in a room situated above a junk shop—a vestige, he thinks, of the bygone world, kept by an authentic old man who, he thinks, is there to aid and abet his happiness. It is there, while taking minute precautions, that the two lovers take refuge from time to time, never ceasing to dread the moment when they will be found out. One day, when Winston exclaims in anguish, "We are the dead," a voice replies, "You are the dead" (230). The picture hanging above their bed conceals the hole through which they had constantly been spied upon. The shopkeeper himself turns out to be an agent of the secret police. Imprisonment, torture, mutual betrayal. Winston comes out of this adventure like a living corpse.

Thus do we have, briefly retraced, the slender plot that would serve as support for the theory. Presented in this way, it seems to justify Thody's opinion, or else again that of Irving Howe, as related by Simon Leys in a recent essay: "When Orwell was writing *Nineteen Eighty-Four,* literature could only have been the last of his worries."[3] Leys, for his part, deems Howe's judgment erroneous. But he says nothing that would bring out the qualities of the novel. On the contrary, Leys concedes:

> It is true that, from an artistic point of view, *Nineteen Eighty-Four* appears somewhat clumsy and it far from possesses the perfection of *Animal Farm;* these minor faults can probably be explained as much by the ambitious breadth of the work as by the difficult physical and moral conditions under which Orwell had to execute it.[4]

What "artistic clumsiness" he is alluding to, I don't know. The vagueness of the statement is what baffles me the most. The balancing between "minor faults" and "ambitious breadth" leads me to fear that Leys, like so many others, is separating the so-called *essential* from the so-called *anecdotal.*

Let us return to the story.

Taking advantage of a shallow alcove hidden from the telescreen in his apartment, Winston sits at his table and begins to write in his diary. Hardly has he jotted down the date — April 4, 1984 — on the top of the page when the following question occurs to him: "For whom . . . was he writing?" (9) "For the future, for the unborn," he tells himself (ibid.). Instead of satisfying him, this answer leaves him perplexed. The unknown persons of future times will not be able to hear what he has to say if they are like his contemporaries; and, if they are different, they will not understand what matters to him. Here we see him panic-stricken when faced with a blank page. The purpose of the diary, we learn, seemed to him to be to transcribe the inner monologue he was carrying on for years. His project had begun to germinate shortly beforehand, after he had discovered, in a junk shop located in a run-down neighborhood, a book he had a sudden desire to possess. There was nothing remarkable about this book except that it appeared to him to be a troubling vestige of the past. Charrington, the shopkeeper, thought it about forty years old, but no doubt in his view it was considerably older. The book had ignited in him a desire to write. Thus is the role the junk shop will play later on announced at the start. Later we shall see Winston, after having again wandered through this squalid (in fact, proletarian) neighborhood, happen as if by chance upon the same junk shop and, as if by chance, again undergo the attraction of an object, this one stranger, more useless, still older than the book: a glass ball that, Charrington tells him, contains a small piece of coral from the Indian Ocean. The object, which will partake in his fate by another path, will turn out to have arisen from his inner ocean, from the ocean of his thoughts.

At the moment he takes up his pen, Winston notices that he, who has never stopped conversing with himself, has nothing to write. And yet write he does. Apparently just some disordered thoughts. He relates an event from the previous evening. It concerns a movie showing. A war film, a "very good" one (10), was projected that showed a ship full of refugees being bombarded somewhere in the Mediterranean. I copy out the following passage:

> Then you saw a lifeboat full of children with a helicopter hovering over it. there was a middleaged woman might have been a jewess sitting up on the bow with a little boy about three years old in her arms. little boy screaming with fright and hiding his head between her breasts as if he was trying to burrow right into her and the woman putting her arms round him and comforting him although she was blue with fright herself, all the time covering him up as much as possible as if she thought her arms could keep the bullets off him (ibid.).

The narrative then mentions the spectators' applause and the indignation of one woman, in the upper gallery, who protests that "they didn't oughter of showed it in front of kids" (11). This woman, Winston notes, undoubtedly never had anything very serious happen to her, for "nobody cares what the proles say" (ibid.).

Once he has written this page, Winston stops himself, surprised. He does not understand "what had made him pour out this stream of rubbish" (ibid.). The reader doesn't know either. Nonetheless, the reader will guess why much later, when Winston recounts to Julia a childhood memory.

Winston does not know why he writes, still less what he should write. He asks himself only for whom he writes, and his answer disconcerts him. Nevertheless, Orwell furnishes the reader with a clue that, after the fact, will let him glimpse the motive and the addressee. Even before delivering to us the content of the first page, he notes that the "small but *childish* handwriting straggled up and down the page, shedding first its capital letters and finally even its full stops" (10). I underscore "childish" since, when Winston writes, he is pulled by the attraction of childhood; he addresses his thoughts, not to people who are not yet born, but to the dead.

Still, it must be pointed out that he does not only feel the pull of the past, he is possessed by the question of the past; he wants to know it. The man who is going to lose all his composure and launch into an adventure that will prove fatal to him—combating the totalitarian power and liberating himself from alienation—this man, we will soon discover, is haunted by the past. His political passion is not to be dissociated from his inner torment. The will to know the regime's secret is one with the will to know about his own secret. We could equally say that what lies before him, apparently on the outside, as an enigma is also in him or *behind* him; or, conversely, that what is buried in him is also before him. And that also amounts to saying that, since what is held deepest inside is himself, what he does not know, in a certain manner he does know; it amounts to saying that he holds the answer to all the questions he poses, while believing that he doesn't know the answer.

Winston's fate is not decided by O'Brien, still less by Julia. It is his own. The ascendancy O'Brien exercises over him may be summed up as follows: this man knows and warns Winston that he knows what Winston believes he doesn't know. Thus, when O'Brien enters his cell and Winston suddenly perceives him as the Party's agent, O'Brien tells him in a few short words: "You have always known it" (251). When this same O'Brien presents his theory of power and derides the hope Winston placed in a proletarian revolt, he declares that the proles will not rise up in thousands or millions of years, adding: "They cannot. I do not have to tell you the reason: you know it already" (274). When, after all varieties of torture, Winston, who has been destroyed to the point of seeing five fingers instead of four, is indulgently invited to ask the questions that torment him, the last one will be the following: What is in Room 101 (the Ministry of Love's room of horror)? And he will hear the answer: "You know what is in Room 101, Winston. Everyone knows what is in Room 101" (273). And indeed, he will ultimately face the test of this knowledge.

Orwell had previously reported a discussion between the two men. While the discussion was taking place, Winston imagined that he was dealing with a conspirator. Orwell notes:

> Even while he was speaking to O'Brien, when the meaning of the words sunk in, a chilly shuddering feeling had taken possession of his body.

He had the sensation of stepping into the dampness of a grave, and it was not much better because he had always known that the grave was there and waiting for him (166–67).

Orwell's artistry is particularly remarkable here, for he attributes to his character only the feeling of having always known. He offers him this simple thought: "The last step was something that would happen in the Ministry of Love. He had accepted it. The end was contained in the beginning" (166). Orwell does not grant him consciousness of what he knows; he keeps him in a state of half-ignorance of what the beginning was, the latter appearing to him only in a "secret, involuntary thought" dating back some years (ibid.). Nevertheless, two chapters later, during the crucial scene that takes place in O'Brien's apartment, the flow of Winston's thoughts are revealed to us in another way. Winston has just sworn allegiance to the Brotherhood, committed himself to obey it blindly and, if need be, to commit any crime in the service of the cause. Before leaving him, his host suggests that he propose a toast: " 'What shall it be this time?' he said, still with the same faint sense of irony. 'To the confusion of the Thought Police? To the death of Big Brother? To humanity? To the future?' 'To the past,' said Winston" (184). What at this moment appears more important than the idea of revolution is that of the defense, the reappropriation of what was. For him, it is impossible to divide the desire for political action from the attraction of the past. What he deems to be particularly ignoble, as is seen elsewhere, is the Party's slogan, "Who controls the past . . . ." Now, it turns out that he cannot condemn this ignominy as a fact that would be foreign to him. It wounds him in the most intimate layer of his thought. He is striving desperately to understand.

We ought not to separate everything Orwell reports about the falsification of history, and everything that testifies to his intelligence of totalitarianism, from the questions tormenting the character in his novel. In the first part of the book, he writes:

What most afflicted [Winston] with the sense of *nightmare* [my emphasis—C. L.] was that he had never clearly understood *why* the huge imposture was undertaken. The immediate advantages of falsifying the past were obvious, but the ultimate motive was mysterious. He took up his pen again and wrote: *I understand HOW: I do not understand WHY* (83).

This last formula appears on three occasions. What constitutes Winston's uniqueness, and his downfall, is the search for the ultimate motive, the desire coursing through him to know *why*. And this desire is inseparable from that of rediscovering the past.

The memory of the Jewish woman enveloping the child in her arms, of a useless gesture, takes on meaning, we said, in light of a childhood memory he recounts to Julia in the hidden room above the junk shop. This story is itself stirred up by a dream from which he awoke in tears, one "too complex to be put into words" (167). In this dream, "his whole life seemed to stretch out before him like a landscape on a summer evening after rain. It had occurred inside the glass paperweight, but the surface of the glass was the dome of the sky" (ibid.). This paperweight is the small object discovered in the junk shop that had captivated him: "a heavy lump of glass," he had then specified, "making almost a hemisphere" (98–99). He attributed to it "a peculiar softness, as of rain-water. . . . At the heart of it, . . . a strange, pink, convoluted object that recalled a rose or a sea anemone" (99). After having the shopkeeper point out that it was a piece of coral from the Indian Ocean embedded in glass, Orwell insists on how charmed Winston was by it: "What appealed to him about it was not so much its beauty as the air it seemed to possess of belonging to an age quite different from the present one. The soft, rain-watery glass was not like any glass that he had ever seen. The thing was doubly attractive because of its apparent uselessness" (ibid.). As if it had come out of a dream when he saw it for the first time on the junk shop owner's shelf, the small lump of glass sank back into the dream, associated with rain water, and it could be said that it contains the dreamer: "It had all occurred inside the glass paperweight," he says upon waking. He then adds, "The dream had also been comprehended by — indeed, in some sense, it had consisted in — a gesture of the arm made by his mother and made again thirty years later by the Jewish woman he had seen on the news film" (167). Such is his emotion, which he confides to Julia: "Do you know that until this moment I believed I had murdered my mother?" (ibid.). The remembrance of the dream brings up the childhood memory we had mentioned beforehand, and it reveals to him that he had not killed her, at least "not physically" (ibid.). "It was a memory that he must have deliberately pushed out of his consciousness over many years" (167–68). In what does it consist? In a vision, the last vision of his mother, which brings back a "cluster of small events" (167). Those events have to do with the period of his childhood following the disappearance of his father. His mother had changed; it seemed as if she had lost all her energy: "It was evident, even to Winston, that she was waiting for something that she knew must happen" (168). "Her large shapely body" (168) comes back to him in memory; or, as he says further on, her "statuesque body bending over the gas ring" (169). He recalls especially his hunger, a hunger that made him despotic, a thief, voracious. All the details are important: notably, he rummaged through trash cans. But let us retain only the final scene, brought on by the sharing of a bar of chocolate between him and his little sister, who was three years younger than he. Furious that he had received only three quarters of the bar, he suddenly snatched from the child's hands the last morsel and bounded from the room but turned around before fleeing. Here is his vision: "His mother's anxious eyes were fixed on his face. . . . His mother drew her arm round the child and pressed its face against her breast. Something in the gesture told him that his sister was dying" (170). If this vision was imprinted on him, it is, we learn, because he never saw either his mother or his sister again. Upon his return, a few hours later, they had disappeared without any trace of their having been taken away. Orwell notes: "The dream was still vivid in his mind, especially the enveloping, protecting gesture of the arm in which its whole meaning seemed to be contained" (171). This word, "seemed," leaves us, the readers, in the same half-knowledge, in the same half-ignorance as Winston. We will have to await his torture in Room 101 to know more about it. To say one more word about this episode in the novel, let us point out that the paperweight dream does not liberate only the childhood recollection; it also makes Winston recall another dream he had two months earlier, that is, if I am not mistaken, after he began keeping his diary but before he was seduced by this now famous object. "Exactly as his mother had sat on the dingy, white-quilted bed, with the child clinging to her, so she had sat in a sunken ship, far underneath him and drowning deeper every minute, but still looking up at him through the darkening water" (ibid.).

We must express once again our admiration for Orwell's artistry, for at the very beginning of the book, he reports a first dream by Winston.

> His mother was seated in some place deep down beneath him, with his young sister in her arms. He did not remember his sister at all, except as a tiny, feeble baby, always silent, with large watchful eyes. Both of them were *looking* [my emphasis — C. L.] up at him. They were down in some subterranean place — the bottom of a well, for instance, or a very deep grave — but it was a spot which, already far below him, was itself moving downwards. They were in the saloon of a sinking ship, looking up at him through the darkening water. . . . He was out in the light and air while they were being sucked down to death, and they were down there *because* he was up here (31–32).

The first allusion to his guilt — "he knew in his dream that the lives of his mother and his sister had been sacrificed to his own" (32) — offered the reader nothing informative. "He could not remember what had happened" (ibid.). No association had been made between the scene in the film and the vision of his childhood. Nevertheless, the two elements whose meaning he will later discover, the look [*regard*] and the water, were present.

If I speak of Orwell's artistry, it is not because he concocts a plot whose meaning is given bit by bit but because he does so in such a way that his reader feels at the same time as his character the strange familiarity of events that mark out his life since he began his diary. Indeed, not only does the reader discover after the fact the reason for the "rubbish" written on the first page but guesses, as Winston does, that there is something to be known in what happens to Winston that concerns the reader most closely. Between the color of the rainwater, the glass ball, the lifeboat where the Jewish woman and the child are standing, and the bottom of the well or the saloon on the ship into which his mother and his sister sink as their looks grow distant is woven a web of images that captivate him. The glass ball exerts an attraction upon us without our knowing why it seduces, but its transparency abolishes the distances of looks, the near-crystallization of the water abolishes that of the inside and the outside, the indestructibility of the tiny piece of coral confers immortality upon the child Winston and upon the being of the past. Winston's dream has no need of being interpreted by him; it itself produces its own interpretation: the dreamer is inside the paperweight and thus pries loose the gesture of the arm — a double gesture, that of the woman in the lifeboat and that of his mother, which upon waking brings back the childhood scene. Orwell makes this gesture itself the emblem, for Winston, of grace — of gratuitous love. When seized by this lost memory, he grows excited; but he cannot communicate his thoughts to Julia, who has fallen asleep at his side while listening to him (a small detail, one to be retained, since, as we shall see, the past doesn't fascinate her). He loves his mother for that gratuitous gesture; similarly, he loves the Jewish woman and he hates the Party:

> If you loved someone, you loved him, and when you had nothing else to give, you still gave him love. When the last of the chocolate was gone, his mother had clasped the child in her arms. It was no use; it changed nothing. . . . The refugee woman in the boat had also covered the little boy with her arm, which was no more use against the bullets. . . . The terrible thing the Party had done was to persuade you that mere impulses, mere feelings were of no account (171–72).

He continues: "What mattered were individual relationships, and a completely useless gesture, an embrace, a tear, a word spoken to a dying man could have value in itself" (172). Carried away then by this love, his thought rebounds abruptly in an unexpected direction:

The proles, it suddenly occurred to [Winston], had remained in this condition. They were not loyal to a party or a country or an idea, they were loyal to one another. For the first time in his life he did not despise the proles or think of them merely as an inert force which would one day spring to life and regenerate the world (ibid.).

One would nevertheless be mistaken if one imagined that Winston's thoughts coincide with those of Orwell. The writer's design is far more complicated. He does not limit himself to describing the intertwining of Winston's thoughts, his two-pronged quest for political truth and for the truth that dwells in him as an individual. He suggests that what most deeply moves Winston's thoughts, the desire that feeds them, is destined to be his downfall from day one not only because that has no place in the universe in which he lives but also because there is something in him that lends itself to the phantasm governing totalitarianism.

Let us return to the beginning of the book, to the writing of the diary. Winston has just written the first page; he is astonished by the "rubbish" that had come forth. Orwell goes on: "But the curious thing was that while he was doing so a totally different memory had clarified itself in his mind, to the point where he almost felt equal to writing it down. It was, he now realised, because of this other incident that he had suddenly decided to come home and begin the diary today" (11). Whereas the story on the first page bore on an event from the previous evening, the memory that comes to him at present concerns an event from that very same morning. That day, there had been a mandatory telescreening: the Two Minutes Hate. Goldstein, when he appeared on the screen, set off as usual a collective hysteria. A first remarkable fact: Winston cannot resist this drive to hate, but, when it reaches its point of paroxysm, that hate changes its object: he sees Big Brother in the place of Goldstein. Then a new transference occurs: he discharges his hate upon a young woman who is in the room, someone he had seen pass by several times who had manifested herself to him by her *look* (a look that he believes is inquisitorial, to the point that he supposes her to be a spy); he is seized by a fantasy of raping her, of destroying her body. The second remarkable event is that during the screening he had a double encounter. I say *double* because the two characters, who are not unknown to him, appear in the same place, in the same field of vision, for one moment. One of them is, as a matter of fact, this woman, Julia; the other is an Inner Party member, a "burly" man with a "brutal face" and a "prize-fighter's physique," O'Brien (12–13). Now, two things have deeply troubled him: a gesture and a "glance" [*un regard*] (20).

O'Brien makes a surprisingly elegant gesture, amid these militants with ugly and vulgar bodies, a gesture of resettling his eyeglasses on his nose that was "in some indefinable way, curiously civilised. . . . It was a gesture which, if anyone had still thought in such terms, might have recalled an eighteenth-century nobleman offering his snuff-box" (12). This is all that is needed to "deeply draw [Winston] to him," and Winston is "intrigued" to the point of imagining that O'Brien's "political orthodoxy was not perfect" (13). Winston is seduced: O'Brien "had the appearance of being a person that you could talk to" (ibid.). But he is most greatly troubled at the moment when the spectacle ends and the spectators stand up.

> Momentarily he caught O'Brien's eye. . . . there was a fraction of a second when their eyes met, and for as long as it took to happen Winston knew—yes, he *knew!*—that O'Brien was thinking the same thing as himself. An unmistakable message had passed. It was as though their two minds had opened and the thoughts were flowing from one into the other through their eyes (19).

Let us add that years earlier Winston had had a dream; a voice that he was later to identify as O'Brien's said to him: "We shall meet in the place where there is no darkness" (27). The dream gave voice to the man with whom one would love to speak. Its meaning will be revealed later.

The double encounter is a double mistake. Julia soon passes him a message he hadn't imagined he'd receive, written on a scrap of paper: "I love you" (113). She therefore wasn't a spy; she will prove to be an independent being, a nonconformist, who hates the Party. Winston will bring about her downfall, for she was in no way dreaming of revolting but only of living as freely as possible, of satisfying her sexual appetites, and of loving—of loving him. As for O'Brien, we have said that after having passed for a fellow conspirator he will catch Winston in his trap and will become, after Winston's arrest, his torturer.

So, one is captured by a glance, by a gesture of the arm. This gratuitous gesture that seems to emerge from the past, this glance that troubles him, they relate to the childhood memory forever imprinted upon him. No need to insist . . . . The consciousness that returns to him from his alienation in Big Brother, consciousness in revolt (he will join in the conspiracy), is a deluded consciousness, spellbound by an image of the body that is buried within him as is the past.

One couldn't finish drawing up a list of Winston's notations about the physical appearance of those beings he frequents, whether the compact, dull, inhuman bodies of the ministry's employees or those of Party militants, or bodies suddenly illuminated by grace, Julia's or the one, though coarse, of a proletarian woman who sings while hanging laundry on a line, in the courtyard neighboring his room of refuge. But let us not lose sight of the essential: Winston is not only the victim of O'Brien, the representative of the totalitarian power; he does not only fall into the trap someone else has set for him. He is first of all his own victim; he is caught in his own trap. And, in fact, it will be seen that, even under torture, the figure of O'Brien won't cease to fascinate him: "He was the tormentor, he was the protector, he was the inquisitor, he was the friend" (256).

The anxious interrogation of the other, of the existence of his body, will ultimately lead Winston to ask O'Brien the following question: "Does Big Brother exist?" (271). Winston's interlocutor answers, "Of course he exists. The Party exists. Big Brother is the embodiment of the Party." Winston insists on the point. "Does he exist in the same way as I exist?" " 'You don't exist,' said O'Brien. Once again the sense of helplessness assailed him" (ibid.). He obstinately asks one more time. " 'I think I exist,' he said wearily. . . . 'I was born, and I shall die. I have arms and legs, I occupy a particular point in space. No other solid object can occupy the same point simultaneously. In that sense, does Big Brother exist?' 'It is of no importance. He exists.' 'Will Big Brother ever die?' 'Of course not. How could he die?' " (272). A few pages earlier, Orwell related a similar dialogue. It was not the reality of the body but the reality of the past that was made the object of Winston's intrepid questioning, of O'Brien's ironic denial. The latter concludes, "Reality exists . . . only in the mind of the Party, which is collective and immortal" (261).

Winston's fierce defense of self-consciousness leans on the certitude of his body circumscribed in space, on the certitude of the past, of the event that has taken place—guaranteed by memory, which is inscribed in intangible documents—and on the certitude of death, tied to the existence of the individual as such. His passion for finitude serves to foster his freedom. And yet, the Self vacillates before the enigma of the body, of the past, of death; it is threatened from within by faith in the indestructibility of appearance as such and of the event. The attraction of the body, the attraction of the past thus silently reconstitutes a belief in immortality—in the sort of immortality to which O'Brien's voice gives resonance in his defense of the Party.

A number of signs go to show that there is a complicity between the torturer and his victim and that this complicity is not established by O'Brien simply as an artifice, the better to subjugate Winston. It is after he has broken all of Winston's resistance, after having extorted from him his own thought, his vision that two plus two make five, that O'Brien asks him: "Do you remember writing in your diary that it did not matter whether I was a friend or an enemy, since I was at least a person who understood you and could be talked to? You were right. I enjoy talking to you. Your mind appeals to me. It resembles my own mind except that you happen to be insane" (271). The two of them are tragically intertwined. O'Brien destroys in himself the individual Winston embodies before him. For example, in an extraordinary scene he obliges Winston to contemplate in the mirror, after months of tortures, his own emaciated body, in part bruised, in part hollow, unrecognizable. He sees Winston seeing himself in the mirror and rains down comments upon him that continue to rip him to shreds. O'Brien thus tears away from Winston the proof of his own power, something no execution would have brought him. What he requires is Winston's gaze [*regard*] on his own body. For O'Brien, the negation of Self passes by way of Winston's gaze.

In the dream Winston had years earlier, the voice later identified as O'Brien's said, "We shall meet in the place where there is no darkness" (27). The moment of their meeting has indeed come, but the dream knew it longer than the dreamer. It takes place at the Ministry of Love, that windowless place where the outside is eliminated. There, the mortality of the detainees maintains the immortality of the Party.

Let us come now to the denouement. After having abandoned all means of defense and contemplated his downfall in the mirror, Winston retains one final thought of his own and dares to speak it: "I have not betrayed Julia" (286). The Self no longer holds to anything but this thought. O'Brien grants him this. Then opens a period of appeasement: he is fed, he regains his strength, is persuaded that the Party is always right, and repeats its slogans. "The mind," he tells himself, "should develop a blind spot whenever a dangerous thought presented itself" (291). This well-formulated statement is put there to suggest that he has imprinted on himself the architecture of the Ministry of Love, that windowless building. But one day, at the end of a long dream — which belongs to the series of dreams of the Golden Country — he is awakened by the noise of the words he himself has just shouted: "Julia! Julia! Julia, my love! Julia!" (293). Terrified, he has no doubt that these words have been heard and are to be his downfall. He then clings to the idea that he will die hating *them,* that *that* is freedom. In fact, these cries, the love of Julia, finally take him into Room 101; he had asked O'Brien what goes on in that terrifying place, eliciting no other response but "You knew the answer already" (296).

The torture, the most intimate one, is now readied, which he could not but know, and which the reader can recognize as Winston's own, since an incident that took place in the refuge room above the junk shop had warned us of what for Winston was the absolute horror: rats. O'Brien has perfect control of the situation. He informs his victim that the worst thing in the world varies according to individuals. He reveals to him that he knows what is the object of his terror. He takes pleasure in pointing out that "by itself pain is not always enough. There are occasions when a human being will stand out against pain, even to the point of death. But for everyone there is something unendurable—something that cannot be *contemplated*" (297, emphasis added). The cage in which the rats are held is brought close, adjusted to fit the mask strapped to his face. A first click signals their passage, through a door, from the back of the cage to the front. Orwell then writes, "Everything had gone black. For an instant he was insane, *a screaming animal.* Yet he came out of the blackness clutching an idea. There was one and only one way to save himself. He must *interpose another human being, the* body *of another human being, between* himself and the rats" (299, emphasis added). Then, after having described the agony of the last seconds, Orwell writes further:

> Too late, perhaps too late. But he had suddenly understood that in the whole world there was just *one* person to whom he could transfer his punishment—*one* body that he could thrust between himself and the rats. And he was shouting frantically, over and over: "Do it to Julia. Do it to Julia! Not me! Julia! I don't care what you do to her. Tear her face off, strip her to the bones. Not me! Julia! Not me!" (299–300).

This shouting saves him. He will later be released. He will live, literally amputated of his self-consciousness. He will love Big Brother.

Such, then, is the secret of Room 101 in the Ministry of Love. At the junk shop, Winston and Julia, suddenly confiding to each other their worry, had granted that they would be caught and tortured, that they would not fail to sell each other out, but one thing remained certain for them: love; one couldn't destroy that. "They can't get inside you" (174). These words, said by one of them, were repeated by the other. Now, how could they have pronounced them if they weren't imagining an entrance? The scene with the rats reveals the door by which *they* enter: the secret door of the phantasm, the one that, one might dare say, is deepest within oneself, for each one, or as if behind oneself. They go in from behind. . . .

With the discretion of a "great writer," Orwell refrains from giving his reader any more explanations. But he has previously said enough for us to know why the rats placed under Winston's eyes not only are ready to devour his face, when the cage door is opened, but come out from himself by an inner door. It suffices for him to note that Winston is transformed into a "screaming animal." What bursts in is the little boy, always famished, vora-cious, cruel, who rummages through trash cans, stealing food on the land-ings where his mother had put him for safety, who devoured everything, up to and including the morsel of chocolate set aside for his sister. The ignoble rat, the object Winston can neither bear nor contemplate is in part himself.

All this would merit more extensive commentaries. It would be worth-while to associate the image of the interposed body with the horrors of a devouring in which the difference between the devourer and the devoured is abolished, as it would be to recall that, during the double encounter (the event that instigated his decision to keep the diary, his labor of reflection), Winston was overtaken by the impulse to rape and destroy Julia's body, a drive whose object had at first been Goldstein, then Big Brother. The love he then brings to Julia comes to him in return by his being chosen by her. But I prefer to give up following this line in order to scrutinize the political and ontological signification of the interposed body.

The author does not leave us any doubt, at the end of the book, as to Julia's fate—without, however, giving us any precise information on this score. One knows only that she has undergone a similar torture. She has had to interpose between herself and the horror Winston's body. Nevertheless, as we pointed out, their cases are not symmetrical. Julia loves Winston; she goes as far as to follow him to O'Brien's, but nothing prompts her to give in to the charm of appearances or of events from the past, and she does not seek the *why* of the totalitarian imposture. She does not separate the love of pleasure from sexuality; she does not pursue any inquiry about her child-hood (at the very most, she retains a happy memory of her grandfather). In short, Julia, like the proletarians, escapes the regime's clutches. She dreams of living, not of changing herself and of changing the world. It is Winston who brings about her downfall. It remains the case that, once tied to his destiny, she is destroyed like him. Orwell shows them, sometime after the torture sessions have ended, crossing each other by chance in the street, like two mannequins. They allude to their mutual treason but are powerless to say more. Though apparently alive, they are without desire, without love, psychically picked clean to the bone. Each, in interposing the body of the other, has lost his or her amorous body and his or her sexed body.

Let us stay close to Winston, since Orwell no longer speaks of hardly any-thing but him. What is suggested to us cannot be summarized in the idea that the destruction of self-consciousness is simultaneously a quasi-destruc-tion of one's own body. The latter is accompanied by the amputation of the image of the loved body. We understand that this other body is not alien to one's own. It was quite necessary, rather, for him to tear that body from his own in order to put it between himself and the rats, to raise it as a screen before the horror. When he cried to throw Julia to the rats, he destroyed the flesh of his flesh. He deprived himself of a flesh that was protecting him, nourishing him, a flesh in which was formed his love, his desire, his self-consciousness. In order to protect himself, he has abandoned a primordial form of protection; he has torn apart his internal tissue. Nevertheless, after having escaped from being devoured, he allowed himself to be invaded by the image of Big Brother. Orwell thus leaves it to us to understand that the body of Big Brother has replaced that of Julia for Winston: Big Brother is, in his way, a new body interposed between him and death. But the difference between the two bodies is clear: that of Julia is a mortal body; he loves it as such and this love is his own; this other gives him the assurance of his own body. In sacrificing it, he destroys what he shaped into reality, the flesh of his flesh, and in the same stroke he destroys his individuality, the consciousness of his own mortality. By way of contrast, the body of Big Brother is immortal; it is neither in space nor in time. This other dispossesses him of himself, drowns him in the togetherness [*l'être-ensemble*] of the Party.

There is no doubt that Orwell is seeking to unveil, through Winston's adventure, something of the essence of totalitarianism. Certainly, Winston belongs to a particular category of individuals. He stands out among the type of men the regime fashions. O'Brien speaks of him as a sick man. But for O'Brien himself this diagnosis does not suffice. We have seen that O'Brien cares about Winston's person, that his mind pleases him, that it might resemble his own, were it not sick. He tells Winston on one occasion: "I am taking trouble with you, Winston, because you are worth trouble" (258). The interest O'Brien shows for him comes from the fact that his case prompts O'Brien to expound upon the principles of the system: indeed, there are nothing like difficult cases to prove its validity. As it turns out, the difficulty resides in the obstinate way Winston pursues self-knowledge and knowledge of the regime. The solution to the difficulty resides in the discovery that the quest for truth is guided by a certitude in the indestructibility of what appears and of what has been, which is both opposed to totalitarian certitude and not alien to it. The meaning of the indestructible is tied to the consciousness of finitude—that of the body's delimitation in space and time, that of the irreversibility of history or of the impossibility of erasing the event. But the consciousness of finitude finds in itself an affirmative strength that takes away from this consciousness of finitude all limits, and this strength always is trying to certify itself in a shared knowledge, in a communion of each one's thoughts. Winston feels secure in the gaze of his mother, in an event from the past forever imprinted on his memory, but the past is not ineffaceable just for having taken place. Winston does not possess only this vision; he is embedded in it, as the coral in the block of glass. Vision is not only in time, but outside time. It is not only the object of his affirmation; he is instituted by it. Furthermore, the recollection he gains through the desire to return to himself is not alien to the attraction O'Brien's gaze exercises, during their first encounter, a gaze that his own one weds, as if *"the thoughts were flowing from one into the other through their eyes."* And the path of his self-consciousness will be such that in the course of his interrogations he will come to prefer, to the certitude of what is, the certitude that the other — be it for his downfall — shares his thoughts: "Perhaps," he says, "one did not want to be loved so much as to be understood" (264). In Winston's case, O'Brien verifies that servitude can be pushed the furthest at the point where freedom seems obstinately sought after.

Sick, in O'Brien's sense, Winston does not belong to another species than the men over whom the power of the Party reigns with ease. But for them to be "normalized," it suffices that Goldstein and Big Brother appear one after another on the big screen. The Two Minutes Hate is but a small episode that reveals the great staging [*mise en scène*] of totalitarianism. Winston's adventure sheds light on the mechanism. Goldstein is not only the figure of the enemy, nor is Big Brother just the friend. Goldstein is the *interposed body* that is thrown to the rats: a body produced in order to be destroyed eternally. Big Brother surges up at the end of this spectacle as the protective body that eternally conjures away the danger of death. It is the fact of *being together* [*être ensemble*], absolutely united before the (visible and invisible) screen of the regime, that allows each to forgo the sacrifice of the loved one, to preserve his sexed body, and to cohabit with the rats. The regime is content, as Orwell notes, just to oversee people's exercise of their sexuality and love relations, and to do so in such a way as to avoid an excessive liberation of energy or an intensity of feeling that would dissociate the collective body and would reawaken in the individual the sense of what he is and of what he has that is his own.

Let us recall that, in the first few pages of the book, Orwell provided a rapid survey of the four large ministries upon which the regime's might is founded: the Ministry of Truth, that of Peace, that of Love, and that of Plenty. He then wrote: "The Ministry of Love was the really frightening one."

The end of the book is contained in its beginning.

Notes

"Le corps interposé. *1984* de George Orwell" was originally published in *Passé-présent* 3. *La force de l'événement* (Paris: Ramsay, 1984), 80–97. Reprinted in *Écrire*, 15–36. [All in-text page references in this chapter, which were provided by me, the translator/editor, refer to the 1989 Penguin edition of George Orwell's *Nineteen Eighty-Four.* Hereafter, "T/E" is used in connection with changes, additions, or explanations by the translator/editor.]

1 T/E: Philip Thody, preface to George Orwell's *Essais Choisis,* trans. Philip Thody (Paris: Gallimard, 1960), 14.

2 T/E: Hannah Arendt, "Totalitarianism in Power," *The Origins of Totalitarianism* (1951), new ed. with added prefaces (New York: Harcourt Brace Jovanovich, 1973), 389–459.

3 Simon Leys, *Orwell ou l'horreur de la politique* (Paris: Hermann, 1984), 52.

4 Irving Howe, *Politics and the Novel* (New York: Columbia University Press, 1957, 1992), 237.

Humanism and Anti-Humanism:
Homage to Salman Rushdie

THE OBJECT OF this colloquium is so vast that it authorizes each person to choose his starting point as it seems best to him. The organizers have certainly wished that it be so. And it is by design, it seems to me, that, instead of the title "The Individual and Society," they have preferred that of "Man and Society." The former would surely have brought us back to those theoretical debates whose origin is mixed up with the birth of sociology or would have prodded us toward the fashionable theme of the dissolution of the social bond and that of the drift toward individualism.

To speak of *man* is to open the field of investigation in an entirely other way. As one knows, "man" was denounced as an abstraction as soon as the Declaration of the Rights of Man was formulated. Although founded upon sometimes different, nay even opposed, premises, the argument was sustained by a call to return to "reality." Men can be known only to the extent that they are defined within a culture, as members of an ethnic group or a nation, as citizens or subjects in a political community, or, yet again, as agents of a process of production and social reproduction. In the absence of a system of coordinates that would allow one to distinguish lines of descent, hierarchies or simply places, functions, that might thus allow one to situate individuals in differentiated ensembles, the image of man vanishes. Man as such, without determination, is not a man. Didn't Aristotle already say that a man unbound from any city would be less than a man or more than a man, a brute or a god?

As forceful as these arguments might be, they run up against an experience, certainly an obscure one, yet undeniable: they are impotent to account for the advent of the idea of man, for its slow advance, then for its irresistible expansion since the end of the eighteenth century. This idea takes on a twofold meaning: it implies that man is not a de facto datum, that he must discover what constitutes his humanity; and it implies that the men who populate the earth are, despite everything that distinguishes them from one another, fellow men [*semblables*]. Undoubtedly, it can be said that this is but an "idea"; that in its first sense humanity, taken connotatively [*dans son comprehension*], is unable to yield a concrete definition of human nature; and that in its second sense humanity, taken denotatively [*dans son extension*], is but a phantom in the absence of any institution that would show the way in which its supposed members participate in it.

Thus have some judged that the rights of man pertained to an ideology that has been grafted onto the real rights of individuals and of citizens in a given place and at a given time (or else only of the bourgeoisie). Nonetheless, this objection does not hold up very well against the fact that all the rights respected within a nation and held to be generative of the existence of a people see themselves at the same time laden with a universal meaning. Let us note in passing that the great Edmund Burke was mistaken when he claimed that the rights acquired by the English were only "the rights of Englishmen," and Tocqueville knew how to denounce his error. Individual liberties and political ones can receive de facto recognition only in a limited space; as soon as they are so recognized, they are revealed to be unconditional, not relative, and constitutive of a properly human mode of existence and coexistence. Such is the apparent paradox of the French Declaration, so disconcerting to its adversaries. It affirms simultaneously the idea of the sovereignty of the people, that of the nation's identity, that of the individual's independence, and that of man.

These ideas do not coincide with one another. Indeed, they give rise to a tension among different exigencies that run the risk of coming apart, as numerous events have shown. It is one thing to be above all a citizen — which presupposes adherence to a political regime — and it is another to be a patriot — which implies, for example, that one would willingly agree to serve under a tyrant after having known freedom, provided that one sees in him the guarantor of national identity (Aristotle was quite attentive to this distinction); and it is a third to want to live one's life as one wishes, whatever one's motives; and it is, finally, another to have, qua man, an idea of freedom and of truth that might, for example, make one feel at certain moments closer to foreigners who struggle against oppression and lies than to one's compatriots and fellow citizens, and even make one run the risk of seeming the traitor for opposing one's government during an unjust war (think of the Frenchman who condemned the Algerian War or the American the Vietnam War).

However, while the tension among the key ideas of democracy can provoke dissension, one must still try to grasp their connection. The images of national identity, popular will, and the independence of the individual are such that they might induce a transference onto *the other* (nation, people, individual). One's way of adopting one's identity in a democratic regime is such that it makes possible an identification with someone who elsewhere sees himself dispossessed of his identity—and this, despite the fact that most of the time this identification is held in check by nationalism or some other form of communitarianism.

The idea of the humanity in man, like that of the humanity that encompasses all men, escapes all definition. Those who criticize it are right on just this one point. But their realism—their conception of the "real" man—hides from them the singular character of democracy, which prevents each person from being at once purely the patriot, purely the citizen, purely the individual, and which, as the other side of this impossibility, allows man to come out. Democracy gives form to a community of an unprecedented kind that could not be confined definitively within its borders but instead opens upon the horizons of a humanity of which there can be no established figure [*infigurable*].

I now come to my principal remarks. Perhaps this preamble will have rendered them less odd. Using the freedom offered us, I would like to draw people's attention to the problems raised by the persecution Salman Rushdie has suffered as well as to the reflections his persecution inspires in him, which testify to a singular conception of the social bond and of the condition of man in our era.

No one has forgotten the death sentence pronounced by the Imam Khomeini, his call for the defenders of the true faith to execute the author of the *Satanic Verses* by whatever means, in whatever place he might find refuge, taking no account of the passage of time. Informed observers have advanced the hypothesis that the imam, finding himself in a difficult position vis-à-vis his Sunni opponents, seized an occasion to trump their intransigent attitude and to affirm his own authority over Islam. However, once Khomeini was gone, Rushdie's death sentence was reaffirmed. In vain would one disregard the fact that Islam professes to be a universal religion and that it is in appealing to a universal mission imposed on its faithful (however contested that mission might be by a number of believers) that Khomeini and his successors have judged and convicted an English writer of Indian origin who was raised in a Muslim culture, finding him guilty of blasphemy. Of course, if the author of the *Verses* had been a Christian or a Jew and purely English, it could be doubted whether he would have stirred up such wrath. But raising this reservation could not make one forget the grand project of human regeneration the imam conceived and the hatreds he unleashed against those hellhounds of Satan, the Westerners. In its own way, the party of Khomeini offers to man a determinate figure of himself—the man who answers to his calling as God's creature, as distinguished from the trivial being who is but the counterfeit version thereof. In its own way, this party also gives a shape [*figure*] to humanity, considered in its full range [*extension*], by affirming its jurisdiction over the entire earth, without caring what laws are in force in non-Islamic lands. By itself alone, this event merits our attention. It has had the virtue of bringing out, or making reappear, a maleficent pole of religious universalism and of reawakening somewhat those who are nodding off into the cult of relativism.

It is an extraordinary thing, and we should not still our sense of astonishment: Salman Rushdie has been living in seclusion since 1989. He has been stripped, if not of his rights, at least of the enjoyment of his rights as a citizen. He finds himself in something like exile within his own country. And as an *individual*, he has lost the secure possession of that property deemed primordial by the liberals who inspired the constitution of that country: the ownership of his body, of his life.

Whoever limits himself to stating the facts is tempted to contrast the logic of a theocratic State with that of a democratic State. The latter respects the principle of noninterference in the affairs of a foreign country, while the former doesn't recognize that principle. Thus, the conflict seems intelligible, though insoluble, short of risking war—an eventuality that has quite evidently been ruled out. Such reasoning is not false. But it allows one to avoid the question that is rightly at the center of Rushdie's work, the question of the social bond and of the way of being or of purporting to be a man in our time.

It is neither qua individual nor qua citizen that Rushdie has written the *Verses,* and it is not only in these capacities that he is to be defended. A writer, he addresses himself to an indeterminate public, to his contemporaries and to a posterity he doesn't know; and he is himself an indeterminate man. His thought, his language cross the boundaries of space and of time, even though they are formed in a certain country at a certain moment. Yes, he writes in English, but his thoughts are not English, nor is that which he expresses English—this, not only because he is also Indian but also because in order to think, in order to write, he must not forget his origins and his present state but instead must find therein the power to bring forth a relationship to things, to others, an experience of the world that detaches itself from him. The work [*L'œuvre*] is that very thing that detaches itself; once done, it suffices unto itself. It is thus that it is *human,* given by right to all men. One is adopting Khomeini's point of view—though it be to defend someone being persecuted—when one takes into account only the difference between two cultures and when one neglects that which is at stake in the existence of the work, an aiming at the universal that, as a consequence, escapes the jurisdiction not only of the imam but of every political authority. Although it is likely that Khomeini was horrified by Rushdie's blasphemy and judged him to be an apostate—in reality, the accusation is dishonest since Rushdie does not share the Muslims' faith and since that is known—his decision presupposes in the very first place a rejection of the literary work, inasmuch as a work of that sort manifests itself as something that cannot be appropriated.

In neglecting this point, the reactions the Rushdie affair has aroused in the West—at least in England and in France, for I am not well informed of the situation in other countries—were disappointing. On the one hand, we have seen religious authorities of various faiths give voice to a revealing sense of discomfort. The call to murder launched by the imam seems to them inadmissible, but they worry about freedom of expression when it is no longer limited by a respect for things sacred. No one, it was stated, has the right to make remarks that offend believers. Thus was Rushdie providing an indication of a decay in mores, of the license that today threatens democracy, of the loss of the sense of *ultimate values.* This is a way of saying that one function of the liberal State, though it is by essence neutral, would be to protect from attacks of unbelief a territory divided between various domains of the sacred. It is also a way of challenging the existence of a public space, since in the end the disturber didn't enter a mosque to insult the faithful or smash objects of worship; all he did was write something addressed to the attention of those who wished to read him. An astonishing spectacle, then, this religious front set up to defend, within society, the common sanctuary of untouchable principles.

Nevertheless, rather than lingering over this point and observing how dogmatism presumptuously asserts itself under cover of a holy alliance among pretenders to the possession of divine truth—how a new religious universalism, purely tactical in character, profits from Khomeini's fanaticism—let us emphasize instead that Rushdie's work isn't being examined. These religious people, so scholarly in matters of dogma, are not worried over a book. Having once and for all drawn the line between the truth of which they claim to be the guardians and that which pertains to opinion, they can only make of the book a manifestation of opinion, in this case a pernicious one, since it transgresses the space generously granted to debate over trivial subjects. I therefore ought not to say that the public space is seeing itself repudiated; it is being reduced to the space of the relative. Thus being substituted for the distinction, constitutive of a liberal society, between the private and the public is the distinction between the public and the sacred. No less significant, let us note, is the reaction of a number of politicians who have shamelessly adopted the language of certain bishops, pastors, and rabbis, or who, like a former French prime minister, have determined that indignation grants too much honor to an insignificant and "pornographic" work.

On the other hand, we ought to rejoice at the mobilization of a broad layer of intellectuals who demand respect for freedom of expression and for the unobstructed distribution of the *Satanic Verses*. The affirmation of liberal principles is a good thing; likewise is opposition to every hypocritical attempt to reestablish censorship. Nevertheless, it is rare that the mere statement of a principle allows one to judge a dispute well. In the present case, it is neither accurate nor well founded to affirm that freedom of expression allows of no limitations. Leaving aside pornography, tolerance of which necessarily has its bounds, falsifications of facts and defamatory statements invite sanction. As one knows, racist remarks may be punishable, as may be, for example, the lies of the pseudohistorians who do everything to deny the genocide of the Jews and the existence of the gas chambers. To defend Rushdie, one had to take into consideration the character of his work, win recognition for the right to literary expression, attack religious taboos, and so on. Failing that, one ran a risk of making a compromise with the ideology of "everything's sayable" and with relativism.

Better than anyone else, Rushdie sensed the equivocations in the debate he had aroused. This debate is revelatory of the mentality of the age; it served as a pretext for controversy in this age, but the age has ignored his work. In an article published 4 February 1990 in *The Independent on Sunday* (and translated in Paris's *Libération* for 8 February), Rushdie expresses his amazement that people on both sides haven't bothered to read him. "At the center of the storm," he notes, "stands a novel, a work of fiction, one that aspires to the condition of literature" (18). Someone who is living under the threat of assassination wants to defend, above all, his work. He thus takes up his pen to explain himself about its design.

The text is dense, sober; it is philosophical without seeking to be so; it touches on many questions, all of them essential, whether it is a matter of literature, of how people relate through language, of the social bond in general, of the spirit of modernity, or of belief and doubt. The reader hears the voice of a singular man who is seeking what this world, as he experiences it through his own history, offers him and what resources he might draw upon in order to think, to write, and to live among others. No concession is made to his adversaries who are in quest of a certitude that risks feeding fanaticism; but no complaisance is shown, either, toward fashionable ideas (the vanity of History, of humanity, of the mind, of the Subject, etc.). Rather, he really feels an attraction for the humanity that, in each person and encompassing all men, is revealed through the ordeal of division and torment.

I shall retain but a few themes from Rushdie's article, the ones that best shed light on his design, fearing not that I am freely reformulating them. Rushdie first places into evidence, against his detractors, the character of the *Satanic Verses*. It is, he insists, a novel, a piece of fiction. Thus does he declare it meaningless to treat this work as one would treat a "work of bad history" or "an anti-religious pamphlet" (ibid). The author recalls that he forges characters, makes them speak, recounts their dreams and that their dialogues or their fantasies testify to their own identity. And he points out that one could not in good faith confuse him with them, believing that he is lending them his own thoughts and his own desires.

This reminder might seem intended to discharge him of his responsibility as a writer when confronted with his accusers. It is nothing of the sort. He claims this responsibility as his own: fiction, he affirms, is a mode of knowledge, a way of exploring our relationships with others and with the world; it is written in order to awaken, to trouble the reader, to stimulate his judgment. "Let me be clear: I am not trying to say that *The Satanic Verses* is 'only a novel' and thus need not be taken seriously, even disputed with the utmost passion" (ibid.). And right away he challenges the conventional distinction between that which would pertain to the imaginary and that which would pertain to the real. What he loves in the novel, he tells us, is that it attempts "radical reformulations of language, form, and ideas . . . , to do what the word *novel* seems to insist upon: to see the world anew" (ibid.).

One could not state any better than he does that the novel, and literature in general, does not designate a fixed mode of expression, set at a distance from other modes of expression, knowledge, and action. It is clear that the writer does not have to serve a cause, be it a political, religious, or anti-religious one, that his speech does not refer to anything that might have taken place or that should have taken place, that it eludes the categories of the true and the false, and that it is self-sustaining. And at the same time it is clear that the writer is in quest of a meaning, even though this meaning might not be delivered in words, that his speech has a power to express that which cannot be expressed otherwise but is given in experiencing the world of life. Still, Rushdie makes it clear that what he is aiming at is not external to language, and language is not a system of available means of which the writer would just have to make good use. What he calls *expression* requires invention. Thus does he bring out his "determination to create a literary language and literary forms in which the experience of formerly-colonised, still disadvantaged peoples might find full expression" (ibid.).

When reading this sentence, how can one avoid thinking of other writers — Frantz Fanon, for example — who believed that they were fleeing the artifices of literature and were making themselves the spokesmen of peoples who were victims of colonization? Claiming that they were going straight to the truth of revolt, such writers leave the reader the choice of a yes or a no, both of which have their share of bad faith. For Rushdie, a full expression implies neither pure assurance of one's own identity nor denial of the other's. His whole book goes to show that; indeed, it presupposes that division is taken up and assumed. When he speaks, in a passage where he justifies himself for having used the name Mahound (a demonic version of Mohammed invented by Christians during the Middle Ages), he observes that the victim's appropriation of the name imposed upon him is a practice that subverts the supposed order of language, stealing its power from the name giver. (Where does the glorious name of *Whigs* or that of *Blacks* come from? From their adversaries. Where does Trotsky's name come from? He took it from his jailer.) The proud claim of the mark of disdain does not signify the conversion of the object into a subject; it testifies to a symbolic destruction of the master, the intrusion into his private world of the speech of the excluded.

What is the image that guides Rushdie's thought? It is not that of man conquering his place but that of man in ceaseless movement. "If *The Satanic Verses* is anything, it is a migrant's-eye view of the world. It is written from the very experience of uprooting, disjuncture and metamorphosis . . . that is the migrant condition, and from which, I believe, can be derived a metaphor for all humanity" (ibid.). Its design is therefore not only to draw from one's own life the resources for a novel whose characters are torn by their attachments to the East and to the West, by a conflict between belief and unbelief, whose "story [is that] of two painfully divided selves" (ibid.). The narrative, both tragic and burlesque, of their adventures also brings out an investigation into the way in which man, whatever his condition, is still put to the test of uprooting and division.

What is this uprooting? It is not a state, that of someone who would have lost his roots. This loss is never consummated or, what boils down to the same thing, it is ever renewed. There is uprooting only for he who in his flesh preserves the memory of himself, for he whose desire to remain in primal proximity to all that surrounds him is forever contradicted by a movement that he does not just suffer but that is also born of him. Rushdie speaks of his own experience and of his characters, Chamcha and Gibreel, each of whom lives uprooting in a different way — one finally becoming reconciled with himself, the other torn to the point of doing away with himself. But he also speaks of man as such, under the features of the Anglo-Indian. Bombay and London serve merely to give shape to *here* and *elsewhere*. To varying degrees, the drive to return and that to escape, the drive to forget and that to remember give rhythmic form to the life of each; and Rushdie again speaks of humanity, of the perpetual migration down through the ages of peoples who for a long time, without knowing that they belonged to the same species, had been caught up in a shared adventure and are ever more so. Linked with the idea of uprooting is that of disjuncture and that of metamorphosis. Likewise, to the idea of division is linked that of *mélange*, intermingling. Here again the portraits of Chamcha and Gibreel only serve to render palpable both the impossibility of coinciding with oneself and the condensation within oneself of different identities. Let us prolong his argument: Is not each person, whatever the culture to which he belongs, the offspring of two lines, and do not the multiple currents that go to make them up produce in him a whirlwind, sometimes a happy fusion of contraries? "Like many millions of people," notes Rushdie, using another image, "I am a bastard child of history. Perhaps we all are, black and brown and white, leaking into one another, as a character of mine once said, *like flavors when you cook*" (ibid.).

Will it be said that not all these ideas are new? So be it. But they take on a singular import when they come to nourish a reflection on the modern world, the social bond, and religion. It is indeed the critical discourse on modernity, and therefore on democracy in its different versions, that Rushdie takes in reverse. "*The Satanic Verses,*" he writes,

> celebrates hybridity, impurity, intermingling, the transformation that comes of new and unexpected combinations of human beings, cultures, ideas, politics, movies, songs. It rejoices in mongrelisation and fears the absolutism of the Pure. Mélange, hotch-potch, a bit of this and a bit of that is *how newness enters the world*. It is the great possibility that mass migration gives the world, and I have tried to embrace it (ibid.).

Rarely has someone rejected so vigorously the ideal of a well-ordered society favoring a shared adherence to secure values, a society that would be delivered from the whirlwind of events, information, spectacles, and artificial pleasures. The mongrelization of which Rushdie speaks is not only that of men; it is also that of all things that go to make up the universe we inhabit. To expose oneself to the outside, to give oneself over to the most varied, the most discordant succession or simultaneity of impressions is for him the opportunity to tap into something of the world, of the passage of time, of the coming of the new—not that which is trivially proclaimed each day as new but that which has not yet been thought or felt and that has the power of *revelation*. In this sense, the attraction exerted upon Rushdie by the big city, the modern city, Bombay already, then London, gives us a better idea of what he tastes in the experience of uprooting and mongrelization: the virtue of the encounter. The city is, par excellence, the site of encounter, the place where the chance encounter predominates, the one of unexpected beings and things—which have the potential to excite surprise, the potential for provocation, and which suddenly awaken our sense of beauty or of horror.

If one concluded from these remarks that Rushdie just enjoys contact with the offbeat [*hetéroclite*], that he is not in the least concerned with judging good and evil, the true and the false, the beautiful and the ugly, it would be easy to challenge his encomium to modernity or to find in it only one more sign of "the crisis of our time"—to use the conventional expression. But the value he sets on the literary work as a mode of knowledge and also as a re-creation of language, so as to give meaning to a human experience, forbids one from thinking so. And how would one then greet the following statement: "I have spiritual needs, and my work has, I hope, a moral and spiritual dimension, but I am content to try and satisfy those needs without recourse to any idea of a Prime Mover or ultimate arbiter" (19)?

Here he says what is of the essence. To those who, faced with the loss of the ultimate bearings of certitude, appeal to the verities of religion, morality, or reason, or else to those who turn this loss into their business and sift back through all the themes of antihumanism, Rushdie opposes a judgment that faces the test of uncertainty. He does not champion a right to state his preferences; he does not hesitate to affirm the moral and spiritual dimension of his work. These are words that one thought were at present the property of conservatives, words that, to an intellectual vanguard, seem to date from the era of metaphysics. For Rushdie, the disappearance of the ultimate arbiter does not take away from man the exigency he is given to decide what is true and what is false, what is just and what is unjust (is not this latter decision already and uninterruptedly at the heart of literary creation?), and to answer for his deeds and his words. Rather, it really stokes this exigency as soon as it finds it has to assume responsibility for the risk it entails, which offers no previous model, no guarantee, and no hope of reward. Addressing himself, at one point, to the Muslim community, the writer declares:

> Life without God seems to believers an idiocy, pointless, beneath contempt. It does not seem so to non-believers. To accept that the world,

here, is all there is; to go through it, towards and into death, without the consolations of religion seems, well, at least as courageous and rigorous to us as the espousal of faith seems to you. Secularism and its works deserve your respect, not your contempt (20).

This statement allows of no equivocation. The image returns of man in movement, without a guide, whose honor it is to think and speak without yielding to nihilism.

Rushdie had said beforehand: "The liveliness of literature lies in its exceptionality, in being the individual, idiosyncratic vision of one human being, in which, to our delight and great surprise, we may find our own image reflected. A book is a version of the world. If you do not like it, ignore it; or offer your own version in return" (ibid.). No more than the previous ones does this statement suggest a relativistic interpretation that would recognize only the arbitrary choices of individuals and would situate them all on the same level. Tolerance is one thing: the believer who has contempt for the nonbeliever is not himself contemptible if he accepts at least the existence of the other; generally speaking, no one has the right to impose his own version of the world. But indifference to the other's point of view is another thing. There is no original individual vision that would not be that of a *human being*. It is because he is a man, whose expression is singular, that the writer is capable of giving rise to the happiness of the encounter, as well as, moreover, to a rejection that also pertains to the encounter.

Rushdie confuses tolerance so little with indifference that he sees in the confrontation of ideas the provocation of the other, the perpetual relaunching of questions, a wellspring of History. In one place, while mentioning the French Revolution and the confrontation between Robespierre and Danton (something he does by design in order to warn that the conflict between purity and impurity cannot be expressed solely in terms of the show of forces presently contending in the East), he exclaims: "I say, let [the argument] continue. Human beings understand themselves and shape their futures by arguing and challenging and questioning and saying the unsayable; not by bowing the knee, whether to gods or to men" (18). Let us leave aside for a moment the last sentence. One could not have better set aside the fiction of an ideal communication held in check only by the interests and passions of men or thwarted merely by the distortions language undergoes as a result of the established relations of domination in society. It is, indeed, pointless to imagine that men are bound to one another with the aid of an exchange of arguments requiring a step-by-step proof of their validity, so that by right they would be promised the attainment of ultimate understanding. They are bound to one another in challenging one another, each trying to grasp in the words of the others only what echoes his own beliefs, his own history being invested in these beliefs. But each, in contact with the others, having to make a move, finds himself touched by that very thing he rejects, and removed, often without even knowing it, from the place where he was trying to take a stand. Men, we would willingly say in commenting Rushdie, understand one another inasmuch as they hear one another, but hearing one another does not mean agreeing with one another; to hear one another is to hold together through the back-and-forth of speech, not abolishing the gap between speaking and hearing, but allowing it to be remade, thus consenting to the coming of the new.

Nonetheless, one couldn't neglect the fact that the will to purity does not easily accommodate itself to debate. Such a will is entirely in the service of might, even among those who live in servitude and get a taste of it only in idolatry. Furthermore, Rushdie exalts the virtue of provocation only in order to make better known the exigencies of freedom. "What is freedom of expression?" he asks. "Without the freedom to offend, it ceases to exist. Without the freedom to challenge, even to satirise all orthodoxies, including religious orthodoxies, it ceases to exist" (ibid.). To say that free speech requires provocation is to say that the social bond is alive only if the difference of positions is recognized, only if this difference is not converted into a pure antagonism, in such a way that it gives to some the power to exclude the others, but also—I believe I can add—only if difference is not degraded because it no longer poses a question and sees itself ratified under the seal of "the right to difference." Provocative speech is the kind that disturbs order, whichever one that might be; it is, par excellence, unexpected speech. In making itself heard, such speech brings people back to listen to what is not said, to listen to everything that, on one side or another, conventional languages cover up. Rushdie's target, certainly, is religious orthodoxy. For him, it is from there that the greatest threat comes. But when he declares that he is combating "all orthodoxies," one cannot avoid mentioning those, less noisy, that proliferate in Western societies, grafting themselves on to good causes, emancipatory causes. Before championing the freedom to offend, Rushdie wrote: "How is freedom gained? It is taken: never given. To be free, you must first assume your right to freedom" (ibid.). In vain would one limit the import of this thought. In democracy itself, the institution of individual and political freedoms couldn't make one forget that freedom is not given; speech always requires an *interruption* of the ordered relations among men, a right that exceeds all definition, a sort of violence. Isn't that what makes itself heard in the formula: Freedom is taken?

This violence is basic. In a sense, it manifests itself in the speech of the writer who attempts "radical reformulations of language, form, and ideas."

He gains his freedom, knowing that it is not connected to the mere use of language, that language itself is *given* to him only in appearance—which does not mean that it *doesn't exist,* as a few of our contemporaries frivolously and funnily state, but rather that it requires of each an invention. This is a singular invention that makes the writer discover himself dispossessed of words, of turns of phrase, of familiar forms of articulation; the writer feels himself growing mute again in order that he might be able to secure his voice, to speak, not better than any other but as no one else, and thus to allow safe passage for what demands to be said. It is no less clear that this violence has a political signification. The social bond, as I already suggested, is not *given,* either; it depends upon the initiative of those who strike a blow against the confidence collective beliefs inspire. And among the latter beliefs, the most dangerous ones are those nourished by what Rushdie calls "communalism" (19).

Rushdie's reflection on literature is constantly intertwined with a reflection on politics. Everything he says about the effects of uprooting, hybridity, mongrelization, and impurity goes to serve the conception of a political society in which the illusion that there is a solution to the human problem sees itself challenged—of a society that welcomes conflict and change. Speaking of India, of the horrors that would be in store for it with the triumph of the communalist ideology, he does not hide the fact that his novel includes a political design. Still, it is true that his battle against the absolutism of purity is directed against religious authority, which claims it can decide about all aspects of the lives of individuals at the same time that it succeeds in subduing the government.

Certainly, he brings to light the intricate connections between the religious and the political, but he is interested in the religious phenomenon as such; and it is perhaps at the moment when he fastens onto this phenomenon that the moral and spiritual dimensions of his work become clear. He doesn't hide his convictions: "I believe in no god," he writes, "and have not done so since I was a young adolescent" (19). Or again: "To put it as simply as possible: *I am not a Muslim.* It feels bizarre, and wholly inappropriate, to be described as some sort of heretic after having lived my life as a secular, pluralist, eclectic man" (ibid.). But this stranger to religion, and to Islam in particular, is not indifferent to them. That is why he wanted to question religion in his novel:

> I set out to explore, through the process of fiction, the nature of revelation and the power of faith. The mystical, revelatory experience is quite clearly a genuine one. This statement poses a problem to the nonbeliever: if we accept that the mystic, the prophet, is sincerely under-

going some sort of transcendent experience, yet we cannot believe in a supernatural world, then *what is going on?* (20).

It is not a question here of a psychoanalytical investigation; what matters to Rushdie is to interrogate man in light of the mystical experience. Does he not say further on: "The point is to try and understand the human event of revelation" (ibid.)? It is regrettable that he does not pursue the question. But cannot one at least reformulate it in another way: What is transcendence, the ordeal of radical otherness, in the absence of God? Rushdie leaves aside the rationalist interpretation; he abstains from calling revelation an illusion. This is not a sign of prudence on his part; in his view, there really is without any doubt revelation of an ability man has, at the edges of the possible, to try to pass beyond his condition, an ability that is the inverse of the one he has to fall below himself, to want abasement. As one knows, the famous satanic verses, attested to historically, indicate that the prophet went astray. They interest Rushdie so much because they allow him to show the troubling moment when the imaginary veers off. Indeed, Rushdie does not exploit this moment in order to point one back toward the real (the sudden attraction for three pagan deities, which destroys the ecstatic posture) but in order to bring out a hint of doubt — not the noble doubt that indicates man's distance from God but the unexpected "uprooting" of mystical speech.

It is not my purpose to speak about the novel itself, of its characters, exposed to the torments of their imagination, who are neither mystical nor abject but float between the adventures of their dreams and those of "reality." In his article, Rushdie shows how denial of the famous verses lends support to an allegedly faultless dogmatism and sustains a machine whose unceasing purpose is to expel doubt and that operates only through the manipulation of lies. In fact, religious leaders, who are presently making themselves into the inflexible guardians of the law, forbid any form of emancipation to the Muslim woman, as if such emancipation would endanger the essence of belief, whereas they have had to abandon, one after another, the barbarian prescriptions their predecessors judged sacred (mutilation for theft, stoning for prostitution, and so on).

Far from attacking the belief of Muslims, Rushdie feels close to Muslim society, inasmuch as that society "questions its own rules daily" (19). His novel is a provocation in that he wants to bring out this questioning and to precipitate it.

Doubt is a word that returns quite often in his remarks on religion. Is this not what, throughout his short essay, Rushdie is celebrating as modernity's most precious good? In reading him, one sees how he differs from contemporary neorationalist or antihumanist currents. But one thinks especially of the philosopher to whom he is the closest by dint of the questions he poses and the furthest by dint of his rejection of that philosopher's responses: Friedrich Nietzsche. Rushdie observes the experience of uprootedness, hybridity, and mongrelization characteristic of democracy as Nietzsche did, but Rushdie does not manufacture the dream of a new aristocracy that would take refuge from the masses, of an authority that, strengthened by the knowledge that it creates its own values, wouldn't have to render any account to anyone but itself. Differing in this respect from Nietzsche, he doesn't deem doubt to be a sign of the baseness of modern man. Quite to the contrary, in his view doubt constitutes modern man's strength, his dignity; and it is what accompanies the exigency to make judgments. Doubt is not the tool of the skeptical virtuoso, the property of the indifferent; still less is it the methodical attempt to provide knowledge with sure foundations. It is, rather, that which protects truth and never lets it give way beneath the weight of belief.

Note

"Humanisme ou anti-humanisme. Au sujet de Salman Rushdie," a contribution to a May 1990 colloquium on "Man and Society" at the University of Lausanne, was originally published in the *Revue Européenne des Sciences Sociales,* ed. Giovanni Busino, 89 (1991): 131–42. Reprinted as "Humanisme et anti-humanisme. Hommage à Salman Rushdie" in *Écrire,* 37–54.

Tocqueville:
Democracy and the Art of Writing

An Exploration of the Flesh of the Social:
Note on Democracy in America

I N THE FIRST BOOK of the second volume of *Democracy in America,* Tocqueville writes: "I need not traverse earth and sky to discover a wondrous object woven of contrasts, of infinite greatness and littleness, of intense gloom and amazing brightness, capable at once of exciting pity, admiration, terror, contempt."[1] What then is this object? Tocqueville goes on to say: "I have only to look at myself." He speaks in this place of democracy's influence upon the intellectual movement and, more specifically, of the sources of modern poetry. These lines certainly would surprise a student who knows our author only via political scientists or sociologists. But how many times would this student not be confounded, were he really to try to read Tocqueville's work (and to read it slowly) while forgetting the ever so balanced, or cramped, portrait the aforementioned scholars have composed. The passion, the heat, or else a sudden and troubling reflection on his own way of thinking all go to show that in Tocqueville we find an astonishingly free speech: it is the speech of an individual who does not remain confined within the circle of his theses, does not fear to overturn his own affirmations, and gladly heads down paths that make him lose sight of the guideposts he had set in place. I would dare say that this individual bears the mark of a democratic temperament — a temperament that rouses one to "restless activity" in the image of the society he is questioning, that precipitates the movement of thought in many directions, and that, simultaneously, is inclined to arrange the facts in line with a small number of principles.

In the book I mentioned, Tocqueville, after having described the penchant of modern writers for general ideas and abstract words, interrupts himself:

> I cannot better illustrate what I mean than by my own example. I have frequently used the word *equality* in an absolute sense; nay, I have personified equality in several places; thus I have said that equality does such and such things or refrains from doing others. It can be affirmed that the writers of the age of Louis XIV would not have spoken in this manner.[2]

Thus, he knows this world whose analyst he claims to be by discovering the imprint of it in himself. At the end of the introduction to the first volume, he notes: "This book does not place itself, in fact, in anyone's train."[3] An aristocratic remark, it has been said. That was to forget what he had written on the new independence of thought and on the rejection of one's heritage, those distinctive traits of the democratic spirit. There are, moreover, a thousand notable signs that reveal his audacity. I wish to cite but one of them that appropriately dispels the image of the conservative who unites the spirit of positivism with a defense of Catholicism: "Most religions are only general, simple, and practical means of teaching men the doctrine of the immortality of the soul,"[4] he writes, adding, a few lines later:

> The doctrine of metempsychosis is assuredly more rational than that of materialism; nevertheless, if it were absolutely necessary that a democracy should choose one of the two, I should not hesitate to decide that the community would run less risk of being brutalized by believing that the soul of a man will pass into the carcass of a hog than by believing that the soul of man is nothing at all.[5]

Let us recall that the work we are questioning is not only an inquiry about American democracy or even about democracy in general. It is an investigation into man and society, into the very becoming of humanity, which, as such, faces the test of the interminable, that is, the fact that nothing is ever entirely resolved.

Few authors, it is true, give such assurance as to the soundness of their design. The clarity of the exposition, the methodical use of comparisons, the concern to offer formulas at the outset and to reformulate them at various stages along the way, the concern, too, to gather here and there an entire development into a conclusion, sometimes making use of the ostensible procedures of proof—all these things lead the reader to attribute to Tocqueville a perfect mastery of his subject. Although he warns us that he has wished only to show the effects of the equality of conditions, without making of that equality the unique cause of the present state of the world, he does not hesitate to declare that, via the path he has traced, he attains his goal.

What goal? To draw up the balance sheet of democracy's virtues and vices, to discern the forms democracy can adopt in various nations and according to circumstances, to spot the advances and regressions humanity has undergone as a result of the democratic revolution, to detect the perils it includes? Undoubtedly, the image of the balance scale predominates and, with it, that of the judge. Tocqueville says this himself: he wanted to paint and to judge. But who would believe that this man, who has so strong a sense of the *contrasts* and the *profound obscurities that accompany singular lucidities,* who tests on himself the clash of feelings, sometimes driving him to exaltation and sometimes disgusting him or giving him a bout of terror, could, whatever he might want, be satisfied with painting his object from the outside and with judging from on high?

Tocqueville is a master in the art of contrast. Modernity stands out against the background of the Ancien Régime. America stands out against the background of the European world. Democracy reveals its physiognomy only opposite aristocracy, its contrary. The effects of the equality of conditions are measured in relation to the inverse effects of inequality. When he is not opposing one figure to another he distinguishes or rather disjoins them: a line is firmly drawn between equality and liberty, or else between the social state and the political institution. Thus does he light his picture [*tableau*] and create the distance necessary for judgment. Nonetheless, one must, I believe, admire him more for his sense of ambiguity and complication, his concern to come back upon his statements of principle, his ability to decipher the singular fact and to extract therefrom a truth that puts the logic of his argument off track.

Take the notion of "democratic revolution." In a sense it encourages one to separate decisively the ancient from the modern. Although this revolution was on the march for a long time, there comes a moment when it reveals something more than a discontinuity, a contrast between two modes of temporality. On the one hand, the action of men, their institutions, their beliefs are stamped in the element of immortality; however diverse the societies under consideration may be, they all show themselves to be preoccupied with assuring the permanence of their existence. On the other hand, the modern world is devoted to change. It lives, knows that it lives, and wants to live in an incessant upheaval of everything that is already achieved. Thus are we confronted, Tocqueville will not hesitate to tell us, with two humanities that are incomparable and that each shed light on the other.

But that is only one aspect of this thought. From the very start of this work, he considers this democratic revolution *irresistible*. It is up to us, it seems, merely to take cognizance of it and to ask ourselves by what means it is possible to master its course. Between these two incomparable humanities we don't have to make a choice: time has *become* irreversible. Is that, however, a mere statement of fact? And does it suffice for us to call upon Providence to persuade us of the inevitability of the change?

No doubt, Tocqueville was convinced that a change had taken place and that he had made a *discovery* that brings into play the very notions of "humanity," "individual," and "society." The other appears to each man as his like [*un semblable*]. The individual possesses by nature the right to decide his own destiny. Society *as such* emerges from the diversity of networks of dependence or of particular communities at the same time that the idea of the sovereignty of the people is affirmed. These are not simple facts; they are so many signs of the advent of a truth that one cannot challenge merely by setting a boundary upon thought. If one cannot go back, that is because one doesn't possess the ability to reject the idea of individual liberty as human liberty. And it is not the ruling opinion that deprives us of this ability; a constitutive exigency of the mind is henceforth imposed on us. Even more, when we form the image of a ruling opinion that would tend to fashion the thoughts of each, we are asserting as a matter of fact our own freedom.

In this regard, Tocqueville's originality is twofold. On the one hand, differing from a number of his contemporaries, he does not join the democratic notion—the modern notion, which he does not fear to call "the just notion of freedom"[6]—to a theory of progress. Although he believes in the perfectibility of man, he is to the highest degree conscious of the ambivalence of the effects of every innovation, be it one of universal significance. The certitude that is attached to the idea of the rights of the individual and of political rights does not exempt one from having to examine the consequences of its being inscribed in reality, in the life of societies. More than that, while Tocqueville does not share Machiavelli's thesis that there would be a constant sum of goods and evils from one era to another, he does suggest, in the latter's wake, that there is no good without evil, that every gain on one point is accompanied by a loss. On the other hand, although he imputes the discovery of the unity of humankind to a spiritual revolution, Christianity, he observes—in conformity, moreover, with tradition, but while placing the accent on the character of the social state at the time of the Roman Empire—that the equality of men, owing to their similar weakness before the prince, disposed them "to listen to the general truths Christianity teaches."[7] In other terms, there is no efficacy to a new idea, even if it were to be the bearer of some sort of revelation, except through its insertion in a definite milieu, a definite epoch.

Tocqueville is not liable, however, to the accusation of historicism or sociologism: what is just is not relative to a particular time or to a form of society; the truth that arises [*advient*] summons men to think what previously was unthinkable—what was unthinkable, for example, for the Greeks, as their conception of slavery testifies—but this truth must be stamped in the social [*le social*]. And when it has become nearly natural, one couldn't conclude from this that the men who had not yet recognized it were in other respects inferior to the Moderns. Tocqueville holds both these ideas together: it is important to understand the American world in itself, starting from its guiding principles (which leads him to say that one would have to burn all books in order to grasp the new); nevertheless, this American world becomes clear only through the contrast it forms with the ancient world.

To a large extent, the opposition between the ancient and the modern links up with that of aristocracy and democracy. The latter opposition, as everyone knows, lies at the heart of his reflections and is restated a dozen times or more. The contrast best makes itself felt in the chapter on *individualism.* On the one hand, there is permanence through the succession of generations, the intensity of intraclass social ties, and the grading of people in such a way that each person always sees above himself someone who might protect him and below himself someone else whose assistance he might be able to claim; people are generally disposed to conceive "something placed outside their own sphere, and they are often disposed to forget themselves."[8] On the other hand, there is the extreme mobility of families that rise or fall or change nonstop, a rift in the woof of time, an ever heightened consciousness that one is self-sufficient and owes nothing to anyone. This opposition is summed up in a formula that has since become famous: "Aristocracy had made a chain of all the members of the community, from the peasant to the king; democracy breaks that chain and severs every link of it."[9]

Nonetheless, right in the middle of the chapter Tocqueville slips in the following remark about aristocratic times: "It is true that in these ages the notion of human fellowship [*du semblable*] is faint."[10] He completes it later on when he specifies that back then "the very image of society was obscure."[11] This remark, rich in consequences, prompts one to shatter the symmetry between the two opposed types. In the aristocratic world, at least such as Tocqueville describes it, relations among men are fashioned locally and are at once both social and political. If there really is, step by step, an articulation of all the networks of dependence, these relations are regulated in the main within the seigneury, the commune, or the corporation. In contrast, and here is Tocqueville's major argument (one that we encounter under a different form in Marx, even though his premises and conclusions are entirely different), democracy implies a disjunction of the social from the political. When conditions are equalized, when men recognize themselves as fellows [*semblables*], society becomes fully sketched out and attains a sort of *sui generis* reality.

Now, this argument lends itself to two interpretations that clash with each other. The text, to which I shall soon return, authorizes both these interpretations, one after the other. According to the first interpretation, society rises above men, while the personal ties they maintain with one another come undone; they see themselves all subordinated to this "immense being."[12] According to the second, the fact that political action and political institutions find themselves circumscribed and that the government no longer disposes of anything but a relative legitimacy that is always being put back into question liberates properly social energies; civil society becomes the focus of invention. Thus can Tocqueville say regarding democratic government that "I am less inclined to applaud it for what it does than for what it causes to be done."[13] In returning to the thesis that opposes the government of the best to the one that remains at the mercy of the whims of the greatest number, he does not shrink from declaring: "Democracy does not give the people the most skillful government, but it produces what the ablest governments are frequently unable to create: namely, it spreads throughout the social body a restless activity, a superabundant force, and an energy that is *inseparable from it,* and that may, however unfavorable circumstances may be, produce wonders."[14] Thus does democracy constitute the antitype to aristocracy each time Tocqueville endeavors to discover therein the germs of a new kind of despotism; it offers the figure, on the other hand, of an original type that does not let itself be known via its contrary when he seeks in it the signs of a new kind of freedom. Still, we must ask ourselves another question: Is Tocqueville completely certain that democracy couldn't retain anything of the aristocracy? Certain passages do not allow one to answer in the affirmative.

Let us note that Tocqueville is imbued not only with the art of contrasts. He also practices the art of surprise through reversals of perspective that strip away truths it was believed had been firmly established. In short, he possesses an extremely singular art of writing that keeps the reader constantly on the alert, forcing us to keep our eye [*regard*] or our thinking mobile at all times and forbidding us from settling into a secure position. The section entitled "The Temper of the Legal Profession in the United States, and How it Serves as a Counterpoise to Democracy" is among those that create the most lively sense of astonishment by shedding sudden new light on the subject preoccupying us. The remarks Tocqueville makes there are not some sort of digression. The sixteenth chapter in which they figure undertakes to discuss the "Causes Which Mitigate the Tyranny of the Majority in the United States" and is connected, as a matter of fact, with the preceding chapter, on the "Unlimited Power of the Majority in the United States, and Its Consequences." That chapter, which has been quoted a thousand times, is too well known for it to be worth summarizing here. It contains a virulent critique of American democracy and of democracy in general. Unstable, arbitrary, endowed with tremendous material and moral strength, the majority seems to have overturned the sort of obstacles against which a despotic prince or even the Inquisition formerly collided.

Now, this ever so terrifying picture becomes entirely blurred as soon as Tocqueville introduces the legal profession. As he describes their penchants and habits, one sees their influence grow and grow. They possess competency; they have a sense of permanency, a sense of forms, and the scope of their action, furthermore, is considerable. Thanks to the institution of popular juries, "the language of the law thus becomes, in some measure, a vulgar tongue; the spirit of the law, which is produced in the schools and courts of justice, gradually penetrates beyond their walls into the bosom of society, where it descends to the lowest classes, so that at last the whole people contract the habits and the tastes of the judicial magistrate."[15] But it is not only thanks to the jury system that the legal profession can flex its power. Tocqueville observed shortly beforehand that "they fill the legislative assemblies and are at the head of the administration."[16] And ultimately their power is revealed to be immense: it "extends over the whole community and penetrates into all the classes that compose it; it acts upon the country imperceptibly, but finally fashions it to suit its own purposes."[17]

What remains of the omnipotence of the majority? Whatever might be the case, it is striking to note that Tocqueville characterizes the legal temper as an aristocratic one: "The profession of the law is the only aristocratic element that can be amalgamated effortlessly with the natural elements of democracy and be advantageously and permanently combined with them."[18] Effortlessly? These words merit one's attention, for they suggest that there is a sort of connivance between the general features of democracy and at least a few aristocratic traits. Now, it seems to me that in a passage such as this one Tocqueville is showing once again how difficult it is to reduce democracy to a social state. The might of the legal profession would not seem to him so extraordinary if he granted that democracy implies the idea of a distinction between opinion and law, however it might be conceived here and there.

Let us linger a little longer over the analysis of the social state that is defined by the equality of conditions. Tocqueville notes that it matters little to specify what the factors are that can explain this phenomenon, but also that, once established, equality can be treated as a fundamental fact. In studying American society, he discovered "the generative fact from which each particular fact seemed to descend."[19] Nonetheless, one cannot fail to observe that the genesis of this social state still matters to him. The references to China or to Egypt or else again the picture he offers of the different figures of equality in the second book show, no doubt without his awareness, what is unique about the advent of modern democracy.[20] Moreover, an entire section of the introduction to the first book summarizes the progress of equality in Europe, and more particularly in France. There one discovers the importance of the leveling process, which kings worked at achieving. This action, which encourages the isolation of citizens, could be compared to that of Asiatic despots only at the cost of oversimplification. The main thing, it seems to me, is that the equality of conditions is indicated in the connection between the four phenomena to which Tocqueville never tires of harking back: independence, isolation, resemblance [*similitude*], and leveling.

There undoubtedly is something schematic in the argument I am proposing, but I will risk stating that Tocqueville is describing two paths, both of which issue upon the same alternative: freedom or servitude. Following the first course, he is guided by the image of independence and isolation; following the second, by the image of resemblance and leveling. In one way or another, and despite his effort to drive a wedge between liberty and equality, he sees himself led again and again to pass from dissociating them to making them coincide. He establishes the split, certainly, at various moments. Equality appears as a social fact. Liberty, on the other hand, although it is expressed differently in one place or another, is not connected to any one type of society; it is alive in aristocratic society just as it lives or can live in democratic society.[21] Equality—at least the kind characteristic of the modern world—develops in History. One can follow its progress through a variety of circumstances; it alone is irresistible. Liberty, on the other hand, burns bright and then is extinguished, then it reignites, but there is no history of liberty; it is timeless. Equality grows naturally, and it seems natural to men. Liberty requires efforts and sacrifices; it is not maintained or even instituted except through voluntary, enlightened action. In Tocqueville's terms, it pertains to art.

Tocqueville, however, is far from settled in this opposition. Not only does he conceive "an extreme point at which freedom and equality would meet and blend," [22] not only does he affirm that "men living [in times of equality] have a natural bias toward free institutions,[23] not only does he admire equality because he sees that it "lodges in the very depths of each man's mind and heart that indefinable feeling, the instinctive inclination for political independence, and thus prepares the remedy for the ill that it engenders," [24] but, as I have already emphasized, he also considers the birth of the very idea of individual independence to be an event whose meaning is irreversible; in a word, he pronounces himself unreservedly in favor of the rights of man. If, however, independence beckons, on the one hand, toward self-affirmation, the will to judge and to act, by emancipating oneself from any authority that claims to be above free enquiry, it beckons, on the other hand, toward isolation. And it thereby lends itself to despotism.

Still, this analysis must be fine-tuned. The isolated man, Tocqueville shows, is the product of the social state; for, having extricated himself from the old networks of dependency, he is led to imagine that he *doesn't owe anything to anyone,* that he possesses the means to be self-sufficient. Beyond the fact that this is an illusion, since the satisfaction of material needs in modern society requires the cooperation of a greater and greater number of social agents, isolation makes each person discover his pettiness, his weakness in relation to society. Thus does society come to acquire in the eyes of the individual a tremendous power; it elevates itself above him as an "immense being."

Yet this argument is combined with another one that seems to us to go to the heart of the idea of "independence." We find this second argument in the second chapter of book 2. It is entitled "Of the Principal Source of Belief among Democratic Peoples": "Obviously," writes Tocqueville, "without such common belief no society can prosper; say, rather, no society can exist; for without ideas held in common there is no common action, and without common action there may still be men, but there is no social body." He adds: "It is necessary that the minds of all the citizens should be rallied and held together by certain predominant ideas; and this cannot be the case unless each of them sometimes draws his opinions from the common source and consents to accept certain matters of belief already formed." [25]

Now, what can this source be when dependence of one person upon another has vanished? Tocqueville poses in this place the central question of authority: "A principle of authority must then always occur, under all circumstances, in some part or other of the moral and intellectual world," and all that one must ask oneself is the following: "where it resides and by what standard it is to be measured." [26] We know the answer. In substance, it is the following: If it is no longer a man or a class that is the repository of authority, it is the mass that becomes this repository and the extent of this authority becomes all the more formidable as it remains invisible. Why this tendency to believe in the mass? Why is it, as Tocqueville says, that "opinion is more than ever mistress of the world"?[27] On account of the equality of conditions. Henceforth, "men have no faith in one another, by reason of their common resemblance; but this very resemblance gives them almost unbounded confidence in the judgment of the public."[28]

Before commenting on this last statement, let us return to the theme of independence. Tocqueville noted in passing: "The independence of individual minds may be greater or it may be less; it cannot be unbounded."[29] An implicit thesis is sketched out here that will be formulated differently at the end of the book:[30] There is in the desire for independence, in the individual's desire for freedom, the illusion of not owing anything to *anyone*, of not owing anything, not only physically but also symbolically. Now, this illusion rushes the Subject, without its knowledge, into dependence upon an *impersonal* power, the mass, opinion. Thus does freedom revert back into servitude.

We began with the fact of independence and the fact of isolation. The text we have just quoted leads us to inquire about resemblance. It is another characteristic of the equality of conditions. So be it! But if we simply granted that individuals have come to resemble one another on account of their equality, we might conclude flatly that each forms spontaneously the same opinion as his neighbors. Tocqueville clearly tells us something else entirely. He knows quite well that, in reality, individuals are not all alike [*pareils*]. Moreover, he doesn't construct society on the basis of relationships among individuals. Authority is not for him the attribute of an individual. Even when, in aristocratic society, authority emanates from a master or from a group, the master or group is only its repository. When authority is exercised by the intermediary of persons, its source lies deeper; let us say that authority is social, on the condition that we don't forget that beliefs in a supernatural power can be invested in the social sphere [*le social*]. To comprehend the mechanism whereby one places confidence in the mass, it must be understood that the social is imprinted on individuals through resemblance. Resemblance is as if detached from those who are fellows, that is to say, from men who are equally deprived of the symbolic bearings of social difference. Now, social power already manifests itself with the aid of the mass's domination. Or, to state it more clearly, the action of the established political power comes to lean on the representation of resemblance.

Tocqueville never lets one forget that power, as soon as it comes to be at the center of everything, tends unceasingly to increase its might, and, in some way, to reduce to the same mold all those who depend upon it.

> Every central power, which follows its natural tendencies, courts and encourages the principle of equality. . . . In like manner, it may be said that every central government worships uniformity; uniformity relieves it from inquiry into an infinity of details. . . . Thus the government likes what the citizens like and naturally hates what they hate. These common sentiments, which in democratic nations constantly unite the sovereign and every member of the community in one and the same conviction, establish a secret and lasting sympathy between them.[31]

Tocqueville adds, "Democratic nations often hate those in whose hands the central power is vested, but they always love that power itself."[32] Thus, the movement that comes from on high is in accord with the movement that is born down below, and each precipitates the other. The effort to level society finds its most efficacious means in administrative centralization; Tocqueville feared that such centralization might be introduced into the United States, where it had not yet taken place, and thus imagined the formation of a sort of despotism that could be worse than the one that reigns in Asia. Without a basis in the facts, his theory suffices for him to sketch the famous picture of the tutelary State, which everyone knows.

At this point, however, we must retrace our steps. Starting from the notion of "independence," we gave a glimpse of how freedom reverts into servitude. At present what matters is to observe that freedom's chances have not disappeared from sight. Assuredly, Tocqueville is more attentive to the perils equality engenders. Nonetheless, it is too often forgotten that he does not stop at a description of the regime in which servitude "might be combined more easily than is commonly believed with some of the outward forms of freedom."[33] It is a fiction, he gives us to understand at the end of the chapter in which the characteristics of a new kind of despotism are described: "A constitution republican in its head and ultra-monarchical in all its other parts has always appeared to me to be a short-lived monster. The vices of rulers and the ineptitude of the people would speedily bring about its ruin; and the nation, weary of its representatives and of itself, would create freer institutions or soon return to stretch itself at the feet of a single master."[34]

The end of the sentence brings us back to the hypothesis of a classical despotism, which makes us break with the new democratic logic; as for the beginning of the sentence, its meaning, it seems to me, is cleared up by a note that was written, it is true, much later and that was to serve as preparation for the second volume of *The Old Regime and the Revolution.* Tocqueville criticizes the confusion created by the usage of the notion of "democracy":

> Now, the words *democracy, monarchy, democratic government* can only mean one thing, following the true meaning of the words: a government in which the people take a greater and lesser part in the government. Its meaning is intimately connected with the idea of political freedom. To give the epithet of democratic government to a government in which political freedom is not to be found is a palpable absurdity.[35]

Let us grant that in *Democracy in America* Tocqueville himself fed the confusion he denounces. The obstinacy with which he reduces democracy to a social state, the equality of conditions, runs counter to his reflection on democratic freedom—without it preventing him, it is true, from scrutinizing all the signs of this freedom.

Allow me to provide another example of his hesitations by mentioning the contrast he establishes between America and the ancient world without my lingering over it. Tocqueville claims that it is in America that one can examine the phenomenon of the equality of conditions in all its purity and gauge its effects. He leaves one to believe that democracy is built there upon a tabula rasa. On the other hand, on innumerable occasions he highlights the distinctive character of the English emigrants and the role of Puritanism, which "was almost as much a political theory as a religious doctrine." [36] So, equality and freedom appear unentangleable from the start.

Tocqueville's art of writing appears, I said, most singular. It sometimes seems that the author is unknowingly straying from the theses he has stated, letting himself be guided by a concern to explore in its detail the democratic fabric [*tissu*]—even to the point of recognizing in it contrary properties. There are, on the other hand, moments when the succession of viewpoints reveals itself to be deliberate. Thus, nothing is more remarkable than the analysis of the function of associations in American life. The second book of the second volume opened with a fresh examination of the relations between equality and freedom. I have already alluded to this part of the text. Deeming that there is an extreme point where one can imagine equality and liberty blending together, Tocqueville seems to go beyond the split between the social and the political. He immediately specifies, however, that there are a thousand other forms of equality and separates anew the social state from political institutions. He then devotes two chapters to individualism so as to bring out one major effect of equality: man's decided isolation within society. It is then that he introduces the thesis that Americans combat individualism through free institutions.

But what are these institutions? At first, the emphasis is placed on local political freedoms. The most important one is said to reside in the political life America's legislators have wisely granted to each segment of territory. In the next section, however, this collective activity appears to supply only one aspect of a more general phenomenon, that of association, which pertains to the most fruitful art, what the author calls the "mother of action [*science mère*]." [37] He then presents civil associations as being the most indispensable ones: "If men living in democratic countries had no right and no inclination to associate for political purposes," he observes, "their independence would be in great jeopardy, but they might long preserve their wealth and their cultivation: whereas if they never acquired the habit of forming associations in ordinary life, civilization itself would be endangered." [38]

It is in defending this right to association that Tocqueville stands in opposition to his contemporaries who, cognizant of the weakness and incompetency of individuals in present-day society, dream only of making government more skillful and more active, that is to say, of subordinating social life to the workings of power. Tocqueville reinforces his argument by setting forth, in a new chapter, the role of the press. Since men are no longer closely tied to one another, only the newspaper gives them a "means . . . to converse every day without seeing one another, and to take steps in common without having met." [39] If at first he judges its role in general terms, he does not hesitate afterward to show its political function. These considerations regarding the press thus introduce an analysis of the relation between political and civil associations. At present, it would appear that where political association is prohibited, civil association becomes scarce; that each supports the other; that, more than this, in political associations people "acquire a general taste for association and grow accustomed to the use of it;" [40] and that they can be considered "as large free schools, where citizens go to learn the general theory of association." [41]

Finally, the judgment is handed down that, without denying the importance of local associations, reverses the priority: "When the members of a community are allowed and accustomed to combine for all purposes, they will combine as readily for the lesser as for the more important ones; but if they are allowed to combine only for small affairs, they will be neither inclined nor able to do so." [42] Tocqueville then sets down the formula that has become so famous: "Thus it is by the enjoyment of a dangerous freedom that the Americans learn the art of rendering the dangers of freedom less formidable." [43] And so as not to leave any doubt about the import of his conviction, after having agreed that a nation may prefer to impose a limit on the right to association, he concludes: "But still it is well that the nation should know at what price these blessings are purchased. I can understand that it may be advisable to cut off a man's arm in order to save his life, but it would be ridiculous to assert that he will be as dextrous as he was before he lost it."[44]

These remarks about associations, which after all are very well known, show at best how, after having seemed to separate the social decisively from the political, Tocqueville is able to reestablish their intricate connection. Without doubt, according to him the work of associations pertains to a science that he even calls the "mother of action." The distinction between nature and art is maintained. It is, however, only half relevant. To which legislators, one wonders, did it fall to discover the science of associations? Hadn't these associations been multiplying since before the American Revolution? Tocqueville seems more inspired when he speaks of political associations as "schools for citizens." But let us not forget that he is always keeping an eye on adversaries in his own country who seek only to reinforce state power and do not understand the new character of civil society.

In our time, don't we still need to denounce the illusion of those who would wish to protect the state administration from the effects of all kinds of associations, since their demands hinder its action and don't easily lend themselves to projects crafted by experts? And don't we likewise still need to denounce the inverse illusion of those who place their only hopes in strictly civil associations and who hold "politics" in contempt?

These questions bring us back to our previous one: To what extent are the ambiguities, nay the contradictions, of Tocqueville voluntary or involuntary? Does it suffice that these reversals of perspective sometimes seem deliberate for them always to be so? Upon reflection, I am not sure that it is so important to decide about the matter. Tocqueville's art of writing seems to me, in effect, to be placed in the service of an exploration of democracy that is simultaneously an exploration of the "flesh of the social." I advance this latter term—which I borrow from Maurice Merleau-Ponty—to designate a differentiated setting [milieu] that develops as it is put to the test of its internal division and is sensitive to itself in all its parts.

Tocqueville lets himself be guided by the exigency of his investigation. He explores the social fabric [tissu] in its detail, fearing not that he might discover therein contrary properties. I would dare say that he performs "cuts" in its tissue and seeks in each of its parts the potentialities that lie hidden within—this, while knowing that, in reality, "everything holds together." Thus, he does not hesitate to draw out all the possible consequences of individualism—which does not mean that democracy's dynamic can be summed up in that of individualism. Or, he brings out all the potential consequences of the fact that opinion has taken on a new function—which does not imply that the only conclusion must be that there is a tyranny of the majority. Or else again, he examines the ultimate effects of the growth of the State, without, for all that, adopting the thesis of democratic despotism (I have recalled in passing that he expressly challenges this thesis).

This exploration requires the formulation of general ideas and, more precisely, of conceptual oppositions, such as equality-hierarchy, freedom-servitude, authority-independence, society-individual, belief-unbelief, and so on. The imbrication of language and experience is such that he must clarify the meaning of words in order to go to the "things themselves." But the concepts don't refer back to "essences"; they allow one to discern the main articulations in terms of which political, social, moral, religious, and intellectual facts are arrayed within a society that is henceforth always in movement.

In this sense, Tocqueville's design is not alien to the inspiration behind phenomenology, at least of the kind of phenomenology that has freed itself from the illusion either that it is only a preamble to a logic of Being or that it would have the power to recover without remainder "mute experience" in order to "bring out the pure expression of its own meaning" (to use Husserl's formula). Tocqueville tries to discover some generative principles of social life, but he does not allow one to believe that one might be able to dissipate the opacity of social life itself. What he sets down is the exigency of an interminable deciphering of the *genesis of meaning*. Of each phenomenon, he seeks to unveil the other side, to comprehend how the oppositions that are discovered on one register of experience are found again on another. And this investigation calls for anticipation, without the latter claiming to abolish the indetermination of History. In the present, he seeks out the trace of time; upon examining what arises and seems to him to be new, to be characteristic of democracy, he imagines what is or can be its counterpart—and again what might be the counterpart of that counterpart.

A Thinking of Contraries:
Note on The Old Regime and the Revolution

There is hardly a writer, a philosopher-historian, more concerned than Tocqueville with stating his theses at the outset of his work, with gathering together an entire development in a limpid conclusion, each time he believes it possible to do so. Hardly is there anyone more diligent about making his observations exemplary, about emphasizing the connections between his arguments as if he were performing a proof. *The Old Regime and the Revolution* obeys, if not the same rules of composition, at least the same requirement as *Democracy in America*.

Let us establish a few benchmarks. The motive behind his research project is presented in the foreword. The author, we learn, has always thought that the French Revolution had been much less innovative than was believed on the outside and than it itself believed. He had been convinced that, despite their efforts "to render themselves unrecognizable,"[45] the French had retained from the Ancien Régime most of the sentiments, habits, and even ideas with whose help they had conducted the Revolution that destroyed this regime and that, without wanting to do so, they had made use of its debris in order to build the edifice of the "new society."[46] To verify this hypothesis, he had to "forget for a moment the France we see and ask questions of a France that no longer exists."[47] The goal is disclosed straight off, and the reader is in no danger of going astray.

Later, the last chapter of the first book presents the general direction of the analysis that has just been developed. The ideas are too well known for us to have to report them in detail. In brief: the Revolution tended "to increase the rights and power of political authority."[48] If one does not give in to appearances, if one keeps one's distance from the accidents, "we clearly see that the Revolution's only effect was to abolish the political institutions that for several centuries had reigned unopposed among the majority of European peoples, and that we usually call feudal institutions. It did so in order to replace them with a more uniform and simple social and political order, one based on the equality of conditions."[49] Finally, at the end of the work we find a recapitulation of all the arguments advanced: "In closing, I want to bring together some of the traits I have already described separately, and to envision the Revolution emerging naturally, as it were, from the old regime whose portrait I have painted."[50]

This picture is equally familiar to the reader of Tocqueville, and there is no point in expanding on it. It is worthwhile recalling, however, what in the author's view are the main articulations of his interpretation. I offer a freely drawn summary.

The feudal system seems to have been preserved under the Ancien Régime, but without its blemishes being balanced by the advantages it once procured. It had become more unbearable there than anywhere else, even though less burdensome, because people no longer drew any protection from it. The nobility, deprived of its political rights, driven from the sphere of administration, had won new privileges that were all the more odious as they were attached to no real authority. Rather a caste than an aristocracy, it had become isolated within the nation and, as an "officers corps without soldiers,"[51] was exposed to an attack that annihilated it in one night. On the other hand, the government of the king held all powers in its hands and had decision-making authority over all affairs. Centralization had made Paris the master of the country and in the same stroke exposed the latter, in the case of insurrection, to the mass concentrated in the capital. In the political void of a nation deprived of free institutions, of classes, of political bodies, and of organized parties, public opinion, in trying to reconstitute itself, found for leadership only the *philosophes*, who were unfamiliar with the practice of public affairs, taken with abstractions, and liable to confuse in the same critique defective laws with necessary laws. The Church was powerless to maintain in people's minds the sense of order; more humane, more tolerant, more sensitive to the public good, it was too tied to the old institutions not to be the target of the reformers and, in the same stroke, not to drag religion into the same disrepute into which it had fallen. Finally, the people, though it had long ago been emancipated and had in its ranks a growing number of small landowners, maintained a condition apart from the rest.

Tocqueville draws two lessons from this picture. He formulates the first one in light of the spectacle of the contrast between the misery and isolation of the people and the general softening of mores: The Revolution "had been prepared by the most civilized classes of the nation, and was carried out by the most coarse and ignorant."[52] Thus does it become apparent why the people almost immediately became the ruling power, as soon as the established authorities were defeated. The second lesson bears on the clash between the dominant passions that developed in the eighteenth century—one, that of equality, of ancient origin, was "violent and inextinguishable"[53]; the other, that of liberty, of recent origin, was powerless to establish itself in a society where all the institutions within which it might have matured had been destroyed. This phenomenon illuminates the course of the Revolution. The two passions, which for a moment intermingled, confer upon 1789 its distinctive character. Later, the tendency of the passion for equality to become carried away annihilated the passion for liberty and instigated the reestablishment of an absolute government. And after 1793, we glimpse the sad repetition of the adventures that cast the French down at the feet of their new masters.

The care Tocqueville takes in announcing his design and, when the time comes, in specifying the ideas that guide his interpretation gives his reader a sense of security. If the reader might have feared wandering off on several occasions, if he had been astounded to see himself carried off sometimes in an unforeseen direction or even running up against an apparent contradiction, all he needed to do, in order to forget his hesitations, was to get a grip back on those firm statements wherein the author has delivered his theses. Now, it is worthwhile asking onself whether this reacquired sense of confidence is well founded, whether the surprises one experiences while reading must yield to the certitude that this or that passage procures, or whether, to put it in other terms, the image Tocqueville composes of his book tallies fully with the actual movement of his research program.

This question is not overbroad. I am not inquiring about the historical exactitude of the author's observations nor about the validity of his interpretations. Can the nobility be restricted, as he wants, to the circle of families of very ancient birth? Does the clergy of the Ancien Régime, when considered as a whole, merit so much praise, and is irreligiosity merely a consequence of the hatred the Church inspired as a political institution? Isn't the presentation of the old aristocratic society as a complex of ties of dependence through which the peasants enjoyed the protection and assistance of their master the result of an idealization? Is the violence of the revolutionary government of the same essence as popular violence? Or, to rephrase the question once again, does not the continuity, so strongly established, between the Ancien Régime and the Revolution, run the risk of rendering the revolutionary event itself unintelligible? There are so many problems that raise doubts and objections. Others, better qualified than myself, have already formulated them.

For my part, I wish only to draw attention to the way in which Tocqueville conducts his analysis of the Ancien Régime and works on his portrait or his picture—two terms that return again and again under his pen—or else again to show how he allows himself to be attracted by the depth and variety of his object and how, acknowledging its complexity, he describes a course appreciably different from the one he has announced or summarized. One is tempted to assume that, in the course of his investigation into the Ancien Régime, Tocqueville witlessly wanders away from the research program he has laid down for himself, but his writing is so controlled, and so clear are the signs of his shifting from one perspective to another, that one is nevertheless tempted to believe that he is consciously aware of his approach. Book 2, to which I shall limit my reflections, authorizes both hypotheses. Perhaps, after all, it isn't of such great import to decide between the two, and it is better, in order to appreciate what is baffling in this approach, to begin by recognizing the strange character of what we were calling his object.

In a sense, his object really is the Ancien Régime. The author, in his preface, notes: "I tried to see into the heart of the old regime, so close to us in years, but hidden from us by the Revolution."[54] This statement is not deceptive. The Ancien Régime is asking to be rediscovered. It is a form of society that has its own consistency. Tocqueville's historical and sociological sense is so lively that he applies himself in earnest to the task of conceiving it such as it was in itself. It is no less true, however, that this proposition could be turned around. It is the Revolution that unveils the true nature of this old regime, which some condemn and others defend. In claiming to have established itself on the ruins of that regime, the Revolution brings out for one to see what it has retained therefrom and, therefore, what, in the murky drawing of its institutions, customs, ideas, and sentiments, constituted the main lines that indicate the shape of the future.

Tocqueville thus undertakes his exploration without taking his eyes off the Revolution. Let us recall one point: he wants to show that the latter came of itself from the society it was going to destroy. Now, such a project assumes one already has an appreciation of the Revolution; it assumes the ability to distinguish within it the essence from the accidents. Still, it must be added that this looking forward and back [circulation du regard] takes place within the horizons of a world that, while itself being the product of the Revolution, is no less new. Knowledge of the Revolution, which intertwines with that of the Ancien Régime, therefore finds the conditions of its possibility in the experience of the present. "What exactly did it destroy? What has it created? It seems that the time has come to answer these questions, and that today we are situated at just the right place to best see and judge this great thing."[55] The present-day observer reveals that he is by and large freed of the revolutionary passions, but he remains close enough to the past in order to enter into their spirit. Nevertheless, in a passage where he admits that passion cannot be set aside when speaking of his country and his time, Tocqueville had also specified: "I admit that in studying our old society in all its aspects, I have never entirely lost sight of the new one."[56] This sentence is to be set facing [en regard] the one we cited previously: We must forget the France we see. Although the two ideas apparently collide against each other, they do not cancel each other out. Tocqueville deems it good to forget the new society, but the study of the Ancien Régime does not permit him to do so: "As I progressed in this research, I often encountered to my surprise many traits of modern France in the France of the old regime. . . . Everywhere I found the roots of present society deeply implanted in the old soil."[57]

The object escapes immediate observation: it is the Ancien Régime such as it was in itself, but one can penetrate into the heart of this society only by the light of the Revolution, and the Revolution, in turn, is intelligible only starting from the Ancien Régime. The latter brings into view at the same time the roots of present-day society, while the experience of the present proves to be the focal point of the investigation, the resource for comprehending the past. The singularity of the object does not stop there. Indeed, Tocqueville compares himself at one point to a doctor who dissects "every organ in order to discover the laws that govern the whole of life." [58] As becomes clear, it no longer is a matter then of investigating in the tomb what no longer is but of rediscovering the principle that doesn't die. In the same passage, he confides that his "purpose has been to paint a picture both accurate and instructive." [59] This last term sends up a warning signal, but it is clarified soon enough. The author does not only wish to know the past and the way in which the Revolution and present-day France emerged therefrom—he is seeking to know whether and how freedom is compatible with modern political society. Furthermore, he intends to show that, the aristocracy being everywhere doomed to disappear and democracy revealing itself to be the regime most favorable to the rise of a kind of despotism that would obtain therein its greatest force, political freedom alone is liable to save the new society from the evils equality engenders.

Without a doubt, Tocqueville does not devise a theory for his approach. Nonetheless, it is a hermeneutics of the political that he is sketching out, and quite a subtle one at that, for he connects an interpretation of the past and of the present with an interpretation of the false representations of the actors of the Ancien Régime, the revolutionary actors, and contemporary actors. Such an undertaking is carried out with the help of a repeated shifting of perspective, a mobile regard, a coming-and-going in time, and also a constancy in the questioning that cannot but trouble the mind of the reader, however firm the general thesis might be.

Let us therefore try to detect the path Tocqueville's thought takes by offering a brief examination of book 2. In the first chapter, as one knows, the author proposes to explain "Why Feudalism Was Hated by the People in France More Than Anywhere Else." He brings out a fact that at first sight is paradoxical: the Revolution broke out in a country where feudal institutions were the least constraining; "their yoke seemed least bearable where it was actually lightest." [60] He gives this observation its full force by sharing with us his discovery: the dividing up of the land did not proceed from the Revolution; from the beginning of the eighteenth century onward, the peasants already owned a large portion of the soil. Their hatred of the feudal regime derived both from this new condition and from the weakening or near disappearance of the nobility's political power. In fact, as landowners the peasants saw themselves being subjected to numerous taxes from which the nobles were exempt and the privileges of the latter seemed all the more intolerable as these nobles were no longer assuming responsibility for the administration of the country.

Although Tocqueville points to the weight of the constraints to which the peasants were subject, his analysis leaves the impression that the image of the evils of feudalism counted more than their reality. Now, it is remarkable to note that the final chapter of the book deals, in large part, with the same subject as the first yet alters the picture quite appreciably. His chapter title speaks eloquently: "How, despite the Progress of Civilization, the Condition of the French Peasant Was Sometimes Worse in the Eighteenth Century Than It Had Been in the Thirteenth." Now Tocqueville offers a detailed description of the constraints hemming in the peasant's life. He shows the peasant both overwhelmed and abandoned by the nobles and the bourgeois, emphasizing the violence that swept down upon him for the slightest of reasons — a practice that contrasted with the softening of mores. The reality of the peasant's fate is depicted in the most somber terms. "The peasant," he writes in particular, "lived in this abyss of poverty and isolation; he was kept there as if it were sealed and impenetrable." [61]

What, then, is Tocqueville trying to prove? That under the appearance of a peaceable regime a formidable danger was growing whose full breadth would later be revealed by the revolutionary explosion. These peasants are impenetrable, no doubt. "However, from all directions the ideas of the times had already spread to these coarse minds; they got there by crooked and underground paths, and in these small and obscure places sometimes took on strange forms. Nevertheless, nothing seemed changed on the outside." [62] The split between the rich and the poor was such that what one sees at a distance, "contemporaries did not see." [63] Worse, they could be heard "talking innocently among themselves about the virtues of the people, about their mildness, their devotion, their innocent pleasures, when 1793 is already before them; a ridiculous and terrible sight!" [64]

But, we ask ourselves, what is the point of this demonstration, which is continued in the considerations already presented about the impoverishment of the nobility, the enrichment of the bourgeoisie, and the tragedy that is class division? To me, the answer seems clear. Tocqueville had just recalled in his preceding chapter (the eleventh) the glamour the society of the Ancien Régime had retained and the virtues of independence it harbored, which are lost in the new France. In particular, he noted in passing that the people "alone, above all those of the countryside, found themselves almost powerless to resist oppression other than by violence." [65] He seizes upon this brief observation in order to adjust his interpretation from the previous chapter. From the first lines of the chapter, he returns to the fate of the people who were "perhaps more isolated than anyone has ever been anywhere else," and declares that "this was a new and unique kind of oppression, whose effects deserve to be carefully considered in themselves." [66] One moment earlier, the reader had been tempted to yield to the attractions of the old society; a final change in perspective suddenly places him back in the presence of the Revolution that is growing within its womb.

Before pausing over the surprising picture of the Ancien Régime that is the object of chapter 11, let us pick out a few of the moments that provoke our sense of astonishment. The initial considerations regarding the condition of the people in a decaying feudal system are followed by five chapters devoted to the way the country was governed. Administrative centralization, Tocqueville states in the first place, "Is an Institution of the Old Régime, and Not the Work of the Revolution or of the Empire, as Is Said."[67] He insists on this thesis to the point of fearing that the reader will judge that he, Tocqueville, has "proved [his] point overabundantly."[68] Reviewing one after another the organs and agents of the State, he attributes to them a limitless power. Of the Royal Council, he says that "all roads led to the Royal Council, and from it came the impulses that guided everything"; of the king, that "it was [he] alone who decided"; of the controller-general, that "gradually he had gained control of everything that had to do with money, i.e., almost all public administration"; of the intendant, that "in reality [he] controlled the government."[69] Comparing the state of things in the eighteenth to that of the fifteenth century, he shows how the nobility was driven from the administration, how municipal liberties were destroyed, how the government gained the upper hand over the judiciary through the creation of special courts. One sentence summarizes the entire development at the end of chapter 3: "Under the old regime as now, there was in France no city, town, or village, no tiny hamlet, no hospital, no factory, convent, or college, which could have an independent will in its own affairs, or freely administer its own goods."[70] The fifth chapter specifies that centralization had been introduced without abolishing the old institutions: "When the Revolution arrived, almost nothing of the old edifice of government had been destroyed; in effect a new structure had been built underneath it."[71]

But that doesn't imply any reservation as to its efficiency. The parlements could very well, under exceptional circumstances, show some signs of resistance, but this was never done in order to demand some responsibility in the administration. The very progress of society, which at each instant gives birth to new needs, operates to the benefit of the central power, which alone is capable of satisfying them. Another remarkable observation: On the eve of the Revolution, improved methods of administration allowed one to do without various means of oppression: "As government became more detailed, more extended, it also became more uniform and more knowledgeable."[72] The analysis of the Ancien Régime seems wholly guided by a concern to show what in it anticipated the revolutionary government.

Then comes the first surprise. In the middle of the sixth chapter, just when he has noted the hatred the administration feels toward all those, nobles and bourgeois, who want to become involved in public affairs, and its feelings of suspicion toward the press, Tocqueville suddenly changes the direction of his description. The government often manifested, he observes, "a great intelligence in its task and always great energy. But its activity was often fruitless and even counterproductive, because sometimes it wished to do things that were beyond its strength, or do something beyond anyone's control." [73] And at that point there bolts out a critique of this government's weakness, of its inefficiency, of its futile agitation, as well as of the confusion it spreads in the minds of its agents. What is characteristic is not only its arbitrariness but its hesitation, its tendency toward improvisation, its lack of rigor: "This is the old regime in a nutshell: a rigid rule, lax implementation. . . . Anyone who judged the government of those times by the list of its laws would fall into the most foolish errors." [74] A moment before, he was showing us a society ever more subject to uniform legislation. The greatest evil now comes from the fact that men have lost the very sense of the law: "Among the men of the old regime, the place that the idea of the law ought to hold in the human mind was vacant." [75]

From then onward, the author's thesis takes a totally different turn. It is not so much the strength of the central power that counts as the representation that is forged of it. One imagines a State whence all movements of the social body must proceed. "Since it had already succeeded in destroying all the intermediate powers, and since between it and the individual there was nothing but an immense empty space, from a distance it already appeared to everyone as the sole mainspring of the social machine, the unique and necessary agent of public life." [76] This argument reminds us of the one Tocqueville formulated in the last book of *Democracy in America:* Once the network of personal dependency has broken down, people, isolated as they are from one another, no longer grasp above them anything but an immense being that dominates them and is presumed to decide their fate. Furthermore, it is no longer a question of domination by the king, his ministers, and his intendants. However, through a stunning reversal of perspective it becomes a question of servitude on the part of those who await everything from the State, those very people who present themselves as reformers, as enemies of established government and who, whatever their goal might be, know but a single means: "borrow the strength of the central power" [77] in order to smash everything and to remake everything according to their own plan.

Nevertheless, one cannot simply set reality opposite the chimerical, since the representation has a certain efficacy: "These ideas did not stay in books; they penetrated all minds, were mingled with mores, infused habits, and spread everywhere, even into everyday life. No one thought that any important business could be well managed without the involvement of the State."[78] Evoking the bundle of expectations issuing from various categories of the population, Tocqueville offers the following formula, which is quite striking for a reader of our time: "The government having thus replaced Providence, it was natural that everyone invoke it in his own needs."[79]

From this last point of view, it appears that one is being urged once again to find in the state of mind of the French of the Ancien Régime an anticipation of that of the French at the time of the Revolution and in the nineteenth century. One will therefore think that the newly constituted State has come to gratify those expectations that were formerly placed in the old one but without being able to respond to them adequately. The uniqueness of the monarchical State remains no less significant, and the reader soon learns that this uniqueness prevents one from completely flattening the new model down upon the old one.

Now, the theme that begins to take shape in his examination of administrative centralization becomes fully developed when Tocqueville comes to show both the progress the equality of conditions made in the eighteenth century and the limits it encountered. Society at that time seems decidedly to be made up of contraries and, in spite of everything it portends, it seems to retain, in his view, a physiognomy of its own. It is the very analysis of two phenomena deemed to be constitutive of the new society that leads one to recognize what is specific to the Ancien Régime and irreducible to the thesis of continuous development. Tocqueville's intention leaves no doubt here. The titles of two chapters, the eighth and the ninth, are devised to bring out a major opposition: one reveals "That France Was the Country Where People Had Become Most Alike [*semblables*]"; the other shows "How Such Similar [*semblables*] Men Were More Divided Than Ever Before, Separated into Small Groups That Were Estranged from and Indifferent to One Another." Furthermore, the author inaugurates the development of his argument with the following words: "Anyone who carefully considers France under the old regime will encounter two very different perspectives."[80] Reading these chapters, one even has to grant that the presentation lags behind the demonstration, for these men who have become so alike are not only separated in fact but are busy making themselves dissimilar.

Once again, I refrain from entering into the detail of the argument and am seeking only to restitute a movement of thought. In the first place, we learn that all those who stand above the people have seen their condition, their education, and their way of living become comparable. Tocqueville relates this fact to the workings of the monarchy, which destroyed all local forms of autonomy: "Across the differences that still existed, the nation's unity was already apparent: the uniformity of legislation makes this clear."[81] Without giving us his proofs, he states that there occurs a continual impoverishment of the nobility and a parallel enrichment of the bourgeoisie. He adds that not only is wealth equalized but that one's riches often become of the same kind, the bourgeois becoming a landed property owner and sometimes holding a seigneury. What arises in the economic domain has its complement in the area of culture. Education and lifestyle no longer distinguish the nobility from the commoners. "The bourgeois had as much education as the nobleman, and, as must be noted, his education had often been received in exactly the same place."[82]

In the second place there appears the other side of the picture. A quick overview [survol] of France's nobility reveals that this class, constituted early on in a caste, maintained itself as such, in contrast to the English nobility, making of birth its mark of distinction. The decisive fact is that, after having lost the offices it exercised under the feudal system, offices that brought into its administration a number of commoners, the nobility owned up to its caste character and thenceforth separated itself off from the bourgeois world. Taking as his point of reference the estates general of the fourteenth century, where the orders decided in common, the author takes it to be the case that since then the noble never ceased to isolate himself more and more from the bourgeois: "In the eighteenth century, this revolution was complete; these two never met except by chance in private life."[83] Privilege surrounds the condition of the nobility—notably that most odious of privileges, exemption from taxation—and distinguishes it from society as a group apart. "When the bourgeois and the noble are no longer subjected to paying the same tax, each year the assessment and levying of taxes marks a clear and precise division between classes."[84]

Far from ignoring the more and more widespread practice of ennoblement, Tocqueville sees in it a new agent of decay for the community. Opposing Burke, who sees in this institution a bit of an analogy to the open aristocracy England has known, he offers the following remarkable argument: "If the English middle classes, far from making war on the aristocracy, have remained so closely united with it, this has not been primarily because of the openness of their aristocracy but rather, as has been said, because the English aristocracy's shape is indistinct and its boundary unknown; less because of how easy it is to get there than because no one ever knows when he has arrived."[85] In short, the distinction between the aristocrat and the bourgeois pertained in England to mores, to a mutual understanding among individuals or families that had no institutional authorization. On the other hand, "the barrier that separated the nobility from the other classes in France, although very easy to cross, was always fixed and visible, always recognizable to those who remained outside by obvious and hateful signs."[86] Finally, if one adds that the nobles of old stock sometimes greeted newcomers with contempt, it must be granted that social mobility renders social difference still more vivid.

Tocqueville does not stop there. From the analysis of the privileges of the nobility he passes to that of the privileges enjoyed by a section of the bourgeoisie. He describes the competition stirred up by the sale of offices, which were a source of prerogatives and of exemptions from public responsibilities: "These miserable prerogatives," he notes, "filled with envy those who were deprived of them, and glutted those who possessed them with the most selfish pride."[87] In every act of the bourgeoisie was manifested "its fear of seeing itself confused with the masses, and its passionate desire to escape from their control at all costs."[88] The notables, as they appear when reading the reports written by the king's officers, become the object of a delectable painting of arrogance, of mutual jealousy, and of the rivalries that in small towns tear apart the different constituted bodies—for example, the wig-makers, the bakers, and the notaries:

> We find within this small portion of the nation, situated apart from the rest, infinite divisions. It seems as if the French people were like those supposedly elementary particles inside which, the more closely one looks, modern physics keeps finding new particles. I have found no less than thirty-six different bodies among the notables of a small town. The different groups, although very small, constantly worked at making themselves smaller still.[89]

And further on, he adds: "Every one of these little societies therefore lived only for itself, and was only interested in itself and in matters that directly affected it."[90] Thus do the workings of separation function. And what the analysis brings out is not only a de facto separation, due to the tax barrier, but also the desire for distinction, the rejection of the similarity of conditions, a phantasmagoria of difference that preoccupies the various categories of the bourgeoisie.

Nonetheless, Tocqueville does not lose sight of the picture's front side. He recalls, in concluding this part of his investigation, that "these isolated people had become so similar. . . . Each of them only held on to his own rank [condition] because others divided themselves by rank; but they were all prepared to mingle in the same mass, provided that no one had held aloof and that no one was above the common level."[91] The main thesis is therefore not contradicted. Yet the Ancien Régime decidedly does not allow itself to be conceived of as merely the preamble to the new society. The efficacy of the imaginary can be glimpsed one more time, but from another point of view. Whereas, previously, the representation of uniformity came to be grafted onto the confused practice of the administration, at present the representation of inequality comes to repress the manifest signs of resemblance.

These changes of perspective prepare us for another, more disconcerting one that is given articulation in chapters 10 and 11. Those two chapters form a whole, we believe, as do the five chapters devoted to the centralization of the French people. In chapter 10, Tocqueville endeavors to bring out all the consequences of society's fragmentation, described previously. He first places the accent on the pathology of the regime: "I have just described the most deadly of all the maladies that attacked the constitution of the old regime and condemned it to death." [92] A fresh comparison of the characteristics of the English system with those of the French one serves as an introduction to a more detailed case against fiscal practices since the sixteenth century that brings out, in passing, the scandalous fate that awaited landed commoners—for example, the right of *franc-fief*—and artisans. The manipulation of the tax and the practice of the venality of offices are at one moment thought to result from the greediness of the kings rather than from a concerted policy; but this judgment is soon corrected: "It was," he tells us, "the desire to prevent the nation, from which money was asked, from demanding its freedom back, that made the government constantly alert to ensure that the classes remained apart from each other." [93] Thus, the sentence pronounced against the Ancien Régime seems to be beyond appeal: "The division of classes was the crime of the old monarchy"—a crime, Tocqueville specifies, that permitted the latter to decide about everything, once all the ancient forms of administration had been destroyed.

What a surprise is then in store for the reader when he undertakes to read the eleventh chapter, entitled: "Of the Kind of Freedom That Existed under the Old Regime and Its Influence on the Revolution." From the very first lines of this chapter, a hitherto unforeseeable switch in the analysis is announced:

> If one stopped reading this book here, one would have only a very incomplete picture of the old-regime government, and one would poorly understand the society that made the Revolution. In seeing these citizens so divided and so withdrawn into themselves, a royal power so strong and wide, one might think that the spirit of independence had disappeared along with public freedom, and that all the French were equally bowed in subjection. But this was in no way the case. [94]

Everything then happens as if the film were being rolled in reverse. We see the vestiges of the past—be they even abuses—take on consistency and value again; we see how they testify to the limits of the central power and to a general spirit of resistance. Here we see how the venality of offices, so disparaged beforehand, procured for their beneficiaries some means of action that allowed them to escape the arbitrariness of royal rule. "This harmful and bizarre" constitution, Tocqueville goes so far as to say, "functioned as a kind of political guarantee against the omnipotence of the central power."[95] One discovers that this government, which seemed, if not capable of regulating everything in "its immense . . . sphere of action," at least determined to penetrate everywhere, "still marched with an uncertain step, as if in strange and foggy terrain."[96] It "backed off at the sight of the least resistance."[97] It no longer suffices to observe that, if the rule was rigid, the practice was flexible; society appears not only confused but also protected in its opacity: "If the formidable shadows that then hid the limits of all powers, and hovered about all rights, were favorable to the attempts of rulers against the liberty of the subjects, they were also often useful in their subjects' defense."[98]

And here again we witness how these classes—who a moment earlier were being discredited for their egoism, their internal divisions, their thirst for privileges—come to see their share of merit fully recognized. The nobles, we learn, "retained, even in the loss of their old power, something of their ancestors' pride, as opposed to servitude as to law."[99] In destroying the nobility instead of "bending [it] under the yoke of the law . . . we have deprived the nation of a necessary part of its substance, and given liberty a wound that can never be healed."[100] The clergy, which is discussed at length, has shone so brilliantly by its courage and its independence in crucial circumstances that it can be asked whether "there has ever been a clergy . . . more enlightened, more national, less confined purely to the private virtues, better provided with public virtues, and at the same time with more faith."[101] The bourgeoisie itself distinguished itself by its spirit of independence. Without a doubt, it coveted public offices, but at least, in buying them, it gained the power to win respect for itself, whereas at present it surrenders to the government, which gives these offices to it. Without a doubt, its vanity was manifest in the establishment of this multitude of bodies, each one jealous of its own prerogatives; yet it is true that, in separating itself from the people in order to form a "pseudo-aristocracy," it retained some of the quality of a "real aristocracy."[102] "The general good was easily forgotten in all the little groups [*associations*] that divided the bourgeoisie into so many parts, but," he goes on to say:

there was always concern for the interest and rights of the group [*corps*]. There was a common dignity, common privileges to defend. No one could lose himself in the crowd and hide his cowardly subservience. Every individual found himself on stage, in a very small theater, of course, but a very well-informed one, and there had a permanent audience that was always ready to hiss or applaud.[103]

This last characteristic holds for society as a whole, with the exception of the people, who were isolated and held in contempt. Means of resistance, Tocqueville will say again later, were offered to everyone, provided that they had "a place in society where they could be seen, and a voice capable of making itself heard."[104] Such is the new light in which the society of the Ancien Régime is presented. The king himself reappears there, no longer as a master but as a leader, as he who could say, "We consider it to be our glory to command a free and generous nation,"[105] and as he who had won the affection of his subjects. Without a doubt, one can be astonished, in passing, that Tocqueville does not connect the layout of a society in which each would want to occupy a place from which he might be seen and heard to the monarchical constitution, that he says nothing about the image of a prince who is supposed to incarnate the realm and who thus focuses on his body everyone's gaze. But what is important to underscore here is that this appreciation of the Ancien Régime is clearly governed by the judgment the author brings to bear on the society of his time. Thus, after having mentioned the theater in which each could move around, he observes: "The art of smothering the sound of resistance was much less perfected then than now. France had not yet become the deaf place where we live today."[106] A little later, he recalls that "the men of the eighteenth century hardly knew that kind of passion for material well-being which is the mother of servitude, a spineless passion, yet tenacious and unalterable, which easily mingles and, so to say interlaces itself with several private virtues . . . and excels at making well-behaved men and slack citizens."[107]

So be it! The plea in favor of the Ancien Régime will be corrected at the end of the chapter we have been examining. It will be pointed out that, although "fruitful," the freedom that reigned there was "disorderly and unhealthy" and was readying the overthrow of despotism but not the foundation of "the free and peaceable empire of the law."[108] Finally, the last chapter, which we have already mentioned, will bring back before the reader's eyes the image of the people abandoned, ready to engage in any kind of fury. But the collision between what Tocqueville at one moment named "two very different perspectives" will not, for all that, be blotted out.

We asked whether Tocqueville strays unwittingly from his program or whether he is fully conscious of how he advances. The answer eludes us. But there is no doubt that his constant attraction for *the other side of the picture* is the sign of his passion to understand and is what gives his work its greatest strength.

Notes

"Tocqueville. Démocratie et art d'écrire." The first part, "Une exploration de la chair du social. Note sur *Démocratie en Amérique*" was originally published in *Écrire*, 55–72. The second part, "Une Pensée des contraires. Note sur *l'Ancien Régime et la Révolution*," was originally published in the *Revue Européenne des Sciences Sociales* 85 (1989): 151–63 (issue in honor of Bronislaw Baczko); reprinted in *Écrire*, 72–90.

1 Alexis de Tocqueville, *Democracy in America*, trans. Henry Reeve, revised by Francis Bowen, corrected and edited by Phillips Bradley, intro. Daniel J. Boorstin (New York: Vintage, 1990), 2:76.

2 Ibid., 2:69.

3 Ibid., 1:16 [T/E: translation altered].

4 Ibid., 2:145.

5 Ibid., 2:146.

6 Alexis de Tocqueville, "L'État social et politique de la France," in *L'Ancien Régime et la Révolution*, vol. 1 of his *Œuvres complètes* (Paris: Gallimard, 1953, 1980), 1:62.

7 *Democracy in America*, 2:24.

8 Ibid., 2:99.

9 Ibid.

10 Ibid.

11 Ibid., 2:328 [T/E: translation altered].

12 Ibid., 2:294 [T/E: translation altered].

13 Ibid., 1:251.

14 Ibid., 1:252 (emphasis added) [T/E: translation slightly altered].

15 Ibid., 1:280.

16 Ibid., 1:279.

17 Ibid., 1:280.

18 Ibid., 1:276 [T/E: translation slightly altered].

19 Ibid., 1:3 [T/E: translation altered].

20 Ibid., 2:94.

21 Ibid., 2:95.

22 Ibid., 2:94.

23 Ibid., 2:287.

24 Ibid., 2:288.

25 Ibid., 2:8.

26 Ibid., 2:9.

27 Ibid., 2:10.

28 Ibid.

29 Ibid., 2:9.

30 "Every man allows himself to be put in leading-strings, because he sees that it is not a person or a class of persons, but the people at large who hold the end of his chain" (ibid., 2:319).

31 Ibid., 2:295.
32 Ibid., 2:296.
33 Ibid., 2:319.
34 Ibid., 2:321.
35 *L'Ancien Régime et la Révolution*, 2:199.
36 *Democracy in America*, 1:34.
37 Ibid., 2:117.
38 Ibid., 2:107.
39 Ibid., 2:112.
40 Ibid., 2:119.
41 Ibid., 2:116 [T/E: translation altered].
42 Ibid., 2:117 [T/E: translation altered].
43 Ibid., 2:119.
44 Ibid., 2:120.
45 *The Old Regime and the Revolution*, ed. François Furet and Françoise Mélonio, trans. Alan S. Kahan (Chicago: University of Chicago Press, 1999), 1:83 [T/E: translation altered].
46 Ibid.
47 Ibid. [T/E: translation altered].
48 Ibid., 1:105.
49 Ibid., 1:106 [T/E: translation altered].
50 Ibid., 1:241.
51 Ibid., 1:242.
52 Ibid., 1:243.
53 Ibid., 1:244.
54 Ibid., 1:84.
55 Ibid., 1:95.
56 Ibid., 1:86 [T/E: translation altered].
57 Ibid., 1:84–85 [T/E: translation altered].
58 Ibid., 1:86 [T/E: translation slightly altered].
59 Ibid.
60 Ibid., 1:111.
61 Ibid., 1:189.
62 Ibid., 1:189–90.
63 Ibid., 1:190.
64 Ibid.
65 Ibid., 1:177–78.
66 Ibid., 1:180.
67 Ibid., 1:118.
68 Ibid.
69 Ibid., 1:119–20 [T/E: translation slightly altered].
70 Ibid., 1:131
71 Ibid., 1:136 [T/E: translation altered].
72 Ibid., 1:137.
73 Ibid., 1:141.
74 Ibid., 1:142.
75 Ibid.
76 Ibid. [T/E: translation altered].

77   Ibid., 1:143.
78   Ibid.
79   Ibid., 1:144 [T/E: translation slightly altered; the English-speaking reader should note that, in French, the "welfare state" is known as *l'État providence*].
80   Ibid., 1:149.
81   Ibid. [T/E: translation slightly altered].
82   Ibid., 1:151.
83   Ibid., 1:155.
84   Ibid., 1:157
85   Ibid. [T/E: translation slightly altered].
86   Ibid., 1:157–58.
87   Ibid., 1:160.
88   Ibid., 1:161.
89   Ibid.
90   Ibid., 1:162 [T/E: translation slightly altered].
91   Ibid., 1:163.
92   Ibid.
93   Ibid., 1:170.
94   Ibid., 1: 171 [T/E: translation slightly altered].
95   Ibid., 1:172.
96   Ibid.
97   Ibid.
98   Ibid. [T/E: translation slightly altered].
99   Ibid.
100 Ibid., 1:173 [T/E: translation slightly altered].
101 Ibid., 1:175.
102 Ibid., 1:176.
103 Ibid. [T/E: translation slightly altered].
104 Ibid., 1:178.
105 Louis XVI quoted in ibid.
106 Ibid., 1:176.
107 Ibid., 1:178.
108 Ibid., 1:179.

Sade: The Boudoir and the City

*J*OUISSANCE, cruelty, knowledge of nature through *jouissance* and cruelty, all these themes are interlaced with that of corruption in *La philosophie dans le boudoir.*

This novel — but is it a novel? — stands out in Sade's work in a paradoxical way, that is, both for its lightness and for its theoretical and political ambition. Here Sade tells us what the Republic should be. What could seem more serious? We are in the Thermidorean period, right after the fall of Robespierre and Saint-Just. Debate is lively between those who think the Revolution is over and those who favor a return to Jacobinism. True, Sade does not speak in his own name. The ideal republic is described in a pamphlet that one of the characters in the boudoir presents to his friends. It is entitled *Français, encore un effort si vous voulez être républicains* (Yet another effort, Frenchmen, if you would be republicans). This text has so whetted the interest of Sade critics that they treat it as an independent tract, and it was even published under separate cover some years ago by Jean-Jacques Pauvert.[1] The fact is that the few political writings by Sade from when he was secretary of the Parisian Section of Piques (1793) do not stand out among the revolutionary writings of the era, although his activity was not negligible. In contrast, *Français, encore un effort* proceeds from an extraordinary will to subvert all established order. I know of no scandalous satire [*libelle*] that testifies to such an upheaval of thought, to such a smashing down of the barriers of the thinkable, to such a groundswell that carries off everything in its path: all positions of authority, the foundations of religious despotism, political despotism, the despotism of opinion, and the despotism that society itself exercises over its members.

Without any doubt, the work bears the mark of the spirit of revolution, but one would have no hope of understanding Sade's design if one forgot that *Français, encore un effort* has its place in *La philosophie dans le boudoir*. True, the relationship between the pamphlet and the dialogues, both cruel and lighthearted, that precede its reading appears somewhat baffling, which is why the famous Sade biographer, Gilbert Lély, imprudently—that is, without proof—surmised that the author had inserted this text, after the fact and arbitrarily, into "an exquisitely constructed whole."[2] Yet, one need only read *Français, encore un effort* somewhat attentively to notice that the pamphlet pursues on the political level the theme of corruption, a theme that is present from the beginning of the work and right up to the very end. Let us not forget that corruption is a great theme of political philosophy. The distinction between a well-ordered society living in conformity with nature and a corrupt society is one of the foundations of classical political philosophy, the philosophy of Plato and Aristotle. Moreover, as unsettled [*ébranlé*] as the classical teachings have become in Modern Times, the political critique of corruption has not ceased to be formulated and reformulated each time one placed tyranny in the dock or charged a monarchy with creeping absolutism, each time one denounced the arbitrary power that the supposed representatives of the people had arrogated unto themselves or described the degradation of peoples who had become accustomed to their servitude.

To take some initial bearings here, we might recall how important the concept of "corruption" was in the Florentine age of civic humanism at the beginning of the fifteenth century and later in the work of Machiavelli. Recall, too, the mobilizing power of the Puritan critique of corruption in seventeenth-century England and, in the eighteenth century, the polemics launched by the radical Whigs, the far Left of the period. An obsession with corruption also haunted the American Revolution and French Revolution. Finally—and especially important for the appreciation of Sade's thought—is the characteristically modern idea of a corruption that could taint not only a city or a particular nation but humanity per se: a sense of corruption concealed beneath the trappings of civilization, beneath the trappings of material progress, of luxury, of refinement and culture. The thing is so well known that it hardly needs emphasizing.

To return to Sade, the author begins to confront us with the question of the corruption of mores by inviting us into his boudoir, an enclosed space, one that is apparently foreign to the city. Four principal characters will move around in there: Mme de Saint-Ange, who has initiated the meeting; her brother, "the Chevalier"; the latter's friend, Dolmancé, a great speechmaker and an expert in the art of *jouissance;* and, finally, an ingenue, Eugénie. It is the desire to corrupt that, at the beginning of this work, guides

Mme de Saint-Ange's singular project to initiate the delicious Eugénie in the liberties of *jouissance*. After being assured by her brother that his friend, whom she does not yet know, "is really the most totally and thoroughly corrupt person, the most evil individual, the greatest scoundrel in the world" (19), she becomes enchanted with the idea of making Dolmancé her accomplice.

What is *La philosophie dans le boudoir?* A sort of novel, in the form of dialogues, presented as a theatrical show; it is a dramatic composition whose theatrical character is underscored by the stage directions given for the actors' movements and by their asides, which are indicated in parentheses. The theme is the education of a young girl or, as I have just said, her initiation in the liberties of *jouissance*. This undertaking, as the lady who has drawn her into the boudoir jokingly says, requires both theory and practice. The practice will induce the most varied exercises, of which Eugénie will be object, agent, and witness. The theory will allow the treatment of similarly varied problems, at the initiative of these wicked instructors, but nonetheless in response to the ingenue's insatiable curiosity.

I'll pass over the elementary teachings. Eugénie wants to know the name and function of everything she is allowed to see, touch, and smell. What is a "prick"? she asks. What are "testicles," a "clitoris," a "vagina"? She acts like a child eager to learn new words. What is "come"? What does "whore" mean? Her philosophical curiosity is no less anchored in the childish desire to know everything; it is she who wants to be enlightened on the utilitarian value of the virtues and who insists that her teachers return to the theme of religion, which they went over too quickly for her liking.

Discussion, however, is interrupted several times for practice in some equally instructive exercises that lead her from discovery to discovery—but without the dialogue ever ceasing. Everything that is done is said. Well before Dolmancé proclaims the "right to say everything"—a formula that Maurice Blanchot emphasizes,[3] but only in relation to Sade's rage for writing—there is an incessant flow of speech. Nothing contracts or discharges in the bodies of the characters, or in their minds (Dolmancé says at one point: "What an imagination . . . she discharges from the head" [180]), nor is there contact or coupling without the accompaniment of a voice. The quest for explanations, which the young girl pursues, conquers all. Thus does Eugénie, deflowered by the Chevalier and then penetrated simultaneously from the front and from behind by the young gardener called to the rescue and by Dolmancé—Eugénie on the brink of annihilation, Eugénie in ecstasy—suddenly recover her voice and find the strength to pose another question. With disarming gravity, the schoolgirl declares: "I would like to know whether mores are truly necessary in a government, whether their influence carries any weight with regard to the genius of a nation?" (189–90). Now, it is at this point, we should recall, that Dolmancé, the most corrupt man, produces the pamphlet he has found (or so he says) at the Palais-Égalité, one of the spots where everyone who is anyone in revolutionary Paris meets.

Sade neglects no detail in what Lély called this "exquisitely constructed whole." The reading of *Français, encore un effort* follows the double rape of Eugénie—who believed herself to be, after her deflowering, at the end of her pains and her joys—and is entrusted to the "fine organ" of the Chevalier, he who had the privilege of executing that most noble task. Eugénie's last cry had been, "Oh, yes, I swear in my present state of drunkenness that I would go, if I had to, and get myself fucked in the middle of the street" (189). The space of the boudoir has thus already opened onto the space of the city. Finally, I myself shall not miss picking up one further indication: before the Chevalier takes hold of the pamphlet, Mme de Saint-Ange dismisses the young gardener, the only character who owed his admission to the boudoir merely to the unusual size of his member, the only one who was not an accomplice, but simply an instrument of pleasure: "Out with you, Augustin, this is not for you; but don't go too far—we'll ring when we want you to come back" (190).

Why, then, shouldn't Augustin listen? To put it another way, what is Sade trying to tell us, the readers, with this stroke? What complicity is he seeking to establish with us, such that he feels no need to justify the exclusion of the man of the people—an exclusion that occurs, moreover, at the very moment when the philosophy of the boudoir opens onto the philosophy of the city? The sign should be kept in mind, whatever its meaning. Something is going to be said that is undoubtedly more serious, something that goes beyond the remarks already made, as scandalous as these have been to a gardener's ears. Could it be that political philosophy exposes one to greater dangers, or is it simply that this "oaf," as Eugénie called him, had already shown that he does not have an ear for listening, so impatient was he to come. At this point, theory diverges from practice; the presence of a body without ideas, as the excellent Sade critic Annie Lebrun says, becomes inopportune.[4] Such little questions are enough to show us that the work is very cleverly conceived—for the pleasure and astonishment of the reader.

I would suggest that the reader who has followed the early dialogues of *La philosophie dans le boudoir* and indulged in the spectacle is disposed in an entirely different way from the reader who approaches *Français, encore un effort* without having been prepared for it and who stumbles upon the first few sentences read by the Chevalier: "I come to offer great ideas. They shall be heard. They shall be given due reflection. If not all of them please, surely a few will. I thus shall have contributed something to the progress of Enlightenment and I therefore shall be content" (190). To be sure, this reader's expectations will be sorely tried when he learns, soon thereafter, upon what foundations the Republic is to be established. But for now, and even for a while longer, he will adopt the tone that the philosophe's speech has insinuated into him, the tone of the Enlightenment thinker. (And how often will we hear about "the torch of philosophy"!)

What I mean to say, in short, is that every reading of a text implies, for the one who reads it, some manner of saying it to oneself—and, always already, some manner of interpreting it, simply by the inflection one gives to the words, the rhythm to the phrase, by a modulation of speech that in oneself remains unpronounced. One does not read Molière as one reads Racine or Descartes. But the difference is not dictated entirely by the text; it also arises from the operations performed by the reader. Indeed, what would be the point of learning to read if not to decipher and to communicate what are called "messages"? The thing is well known, but usually everything happens as if this knowledge served no purpose. Ordinarily, we are reluctant to admit that the interpretation based on one's understanding, the learned interpretation, is inseparable from this first sensible interpretation of which every reading is made. And there is an indefinable shuttling back and forth between them. It is one's manner of reading that leads to understanding, and it is also one's understanding that leads to rereading, to rearticulating, to scanning the text in another way. Of course, the distance between the actor-performer [*l'interprète-acteur*] on stage and the scholar-interpreter may be unbridgeable, but there is still a sort of mediation: the art of reading, which is impossible to define. And since I have just advanced the idea that the manner of reading is not dictated entirely by the text, I must qualify this statement by adding that it is nevertheless from the power of a piece of writing that a reading draws its power. For, the reader knows that there has to be a proper reading [*une bonne lecture*].

Why this digression? There are certainly no writers, by which I mean genuine writers, who exempt us from the task of interrogating ourselves about our manner of reading, no writers whom we do not have to reread and reread again in an effort to harmonize our voices with theirs—unless we just collide against them, which sometimes happens. And it is not some knowledge about what genre their literature, their writing, belongs to that will deliver us from the insecurity of reading. But, this being granted, we still must recognize that among these writers are a few who throw us into a state of the greatest insecurity. Sade is one of them. Not primarily because he escapes all academic classification, but because even *the abysses he opens up are not always reliable;* and because, by the same token, we cannot always rely, either, on the operation whereby we think we have discovered in the damned part of his work the sacred part, or in the omnipotence of the desire he affirms the pure denial of the law, or, yet again, in the exorbitance of what he calls "insurrection" the "intransigence" of Saint-Just. (I am alluding here to an interpretation advanced by Blanchot, an otherwise admirable critic.)[5] But as it is neither among my intentions nor within my power to pronounce on the work as a whole, I will return to the manner of reading *Français, encore un effort*—to the manner of reading that I believe I have learned in letting myself be guided by the early dialogues of *La philosophie dans le boudoir*.

These dialogues are highly troubling owing to the variety of impressions they procure. I have already mentioned the variety of exercises practiced and the variety of themes subjected to discussion, but now it is time to note the relationship that Sade establishes with us, his readers. He allows us no rest. He exacts from us an extreme agility, suggesting this or that position only to yank us immediately out of it. "Dissolved positions [*attitudes rompues*]," he says once, speaking of his characters. This is a theatrical term, but it also applies to us, the readers, for he is constantly disrupting our own progress. For brevity's sake, I shall simply say that this agility is stimulated by the devices of comedy. Annie Lebrun rightly observes that *La philosophie dans le boudoir* is a "very merry [*gai*] book."[6] To me, it seems somewhat more than that. It is at times irresistibly funny, despite its cruelty—which does not mean that it is not serious and, again, even somewhat more than that: in short, it is a book that torments our thought. What is this torment?

The first words exchanged between Mme de Saint-Ange and the Chevalier are those of libertines. They presage an intrigue that is consonant with an established tradition. Our expectations are undone as soon as Mme de Saint-Ange discloses her project—a kind of education—and her intentions: "I'll have two pleasures at once: that of enjoying [*jouir*] these criminal lecheries myself and that of giving the lessons, of inspiring a taste for them in the sweet innocent I am luring into our nets." She adds: "Of course, I'll spare nothing to pervert her, degrade her, upend in her all the false ethical principles people might already have used to dazzle her" (24 and 25). Seducing an ingenue in order to enjoy her and to see her deflowered and sodomized, thereby satisfying one's own criminal desires—the game is not surprising when one knows about libertinism, the literature of libertinism. On the other hand, the reader is caught in the net when wickedness and education, initiation into *jouissance* and emancipation, come to be conjoined. The net's mesh may seem too large, too visible, for Sade is obviously inverting the old Socratic formula: *No one does evil voluntarily;* but it becomes clear in what follows that, beginning with the premises he has laid down, Sade is empowering himself to seize upon those ideas that are considered the most noble, those that are the attainments of civilization—and this he does precisely in order to discredit the principles of morality. These fine and noble ideas partly contradict the ones that guide Eugénie's emancipation, yet he does not wish to do without them, and perhaps he cannot do without them. He must invoke natural law, liberty, and equality—essential attributes of human nature.

But what is human nature, if "nature" implies no norm? What is liberty, if the sexual drive alone dictates the worth of any act? And what is equality, if it excludes the recognition of like by like? And the whirlwind does not stop there, for we cannot forget Mme de Saint-Ange's desire: "I want," she says of Eugénie, "to make her as wicked as I am . . . as impious . . . as debauched" (25). The object of her desire, in other words, is Eugénie's desire, but in a quite particular way. To want to corrupt her is to want to form her in one's own image, to seek to see oneself in her. This whirlwind has already dizzied the reader. But there are several sorts of dizziness: the image of the educator-corruptor is also troubling. There is, in fact, in every educational undertaking a sort of violence that cannot be measured, that lies hidden, that is only indicated by the *obligatory* distance between teacher and pupil; it is only indicated by the resistance that the teacher opposes to the drive for knowledge so as to neutralize it, to temper a drive that could get the better of the student. And, correspondingly, this undertaking entails a violence in the pupil's expectations: an impatience for what, beyond the things the pupil is told, his senses are avid to know. This is, indeed, the twofold relationship that Sade makes manifest, that he is showing us.

The bodies embrace, interpenetrate, and the movement of thought couples upon the movement of the organs. From the erogenous zones emerge ideas. But the characters' words are just as troubling, these words that accompany and that name the movements of the bodies and the successive combinations of positions, governed always by the orgasmic imperative [*l'impératif de la jouissance*]. For, starting with injunctions, responses, commentaries, and exclamations, a sense of bewitchment such as few physical spectacles produce overtakes us, the readers. Then the boudoir, the enclosed space of pleasure, captivates the reader, who becomes the target of the desire to corrupt. Yet this is only one moment of the reading process. What could be more comic than this schoolgirl who is so quick to satisfy her sense of perversity, so enchanted with her own progress: "Oh, how well I now understand what evil is . . . how much my heart desires it!" (91). Or: "How easily do I see that what you exact is for my own good" (60).

And one cannot help but laugh once more when, after having justified murder, rape, incest, and parricide, Mme de Saint-Ange, hoping to free Eugénie from all scruples toward her mother, solemnly declares: "During this age when the Rights of Man have been broadened at so great a cost, girls ought not to continue to think that they are the slaves of their families" (66). Or, yet again:

> Let us hope that people's eyes will be opened and that, in guaranteeing freedom for all, the fate of these unhappy girls will not be forgotten; . . . they will soon triumph over custom and opinion. Man, becoming wiser because he will be freer, will sense the injustice that would exist in heaping scorn on girls who act thus. May the act of yielding to nature's impulses, which a captive people viewed as a crime, no longer be so regarded among a free people (68).

All this noble talk—which is attributed to an ignoble character—how can we read it, and hence say it to ourselves, without adopting a declamatory tone, as I have just done? Even more, how can we avoid seeing in the statements, the refined speeches delivered by Dolmancé, which are placed in the service of the critique of morality, the pretensions and the dogmatism allegedly connected with the ideology of the age?

La philosophie dans le boudoir is a title that by itself is already blasphemous. Where it finds a site to work, philosophy plies its trade within a learned society. No doubt, during that century philosophy was widely practiced in the salons. But it went there without—at least in the eyes of its faithful supporters—losing sight of its primary destination. To philosophize in the boudoir, on the other hand, presupposes a singular manner of conceiving wisdom: what the ancients called "a life lived in conformity with nature"—which presupposes an even more singular manner of testing principles in the light of facts. This entails not only, as someone will later say, bringing philosophy down to earth from the heavens, but setting it in a place of lust.

But knowledge does not lose its rights for all that. In the boudoir, one discusses virtues and vices; one discusses, too, the foundations of religions, the paths to happiness, the classical distinction between nature and convention. Nevertheless, the great traditional themes are subjected to the viewpoint of the boudoir. Philosophy in the boudoir is philosophy sifted through the screen of the boudoir. True, just as in a learned society, the society of the boudoir includes members who hold some title that authorizes them to participate in the dialogue. It requires walls that separate it from the vulgar. Perhaps this is why the gardener is chased out. Nevertheless, this society is also distinguished by the fact that it is a secret society and one that intends to remain so, since its debauchery contradicts the rules of every political society.

Although Eugénie's curiosity incites her to ask whether "mores" are truly necessary to a government, and although Dolmancé—as an enlightened man with views on all subjects—would not want to leave any question unanswered, it is unclear what motive would drive the tiny world of the boudoir to develop the model of a Republic that would respond to its wishes. Surely, the society that would come closest to its wishes is precisely the one that would ignore it. Moreover, Sade very cleverly introduces political philosophy here through the reading of a pamphlet that comes from outside the boudoir. Not only does this device meet a need, but it also serves a ruse that momentarily disconcerts us, the readers.

To summarize, as briefly as possible, the pamphlet's argument: From his very first words, the author of the pamphlet appears to be a patriot and a staunch republican, as well as an ardent defender of the Revolution—with, however, one reservation, namely, that he deems the Revolution unfinished (hence his appeal to the French: "Yet another effort!"). He speaks, at length, the language of virtue; then, while examining the best means to found the Republic, or rather to set it upon indestructible foundations, his words again link up, little by little, with the words uttered in the boudoir, those of Dolmancé, those of Mme de Saint-Ange. The anonymous author, a stranger to the boudoir, in some sense reinvents it, proposing to multiply this boudoir under the form of establishments created by the government. Men and women who noticed some attractive individual in the street could summon that person to appear and assert their right to take their pleasure [*jouir*] with him or her, ultimately to use him or her as they liked in guaranteed secrecy. Finally, there is a description of licentiousness, which is defined as the condition for the safety of the Republic. What makes this even more comic is that the point of departure for this new philosophical, or philosophical-political, agenda is the opposite of the previous one, that is, the one at the beginning of the dialogue. We are led back, under the sign of pure reasoning, to a panegyric on corruption. Ignominy was evident from the start of the dialogues, although not without being combined, at times, with the new themes of emancipation: liberty, equality, and natural law. Here, the ignoble is first concealed under a pompous display of grand principles, then it reappears innocently draped in the folds of virtue. Simply speaking, virtue is transformed into vice. Now, if we do not recognize that this is a deliberate move on Sade's part, we will inevitably fail to grasp a weakness in his arguments. That is, we will fall into the trap of attributing to him ideas that he seizes upon only to pervert, of taking literally arguments and maxims from the first part of the text—the section on religion and the one on mores—without noticing his playfulness there. I have already quoted the beginning of the very first sentence: "I come to offer great ideas"—which many other phrases will come to echo. For example:

> Let us therefore annihilate forever everything that might one day destroy your work. Imagine that the fruits of your labors were reserved only for your grandchildren; duty and probity command that you bequeath to them none of those seeds of disaster that could plunge your descendants back into the chaos from which we have with such pains just escaped (194).

Or:

> Rather than fatigue your children's young organs with deific stupidities, replace them with social principles of surpassing value; . . . teach them to cherish the virtues you scarcely ever mentioned in former times . . . ; make them feel that this happiness consists in making others as fortunate as we ourselves desire to be (204).

Finally, and I shall stop here:

> Return next to the utility of morality: give them [your pupils], on this vast subject, many more examples than lessons, many more demonstrations than books, and you will make good citizens of them; you will make them into fine warriors, fine fathers, fine husbands; . . . Patriotism will then shine in all spirits (207).

Each and every one of these sentiments will be contradicted in the rest of the pamphlet, not a word of which proves credible. The generations to come merit only indifference, we learn; morality is not only useless but dangerous; the family is destined for destruction; children will not know their fathers. It thus seems to me that Blanchot is mistaken when he chalks up to reason in Sade—a reason that is always in excess, he says—what must really be seen as "the most shameless contradictions, arguments that turn into their opposites, statements that do not hold up,"[7] yet adds: "Sade speaks in order to convince. He is searching, he is always manifesting, here and there, his sincere conviction."[8] To say this is to run the risk of passing Sade off as either a madman or an imbecile. I maintain, again, that it suffices to set the tone in order to give these phrases the effect the author is expecting from them.

In short, I maintain that Sade exploits philosophical-revolutionary discourse in order to bring out the consequences that undermine its principles. Moreover, once we uncover this process (which again draws on the art of the theater), we must grant that the author never stops exploiting it, even when he seeks to demonstrate that vices exist in conformity with the laws of nature (in the classical sense) or with natural law (in the modern sense), or with the ultimate ends of the Republic. It is not only revolutionary discourse that Sade deliberately distorts, but philosophical discourse in general and republican humanism in particular. While Sade does not mention Plato, he invokes the theory of the community of women—but only to distort it by basing the legitimacy of incest on it. He does not mention Machiavelli, but he follows the latter in observing that Rome was founded upon crime; and while affirming that an old and corrupt republic cannot save itself by virtue, he neglects to recall what Machiavelli viewed as the greatness of the Romans, that is, the fact that law thrives only when it is combined with the desires of a free people. He also forgets that corruption cannot be abolished by granting individuals a license to indulge their private pleasures. He does not mention Hobbes, but he makes his own the thesis that the state of nature is a war of all against all—except that he takes care not to point out that civil society originates and evolves from man's inability to sustain this war, this terrible ordeal. He does not mention Rousseau (whom he invokes only apropos of the death penalty and adultery), but he makes his own the case against civilization—except that he uses this case to serve an end that runs contrary to Rousseau's since he denies man's natural goodness.

Sade's concern is not to subject the ideas of the philosophers to examination but to extract formulas from them that will allow him to dress up his own discourse in philosophical garb or rather to drape himself in the tatters of philosophy. He renders this travesty of philosophy almost convincing by throwing about himself some of the references in which it is clothed. He makes the legislators of Greece, along with Seneca, Charron, Plutarch, and many others shine, one after another. He does so, however, in order to exculpate calumny, rape, and sodomy. Why speak of contradictions? Contradiction, because it reestablishes the exigencies of logic, is a serious thing. Now, it seems to me that in Sade this is an authorial ruse. Philosophical discourse, moreover, has never been exempt from such tricks. The Platonic dialogues or the works of Machiavelli offer some great examples. It is not certain (nor has it been disproved) that Sade was inspired by them, but he is pleased above all to *divert* [*détourner*]—I insist upon this term because it had so much success in 1968—ideas from their original destination, and he endeavors in other respects to weaken the authority of the argument, of all argument. He does so by advancing, with equal seriousness, a thesis and its contrary, or by thoroughly exploiting the resources of an infantile intelligence.

Take incest. It is not an evil, he tells us, since procreation, a fact of nature, does not result in any tie between the child and those who begot it. And furthermore, experience proves how this purely conventional relationship can arouse feelings of hatred. Nor is it an evil, he tells us later, because it is quite natural that a being should feel attracted by its closest object, the one that resembles it most. Take another example: the defense of calumny. The slanderer has every merit on his side. If he attacks a perverse man, he usefully attracts attention to the latter, and, in imputing to that man crimes he did not commit, the slanderer helps to unmask him before public opinion; if he attacks a virtuous man, he incites that man to redouble his zeal in order to defend his honor. After this, can we say that Sade wants to convince anyone? And yet I note that Jacques Lacan, who did not ordinarily lack a sense of humor, complained that in this case the demonstration was a bit abrupt.[9]

What there is no doubt about is that before or behind the arguments, Sade is pursuing his own design. The determined, deliberate movement of his discourse does not lead one to believe that it is just some incoherent blathering. The cumulative effect produced by the pamphlet seems to me quite remarkable. Indeed, the philosophical demonstrations come to resemble the exercises practiced in the boudoir. The ideas copulate, part, and are rearticulated in accordance with the multiple positions of the person speaking. The learned profligacy seems aimed precisely at arousing the reader to orgasm [*une jouissance*]. I am not talking about metaphysical orgasm. Sade employs *jouissance métaphysique* once when denouncing the futility and horror of the kind of love that fosters a disagreeable burning sensation, he tells us, in the absence of all real pleasure, which is to say, a love that corrupts. No, it is rather an orgasm that proceeds from excitation of the head—this head that "discharges," to use Dolmancé's expression—an orgasm that is apt to spread into the body and one that, perhaps, was already brewing within the body.

In a sense, the reader is put into a state somewhat reminiscent of Eugénie's condition. Mme de Saint-Ange confided to her brother that she wanted to upend [*culbuter*] all the false principles of morality in Eugénie. Does not Sade want to upend philosophy in the reader? Of course, Eugénie and the reader do not occupy the same place; the reader is not necessarily an ingenue. Indeed, Sade is probably counting on the reader's complicity, perhaps even more on his complicity than on his conversion. Provoking laughter from the reader is already a way of corrupting him, for laughter is not always the best medicine, contrary to what is often said. In luring him into this debauchery of ideas, Sade is seeking to stir up an agitation of the body that is already within the reader, to insinuate into thought the drives that thought restrains. And in fact he suggests at one point, in the voice of Dolmancé, that his philosophical saraband contains seething desires. Dolmancé has just expounded a long dissertation on *jouissance,* the will to domination that accompanies it, and the absurdity of wanting to thwart it. Suddenly, he exclaims: "Fuck! I'm hard again! . . . I beg you to call Augustin [the gardener] back in here. 'Tis amazing how this fine lad's superb ass does preoccupy my mind while I talk! All my ideas seem involuntarily to relate back to that masterpiece, Augustin" (279).

Be that as it may, we should not lose sight of Sade's relationship to the Revolution and the Republic, to which I now return. I do not want to give the impression that Sade was counterrevolutionary, antirepublican, or indifferent to politics. I doubt that his radical critique of religion has ever been equaled; his rejection of all forms of deism, his attraction to all forms of insurrection, necessarily puts him on the side of the Revolution. The general uprising, the tremendous upheaval in institutions, all that has stirred up a new phantasmagoria—raging floods, volcanic eruptions, earthquakes—none of this was alien to him. Yet he detested the revolutionary ideology and everything that smacked of new, constraining norms, of pretensions to virtue. On the other hand, without being republican, he was nonetheless biased, I would say, toward this regime owing to his hatred of royalism and of the eighteenth-century aristocracy. In order to try to catch up with his thought, we need to focus on the passage in the pamphlet where its author calls for, indeed demands, immoral citizens. At this point, the argument is aimed at defending the thesis that prostitution, adultery, incest, rape, and sodomy should not be considered offenses.

> We certainly should not for one moment doubt that all those so-called morals crimes . . . would be of absolutely no importance under a government whose sole duty consists in preserving, by whatever means necessary, the form essential to its continuance: there you have a republican government's sole morality. But, since the republic is permanently menaced by the despots surrounding it, one cannot reasonably imagine that the means for its preservation might be *moral means,* for the republic will be preserved only by war, and nothing is less moral than war. I ask now how one will succeed in demonstrating that, in a State rendered *immoral* by its very obligations, it is essential that the individuals who make up this State be *moral.* I will go further: it is a very good thing that they are not. The Greek lawgivers perfectly appreciated the capital necessity of corrupting the member-citizens so that, their *moral dissolution* influencing the dissolution useful to the machinery of State, there resulted the kind of insurrection that is always

indispensable to a government that, perfectly happy like a republican government, must necessarily arouse the hatred and envy of all that surrounds it. Insurrection, these sage legislators thought, is not at all a *moral* condition; it nevertheless has got to be a republic's permanent condition. Hence it would be no less absurd than dangerous to require that those who are to insure perpetual *immoral* upheaval in the machinery of State themselves be very *moral* beings, for the *moral* state of a man is one of peace and tranquillity, whereas the *immoral* state of a man is one of perpetual unrest that brings him nearer to that necessary state of insurrection in which the republican must always keep the government of which he is a member (224–25).

This passage is also quoted by Blanchot, who draws conclusions from it that I do not share.[10] First of all, Sade attributes to republican government a characteristic that he ought to acknowledge as true of any government. Indeed, that its sole duty consists in preserving itself is a formula that has a Machiavellian resonance to it—although the Florentine did not express himself in those terms—but the author of *The Prince* did deem, as Aristotle did before him, such an imperative indispensable to any power. It is equally obvious that, whatever the regime, a State is surrounded by potential enemies and forced to have recourse to immoral means and that, therefore, it encourages a tendency toward violence among its members that is alien to the virtues celebrated by philosophy. If Sade wants to distinguish the Republic from other regimes, he has undoubtedly made it his target because it claims a morality that it can only fall short of achieving; it pretends to obey the animating principles of virtue, and not those of fear or of honor, as Montesquieu noted. Sade counters this pretense with the idea that liberty implies a permanent state of insurrection—that is, not harmony, as republicans presume, but, one would think, a constant state of agitation among its citizens, each one of whom is ready to rise up against the threat of oppression. After all, this language could still be considered Machiavellian while also recalling that of numerous revolutionary writers equally convinced since the seventeenth century that the people should never prostrate themselves before a master, nor even before their own representatives, mere delegates at risk of turning into tyrants. Nevertheless, these writers never associated insurrection with immorality; insurrection is the sign of the desire for liberty, whereas vice is the weapon of despotism. To understand what Sade means by insurrection, one must read on a little further and pause at his examination of lust: "We must endeavor to introduce some order into this sphere," he then writes, and "establish all the security necessary so that, when need draws the citizen near the objects of lust, he can give himself over to doing with them all that his passions demand, without ever being chained down by anything, since there is no other passion in man that has so great a need for full and free extension as this one" (227). Then, after having recommended the creation of those famous establishments I mentioned earlier, Sade suddenly lets his own views break through:

> Although, as I told you just a moment ago, no passion has a greater need of the widest horizon of liberty than has this one, none, doubtless, is more despotic: here it is that man likes to command, to be obeyed, to surround himself with slaves compelled to satisfy him. Now, whenever you withhold from man the secret means whereby he exhales the dose of despotism nature instilled in the depths of his heart, he will return to exercising this despotism over objects near to him and he consequently will trouble the government (228).

In contrast, if "his tyrannical desires" (ibid.) are satisfied, he will conduct himself as a citizen. Sade turns over this argument again and again, but I do not want to quote it at too great a length; his attitude toward the Republic, it seems to me, is sufficiently enlightening here. He violently weds the Republic, joining with it on the ruins of a regime he hates. But somehow he penetrates it to touch bottom, what he thinks is the bottom: the despotism of the human being, which only the Republic can authorize. I say *touch bottom,* but it would be better to say *open an abyss.* There is for Sade, in effect, an abject despotism, which is that of the prince. Man makes an idol of the prince, just as he makes an idol of a despotic god. But then man is unaware of his abjection. In contrast, the despotism of passion, if made his own, leads man to discover his abjection. Why, one might ask, is Sade interested in the political sphere? But is it not precisely because the possibility of conceiving despotism depends on the form of government— depends on the Republic? The Republic does not institute a virtuous community for itself. When it claims to do so, the Republic in turn becomes a machine for producing idols: the very machine that Robespierre tried to restore. No, the true merit of the Republic is its fitting out, or furnishing, the space of people's solitudes. Therefore, it is hardly possible to affirm freedom. The liberty to take one's pleasure is achieved, is won, only through the blooming, through the blossoming forth, of tyrannical desires. But it is also impossible to affirm equality, for if it is true that each person naturally possesses the same right, the exercise of that right is accomplished by the enslavement of the other.

The speech Dolmancé addresses to Eugénie echoes these sentiments from the pamphlet:

What is it that one desires when taking one's pleasure? That everything around us be concerned with nothing but ourselves, think of naught but us, care for us only. If the objects that serve us know pleasure too, you can be very sure that they are less concerned for us than they are for themselves, and lo! our own pleasure is consequently disturbed. There is not a living man who does not wish to play the despot when he is hard; . . . the idea of seeing another enjoy as he enjoys reduces him to a kind of equality with that other, which impairs the unspeakable charm *despotism* caused him to feel (276–77).

These sentences no longer seem to me to pertain to what I called a "philosophical saraband." Sade's own thinking breaks through, as it does when he has Dolmancé say: "So long as the act of coition lasts, I may, to be sure, continue to need that object [the other] in order to participate in the act. But as soon as the need is satisfied, what, I beg you to tell me, remains between me and that object? And what real obligation will bind the result of this commerce to it or to me?" (173).

This is, let us note, a good summary description of the Cartesian notion of a space that is *partes extra partes;* it is the notion of a "time pulverized into instants" that comes back to us via the unexpected detour of a theory of eroticism. Pure exteriority of one person in relation to another, pure discontinuity, pure contact of self with self: such would be the "original truths." But at this point mustn't we grant that Sade's thesis, if thesis there be, is virtually overtaken or turned inside out by his work? Indeed, his own characters do not couple with each other like mere automatons. The movement of bodies is associated with the imagination of figures and also with the imagination of orgasmic pleasure. They speak, they are caught up in the duration of the dialogue. Ultimately, the work itself addresses readers and requires at some unspecified future time the renewed presence of an interpreter. It unleashes in each reader a process of incorporating thoughts that have escaped the author's mastery.

But perhaps this conclusion at which I am tempted to halt, shouldn't it too be doubted? Is Sade entirely captivated by the image of the individual despot? And by the image of a humanity populated with beings who are strangers to each other? Does he not know that he is writing? Why does the idea of corruption matter so much if freedom merges with the expression of tyrannical desires? And, in terms of this hypothesis, what does the desire to write, Sade's desire to write, signify?

Does not Sade suggest that the desire to corrupt exceeds the desire to take one's pleasure and to dominate in taking one's pleasure? Assuming that this last desire would be natural, the first must be deviant since the desire to corrupt recreates a tie with the other, tends to make of the other an accomplice, and in a certain manner remakes sociability. And furthermore, if civilization is the process of corruption and if moral teaching is the perversion of the human being, what are we to make of a corruption that is a counter-corruption? Is not Sade exploiting the phantasmagoria of the revolutionary era, the phantasmagoria of plot and counterplot?

I thus return, in conclusion, to my initial remarks about the role that the concept of "corruption" plays in political life. Classical philosophy as well as modern philosophy, though in a different way, established the distinction between nature and corruption via an idealization of nature, by which I mean via a purification or purging of the idea of nature. Sade does not abolish the distinction, let us note, but he reestablishes it via an idealization of corruption. Whereas Plato arrived at the analysis of real society by starting from an idea of the nobility of human nature, Sade returns to real society by disclosing what is basest in human nature.

In doing so, he renders the distinction obscure; its terms can no longer be grasped. We, the readers, are deprived of the image of a "good society." We are incited to reject ideology of any kind whatsoever, as we glimpse the abyss that ideology covers over. But I do not want to say any more for fear of attributing to Sade a new moralism; and I would much rather preserve his enigmas.

Notes

"Sade: Le Boudoir et la Cité" was originally published in *Petits et grands théâtres du Marquis de Sade,* ed. Annie Lebrun (Paris: Paris Art Center, 1989): 217–21; reprinted in *Écrire,* 91–111. [T/E: The present translation originally appeared in the *South Atlantic Quarterly* 95, no. 4 (fall 1996): 1019–28. I thank *SAQ* editor Candice Ward for her incisive editorial suggestions and special issue editor Vassilis Lambropoulos for all his interest and support. I have consulted and made extensive use of Richard Seaver and Austryn Wainhouse's translation, "Philosophy in the Bedroom," in *The Marquis de Sade: The Complete Justine, Philosophy in the Bedroom and Other Writings* (New York: Grove Press, 1965), but I take responsibility for the final form of the translations from Sade quoted in the text; in-text page references are to the French edition, *La philosophie dans le boudoir (Les instituteurs immoraux),* prefaced by Gilbert Lély (Paris: Union Générale d'Éditions, 1972).]

1 *Français, encore un effort,* preceded by Maurice Blanchot, "L'inconvenance majeure" (Paris: Jean-Jacques Pauvert, 1965).

2 Gilbert Lély, *Vie du marquis de Sade,* 3rd ed. (Paris: Jean-Jacques Pauvert, 1982).

3 Blanchot, "L'inconvenance majeure," 20.

4 Annie Lebrun, *Soudain un bloc d'abîme. Sade* (Paris: Jean-Jacques Pauvert, 1986); see also *Sade, A Sudden Abyss,* trans. Camille Naish (San Francisco: City Light Books, 1990).

5 Blanchot, "L'inconvenance majeure," 32–38. [T/E: The phrase "the damned part" in the text is probably an allusion to Georges Bataille's 1967 book, *La part maudite,* translated

by Robert Hurley as *The Accursed Share: An Essay on General Economy,* 3 vols (New York: Zone, 1988–91).]

6   *Soudain un bloc d'abîme. Sade,* 257.

7   Blanchot, "L'inconvenance majeure," 11.

8   Ibid., 10.

9   Jacques Lacan, "Kant avec Sade," in *Écrits* (Paris: Seuil, 1966), 788; see also "Kant with Sade," trans. James B. Swenson Jr., *October* 51 (1989): 55–75.

10   Blanchot, "L'inconvenance majeure," 29.

U NTIL A PEOPLE which has gone through a great revolution has passed on the principles, the passions, and the doctrines which have led to this revolution, a sentence like that which shall be passed on all human things at the Last Day, "severing the wheat from the tares, and the corn from the straw that shall be cast into the fire," it can never surmount the perils, nor reap the advantages, of the struggle in which it has been engaged. So long as this judgment is deferred, chaos reigns; and chaos, if prolonged in the midst of a people, would be death. Chaos is now concealed under one word: Democracy. This is now the sovereign and universal word.

These lines are taken from *Democracy in France,* the pamphlet Guizot published in January 1849.[1] A year earlier, Marx proclaimed, in the opening lines of the *Communist Manifesto,* that "a specter is haunting Europe— the specter of Communism. All the Powers of old Europe have entered into a holy alliance to exorcize this specter: Pope and Czar, Metternich and Guizot, French Radicals and German police-spies."[2] Clearly, Guizot was condemning along the way anarchy, socialism, and communism, which moreover he confused with one another. But these are for him only byproducts of democracy. The last of these is his target. So far as I know, Marx never questioned this other alliance into which he entered with the person he identified as one of the masters of old Europe.

Democracy in France is disconcerting because of its feebleness and its extreme conservatism. Chased out by the February revolution, Guizot took refuge in England. From there, he sketched a dramatic picture of the state of France and entreated his contemporaries to repudiate their errors. But of those errors that he himself might have committed, the man who occupied the leading role under the July monarchy and who during its final years led the government breathes not a word. One might believe, in reading his pamphlet, that political and social facts hold no importance for him. He doesn't analyze the event that brought about his downfall, nor does he understand it. It is hardly even named. An "explosion," he says, once. If he speaks of revolution, it is in order to state that nothing new has happened for fifty years. The revolution arose in the past; at present, it is "afraid of [its] own work, and would fain to change its character and aspect; but [it] can produce nothing but a copy."[3] Everything happens as if thenceforth History was being erased and only the repeated clash of ideas counted. Thus does society appear as torn, as always, between its good and bad inclinations, like the human soul. Today, the crazy idea of an equal right to happiness, beneath which are stirred up all the passions, opposes the idea of the unity of the laws and that of the equality of civil rights, which, though recognized only recently, simply proceed from the nature of society—a society that can be "tortured, perhaps destroyed; but you cannot force it to assume a form and mode of existence foreign to its nature."[4] Social war, the same one, continues on, although it now brings about the appearance of a new protagonist: "The workmen are now arrayed against their masters, or the people against the middle classes."[5] The fundamental data of the human problem do not change. The principle of order has to unite with the principle of movement in order to subordinate the latter to its authority. The democratic principle has to be granted; it is right to make a place for it, but the aristocratic principle is only that much more necessary, provided that it is removed from all belief in a fixed classification of people. Order and stability require a strong power that depends on all social classes but that is tied mainly to the natural "guardians of society,"[6] since "it is absurd to seek the principle of the political stability of government in the mobile elements of society."[7]

Guizot embraces French society from on high. He disdains the detail of the class conflicts running through it. He is content just to chase away the illusion of the sovereignty of the people as well as that of an egalitarian society. He brings out the natural foundations of civil society: real estate, personal estate, labor. He finds the true guardians of society in the possessors of the earth who, in contact therewith, have recognized what is immutable in the order of the world. He implants civil society in the primary institution, the family. Religion, finally, provides him with the condition by which humanity becomes capable of accepting inequalities, diversity, the law that imposes upon each person his own destiny, and of resisting self-idolatry.

Democracy in France is a plea in favor of conservatism. It will not be heard. The conservatives he addresses know better than the author by what way the defense of their interests henceforth passes. After 1848, Guizot ceases to be a political actor. Now, it must be granted that he ceases to be, at the same time, a political thinker. The ideas are not developed to any significant extent, and they are linked together with the aid of dogmatic belief. A fact worth noting, the style likewise goes downhill. It becomes sententious, emphatic—let us say it: boring. In short, at the moment when the event calls for imagination, whatever might be the interpretation it prompts, Guizot loses, along with political power, the powers of intelligence and language. The reason for this is undoubtedly that the theoretician, the historian, the practician, and the writer were so intimately bound up in the same man that they could only falter together. When History exceeds the boundaries he had assigned to it, when social and political life steal away from the interpretation of representative government he deemed to be definitive, when this art of "dealing with the masses"[8]—which he called the most difficult and of which he believed himself to be the master— is taken away from him, while the art of dealing with individuals—which he believed was easy and which he held in contempt—reminds him of the signs of his sudden isolation, it is then that Guizot doesn't know how to do anything but take refuge in eternal ideas.

His failure is on a par with the hopes he had placed in the July regime. To be honest about it, we should note that these hopes had in large part been shared by a number of liberals. More than anyone else, nonetheless, Guizot believed that he had drawn the proper lesson from the insurrection of 1830. It is not that he liked the image of the crowd taking to the streets. Great jolts remind him of the permanent danger threatening societies. Mentioning, in 1849, these revolutions, he exclaims: "Over what an immense extent, and with what fearful rapidity, have all the causes of social war and social destruction, which are always fermenting in the midst of us, each time burst forth!"[9] No doubt he rejoices at having witnessed in July 1830 "the purest, the wisest, the gentlest, and the shortest of these formidable convulsions."[10] But, he adds, "I shuddered as I saw a mighty tumult of insensate ideas, brutal passions, perverse inclinations, and terrible chimeras, rise and swell, minute by minute, ready to overflow, and submerge a land where all the dikes that had contained it were broken down."[11] A moment earlier, he was asking: "Which of us has not shuddered at the sudden revelation of the abyss over which society lives?"[12] This revelation, however, was two-sided. Once the abysses were closed back up, the new regime bore the signs of the natural order of society. What Guizot discovered in the aftermath of July is that the Revolution, the great Revolution, had, at the cost of one ultimate dramatic episode, finally been completed. To borrow

his formula, let us say that the people had, in submitting to a fully constitutional regime, pronounced the sentence of the Last Judgment. The end
of the Revolution signified the "end of History" (Guizot had some knowledge of Hegel, thanks to Victor Cousin): France's gestation period, which
he had described in following the ups and downs of the class struggle since
the Middle Ages, reached its term in the present social and political state,
with the establishment of civil peace and the reconciliation between liberties and power. Whence the disenchantment that comes in 1848: one must
grant that the people has reconsidered its sentence or admit one's mistake;
the hour of the Last Judgment had not sounded. From then on Guizot no
longer sees himself as the interpreter of the movement of History; he takes
himself to be the witness of eternal truths, those truths that, forever anew,
men fail to recognize.

We had to take a moment to cast the figure of the man who became democracy's great adversary, the better to shed light on the figure of the man who
was one of the most ardent, the most talented of liberals, but also one of
the most capable of working out a modern conception of the political. I do
not mean that Guizot ever ceased to be a liberal, nor that he failed to manifest, as early as his first writings, a love of order and hierarchy. But it is a far
cry from triumphant liberalism, from the era of the Restoration, whatever
its conservative tone might be, to the defensive liberalism, haunted by the
image of a dissolution of the social, that becomes petrified in principles and
precepts after 1848.

In our view, *Democracy in France* retains the value of a document. Nothing more. *Des moyens de gouvernement et d'opposition dans l'état actuel de
la France* (On the means of government and of opposition in the present
state of France), written in 1821, during a critical period, is to a great extent
devoted to analyzing the facts, to describing the main actors of the moment, to bringing out the true stakes in the conflict between the party of
the Ancien Régime and the opposition as well as the reasons for their respective weaknesses and blindness, and to denouncing the impotency of the
new government. But this work, so reliant on circumstance that one might
think that it should be reserved for historians alone, actually retains an astonishing freshness. Thought-provoking, it includes a reflection on modern society and power and settles accounts with most of the other liberals'
writings.

Guizot, we noted, combines in one person a historian, a theorist, a man
of action, and a writer. His renown as a historian is established. We know
that, with Augustin Thierry, he stood in the first rank of those who founded
what Chateaubriand called the "new historical school," which in fact is

the modern science of history. It is to him that we owe the idea of a history of European civilization, the first attempt to reconstitute the genesis of the great modern States and to compare the French model to the English one, as well as an intelligent understanding of how class struggle functioned in the rise of the monarchy. It is to him, too, that we owe the idea of unearthing, registering, and exploiting everything, documents and monuments alike, that bore witness to France's past. The writer's talent and prolificness, moreover, have not ceased to garner recognition, nor has one forgotten the breadth of his interests, which made of him one of the pioneers in fields as diverse as the new pedagogy, public education, administrative science, and constitutional law. Who hasn't encountered him as a political actor in the course of his studies? No textbook fails, in its chapters on the Restoration and the July monarchy, to highlight the major role he played. On the other hand, a certain silence has fallen upon the theorist, which was broken only recently by Pierre Rosanvallon's excellent book.[13] When Benjamin Constant and Alexis de Tocqueville began to attract the attention of our contemporaries, Guizot remained in the shadows, even though, like them, though from an entirely other point of view, he was able to grasp an essential aspect of modernity. The fact is that Guizot wrote only one text of political philosophy, an incomplete one at that, of which the public has had some knowledge only for a short time. His reflections on politics are formulated only within the confines of historical studies, basically in his *History of the Origins of Representative Government*[14] and his *History of Civilization in Europe*,[15] or else in his speeches, or else again in works written under the influence of events, hastily; of these, one is tempted to retain only the objective they had at the time of their writing and their polemical character. Undoubtedly, it is on account of its close connection with history, on the one hand, and with practice, on the other, that Guizot's political thought allows itself to be forgotten, whereas in fact it is from these that it drew its greatest strength.

Guizot intervened in the political debate by publishing, one after another, *Du gouvernement de la France depuis la Restauration* (On the government of France since the Restoration) in October 1820 and *Des moyens de gouvernement* in January 1821. The author himself describes the conjunction of circumstances clearly enough so that a reader of our time might follow him without any great difficulty. Let us recall at least that the regime had just undergone a sudden change in orientation. The new monarchy had been bound to a charter since the adventure of the One Hundred Days. After the episode of the "incomparable chamber" [*chambre introuvable*] — that legislative chamber entirely dominated by ultraroyalists who were seeking to reestablish the privileges of the nobility and the clergy—Louis XVIII decided to lean on the moderates for support. Starting in 1816, it was these moderates, the constitutionalists devoted to defending and consolidating the guarantees of civil equality and various liberties, who were behind the ministry's policies. Under the government, whose most influential personality was Decazes before he became its top leader, a reform allowed for a slight enlargement of the electoral body, new laws favored the freedom of the press, and the spirit of constitutionalism asserted itself. During this period, the young Guizot placed his convictions in the service of an effort to make progress toward greater liberties. Entering early upon an administrative career, he had already become, at age twenty-seven, secretary to the minister of the interior under the first Restoration, then general secretary of the Ministry of Justice at the beginning of the second Restoration. But it was beginning in 1816 that he started to play a political role. He participated in the drafting of the electoral reform and of the law on the freedom of the press, entered the Council of State, was consulted on several occasions by various ministers, and, at the same time, joined the group of *doctrinaires*. His first writings assured him a precocious notoriety. In 1819, Decazes placed him at the head of the administrative office for communes and departments.

The ultras' return in force after the assassination of the Duc de Berry (14 January 1820) therefore ushered in a new era. With Decazes ousted, the moderates evicted from the new chamber, Guizot himself forced to vacate the Council of State, and the press laws suspended, it was then that the liberal opposition was formed. And it was then, too, that the author of *Du gouvernement de la France depuis la Restauration* and *Des moyens de gouvernement* found his style and won his place. He had the style of a political leader and the place of a master thinker. Guizot was not content just to polemize against his adversaries; he had a sense of the occasion. He seized upon the new course the regime had taken and upon the defeat of the liberals to formulate his message, and in the same breath he denounced the futility of the government in place and the pusillanimity of those who trembled at the word *freedom*. He situated the troubles of the present back within History with a capital *H* and reawakened the spirit of social war. And he stated, finally, what power requires of those who are destined to grab hold of it.

Nothing teaches us better what separates *Des moyens de gouvernement* from *Democracy in France* than the way in which the author of these two books speaks of power and of freedom. In 1849, the antagonism between the two is supposed to reveal the tragic essence of History. Now, the very first lines of his 1821 pamphlet sound another note: "Two things are today equally feeble, equally fearful of their future, power and freedom. Whence comes this evil? Is not its cause but the eternal problem of human societies: the difficulty of reconciling freedom and power? Would to heaven that this were the only problem given to us to resolve! But we have much more to do!"[16] Undoubtedly, Guizot is not impugning eternal truths, but he makes mention of them quite lightly, even suggesting that such truths run the risk of masking the task at hand. He will not put off naming it: "We have, both together, the constitutional order to found and the Ancien Régime to repel."[17] Likewise, he doesn't delay in revealing his motive. The Revolution is only half done:

> The Revolution is still, so to speak, living out of doors. On all sides, it is open and dismantled. The institutions it has proclaimed have not at all been converted into practical institutions, into effective laws. The interests it has established are in disarray and have not been cemented together well.[18]

To bring the Revolution to its conclusion, *that* is the objective that requires at the same time that one confront the party warring against it — that is, the counterrevolution that has reawakened. Guizot does not mince his words in his first chapter: "I have had the occasion to say it elsewhere: Our history from 1789 to 1800 is that of a war. . . . Under Bonaparte, the Ancien Régime had been happy to obtain peace. In 1814, it resumed the war. . . . I persist in thinking that this really is war and that the war continues."[19] He does not hesitate to formulate the twin tasks he sees before him. For example: "Like the Israelites, we therefore have to both establish ourselves and defend ourselves; all of us together undergo the necessities of war and that of peace."[20]

By his eloquence, the liveliness of his remarks, which matches the urgency of action, by his constant invocation of a *we* who are in peril, by the call to know where right and force are located, *Des moyens de gouvernement* takes on the character of a political manifesto. The author addresses himself to the middle classes — or, more precisely, to the bourgeois elite — and at the same time speaks in their name, declaring what their interests and aspirations are. He does not so much situate himself within the already constituted opposition; some who profess to be a part of it are not spared his criticism. His entire concern is to show that a new France exists in fact, but that only when the most dynamic elements of society achieve an awareness of its full legitimacy will the power that can definitively guarantee it finally be secured.

With this intention, Guizot's art consists in his articulating in one and the same argument the description of what he is presenting as the actual state of fact, the elucidation of the principles that preside, partly without its knowledge, over the government's action and that mistreat its opponents, and, finally, a general reflection upon the nature of social power. The primary objective of the description—or, better put, the establishment [constat]—of actual facts is to note the weakness of the new government. There is no need to linger over the brilliant portraits he draws of the men in positions of power. The main point lies in the following: the power in place has been moved to the side of reaction; apparently, it is turning its back on the Revolution, which it deems ungovernable, but at the same time it retains the conviction that counterrevolution is impossible. Such is the contradiction within which it remains confined. It seems to the established power [le pouvoir] that the regime's survival depends upon the support of the ultras, but in espousing their cause it forbids itself from making any movement. Irritated by its own impotency, it seeks the cause of such impotency in the state of society, whereas in reality it is merely communicating to society its own weakness. The effect of its policy is to inhibit any initiatives that seem to it to be independent, to discourage everywhere the will to participate in public affairs, to curtail freedom of expression. Constantly haunted by the peril of revolution, it lives upon the illusion of a time that has stopped and of a space that is compressed. Precisely because it needs the cooperation of collective energies and because these are what it lacks, it never stops complaining about the crumbling of a society for which it bears the responsibility.

His statement of the crisis therefore leads him to ask the following question:

> Why this system? Why does a new power, one that has just opened to these peoples, and to itself, a new career, reveal itself, from the outset, to be stationary and impotent? Around it everything moves, everything works. However deep may today be the calm, the social movement has not ground to a halt. Its direction has not changed in the least. The classes that throw themselves into the fray continue to rise up, those that refuse to take part therein remain each day further back. Land reform, industrial development, the rapid circulation of wealth, the spread of ideas—all these elements that are constitutive of the new order expand and develop from day to day. People's minds do not stop or do not regress any further.[21]

Guizot's statement bears on the facts. He is not satisfied, in the interpretation he is offering, simply to unveil the complicity of interests that unites the new ministry with the party of the Ancien Régime. To be sure, there is nothing innocent about joining the camp of reaction. Nor is there any doubt that ignoring those aspirations that were born of the Revolution constitutes a serious error of judgment. What is more important for Guizot, however, is to spot in the present situation the traces of a failure to recognize the nature of power, which is not the simple effect of a crisis, for it is in analyzing this failure that one can gauge the exigencies of all political action. The opposition itself, indeed, is not exempt from this failure of recognition, and the opposition has everything to learn from the shortcomings of the new ministry.

At this point, we find ourselves faced with the question announced in the title of the work. In brief, the government is mistaken about the meaning of its position, of its function, and of its means. It confuses power and command. Imagining itself to be situated above or outside society, it claims, from this standpoint, to be deciding about its organization and its operation. The government's opponents, for their part, most often dream only of defending existing liberties and recoil at the idea of having to exercise power, for fear of betraying their convictions, for they themselves reduce the exercise of power to that of command and coercion. The opposing sides, it is thus suggested, are caught up in the same illusion. Now, in order to dissipate that illusion, one must acquire an intelligent understanding of the complex relations between power and society; one must comprehend, both at once, that power is engendered within society and that society finds the form toward which it tends, and gains stability, only in the deed of its action.

Thus does Guizot's thinking proceed from the examination of a given situation, of a crisis everyone is observing and commenting upon, in order to advance an interpretation that requires what we must call a dialectic of the political and the social. The constant reference to the actual facts supports the account of this dialectic. On the one hand, the facts teach one of the distinction between the two orders of phenomena, social and political. Guizot points out that in society everything is moving, that the new France is currently in gestation, whereas in the governmental sphere impotence and immobility reign. On the other hand, this distinction does not imply a separation: on the de facto level, society does not succeed in expressing its own movement; it fails itself to the extent that it lacks power. Moreover, the imprint of the political upon the social is still manifest in the moment of their discordancy: the government is propagating a sort of passivity within the social sphere on account of the constraints it exerts; it prevents the constituent elements of the new order from identifying with one another as participating in the same force. For genuine political reform to become possible, it would suffice therefore that these elements achieve awareness of their unity and of their vocation to lead. Such reform alone would allow one to bring to term the silent labor taking place within society. Nonetheless, the facts teach one only because the interpreter grasps in them the signs of a logic that refers back, beyond the current circumstances and beyond every specific situation, to the generative principles of political society—even though at the same time this logic, these principles, can be revealed only in the present, in an age when power has ceased to veil itself with a de jure sovereignty, so as to be in accord with a society that is on the way to overcoming the divisions that formerly blurred the image of its unity.

Let us return, in the first place, to the critique of a power that imagines itself to be lodged at a distance from society and claims to command it from the outside. The political leaders' weakness seems to result from a philosophical illusion, whatever might, in other respects, be the nature of the motivations determining their alliance with the party of the Ancien Régime. They believe that they can intervene in society only by multiplying the number of agents occupied with its administration and with the surveillance of its activities. That is their conception of the means of government. Their policy is wholly instrumental, their theory artificialist. The only thing that counts in their view is the ability to obtain from individuals and groups obedience to directives whose purpose is to assure society's cohesion. Nevertheless, they are fooling themselves. Indeed, "the true means of government are not in these direct and visible instruments of the action of the established power."[22] Among such instruments, Guizot ironically enumerates "ministers, prefects, mayors, tax collectors, soldiers."[23] Where are these means to be found, then?

> They reside within society itself and cannot be separated therefrom. It is there that one must seek them in order to find them, there that one must leave them in order to make use of them. Thanks be to heaven, human society is not a field that a master comes to exploit; it lives another kind of life than does the movement of matter. Society itself possesses and produces its own sure means of government; it gladly lends them to he who knows how to handle them. But it is to society that one must address oneself in order to obtain them.[24]

This language sheds the best light on how Guizot conceives the overlap and interconnection between the political and the social. He speaks of the true *means*. He in no way wants to minimize the action of government, as other liberal thinkers wish to do. He will specify, moreover, later on that the formula then in vogue, laisser-faire, laisser-passer, strikes him as detestable. His conviction is that the government's relation to society could not be formulated in the traditional terms of the opposition between mind [*esprit*] and matter, subject and object, active and passive. The social world is a world of life and of spirit [*esprit*]. "The serious fact," he observes, "the overriding one, is the movement of the human spirit which today makes of thought a so to speak temporal power [*puissance*], a delicate and proud power, which wants, if not to be obeyed, at least to be understood and respected."[25] To hear him tell it, power [*pouvoir*] is active only inasmuch as it draws the resources for its action from the social movement, which presupposes that power endeavor to detect that movement. Its capacity for action is a match for its capacity for reception. And its goal is not to attract to itself, to subdue, social agents, but—to borrow his expression—*to leave them where they are in order to make use of them,* to use the means a confident society lends to it in order to handle them. In other terms, he speaks of an authority that is exercised for the public interest, that tends toward the greatest efficiency and renounces none of its prerogatives, that fully assumes responsibility for its office, that knows it is inserted within society and is dependent upon society. This authority has a hold on society owing to the fact that it is held by it—owing to the fact that it knows itself to be held by it. And this knowledge is never definitively achieved. It can't forgo the task of incessant exploration, the twin goal of which is to bring out the sources of power and to reveal to society itself its force and its right.

Speaking of the masses, who matter or should matter to power much more than individuals, Guizot declares: "It is in the masses, in the people itself, that it [power] is to draw its main force, its primary means of government."[26] Or again: "The public, the nation, the country, that is where the force is, where one can obtain it. Dealing with the masses is the great wellspring of power."[27] And, more explicitly, with a singular eloquence he writes: "Every people, every party, viewed in general, has opinions or, if one wants, prejudices that predominate, interests that direct it, passions that are seething within its bosom. It is through these that it allows itself to be led; these are the levers by which one can take it; it is here that reside the means of government it offers to power."[28] In another spot, where he demonstrates the virtues of representative government, the image takes over of an investigative power whose function is to be revelatory:

> The legislative chambers, the openness of public debates, elections, freedom of the press, the jury, all the forms of this system, all the institutions that are regarded as its necessary consequences—the design and the result of all these is to *probe society endlessly,* to bring to light the superior qualities of all kinds that it contains, to bring them to power.[29]

One thus cannot stop at the idea of an autonomy of the political sphere. Guizot is suggesting the image of a single space that is doubled in such a way that, heading in one direction, politics invests itself in the social and, heading in the other direction, the social invests itself in politics.

Now, such an image equally forbids one from separating, within society itself, that which would be of the order of the real and that which would be of the order of representation. A government, we said, adopts this pretension when it believes itself to be placed at a distance from society and apprehends society as a surface (the term is our author's). He who perceives only a surface likes to distinguish matter from its appearance, and it is upon matter that he wishes to inscribe his action. Thus, interests alone are attributed with having some consistency, and these interests seem unconnected to ideas, opinions, and passions. That is the illusion's flip side. Important as it is to understand that power is in a close, intimate relationship with society, it is of equal importance to know that society is already in relation to itself, that the social is sensitive to itself in the variety of its manifestations: it is thick, deep, and, for this very same reason, both generative of power and offered up to its hold. "Nothing," Guizot observes,

> is more futile, more false, than these distinctions by which one claims to take society apart, isolate from one another the forces that move therein, give a name to each of them, and then call to oneself only those ones that most conveniently allow themselves to be handled. . . . It is not true that interests might thus be separable from opinions, or opinions from interests; it is not true that the latter are everything and the former nothing. Both are closely, tightly interwoven [*fortement tissus ensemble*]. A sort of nervous irritability is common to them both and unites them. And when power acts upon society, I would defy it quite often to say whether it is through opinions or through interests that the former has reached out and touched the latter. It touches everything at once, for in the social body, as in the human body, nothing is insensible and everything holds together.[30]

This last image would merit a long commentary. Let us recall only that the metaphor of the body, as one knows, played a key role under the Ancien Régime, in a theological-political context. It was advanced in the service of the monarchy. Now, what was this reference? Either it was that of the functional body (with the prince taking on the figure of the head and his subjects the members or organs) or else it was that of the mystical body (a body without organs, a replica of that of the Church, the latter being itself a replica of the body of Christ). One can gauge the novelty of the representation that arises in the course of the nineteenth century, and which Guizot formulates so well. This representation no longer comes to support the idea of a natural hierarchy, nor does it celebrate the invisible unity of a community embodied in the immortal Sovereign. Instead, it testifies to an intricate connection between practices and thoughts, and it bears witness to the existence of a setting [*milieu*], wherein what one is tempted to grasp as purely material is spiritualized and what one is tempted to grasp as purely spiritual is changed into a force and wherein the division between the active and the passive is not settled. This milieu, it seems to us, is what Merleau-Ponty will later try to describe under the name of *the flesh*.

Guizot's philosophical considerations and his interpretation of the present are, we observed, closely connected — *interwoven,* to use his expression. It is worth specifying at this point what they gain from this connection. Remarkable, indeed, is the subtlety of his argument when he analyzes the relationship between interests and opinions. In the first place, the author denounces once again the error of the present government. The latter doesn't comprehend that the new interests (in particular, the most powerful one, that of those who have acquired national property) cannot be dissociated from the new ideas. It feigns to respect these interests while pretending to proscribe all the doctrines, all the theories of the Revolution.

Now, let one judge, based on the facts: "Take away from the mayors, hand back to the *curés* the keeping of the civil registers, and those who have acquired national property will be filled with alarm. You can try this out on the whole revolution. You will find everywhere ideas at the heart of interests, interests beneath ideas." [31] The critique is then expanded: "One is dead set against principles, doctrines, theories; one hunts them down like a scourge of a new sort; one imputes to them all the evil we have suffered and at the same time one treats them as vain dreams!" [32] The disdain power affects for ideas is like that of the king of Siam. Thus is it forgotten that opinions of so light a weight have overthrown or founded empires. Here is the conclusion: Opinions are an integral part of reality; they are a force to be dealt with.

Nevertheless, Guizot does not stop there. Demanding that one acknowledge and recognize opinions, he specifies immediately that one must, in order to deal with them, try to discover the sentiments they express. Power, we noted, is an investigative organ, an organ for deciphering the social. In fact, even if society is sensitive to itself, that does not mean that its own movement is immediately intelligible. It gains such intelligibility when power succeeds in extracting from common parlance the meaning that dwells therein. In other words, the important thing for power to do is to distinguish the latent content from the manifest content of opinion. If the social is not a surface, if it has a depth, it must grasp under the appearance the thought in actuality. Opinion knows not whence it comes; its formulation is falsified by reason of the impotence of the power in place to make known to it its motives — still more, by reason of the fight power leads against it, which both wounds it and confers upon it false claims to truth, thus reinforcing its obstinacy.

Guizot's subtlety resides in the relationship he establishes between these two forms of obstinacy: the established power obstinately treats new doctrines as mere dreams; its opponents obstinately become fixated upon a theory whose force their adversary confirms while claiming to destroy it. Without entering into the detail of the argument, let us indicate the line it takes: Guizot at first reduces the new opinions to three articles of faith — what he names the *popular credo:* sovereignty of the people, rejection of aristocracy, the image of a humble power that will take its public charge on the cheap.[33] Then, in a second move, he strives to demonstrate that these beliefs proceed from legitimate sentiments, though ones that have not found their adequate expression. In short, no one believes in a "constant and direct exercise of power by the citizens as a whole,"[34] any more than in an election of all powers by universal suffrage. Taken literally, the sovereignty of the people is a chimera; converted into the sovereignty of number, it is an iniquity. The formula of the sovereignty of the people, under the given circumstances, was tied to a combat against the small number who, "sole master of force, arrogated unto itself also all rights."[35] Once the Revolution is over, one preserves the principle, and one demands simply a "government of general interests, as opposed to government of these or those private interests."[36]

One doesn't want power to be monopolized. That's all that is legitimate and also all that retains any potential today in a principle that in itself is "absurd and barbaric."[37] The task is therefore to show that, under cover of the sovereignty of the people, what is seeking to affirm itself is the idea of the sovereignty of justice, of reason, and of law. Likewise, the French seem to condemn all aristocracy. The doctrine of equality they profess is a "confused dogma,"[38] but a powerful one that, without really being able to account for itself, "inspires antipathy and distrust for every measure that would tend to fix in place once and for all the higher ranks of society by giving them the sanction and support of the law."[39] What they think is that "no artifice should disturb, in the social order, the upward or downward movement of individuals."[40] Opposed to any fixed classification, they remain convinced that superior qualities, provided that they are based on merit, are to be recognized. Finally, the French do not wish to have a weak power; they feel the need to be governed, provided that the government would act in conformity with the new interests. Power therefore has to own up to its basic function: it goes along with and reveals superior qualities. "There we find its origin," Guizot specifies. "Between equals it would never be born."[41] The same reasons therefore militate in favor of a new conception of equality, the equality of opportunity, or a new conception of inequality, the inequality of merit, and a new conception of power, that of *representative government.*

In sum, without using a term whose meaning Marx will be the first to define rigorously—and with quite another intention, need it be said—Guizot traces out the line dividing ideology and social consciousness. The sovereignty of the people, equality, and the narrow limitation of power pertain to ideology. This ideology inspired the Revolution and survives it. The victory of the bourgeoisie must at present allow it to extract, from the language that at one moment was necessary to it, the truth of its practice and of its aspirations. As Rosanvallon has rightly observed, Guizot calls upon the bourgeoisie to assume its role and to shoulder responsibility for its ends; he pushes the bourgeoisie to demand power and to become in right what it is in fact, the dominant class. He reasons in *realist* terms. Whence the singular character of what we called his 1821 Manifesto.

The connection between right and force that Guizot is constantly endeavoring to bring out is in this regard instructive. Presently, he observes, interests are struggling with one another: it is a fact, and it matters little that one deplores this fact. Unless it is to make society weak, power has to ally itself with the strongest interests. That doesn't mean that force is in itself a good thing: "Let the moralists hold back their anathema. In no way do I adore force, and I know that there are cases where an honest man has to renounce his empire."[42] Yet it must be agreed that when the expansion of the social elements conveying powerful interests becomes irreversible, a new right asserts itself. The force of which Guizot speaks is by nature social. It testifies to what is alive in society, and what is alive is of both a material and a spiritual order. Force does not, except in secondary circumstances, become attached to the means of coercion—which, we remarked, presupposes an external relationship between dominator and dominated. Conceived thus, it would be violence. It connects up with what is growing within the social sphere. And, although it sometimes happens, when a revolution of the breadth of the French one occurs, that one can be mistaken about some specific tendency taking shape under this or that particular set of circumstances, one cannot think that force might be something accidental. "When [force] appears with the sway of a decree from Providence, when it is clothed in the characteristics of necessity, it would be folly to separate oneself from it, to try to establish oneself beyond its bosom."[43]

Without a doubt, force thus understood, as a potentiality of life, requires the destruction of all that is opposed to it. But this destruction entails violence only when power has been unable to ally itself with force. That, as a matter of fact, is the origin of the Revolution. Still, it must be reiterated that social force, even without the knowledge of those who hold it, tends to imprint itself onto institutions. It harbors within itself a new right, but it doesn't fulfill itself; its legitimacy remains in abeyance, inasmuch as it is still lacking power. The active part of society must in some way communicate its strength [*force*] to power, in order that the latter might in return reveal to it its vocation to lead. Similarly, power must detect in the manifold of elements that make up this active part the unity of a class, so that power may borrow from this class its force. Guizot identifies these elements as landowners, lawyers, notaries, capitalists, manufacturers, merchants, and so on, so many agents who at present "possess a considerable existence [but] keep public affairs at arm's length" and fail to perform their task;[44] and that is the fault of the government in place, which neglects them. Society remains divided so long as the division between power and the socially dominant forces subsists. This crisis can be resolved only by the establishment of *representative government.*

This concept designates much more than a new constitution in the legal-political sense of the term. In truth, Guizot does not use it only to describe a new form of government but to bring out the principles that have always governed the organization and history of societies. He is fully conscious of the originality of the theory he has elaborated in his *History of the Origin of Representative Government in Europe* and in his unfinished manuscript "Philosophie politique," where he makes one realize that his theory breaks with tradition.[45]

In these works, the distinction between political regimes (government of a single one, of a small number, or of a multitude) seems to him in effect irrelevant. He reproaches the great authors for being interested only in the form of government, not in the thing itself, in the principle, in the inner nature, in the laws of government. And this formalism remains when one thinks that one has spoken in concrete terms by distinguishing between despotism, monarchy, aristocracy, and democracy. Montesquieu doesn't escape criticism, even though the latter wasn't satisfied with borrowing the usual categories and wanted to detect the wellspring of people's conduct in each political system (fear, honor, moderation, virtue). He thought he had reached the principle, and yet missed it, touching only upon secondary phenomena. His mode of analysis blinded him to the kinship that remains among various regimes as soon as in each one a de jure sovereignty sees itself affirmed. Guizot goes so far as to say that every government that appeals thereto bears the mark of despotism.[46]

The comparison he makes between monarchy and democracy is of more particular import to us. These are, according to him (as they are already for Plato in *The Statesman,* let us recall in passing), the two mother species. Now, they obey, despite their apparent opposition, the same principle. Indeed, it doesn't change things that de jure sovereignty, first attributed to the prince, might be transferred onto the people. What alone is true is that monarchy, as its endurance within History demonstrates, is better made to make this claim. "In placing sovereignty in the land, [monarchy] personifies it, lends it a body, a place, a name, luster, all that might induce men to believe." [47] In democracy, by way of contrast, this sovereignty is fastened onto a phantom or onto an abstraction, the people or number.

The argument he develops shines again on account of its subtlety. On the one hand, it appears that men are possessed by the desire to make idols, to make gods of these idols, and to adore them in such a way that they give themselves over to despotism: "It is all fine and good that they dread despots, but somewhere they want despotism at any price." [48] So intense is this desire that when they discover the impotency or obsequiousness of the venerated being, they have to transfer it onto a new object. "In renouncing the fallen master, men have in no way lost hope of finally obtaining the master who could not fall." [49] And again: "There is no reform of ideas that would not have set in some place the mark of infallibility." [50]

Nevertheless, while he denounces the power of the imagination—the sovereignty of the prince or of his substitutes merely makes use for its own ends of the people's obstinate tendency to delude itself—on the other hand he discerns in the endless search for an absolute in this world the indication of a natural sentiment, the need to secure the permanence and the unity of the social body. Thus does one read his remarks on idolatry (in particular in his "Philosophie politique") at first as if they came out of La Boétie's *Discourse of Voluntary Servitude,* glimpsing later that they offer only a half-truth. Men are not only prey to a phantasm; they are guided by a legitimate exigency, even though they do not know how to respond to it correctly. It remains the case that, whatever its motives, their belief chains them to an untenable principle. De jure sovereignty does not exist on earth. It can reside neither in the prince nor in the people. Power is not an invention of man; God alone is sovereign.

Perhaps it is worth noting that this very last assertion, which is repeated several times by Guizot and which is one he undoubtedly deems decisive, is not necessary to his thesis. It suffices for him to establish that society, and man as social being, are inconceivable when lacking a reference to the law and to power. Man's bond with man implies, he tells us, a reciprocity, a recognition of the one by the other, and its institution could not be imputed to them. One would search in vain for the nature of the law *within* society, for, whatever might be the character of the positive laws, these positive laws derive from an originary and universal notion of the Law. Likewise, the birth of power cannot be located therein, for, in whatever way it might be represented and however it might be exercised, power marks the place of the enunciator and guarantor of the Law. Also, it is significant that Guizot invokes in support of his thesis the example of the paternal power. He doesn't do this at all in order to find therein the most rudimentary figure of political power but, rather, in order to shed light on what in our day would be called the distinction between the symbolic and the real: beneath the most varied traits imaginable, the father, being not the inventor of paternity, but assuming it as his own, and identifying himself as father, sees himself instituted as such.

Rather than the affirmation of a divine sovereignty, it is the critique of the belief in the absolute legitimacy of any human power that allows political society to become intelligible.

> Here, then, resides the fundamental and truly distinctive character of governments. On one side are lined up those governments that believe in the presence of a sovereign on earth and that regulate their organization according to this belief, subject later to painful and inadequate efforts to escape its results. On the other stand those ones that refuse to attribute de jure sovereignty to any de facto sovereignty; they are constituted on the basis of this maxim and endlessly seek legitimate power, the true law, whose existence they recognize but which they never boast of possessing in a reliable manner and forever. These latter governments alone conform to the interests of freedom as well as to the interests of reason.[51]

This second series of governments in reality boils down to a single model, representative government, whereas one has to admit that the first series is highly differentiated, despite the principle that constitutes it. As defined, representative government seems to be the sole kind capable of welcoming change and preserving itself through change because it is set up in such a way as to give expression to the interests and aspirations that are born within society and to regulate itself according to the forces that develop therein.

What Guizot is suggesting is that such a government can assert itself fully only in Modern Times, consequent upon the destruction of any fixed classification, of any alleged natural order, and upon the incessant increase in social mobility. In continual debate over how to define the legitimate and the illegitimate, it adjusts itself to a society that secretes its own history, seeking its balance without ever finding an ultimate guarantor in the authority of tradition, which is recognized as always being in gestation.

Nevertheless, the formula of representative government is not contingent. It prompts one to take on the burden of an exigency that has always been constitutive of government: namely, that the de facto power be distinguished from the rightfully absolute power and that, on each occasion, there be a power that decides—according to Guizot's expression: a "definite, that is to say, in fact absolute" power.[52] Although, in the past, governments might have claimed de jure sovereignty, they have had, even when they were apparently despotic, to come to terms with the resistances of the governed and, in some way, to make an effort to give some proofs of their legitimacy. Representative government is therefore not alien to the former types of government; it unveils the obstinate denial of an unending need for legitimation. On the other hand, it inherits the obligation to take responsibility, from moment to moment, for decisions that will have the force of law.

Representative government faces a problem all other governments run up against, but it is the only one to maintain it as a problem instead of stealing away under cover of a fictive solution. Guizot writes in this sense:

> To make de facto power, as far as possible, identical with de jure power, by imposing upon it the abiding necessity of seeking for reason, truth, and justice—the de jure source; by investing it with practical power only when it has proved, that is to say, given a presumption of, its success in this search; and by compelling it ever to renew and confirm this presumption under penalty of losing power if it is unable to do so, this is the course of the representative system,—this is the end at which it aims and according to which it directs, in their relations and their movement, all the resources which it brings into action.[53]

He then specifies that, "in order to attain this end, it is indispensable that the de facto power not be simple, that is to say, that it not be suffered to confine itself to one single force."[54] Then, later, he states that it will be only when the various ruling elements are in accord that "there will be a presumption that the de facto power knows accurately and is well disposed to the legitimate rule which alone confers de jure power."[55] Here his thinking is best revealed: legitimacy is never assured; there is only the incessant legitimation of the success of a *search*.

It is still worth noting, however, the slippage from the concept of representative government, generally used, to that of a representative system. Most often, the reader may judge that they are equivalent. In the passage mentioned, the difference captures one's attention. The system has an immutable value; it does not depend upon the circumstances and the character of action, on what could be called by convenience *politics,* meaning by that the complex play of opinions and decisions that are those of the king, his ministers, the members of the Chambers, and the electors themselves. This is the system that places those who exercise a power of some sort before the necessity to search constantly for reason and for justice and that, in the same stroke, places them under the threat of losing their force in case of failure. The government, in turn, is that organ which is subject to change. This is what leads one not to attribute sovereignty to the system: an assertion like that would be meaningless. But it is apparent that the distinction between de facto power and de jure power does not exhaust the question.

The system Guizot is talking about cannot be reduced to legal mechanics, still less to a set of playing rules. It bears the mark of a spontaneous elaboration of social life that has a philosophical signification. Its virtue is to put society in communication with itself while depriving it of the illusion that a power of some sort might embody it. Its virtue is to procure for society an image of its general layout without this image being able to become fixed and to remove itself from a constant questioning about law and truth.

In considering this analysis of the representative system, one is led to reexamine Guizot's opposition to democracy. There is no doubt that his critique of an absolute sovereignty, the notion he advances of a power incessantly in quest of legitimacy and of an intertwining of the political and the social ushers in an intelligible understanding of modern democracy. Yet he always wanted to bar the way to the latter. Is this only because of his social condition, because of his desire to justify and to defend class interests, ones that were also his own? It is more worthwhile to try to comprehend the theoretical motivation for his hostility.

Guizot's constant target is the principle of the sovereignty of the people, which he makes the generative principle of democracy, and he interprets it, we believe, in two ways. Such sovereignty is conceived either as the sovereignty of a new monarchy or as the sovereignty of number. In the first case, this monarch is an idol, and it doesn't even have the advantage of appearing in a glorious body liable to fascinate its subjects. Since it is absurd to imagine a sovereignty exercised in fact by the citizens as a whole, either democracy manifests itself in the street, with the characteristics of a mass loudly proclaiming that it *is* the people in order to impose its whims, or it is summed up in the power of an assembly that claims to legislate and to decide in the name of the people. The thesis is definitely based on the experience of the French Revolution. One will never say enough how much liberalism, which in France is basically political in inspiration, owes in its diverse variants to a reflection upon the disorders of the Revolution and in particular upon the Terror. Guizot, for his part, is haunted by the memory of the crowd in arms and that of the all-powerful Convention. In the second case, that of the sovereignty of number, the curse of democracy consists in its legally crediting a majority with the possession of law and of reason. What Guizot is combating, then, is universal suffrage, the abandonment of the direction of society into the hands of abstract individuals who elude every criterion of competency, wealth, or respectability and benefit therefore only from the force of number. It is senseless, in his view, to claim to draw from universal suffrage a legitimate form of representation. He states this second thesis with complete clarity when he writes:

> The principle of the sovereignty of the people applies to all individuals, merely because they exist, without demanding of them anything more. Thus it takes the majority of these individuals, and says, — Here is reason, here is law. Representative government proceeds in another way: it considers what is the kind of action to which individuals are called; it examines into the amount of capacity requisite for this action; it then summons those individuals who are supposed to possess this capacity, — all such, and such only. Then it seeks for a majority among those who are capable.[56]

A quite remarkable fact: Guizot takes no account of the American example and learns nothing from Tocqueville. The man who recognizes the intricate connections between social and political facts does not want to know that the right to initiative is indivisible and that, as Tocqueville shows so well, the restriction of political liberties discourages the exercise of civil ones. Evoking America in his *Democracy in France,* Guizot emphasizes that America founded a republic without wanting to make it democratic. In short, its regime seems to him to be analogous to the July one, a constitutional regime that, on account of peculiar circumstances, succeeds in functioning without a monarch. He prefers to ignore the fact that Americans hold the people to be sovereign, that they consider the people to be the "Fountain of Justice," that they place the people at the origin of all powers at the very moment when they leave the people outside the system of government ("out of doors," according to the expression of the period taken up by the historian Gordon Wood). And whereas the American Constitution could have provided him with the most precious illustration of a representative government, he does not examine it because it would reveal that the most perfected form of representation requires not only the abolition of every "fixed classification" but also the abolition of every criterion of social distinction so that power might not become prisoner of some coalition of interests, that is to say, of a determinate social category. In short, that very place where democracy is connected neither with the sovereignty of the people-monarch nor with the sovereignty of number—Guizot does not *see* it.

This blindness is a powerful indication of the distance separating liberalism from democracy. Nothing apparently forbids liberal thought in principle from recognizing in democracy the formula for a political society in which power is not appropriated by anyone and where justice and reason are always under debate. Nothing apparently holds liberal thought back from giving democratic demands their due, though it might judge that, given a certain social state, the people in their immaturity are not ready for universal suffrage. Nothing, we say, if not the belief that once the power of the Ancien Régime, whose function was to embody the nation, has disappeared, there remains a substantial society with new characteristics, that that society must be discovered, that its contours must be set, and that it must be released from a dubious, floating humanity that is lacking in all determination. Before designating as *number* the electors whose universal suffrage will make a majority, Guizot has already deprived of their identity those who hold no power, no honor, no wealth, those who are not caught within the social *fabric* [*tissu*] of which the community he imagines is made. There is, we observed, no doubt that he has given up the image of the organic body or the mystical body; nevertheless, he confers *flesh* only upon a carefully circumscribed society, within a social ocean that is ever ready to change into an abyss.

It is astonishing to see how he formulates the opposition between democracy and representative government in the passage we quoted. The principle of the sovereignty of the people, he writes, takes in all individuals solely owing to the fact that they exist, without asking anything more of them. Can he then forget that they belong to the same nation, live on the same soil, participate in the same history, maintain a thousand ties with one another, enjoy in principle the civil equality and the liberties instituted by the Revolution? And if it is true, as he says in the same place, that the task of representative government is to detect superior qualities, to separate out those who do from those who don't have the right to have political rights, whence comes to such a government this very first right? Whence does this right come to it, when we know from Guizot himself that a government acting from the outside upon society fails to recognize the nature of power? The answer doesn't seem to leave any doubt: Through its institutions, a ruling social class inspects itself, remodels itself, and decides about its hierarchies.

In affirming, against the principle of the sovereignty of the people, that of the sovereignty of reason and justice, Guizot wants to restore a transcendence that is threatened by the ultimate form, the most subtle form of idolatry. At the same time, in specifying that justice and reason allow of no definition, that no one can make of himself the supreme guarantor, he forbids anyone from giving any shape to this transcendence. But as soon as public debate upon what is just and unjust, true and deceitful, sees itself limited to the boundaries of a class, a new guarantee sees itself reestablished. If reason and justice will never be revealed in statements, at least the labor of their enunciation will be reserved to those with superior qualities. No one, therefore, who is not duly qualified should disturb that place where members of the ruling class evaluate and judge one another.

By his fecundity and his contradictions, Guizot continues to instruct us about the principles of liberalism and about the equivocal relationship it still entertains with democracy, once the latter is established.

Notes

"Guizot. Le libéralisme polémique" was originally published as the introduction to the reprint edition of François Guizot's *Des moyens de gouvernement et d'opposition dans l'état actuel de la France* (Paris: Belin, 1988), 7–34. Reprinted in *Écrire,* 113–39.

1   François Guizot, *Democracy in France* (New York: D. Appleton, 1849), 10.
2   "Manifesto of the Communist Party," in Karl Marx and Frederick Engels, *Selected Works in One Volume* (New York: International Publishers, 1974), 35.
3   *Democracy in France,* 28 [T/E: translation altered].
4   Ibid., 39.
5   Ibid., 57.
6   Ibid., 73.
7   Ibid., 61.
8   *Des Moyens,* 108.
9   *Democracy in France,* 16.
10 Ibid.
11 Ibid.
12 Ibid. [T/E: translation altered].
13 Pierre Rosanvallon, *Le moment Guizot* (Paris: Gallimard, 1985).
14 François Guizot, *History of the Origins of Representative Government in Europe* (1821–1822), trans. Andrew R. Scoble (London: Henry G. Bohn, 1861).
15 François Guizot, *The History of Civilization in Europe* (1828), trans. William Hazlitt (London: Penguin Books, 1997).
16 *Des moyens,* 37.
17 Ibid., 37.
18 Ibid., 38.
19 Ibid., 40.
20 Ibid., 41.
21 Ibid., 101.

22 Ibid., 106.

23 Ibid.

24 Ibid., 106–7.

25 Ibid., 114.

26 Ibid., 107.

27 Ibid., 108.

28 Ibid., 108–9.

29 Ibid., 126 (emphasis added).

30 Ibid., 112.

31 Ibid.

32 Ibid., 113.

33 Ibid., 114.

34 Ibid., 115.

35 Ibid., 116.

36 Ibid.

37 Ibid., 117.

38 Ibid., 120.

39 Ibid.

40 Ibid., 122.

41 Ibid., 125.

42 Ibid., 136.

43 Ibid., 137.

44 Ibid., 179.

45 "Philosophie politique. De la souveraineté," in François Guizot, *Histoire de la civilisation en Europe,* ed. Pierre Rosanvallon (Paris: Hachette, 1985).

46 Lecture 6, *History of the Origins of Representative Government in France,* 55–64; "Philosophie politique," 335.

47 "Philosophie politique," 340.

48 Ibid., 320.

49 Ibid.

50 Ibid.

51 Ibid., 336.

52 *History of the Origins of Representative Government in France,* 78 [T/E: translation altered].

53 Ibid. [T/E: translation altered].

54 Ibid. [T/E: translation altered].

55 Ibid., 79 [T/E: translation altered].

56 Ibid., 72.

Machiavelli and the *Veritá Effetuale*

I N THE PREFACE to the first book of *The Discourses on the First Ten Books of Titus Livius,* Machiavelli makes a bold claim to originality. He says he has embarked upon a path that had not yet been followed by anyone else, and he compares himself to the audacious navigator who has departed in search of unknown lands and seas. And, as soon as he has made this declaration, he seems to state his intention. That intention would be to convince his contemporaries to extend to the domain of politics the imitation of the Ancients that seems to them to go without saying in other domains. A paradoxical proposition, as historians will emphasize: the thinker who was aware of innovating absolutely and whom posterity has indeed judged to have opened a new path to political thought, this man wished to erect Antiquity into a model. Everything happens as if the discovery of the unknown continent was in his view issuing an order to return to the ancient world or even coincided with the rediscovery of that world.

Let us pause for a brief moment over this part of the text. Imitation of the Ancients, the writer declares, is at present the deed of artists, jurists, and doctors, but those who run public affairs or take part therein regard that as impossible. The admiration borne for Antiquity doesn't give rise to any desire to be inspired by its examples in order to regulate institutions and guide political action. "In constituting republics, in maintaining States, in governing kingdoms, in forming an army or conducting a war, in dealing with subjects, in extending the empire, one finds neither prince nor republic nor captain nor citizen who repairs to antiquity for examples."[1] In a single phrase, Machiavelli gives two reasons for this phenomenon. The first relates to "the weak state to which the vices of present-day education have brought the world [and] to the evil wrought in many provinces and cities of Christendom by ambition conjoined with idleness."[2] The second relates to the absence of genuine knowledge of the historians, of *storie,* from which one no longer knows how to pick the fruit and "taste . . . the delicacies it comprises."[3] Indeed, men of today are inclined to derive from the reading of *storie* merely the pleasure the "various incidents" procure for them.[4] Thus do they turn themselves, we are given to understand, into mere spectators of the scene of the past without glimpsing that ancient times are no different from the ones in which they live. They do not dream of imitating, because they cut themselves off from the past by a contemplative — or, better put, an aesthetic — attitude. They do not know that they are inserted into the same world as their predecessors. They hold such imitation "to be not merely difficult but impossible . . . as if the heaven, the sun, the elements and man had in their motion, their order, and their potency, become different from what they used to be."[5]

Fortified by this report, Machiavelli offers to bring back a taste for *storie.* And, since there exists a great, though mutilated, work devoted to Rome, that of Livy, he wants to encourage people to read it, leaning, in order to gain an intelligence of it, as much on a knowledge of present facts as of past ones. His argument, therefore, is complex: the ability to imitate not only seems strangely associated with the discovery of the unknown — it is subordinated to an ability to grasp the identity of past and present. Such an identity is not immediately palpable, but it will unveil itself if one knows how to make the one speak through the other; and that will happen with the aid of the interpretation of a text. This text is itself intelligible only if the reader vests in it the knowledge he possesses of the institutions and the mores of the Ancients and the Moderns.

The paradox I mentioned above is transformed if we follow the sinuous meanderings of Machiavellian writing. An encomium to Antiquity, an appeal to imitation, an obligatory passage by way of the reading of a great author — this is indeed the opening theme of the *Discourses.* But neither the past, notably the Roman past, nor the text that governs access to it, Livy's text, reveals itself to be open to the acquisition of immediate knowledge. Both demand to be deciphered. Their meaning is given only to he who knows how to comprehend the facts through the book and the book through the facts and to combine present facts with past ones.

Many readers and commentators do not feel particularly embarrassed by these subtleties. They have been struck by what they deemed to be a contradiction within the *Discourses,* which becomes more vivid when one compares the teachings in this volume with those of the *Prince.* On the one hand, Machiavelli, a republican by conviction who dreams of Florence's liberties being restored, is supposedly seeking in Antiquity a model; on the other hand, carried away by his passion for the *veritá effetuale* and bewitched into reducing all people's actions to the same denominator, he is supposedly abandoning any concern with what ought to be. Moreover, the exploration of the politics of the Ancients is said to offer him merely the means to enlarge the field of his inquiry and to pursue the task of objectivating politics, which he had already undertaken in his first work. Nevertheless, the contradiction supposedly remains masked, in part, from his own view: while he is apparently commending the virtues of the Romans, insofar as these virtues combine with the art of political action, the knowledge of this art is also said to lead him to silence his convictions and to make him transgress every moral norm.

One must pay the homage that is due to Leo Strauss. He was the first to show that the *Discourses* merely harbor in places the same principles as *The Prince,* while the encomium to the Roman Republic and to the virtue of its citizens had a philosophical design whose purpose was to break with the teachings of the Tradition. Indeed, the encomium to the Roman Republic hatches a corrosive critique of the good regime as the classical authors had conceived it—a regime whose excellence results from the wisdom of the government of the best or of its legislators and is measured by the criterion of the order that reigns in the city and by the stability of its institutions. The encomium to citizen virtue hatches a no less excoriating critique of the norms of conduct of the actors, who deserve praise or blame only on account of their ability to interpret what chances their actions will have within the framework of established institutions and amid the conditions of the moment. Ultimately, the authority conferred upon Livy at the beginning of the work should fool us no more: Machiavelli invokes him in order to win over his readers and to lead them, by stages, to place in doubt this historian's interpretation and, finally, to disengage from the aristocratic principles governing that interpretation.

One argument from the first book of the *Discourses* attracts our attention. After having weighed the comparative merits of Sparta and Rome, apparently without taking sides, Machiavelli observes that Rome's greatness was not the product of wise legislation but was built up, rather, with the aid of events. He suggests that the goodness of a constitution does not necessarily reside in the principles determining its foundation and that time is not necessarily a factor of corruption. He connects the lucky events from which Rome benefited with the conflicts that set the Senate and the plebs in opposition to each other, ultimately discovering in these conflicts the wellspring of the Republic's greatness and celebrating the virtue of discord, or *desunione.* He then rises up against the most widespread opinion, the *opinione de molti,* in order to affirm in his own name (*io dico*) that "those who condemn the quarrels between the nobles and the plebs seem to be caviling at the very things that were the primary cause of Rome's retaining her freedom, and that they pay more attention to the noise and clamor resulting from such commotions than to what resulted from them, i.e., to the good effects which they produced."[6] Turning upside down the traditional thesis that finds the sign of the wisdom of the laws in their effective ability to contain the desires of the multitude, he deems these desires fecund when they are the deed of free peoples, specifying that they are "very seldom harmful to liberty, for they are due either to the populace being oppressed or to the suspicion that it is going to be oppressed."[7] The idea of law is then dissociated from that of proportion [*mesure*]; it no longer necessarily results from the intervention of a reasonable instance of authority. Instead, the law reveals itself to be connected with disproportion [*démesure*], an excess of desire for freedom. This is a desire that certainly could not be separated from the appetites of the oppressed; such appetites are always rife with envy, but they cannot be reduced thereto since, in its essence, that desire is pure negativity, a refusal to be oppressed, a desire to be and not a desire to have. Finally, in one of the last chapters of this first book, at the end of a long discussion about the nature of the multitude, Machiavelli does not hesitate to attack Livy—he whom he calls "our Titus Livy"—and, with him, all the other historians, so as to affirm that the multitude is wiser and more steadfast, *più savia et più constante,* than a prince.

In recalling this argument, to which many others would have to be added —notably the one about how Rome's greatness and freedom were paid for by the oppression of Italy, or the one about how the favorable effects of tumults in Rome related to the Senate's need to make concessions to the plebs in order to satisfy its policy of conquest—we want only to shed some light upon Machiavelli's singular reading of Roman History. Its institutions, he suggests, are not intrinsically good, nor are its citizens intrinsically virtuous (a number of examples are given to us of the ambitions of certain ones among them, even their conspiratorial ventures). Rome offers the image of a city that, rather than falling back upon itself and withdrawing, welcomes conflict and invents, amid the ordeal of events and tumults, "answers" that allow it to hold in check both the constant threat of tyranny and the constant threat of licence. Thus, the dynamic schema of the Roman Republic renders readable for its citizens the conditions for meaningful political action, or, one can perhaps also say, the conditions for intelligent and disciplined conduct—with discipline not excluding transgression of orders

deemed inapplicable in a given circumstance, since authority is never petrified, and with the intelligence of the actors not eliminating respect for the
laws since the weight of suspicion falls upon the ambitious.

If one wanted at present to try to define Machiavelli's relationship with
the Ancients, one would have to, it seems, combine the following four
propositions:

1. The Ancients are superior to the Moderns since the latter are victims
of the Christian ethic, which forbids them from seeking in this world the
ultimate measure of their action and from fully investing their desires in a
citizen's life—desires that for the few are at once a desire to act and a desire
to know. In the modern world, men voluntarily accept servitude, and those
who command are tempted by tyranny.

2. The wellsprings of freedom were effectively real in the Roman Republic, but they were not known. They were, rather, very much concealed by
a discourse on the good of the city, which is measured by the criterion of
concord, and on the moral virtue of its eminent citizens—a discourse of the
philosophers and of most of the historians, which proceeded from an aristocratic prejudice and gave the wisdom of the dominant class a good name
by imputing its moderation to its advantages that sheltered it from envy.

3. Men do not change: Ancients and Moderns are made of the same stuff.
What alone changes is the way in which men respond to the permanent
questions posed by the arrangement of a city and, in the first place, by the
division between those who want to command and those who desire not to
be commanded, not to be oppressed. The ancient world makes us discover
the variety of responses that have been given to these permanent questions
as well as the superiority of the Roman model.

4. While, on the one hand, the Moderns show themselves to be inferior
to the Ancients, inasmuch as they remain prisoners of the Christian ethic
and are incapable of recognizing their kinship with the Ancients, on the
other hand, however little their desire to act, which is stirred up by the spectacle of the miseries of the time, ignites in them the desire to know, they
are nevertheless liable to discover the principles of politics that have always
been concealed, for they can comprehend the meaning of actions and institutions that had escaped the awareness of the actors themselves and that
the classical historians endeavored to disguise.

Reformulating in these terms Machiavelli's design, or part of his design,
I am exposing myself to an objection. Machiavelli, it would be said, was
in no way interested in the ancient and modern virtues, as common sense
has understood them in all ages—that is, in opposition to vices—and as
still supposedly ruled by a concern for what is good. He could only be con-

cerned by what he calls *virtù,* a virtue that gives the subject its greatest strength in order to resist the trials of fortune and to assure that subject the greatest power of action. Or, one might say, Machiavelli is completely breaking as much with classical philosophy as with Christian thought in order to fall back on positive truths, the celebrated *veritá effetuale.*

In order to judge how well founded these objections are, it seems to me that we will have to reexamine the reasons why the author of the *Discourses* decided to make of the Roman Republic the central object of his study. (I say *central object* since, speaking of Rome, he doesn't deprive himself of the opportunity to expatiate on other States ancient and modern.) This re-examination requires a few brief considerations of a historical nature. I hasten to specify one thing: being interested in History is not yielding to historicism. Leo Strauss has already made what is the fitting remark about that. But I would like to give that remark its full weight. If one wants to know the intentions of a writer, it seems worthwhile to ask oneself who are his privileged interlocutors, what are the opinions he targets, what are the circumstances that summon up his desire to speak. Let us note in passing that, in order to account for his thinking, it doesn't suffice to answer these questions, supposing that one could, for it is equally true that he writes for no one, that he becomes intimate with a reader who has no definite identity. The reader's place will be occupied, in a future he could not imagine, by unknown people. And again it is true that he draws on circumstances for an ability to think that transcends the contingency of his situation.

A first indication: The *Discourses* are in part the product of discussions that took place in the Oricellari gardens, in a circle whose exact composition is unknown but that included educated young people who were impatient to act. The host was Cosimo Rucellai, cooped up in his home on account of an infirmity, and among the auditors figured notably the future authors of the plot mounted in 1522 against Cardinal Guilio de' Medici: the poet Luigi Alamanni, Zanobi Buondelmonti, Machiavelli's former collaborator at the time he held important offices in the Soderini government, the brothers Diaceto and Battista della Palla, these last two forced into exile or executed after the conspiracy's failure. This information is certainly not negligible. Machiavelli was not unaware of the feelings of this small public; he undoubtedly had to weigh carefully the import of his remarks when broaching the highly perilous questions of rebellion and civil disobedience. Such was the case, for example, when he painted the portrait of the first Brutus, when he analyzed at length the chances of conspirators, when, highlighting the role of young captains under the Roman Republic, he evoked the audacity of Fabius, who didn't hesitate to disobey the Senate's orders in order to engage his troops in a forest that was reputed to be impenetrable, or again when he praised Epaminondas, who, under cover of training young Thebans in gymnastics, secretly prepared them for struggle against the occupier. Wasn't his own teaching semiclandestine? Didn't he propose that one combine the exigency of knowing with the exigency of acting, persuading his listeners of the futility of a political fight that would be lacking a knowledge of History?

A second indication: We know, too, that the Orti Oricellaris had become illustrious a decade and a half earlier as an antidemocratic household. Cosimo's uncle, Bernardo Rucellai, had brought together there the most resolute adversaries of the reformist—today one would say "progressive"—policy conducted by Soderini. Lorenzo the Magnificent's brother-in-law, one of the leaders of the oligarchy's hard-line faction—that is to say, of the faction that rejected all compromise with the government in place— is known to have been the author of a commentary on Livy. I do not believe I am mistaken in assuming that Machiavelli was developing a counter-teaching at the very place where Rucellai had held the position of master teacher. Machiavelli was endeavoring to dislodge Rome and Livy from the conservative interpretation, demonstrating through various hints the ignorance and servility of the older generation as well as suggesting that Roman History accredited not the Medicis' titles but those of democracy and that the restoration of liberties sometimes required disobeying the laws.

A third indication: The *consulte* or *pratiche* were informal sorts of councils composed of influential Florentines summoned periodically by the gonfalonier. Soderini had broken with Medicean tradition by opening them up to a large number of citizens. The minutes of these councils (which have carefully been analyzed by Felix Gilbert[8]) testify to how frequently references were made to Roman examples. Now, one can easily distinguish, in reading these minutes, three main currents of opinion. They enliven, on the one hand, a rationalist, and intentionally cynical, discourse that deals with politics in terms of relations of forces; it is that of those famous "sages of our time,"[9] whom Machiavelli loses no opportunity to expose. These are the sages whose supreme maxim is to know how to "take advantage of the passage of time."[10] There is, on the other hand, a discourse inspired by Christian values, which makes Florentine civic feeling rest on virtue. This is the discourse Machiavelli denounces as that of snivelers (*piagnoni*). Finally, there is a humanist discourse that praises the prudence and moderation of those who govern and always boils down to the idea of a stable, hierarchized political body. Despite their divergences, these discourses share great affinities with one another. Their referents are easily interchangeable: what one names Necessity the other names Fortune, and the third God. The invariant themes are: concord among citizens (*unione*) and the peril of dissensions, these latter always being imputed to factions; the inherent goodness of the original institutions and the peril of modifications; the defense of the status quo in Italy; and, also, the virtue of the happy medium, as well as those of taking the least risk and of temporizing. Once again, I do not believe I am mistaken in observing that Machiavelli meant to denounce before young Florentines enamored of change a threefold set of illusions: the one that the leaders would possess a mastery of political science (they are, he shows, rotten calculators); the one that the city would be benefiting from the special protection of Providence; and the one that the city would be the inheritor of Rome and of the ancient wisdom. We see very well, when reading him, that these illusions serve to cover up a defense of an oligarchic system, one that deprives a large portion of the people of its political rights, keeps it disarmed, and, in order to survive, readily consents to the domination of foreign powers.

Let us move forward in our rapid investigation. The idealization of Antiquity, and more particularly that of Rome, appear to us to be a dominant trait of Florentine thinking. That does not inform us completely, it is true, about its real political import. Quite often, the men who cited Livy or who invoked the authority of Aristotle did so only to indulge in mere figures of rhetoric. This, moreover, is why, in the foreword I mentioned, Machiavelli deplores an indifference to the past in matters of politics that is not the product of ignorance but signals, rather, an inability to seek in the spectacle of the past anything other than some bit of pleasure. However, we have solid reasons for imagining the force of the emotional attachment to Rome. It is, indeed, quite ancient. Since the bourgeois gave the city its de facto independence by attacking the nobility and razing the surrounding castles, the Florentines have identified with the Romans.

The word *identification* should be taken in its strongest sense. The Florentines were not thinking only, like the French revolutionaries a few centuries later, of seizing hold again of Roman virtue, of conducting themselves in the image of the Romans: they claimed to be their descendants and affirmed that Roman blood flowed in their veins. I borrow these formulations from a study by Nicolai Rubinstein.[11] An old chronicle written around 1225, the *Cronica de origine civitatis,* which the celebrated chronicle of the Villanis was to draw upon a century later, offers a rich description of the foundation of Florence by Rome in the time of Caesar. Florence is supposed to have drawn its name from a consul called Florentinus, killed during the siege of Fiesole, and to have been conceived on the model of Rome, so much so as to merit the name of *parva romana.*

Let us skip over the details—the legend of the destruction and reconstruction of the city five hundred years after its foundation, the changes the Villanis imposed upon the first narrative as a function of new vicissitudes occasioned by the opposition between Florentines and Fiesolans—and simply retain the fact that very early on Florence saw itself assigned the destiny of taking on the legacy of Rome, a legacy both spiritual and *real*. Dante himself proclaims in the *Convivio* that it is the "*bellissima et famosissima figlia di Roma*" and, in the seventh *Epistola*, that it has been made "*ad imaginem suam atque similitudinem.*" In his *De Monarchia,* he boosts to an even higher level Florence's mission by combining the "truths" of History and religion, for he makes of ancient Rome the work of God: the Roman people, he affirms, were chosen by divine Providence for the world monarchy, without which it would be impossible for humanity to attain earthly happiness and which prepared the ground for the coming of Christ. The Roman people is thus the *populo santo.*

To ignore Dante's shadow when reading Machiavelli would undoubtedly be to deprive oneself of a precious element for reflection. Machiavelli thinks, of course, that the advent of Caesar was inevitable; with the coming of the Roman Empire, on the other hand, he sees the installation of the reign of corruption. Generally speaking, Machiavelli, like Dante, thinks that the Roman people were exceptional, but Machiavelli does not hesitate, as I have noted, to point out that its greatness was paid for by the enslavement of other peoples. He goes even further, since he remarks that the Romans brought about the disappearance of the traces of free institutions in all of Italy from previous times, thus suggesting that the founders are perhaps only the imitators of the Etruscans. But the main point does not lie here. I have already intimated that one of his privileged targets is what we called the humanist political discourse, by which I mean the republican humanist discourse. Why? Because the latter is the vehicle for all the themes that continue to mobilize men enamored of freedom and because it leads them astray by travestying the nature of the Roman Republic and preventing his contemporaries from comprehending what direction change ought to take and what means should be adopted for obtaining that change.

This humanist discourse—what Hans Baron has called *civic humanism*[12] —was constituted during the last third of the trecento and developed until the rise of Cosimo de' Medici, who, capably thrusting aside the image of the tyrant and contenting himself with appearing as the first citizen of Florence, equally succeeded in exploiting for his own use the reputation of the greatest spokesman for the Republic, Leonardo Bruni. As I have just indicated, the humanists in particular did not originate the myth of Florence's Romanness, nor were they the source of an identification with

Rome, signs of which are also to be found in other cities but which was worked out nowhere else in such rich detail. What, on the other hand, they are responsible for doing is to have forged a new representation of Florence's origin, its history, its regime, and its mission by claiming an exact, scientific knowledge of the texts of the historians and philosophers of Antiquity. A new representation of origins, I say. Bruni, in particular, denounces in his *Laudatio fiorentinae urbis* the fictitiousness of the old chronicles; it was not, he shows, the legions of Caesar sent in pursuit of Catiline who had instigated the founding of Florence; the latter had its birth as a colony created by veterans of the army of Sulla during the Social War. Florence is not daughter of imperial Rome but rather daughter of the Roman Republic. Roman blood flows in the veins of Florentines, but it is the blood of ancestors who were free men. Here the identification takes advantage of some new resources; it is sustained by an image of transmitted *virtù.*

The conjunction of the good and the ancestral persists, although it is expressed differently and now enlisted in the service of change. Indeed, a new representation of History and of the mission of the city is instaurated: in a time when Florence saw itself threatened by Milan, the humanists presented its fight against Visconti as that of freedom against despotism and assigned this fight a universal import. They conferred upon the city the task of supporting the cause of all who are oppressed. In the successive struggles Florence was to lead in the course of the century in order to defend its institutions or its independence, they deciphered the episodes of a single History that makes the latter into a continuation of the Roman Republic: the war against Martino della Scala, the tyrant of Verona, the popular revolt against the Duke of Athens, a pretender to tyranny, the conflict with Pope Gregory V, the resistance against Milanese imperialism, and so on.

Similarly, a new representation of the regime and, it must be added, of the citizen was born: *virtus romana* is maintained only because it dwells in the citizens who, in each of their activities as merchants, as captains, as magistrates, or as scholars devoted to the *studia humanitatis,* put their energy in the service of an active life and endeavor to contribute to the glory of the city. Reciprocally, this virtue of the citizens, manifest in their devotion to the public good and sanctioned by the rewards they receive in this world — honors, wealth, knowledge — is revealed to be the product of institutions: the equality of all before the law, the sharing of public offices among those who are legally capable of exercising them, and the value accorded to individual labor as opposed to that of birth. All these result in a noble emulation in search of virtue.

Undoubtedly, the *credo* of civic humanism didn't resist the change in regime, that is to say, the reign of Lorenzo the Magnificent. In fact, the proclaimed republican ideal—which was worked out starting around 1375 by men of the first rank, such as Coluccio Salutati, at first, and then Leonardo Bruni, and which was embraced by a number of important members of the Florentine bourgeoisie (Lauro Martines's sociological investigation is highly instructive on this point)[13]—could no longer with impunity find spokesmen under a tyranny, even a disguised one. Nonetheless, we know that a republican opposition persisted in Florence and above all that the themes dear to civic humanism blossomed again after the fall of the Medicis.

Now, it very well must be granted that these themes had for the first time been propagated under a set of circumstances that were marked by the failure of democratic demands, but such a paradox will surprise only the naive. The struggles for the extension of the rights of the lower classes had been most intense beginning in the middle of the trecento and had reached their point of culmination in the famous revolt of the *ciompi* (the wool workers). It is as a consequence of this revolt's defeat—a defeat to which the middle classes had actively contributed—that a narrow oligarchy succeeded in taking over the government for itself. It does not seem exaggerated to state that considered in its own time, under the singular circumstances in which it was practiced, civic humanism, whose work was decisive for the formation and spread of republican principles in modern Europe—or for resistance to absolutism—furnished the counterpoint to an antipopular reaction.

Or, let us state it better: Its work appears eminently ambiguous. In part, it formulated a new political ethics that emerged from a series of conflicts. These conflicts culminated in: the elimination of multiple centers of power (in the first rank of which were the Guelph party and the Church); the imposition of the law of the commune over the entire territory and the protection of citizens against exactions committed by large-scale rival bands; the concentration of power in the organs of the commune; the rout of families whose authority was based on the seniority of their rank; and the affirmation of the value of the individual as measured by his personal ability. In another part, this ethics masks a new order wherein the many are expected to hand over to a narrow ruling stratum the conduct of public affairs.

Humanist praise of the Roman Republic and of ancient authors takes on, from this perspective, a quite specific import. The Florentines were held to be the new Romans because they would not suffer to obey the power of one man, because they therefore abhorred Caesar (as was said of them) and praised Brutus, and because they placed the law above private interests, but also because they understood that the greatness of Rome was the work of the wisdom of its Senate and that Rome's ruin was the result of its divisions, instigated by the insatiable envy of the plebs, and because, instructed by this ruination, they discovered the virtues of concord, stability, moderation, the *via del mezzo,* and so on.

There is no need to go on at length about Machiavelli's argument in order to gauge the distance he has set between himself and civic humanism. Let us state only that if one wants to locate the first moment when there is an articulate appeal to imitate the Romans, a vindication of the ancient virtues, a conception of man's fate as being played out within the confines of the terrestrial world, and an idea of the superiority of the active life over the contemplative life and of the excellence of free institutions (which guarantee at once the security of the citizens, their de jure equality, the full development of their faculties, and the collective exercise of public offices), one must turn toward the very beginning of the quattrocento.

Machiavelli links up with this conception in part, but at the same time he allows one to get a glimpse of the lies that accompany it. A first lie: The idea of virtue, which finds its raison d'être and its reward within the confines of terrestrial life, accommodates itself to a social order in which the Christian religion retains all its power, for it offers the advantage of keeping the people obedient by persuading them that "it is an evil thing to talk evilly of evil doing."[14] A second lie: The idea of the superiority of the active life conceals the split that has arisen and been maintained at Florence between the bourgeois and the citizen. This split reveals, in the very first place, the practice of paying foreign armies or mercenaries to assure the city's defense. A third lie: The idea of a collective exercise of public offices masks the monopolization of power by an oligarchy. The few present themselves as the guardians of free institutions, when in fact they confuse the preservation of these institutions with that of their own prerogatives.

As he is breaking with the humanist discourse Machiavelli brings out what Florence can learn from Rome. But what Florence can learn from Rome is something of which the Romans themselves did not have a theoretical knowledge because their institutions had been improvised in response to events: namely, the beneficial effect of tumult in a republic, of a sort of political effervescence that thwarts the ambitions of the ruling stratum and makes it seek its security in granting concessions to the legitimate aspirations of the many. What Florence can learn from Rome is also the meaning of the events that mark its own history, in particular of the great event, still quite close, that was the regrettable collapse of the last free government, that of Soderini. A policy of reforms is disastrous when it is conducted by gullible men who retain confidence in the honesty of their adversaries, in their patriotism, and in their desire for concord. What the Florentines can learn from the Romans in questioning at once the present as well as the past is that the art of politics requires one to know how to identify one's enemies, choose one's camp, and make opportune use of cunning and force; in short, what they can learn is that the art of politics pertains to the art of war, even though it couldn't be reduced thereto.

Certainly, these considerations do not dispense one from having to appraise Machiavelli's break with classical philosophy. Sounding the depths of this break is beyond my present purpose. I shall be content to formulate a few remarks while making reference to the most penetrating critique of the Machiavellian oeuvre, Leo Strauss's. In his essay on "The Three Waves of Modernity," Strauss brings out two assertions that are said to be revealing of the "broad intention" of the author of the *Prince* and of the *Discourses* and to have revealed themselves to be at the basis of modern political philosophy.[15] The first is said to indicate his disagreement with previous writers on the way to judge what a prince's conduct is to be. According to Strauss, Machiavelli would be declaring that he wants to know only the factual truth and isn't interested in fictions forged in former times. Thus would he be challenging idealism in order to lay a claim to "a realistic approach to political things."[16]

The novelty of his teaching would best be grasped in the first lines of the fifteenth chapter of the *Prince,* where it is said:

> Our next task is to consider policies and principles a ruler ought to follow in dealing with his subjects or with his friends. Since I know many people have written on this subject, I am concerned it may be thought presumptuous for me to write on it as well, especially since what I have to say, as regards this question in particular, will differ greatly from the recommendations of others. But my hope is to write a book that will be useful, at least to those who read it intelligently, and so I thought it more fitting to follow the real truth [*veritá effetuale*] of the thing than one's imagination.[17]

These remarks have rightly been underscored by a number of commentators. After having examined various cases, Machiavelli boldly advances beyond the paths of tradition and unveils his intention. Nevertheless, if his approach can be said to be realistic, one must agree, as Strauss himself observes, that he is not content to adopt the position of observer or analyst; he is claiming to discover rules of conduct through the examination of what is. Thenceforth, he abolishes the distance, always preserved by the classical philosopher or the theologian, between the data of sense experience and what ought to be; and by this very deed, he reabsorbs morality into politics and reduces politics to a technique. Strauss very much seems to rally to the widespread opinion when he finds occasion to write: "The political problem becomes a technical problem."[18]

This formula is nonetheless the sign of a concession to opinion much more than the expression of Strauss's own thought. Indeed, he comes back on this point in his great work, *Thoughts on Machiavelli*.[19] The genuine, the underlying intention of the writer—which is different from his "broad intention"—Strauss gives us to understand here, is not to convert politics into a technique, nor does it even concern chiefly politics. The target at which he is aiming is the teachings of the Bible and the teachings of classical philosophy, and basically the latter beyond the former. Machiavelli takes himself to be the founder of a sure science that obtains an intelligible understanding of society and of the things of the world; he claims to be uprooting the idea that there would be virtue in itself, justice in itself—which, though they may have been inaccessible in fact, were said to constitute a norm for human conduct and social organization. He claims to be destroying what he treats as a prejudice, the belief in a hierarchy within the soul and within the city that is said to correspond to the hierarchy of beings within the *cosmos*—the belief, therefore, in a distinction between the *high* and the *low* that would not be created by man but would be constitutive of his nature. Against the classical thinkers, Strauss also notes, Machiavelli is accounting for the high by the low; he is reducing virtue and justice to effects of necessity. Moreover, his project is to show what the conditions are starting from which men are placed before the necessity to conduct themselves as good citizens or as good subjects. By the same stroke, the political art derives from the knowledge of necessity—a knowledge guided by the examination of extreme situations. Upon these premises, he can, without contradiction, on the one hand objectively conceive of the imperatives that arise for building up and preserving a tyranny and those ones that arise for building up and preserving a republic, and, on the other hand, he can express his preference for the Republic, with the conviction that it takes better account of the need to reconcile the ambition of the few with the needs of the many.

True, one can inquire as to the motive that prompts the prince or a small number of persons to attain this knowledge of necessity. According to Strauss, it is not so much concern with their security, awareness of the danger in which their appetite for power places them, that pushes them to take responsibility for the interests of the multitude as it is due appreciation of the means for obtaining from the people the support that is indispensable for the satisfaction of their desire for glory. In this regard, the Roman Republic still seems exemplary. For having wanted to gain renown through a policy of conquest, the patricians deliberately conceded advantages to the plebs. Let us leave aside the analysis of the motives of Machiavelli himself, pretender to the foundation of an entirely new science, as I have discussed this elsewhere.[20] Let it suffice to retain in our mind the fact that the common good sees itself rigorously cut off from the domain of morality and that it is established as a result of an "enlightened" necessity, which testifies to the reign of needs and passions.

It is from another angle that Strauss discerns Machiavelli's broad intention in the "The Three Waves." Without a doubt, it seems to him the most propitious way of bringing out his role as initiator. The writer's second principal assertion concerns the power of fortune. He is said to be breaking with the entire classical tradition when he affirms that man can beat chance. Strauss limits himself here to summarizing a passage from the fifteenth chapter of the *Prince*—fortune is a woman who can be mastered by the use of force—whereas in his major book he goes on at length about this subject. The main point, however, is made: the elimination of fortune signals an entirely new idea of man's potential, of his capacity to dominate nature.

Here was the teaching of the Bible: Man is God's creature and, while it has been granted to him to reign over other earthly creatures, limits have been set that he cannot exceed; the designs of Providence escape him. As different as its project was in other regards, classical philosophy, all the while granting man an eminent position, subjected him to an order of the world of which he can have an idea but which he could not fully conceive and still less modify. Fortune is then the name given to what foils and will forever foil his calculations; it is the name given to this force that, independent of his will, raises him up or proves to be his downfall.

As Strauss rightly recalls, the famous proposition "Man is the measure of all things" is the opposite of "Man is the master of all things."[21] As measure of all things, he is the sole being open to "all"; he possesses in himself the idea of the "all" and of the specific difference of the beings within it. But he cannot place himself in the position of the principle of the generation and reproduction of that with which he is in relation. The meaning of measure prohibits him from abandoning himself to the unbridled desire to appropriate for himself, and therefore to deny, what is outside himself. For someone who lives in conformity with the teachings of religion, Providence remains forever *inscrutable,* and for he who trusts in reason, fortune remains forever *elusive.*

Machiavelli therefore violates the divine commandments and perverts the project of philosophy, the very idea of reason—which is reason, *logos* or *ratio*, only upon the condition that one maintain a gap between thought and being. *Elusive* is the label Strauss associates, here and there, sometimes with fortune, sometimes with nature, sometimes with everything. These notions are not equivalent, but for man they are inseparable. As symbol of what cannot be grasped, to man fortune signifies the irreducibility of the whole to its parts and the irreducibility of the supreme norm to the various social representations of the norm. Thus, in grappling with the power of fortune, Machiavelli heralds the reign of modern science, which converts nature into matter—treated by right as fully intelligible and "manipulable" —and claims to free physics from cosmology. In the passage from "The Three Waves" previously mentioned, Strauss suggests that, with Machiavelli, modern political philosophy anticipates the revolution that would soon take place in the natural sciences. We witness his audacity in the hypothesis (Strauss is tacitly referring to the *Discourses* 1.26) that the instauration of the most "desirable political order" does not depend upon chance— this is the happy and very improbable association of power and philosophy in conjunction with the desire of a people enamored of wisdom—but rather upon the clever ability of an outstanding man to "transform a corrupt matter into a good matter."[22]

Nevertheless, doesn't one have to ask onself whether the Straussian portrait of Machiavelli isn't guided by the principal concern of assigning to the latter the responsibility for the vices of modernity? Shouldn't one be surprised that so subtle a reader, sensitive as no other to Machiavelli's writing art, would take so many liberties when he tries to summarize the latter's teaching; that he retains from the passages deemed most revealing only what comes to support his own theses, that he deliberately omits those arguments that would run counter to these theses, or that he lifts certain statements without worrying about a context that at first sight alters their meaning? In fact, it happens that, in observing the rules of reading to which Strauss so firmly invites us to conform, one might be led to follow a direction that would not be his own. This, after all, is something that would perhaps not have displeased him.

Was Machiavelli's plan to destroy belief in the powers of fortune and to reveal to men that nothing could oppose their domination over nature, provided that they manage to abandon the principles of morality? To be honest, however superficially one goes through the *Prince* and the *Discourses,* the passages in which Fortune turns up turn out to be so numerous that they would require a study of their own. Let us linger over a few of them. And in the first place, let us consider the one Strauss deems to be of decisive import. Here is what Machiavelli writes in the last paragraph of chapter 25 of the *Prince:*

I conclude, then, that since fortune changes and men stubbornly continue to behave in the same way, men are happy when both [these situations] are in harmony and, as soon as they enter into disharmony, unhappy. I do think, however, that it is better to be bold than prudent, for fortune is a lady. It is necessary, if you want to master her, to beat and strike her. And one sees she more often submits to those who act boldly than to those who proceed coldly. Moreover, since she is a lady, she smiles on the young, for they have less respect, more ruthlessness, and command her with their boldness.[23]

My first remark, which is not the least of them, is that Machiavelli has the gift of speaking of serious things with humor and that it isn't good to neglect the gracefulness of an image used to deliver an alleged message in which the signification of the modern project is said to be deciphered. The image here is that of an amorous relationship; Machiavelli is suggesting that the conquest of a woman is never certain, but he specifies that he who is *impetuoso* has more of a chance of succeeding than he who is *respettivo*. This certainly does not mean that man has at his disposal a form of knowledge that guarantees he will achieve his ends; nor does it mean that he has been given the faculty to reduce every situation down to physical data, to the data of a problem whose solution would depend upon a correct calculation of the means. Machiavelli is really taking the side of risky initiative against calculation. If one wants to understand him, one must recall his critique of the "*sages of our time,* who have in their mouths from morning until evening: *Take advantage of the passage of time,*"[24] that is to say, the conservatives tethered to their alleged science of politics, impotent to understand that "time chases everything before itself" and can bring with itself good mixed with evil and evil mixed with good.[25] One must also recall the admiration he bears for Cesare Borgia and for the boldness of his undertaking.

My second remark, which again the example of Borgia supports—and which is confirmed by his reflections on the inconveniences of age in the preface to the second book of the *Discourses*—bears upon Machiavelli's confidence in youth. Very young indeed was the conqueror of Romagna; very young, too, was Lorenzo de' Medici, to whom the *Prince* is dedicated; and again, very young were most of the Roman heroes whom the Roman Republic did not hesitate to entrust with tasks of the highest importance. There is no doubt that the desire for new things and the disrespect for traditions relate to those who have not yet given up on the possible and still dream of being fortune's chosen ones. Machiavelli notes that fortune is fickle whereas men remain stubborn. This is a conviction he counts on several times, although he happens to recognize that men are changing too.

Now, the character of young people seems to him to have not yet become entirely petrified under the weight of habit. He goes so far as to say of his new prince that "he must have an understanding ready to turn according to how the winds of fortune and variations of things command him and . . . not to move away from the good if he can but know how to enter into evil, if it is necessary."[26]

How could one grant a greater role to the event, to the incessant mobility of things in the world, to the ever renewed test of complexity? Knowledge of necessity proves to be in part indissociable from the exigency that one interpret what is produced *here and now,* in constellations of unwanted facts that call for an invention of action. Nonetheless, let us not allow ourselves to be guided by a single image. In the very same chapter we had already, after Strauss, mentioned, one finds another image, one familiar to the humanists and already exploited by Leon Battista Alberti, that of Fortune as a wild river. Opposing those who deny "our free will," Machiavelli reckons that "it may be true that fortune is mistress of one half of our actions, but that, *etiam,* even so, she leaves us to control the other half, or thereabouts."[27] He then compares fortune to a river that, lacking a barrier to contain its course, periodically ravages everything in its path. "The same thing happens with fortune: She demonstrates her power where no force [*virtù*] at all is lined up to resist her."[28] This is what Italy's situation appears to be: in contrast to Germany, Spain, and France, it is the theater of many upheavals. "And what I have said is enough, I believe, to answer the general question of how far one can resist fortune," Machiavelli then notes.[29]

Surely he is here confiding a thought that governs his analyses of the exploits or errors of Cesare Borgia as much as of the wisdom of the great founders. *Virtù* consists in foreseeing, in forging institutions that resist adversity. But let us not conclude from this that man can eliminate Fortune. Moreover, one must heed the first words of the chapter. Machiavelli is combating those who think that the affairs of this world are governed by God and by Fortune and conclude therefrom that the wisdom of men has no power to rectify them. He gleefully derides those who, steeped in their wisdom, do not know that "time chases everything before itself," just as much as he condemns those who abdicate their political responsibility by invoking the secret designs of Providence or Fortune.[30]

What target is he aiming at when he speaks of fortune and of *virtù* in one place or another? This question has to remain always in our minds. The sole passage that seems to me to be liable to justify Strauss's thesis is located in chapter 6 of the *Prince,* where the author cites the *very great examples of the founders:* Moses, Cyrus, Romulus, Theseus, and a few others like them. Machiavelli declares there that "if you look at their deeds and their lives, you will find that they were dependent on Fortune only for their first opportunity. They seized their chance to make of it what they wanted."[31] Now, in this instance once again there is room for scrutinizing the context. Concerning those founders whom Machiavelli deems admirable, he specifies that no one can dream of equaling them. In giving them as examples, he acts in the manner of "an experienced archer, who, trying to hit someone at a distance and knowing the range [virtù] of his bow, aims at a point above his target, not so his arrow will strike the point he is aiming at, but so, by aiming high, he can reach his objective."[32] The reader is thus being warned that we no longer find ourselves on the terrain of the verità effetuale. Moreover, Machiavelli waxes ironic and irreverent about Moses in such a way that the surest lesson of the chapter seems to lie in the condemnation of unarmed prophets. Savonarola provides the cheerless model to which one faction of Florentines still remained attached.

In a parallel vein, in his Discourses (2.1), Machiavelli forcefully contests the idea that fortune, more than virtù, might have contributed to Rome's greatness. He lines up against the opinion of Plutarch as well as the opinion that Livy also seems to have supported. But his argument concerns only the military institutions of Rome. What is therefore essential for him to demonstrate is the superiority of a republic whose existence rests on the force of the people in arms. Nothing is said there that goes beyond this thesis. It is accompanied, in the following chapter (2.2), by a picture of the ravages inflicted upon Italy by Rome, of Rome's destruction of all free regimes, notably that of the Etruscans, the ancient Tuscans whose memory is dear to the Florentines. Let us note in passing that the idealization of Rome is put to a rough test. The author's subsequent return to the powers of fortune (2.29 and 2.30) persuades us that he conceives of these powers as he did in the Prince and even extends their range: "I assert once again . . . that men may second their fortune, but cannot oppose it; that they may weave its warp, but cannot break it. Yet they should never give up."[33]

Machiavelli uses another sort of language in the first book of the Discourses when he discusses the causes of the Roman Republic's greatness. Let us point out first that in the first chapter he inquires as to where the best sites are for implanting a city. It is then that he speaks of necessity. The choice of barren sites seems at first preferable "since men work either of necessity or by choice, and since there is found to be greater virtue where choice has less to say to it."[34] But he endeavors to refute this opinion right away. That kind of establishment would in effect be good if men were content with what they possessed and didn't have a desire to command others. Now, that is not the case. The inhabitants of a new city are therefore exposed to possible aggressions from their neighbors; it is thus better to choose a fertile country that offers the means to gain strength. The danger, it is true, then comes from within; the consequence of the site's advantages is to favor the increase of wealth and, in its train, idleness as well as softness of souls. Machiavelli's response is that it is up to the laws to constrain the inhabitants to recognize necessity. In other terms, enlightened necessity is the kind fittingly imposed upon men in order to make them forgo the licence to which they would of their own accord be disposed to abandon themselves. The constraint of law is greater than "natural" constraints.

Chapter 2, clearly inspired by Polybius, takes note of the distinction between six forms of government, three of which are good with the three others being flawed, and relates the episodes of the initial settlement of the earth. Let us retain only the following two indications: the first is that Rome, in contrast to other cities, notably Sparta, did not benefit at its outset from the best laws but instead had them owing to chance and received them in the wake of events, at several times; the second indication, more specific than the first, is that the *desunione* that reigned between the Senate and the people operated in its favor, something that the law had not foreseen. Following Polybius, or feigning to follow him, Machiavelli suggests that a regime was thus instituted at Rome that combined the virtues of the three good forms of government (royalty, aristocracy, popular government).

Let us now come to the third chapter. There one finds the initial theme reformulated in the following terms: "Men never do good unless necessity drives them to do it; but as soon as they have the choice to commit evil with impunity, turbulence and disorder become everywhere rampant." [35] The author adds: "Hence it is said that hunger and poverty (*pero si dice*) make men industrious, and that laws make them good." [36] Nonetheless, what is said does not coincide with what Machiavelli wishes to make understood. His final considerations, which might provide support for Strauss's interpretation, are in effect justified by the spectacle offered by Rome after the death of the Tarquins. The nobles feared the might of the Tarquins and thus they remained quiet. After the Tarquins were gone, "they [the nobles] began to vomit forth against the plebs the poison hid in their hearts and to oppress them in every way they could." [37]

The path Machiavelli is following now becomes clear. He gives certain statements a general import that is in conformity, he claims, with a commonly held opinion. For example, he declares at the beginning of the third chapter that "all writers on politics have pointed out . . . that whoever wants to found a State and give it laws has to take for granted that all men are wicked and that they will always give vent to the malignity that is in their minds when opportunity offers." [38] Then, he makes a distinction between the great men and the people. So long as the former have to fear the might of a tyrant, they "seemed to have set aside their pride, to have become imbued with the same spirit as the populace";[39] as soon as they are freed from this fear, they give free reign to their wickedness. A tyrant governs arbitrarily. He is not the repository of the law. Everyone bows before him, so that he makes a semblance of equality reign. But one should not trust in appearances. Law is required as soon as the great let loose the ambition they previously had to hide.

Are all men wicked or are they not? Is human nature in itself bad? Such questions hardly matter to Machiavelli. And if one insists on posing them, one will run up against contradictory statements that in fact acquire their meaning only once they are put back into context. In the *Prince*, the author declares: "For of men one can, in general, say this: They are ungrateful, fickle, deceptive and deceiving, avoiders of danger, eager to gain. As long as you serve their interests, they are devoted to you"; on the other hand, when danger approaches, "they steal away."[40] His desire, then, is to show that the prince will be lost if his primary concern is to make himself loved (chapter 17). Previously, however, in chapter 9, when he wanted to convince the new prince that he ought not to disarm the people, his advice was entirely different: he says in substance that, if the prince knows how to command, to give his subjects courage, and to be a *great-hearted man,* "never will he find the people deserting him."[41] And better still: the conclusion of chapter 10 is that if the prince has been able to make himself not hated at all by his subjects, he will find in them the most firm support during times of calamitous fortune. It matters little that a foreign army is ravaging the territory and that he sees himself at their mercy. "It is in men's nature to feel as obliged by the good they do to others as by the good others do to them."[42]

There is no need to multiply the quotations. The question Machiavelli poses does not bear on human nature but on the nature of the city. But this time his response leaves no doubt: It is the same in the *Prince* (chapter 9) and in the *Discourses* (chapter 4): "There are in every city two humors, that of the people and that of the great men; the people do not want to be commanded, oppressed by the great; the great want to command, to oppress the people."[43] But, more clearly still in the *Discourses* than in the *Prince,* Machiavelli draws a lesson from this assertion: It is only where conflict happens to manifest itself, that is to say, where the people shows itself to be capable of resisting the oppression of the great, that good laws are forged, that the Republic is truly deserving of its name. I have already mentioned the passage where Machiavelli, *in opposition to all historians,* praises the tumults of which Rome was periodically the theater. It is better to believe Machiavelli when he launches into an *as for me, I say,* than when he is exploiting the opinions of others. Indeed, the remark I am mentioning receives a faithful reply in the preface to his *History of Florence:* "No example to my knowledge better proves the strength of our city than that of our dissensions, which would have sufficed to annihilate a greater and more powerful State, whereas Florence seemed always to draw therefrom new strength."[44] It is not by starting from an "idea" of necessity, from an "idea" of *virtù,* from an "idea" of fortune that Machiavelli's analyses are laid out; all these "ideas" that, let us not forget, are conveyed by discourse — or, rather, by the various contradictory discourses that ruled in his time — become operative only once the constitutive division of the city, of every political society, is recognized, only once the problem this division poses is recognized and the responses different types of regimes bring to bear on the problem are examined.

Certainly, Machiavelli's break with the principles of classical philosophy is manifest. Not that Aristotle is unaware of the fact of a universal division: that of the rich and the poor. A citizen, he notes, can be ranked in several categories at once; but he cannot be at once both rich and poor. Machiavelli knows about this division, but it does not seem to him to be primordial. The division by which society fits together is not a de facto division; it is not a division that is the effect of a "natural" necessity arising from a scarcity of goods. It is that of two desires (to command, to oppress; not to be commanded, not to be oppressed), each of which is defined only by the other. From this "truth" one must not draw the conclusion that discord is good in itself. Every political society presupposes a certain amount of concord. But if the latter is attained at the price of having institutions that mask the division of these desires, that forbid the people from satisfying its "humor," concord becomes the sign of a *mutilated* society. I employ this last term expressly, for, under such conditions, a regime can very well prove to be stable over a long run, efficiently ruled by laws; it doesn't permit society to develop everything that it potentially contains.

If one really wants to grant that this is Machiavelli's conviction, how would one judge the fact that he observes the different regimes with an air of neutrality and that his remarks in favor of the Republic testify to a mere *preference?* Against the opinion of most historians and saying it emphatically in Machiavelli's own way, I maintain that he is treating the Republic as a regime that conforms to the nature of the city; this regime is in conformity with political society as defined, always within limits, by a certain mode of constitution (in the largest sense of the term) and under a proper name (that of Romans, Athenians, or Spartans, Florentines, Turks, or French). What does *in conformity with nature* signify? The uses of the word *nature* are varied. For example, when speaking of Louis XII's Italian projects in chapter 3 of the *Prince,* Machiavelli notes that the desire to conquer is "certainly a quite ordinary thing and is according to nature."[45] This assertion seems to reduce nature to the level of impulses. The idea loses all normative meaning. In order to be fully satisfied, the appetite for conquest requires a political art, which alone is liable to ensure the preservation of what is acquired by force; the possession of this art is a sign of the *virtù* of the prince. Here we have what seems to indicate that the *high* is being engendered by the *low*. It is said in the same passage, however, that, in the conquered country, the desire to dominate runs up against the desire of the great men already in place there or else against the people's own desire. The explanation of Louis XII's failures tends to show that he failed because he did not understand the nature of political society, generally speaking, and the particular characteristics of the regime to which the territories he coveted were subject. Implanting oneself in a society subject to a despot or a tyrant is not the same thing, Machiavelli observes, as subduing a people accustomed to obeying a hereditary prince; and neither is confronting a State in which powerful barons dispose of a force of their own, independent of that of the monarch, the same thing as combating a Republic. Returning to the difficulties of conquest in chapter 5, the author judges that these difficulties become most arduous in the very last of these cases. Whence the following judgment: "He who becomes the ruler of a city that is used to living freely and does not destroy it at all, must expect to be destroyed by it."[46] This remark seems cynical only to readers who remain inattentive to Machiavelli's overall design. After having argued from the standpoint of the conquering prince and presented various instances and examples that shed light on the reasons for his failure or his success, he concludes: "In former Republics, there is more life, more hatred, more desire for revenge. The memory of their former freedom gives them no rest and cannot leave them in peace. So, the best thing to do is to demolish them or go and live there oneself."[47]

Thus, even in a work devoted to the government of a prince and addressed to a prince, the superiority of republics is firmly established. In them, we learn, there is more life (*è maggiore vita*) than in any other regime. Now, to what is a city's vitality due? To its attachment to freedom. And what is the distinctive trait of a free city? There, man does not depend upon man; he obeys the law. The Republic is the regime in which the equality of citizens before the law is recognized. So be it; this is an equality in principle. In reality, men are unequal there: the great want to dominate; the people defends itself. Nonetheless, on the basis of equality positive laws are exposed to the effects of social division, that is to say, to conflicts. Sheltered from the established laws, the great seek not only to preserve their wealth and their might but also to acquire more of the same — for, according to Machiavelli, it is highly naive to believe that the fact of possessing inclines one toward moderation; the desire to have is insatiable. The people oppose this desire with its own demands; it wishes to be safe and secure, to benefit from material advantages and especially not to be oppressed. It is only on account of the fear it inspires that the few see themselves constrained to be prudent and that new laws favoring concord may see the light of day.

Machiavelli does not maintain that the law *as such* is the product of men. Truly speaking, the question of the origin of law hardly interests him — any more than that of human nature, or necessity, or virtue in itself — and when he does mention it, he does so in order to take into account theories that for his contemporaries have the force of authority. What matters to him is to bring to light the tie between liberty and law, to show that, in a genuine Republic, men have a hold upon the laws and that their dissensions, far from being destructive of all civil life, are generative thereof. From this perspective, it appears that there is a fundamental opposition between two forms of government: the government of a *single one* — a prince whose power is limited, a tyrant, or a despot — and the Republic.

What then is his intention when he is addressing himself to a prince and fears not to recommend to him ways of governing that would be most profitable to him? He is suggesting that the prince be inspired by the model of the Republic. Let us not be in awe of the word: the Republic can furnish him with a *norm*. This project would be unintelligible if the Republic were good under every circumstance. Now, that is plainly not the case. On one side there exist republics so corrupt that they have no chance of reforming themselves; on another, there exist some that are in such a state of turbulence that the very independence of the city is threatened, so that a quasiroyal authority alone can, in the specific combination of circumstances, guarantee its salvation; on yet another side, there are peoples so accustomed to inequality — to man's subjection of man — that it seems vain to dream of their rallying to the principles of a Republic. In all the cases where law would no longer be anything but a hypocritical reference favoring a hidden form of oppression exercised by a few, either because the law has proved to be wanting or because the very idea of law has never truly been formed, the name of the prince can furnish a substitute that allows one to bring men as a whole back into a state of obedience and to inspire them with a shared feeling of belonging to the city or to the nation.

Certainly, the best ordered monarchy remains different from the Republic, whose essence is to contrast the reign of law — the principle of equality before the law — to the reign of a master, and all of whose institutions are made to prohibit anyone from monopolizing power. But it is possible that a new prince, sufficiently instructed in past and present facts to understand what confers upon the Republic its greatest strength, might create institutions that bear its mark. The sole thing he cannot offer his subjects is free-dom. Moreover, even if he wanted to do so, how could he? Freedom is not granted. The Roman Senate did not make a gift of it to the people. On the other hand, the prince can, all the while remaining in command, avoid the appearance of being an oppressor and therefore avoid making himself hated; he can draw benefit from the security he procures for the little people while keeping a tight reign on the ambition of the great; he can entrust his subjects with the defense of the city instead of disarming them, thus giving them the feeling of almost being citizens; he can feign to act in accordance with the principles of morality and religion, making people believe in his appearance—which is essential, since in such a regime all eyes are fixed upon him and since each depends upon his person and not on the law.

Once again we gauge the distance Machiavelli sets between himself and the political philosophy of the Ancients. If we grant that the Republic is in its very principle the best regime and that it can serve as norm for a prince's government, if we grant even that there is a gap between the Re-public such as it ought to be and all the republics that have ever existed, including the Roman Republic—which, let us not forget, sank into Caesar-ism—it remains no less certain that Machiavelli is abandoning the idea of a harmonious society, one governed by the best, whose constitution would be conceived as a way of warding off the danger of innovations and would proceed from the knowledge of the ultimate ends of man and of the city.

Supposing that Machiavelli does retain the concept of *end,* the latter takes on an entirely new signification. That toward which the city *tends* is the securing of its freedom. The latter is not to be confused with license; or, to employ a more moderate language, it does not consist in the public recogni-tion of the right of each to do as he pleases. Political freedom is understood through its opposite; it is the affirmation of a mode of coexistence, within certain borders, such that no one has authority to decide the affairs of all, that is to say, to occupy the site of power. Public affairs cannot be the af-fair of a single person or of a small number of people. Freedom, posited as end, implies the negation of tyranny, whatever its variants might be. But it implies, too, the negation of every instance of authority that arrogates unto itself the knowledge of what the common good is; that is to say, it implies the negation of philosophy *inasmuch as philosophy claims*—be it by distin-guishing the ideal from the reality—to set the norms of social organization, to conceive what the good life of the city and of the individual in the city is.

In taking into consideration the famous statement according to which it seems "more fitting to follow the *verità effetuale* of the thing than one's imagination," one concludes too quickly that the concern for what is erases the concern for what ought to be. Focusing on the critique of the imagination, one thus neglects a more profound critique that bears on the status of knowledge, not so much that of the legislator — who, it is suggested to us, is, however extraordinary may be the loftiness of his view, guided as a matter of fact by the *veritá effetuale* (using force and proving skillful at exploiting belief) — but, instead, that of the philosopher. Hadn't he reproached him, rather than for being a dreamer, for yielding to the attraction of the omnipotence of thought? Such a doubt does not strike only, or even principally, at Plato's construction in the *Republic,* for that work bears the clear signs of being a logical fiction; it is a doubt that strikes a blow against every representation of a regime that is said to be good in itself, notably the one Aristotle sketches in the final chapters of his *Politics.*

If division is not de facto, if every city, every political society, is laid out in terms of the effects of division, the posture the philosopher adopts in drawing his picture of the good regime arouses suspicion. Cannot one assume that this suspicion is, for Machiavelli, tied to the critique to which Florentine republicanism, the sort of republicanism that seeks its seal of legitimacy in classical political philosophy, gives rise? The fact that this philosophy may be converted into an ideology, or at least that it might be nourishing one, can be explained by a number of events, not the least of which is the birth of a new religion, which itself has arisen out of the formation of the Roman Empire and out of the decay of that empire.

But granting that the intentions of the founders of political philosophy are at present unknown, one cannot dispense with an investigation into the reasons why the principles formulated in previous times lend themselves to a certain type of distortion. Is not this investigation itself philosophical? It is not the course of events that has belied the ancient philosophers' ideal, since they never stopped warning that the instauration of a good regime was either improbable or impossible. It is quite rather the persistence, if not always of this ideal, at least of the notion of a regime that would be approaching it, the *mixed regime,* that prompts one to discover in philosophy itself some "unwanted effects" that are not, however, without causes.

Machiavelli's audacity, his will to "follow the *veritá effetuale,*" can best be spotted, we think, in his conception of social division and his conception of political freedom. Why are these indissociable? At its most profound, this division is, let us repeat, that between two desires, that of commanding, of oppressing, and that of not being commanded, of not being oppressed. In a sense, the second desire, that of the people, is a desire for freedom. This conviction is reinforced by reading chapter 5 of the *Discourses,* where Machiavelli asks himself: "Into whose hands is it best to place the guardianship of liberty," those of the great men or those of the people?[48] In the course of this argument, Machiavelli establishes that the guardianship of anything should be placed in the hands of those who are less desirous of violating it. And unquestionably, if we ask what it is the nobility are after and what it is the common people are after, it will be seen that of the two orders of citizens there is in the former a great desire to dominate and in the latter merely the desire not to be dominated. Consequently, the latter will be more keen on liberty.[49]

Nevertheless, does it suffice to consider the character of *two orders of citizens,* or must one consider the character of the city? At this point, the argument forks off. The author makes a distinction between the cities whose main goal is to preserve themselves and those whose main goal is to extend themselves. Once again, he seems to adopt the position of a neutral observer. Because they belonged to the first category, Sparta and Venice limited to a small number of citizens the right to participate in public affairs; Rome, in contrast, was able to satisfy its appetites for conquest only by seeking the support of the people. Let us not follow this trail—which, moreover, contrary to a widespread interpretation, doesn't lead to the statement that imperatives of power alone decide the role the people are to play in the service of freedom. Rome is more lively than Sparta, Florence more lively than Venice. Finally, at the end of chapter 6, Machiavelli judges that "one should take for a model Rome rather than the other republics."[50] He no longer is balancing between the advantages and inconveniences of two forms of society: "To find," he says, "a middle way between these two forms I do not think possible."[51] The divisions that exist between the Senate and the people therefore prove to be at the origin of the Republic's greatness.

It seems to me more important, however, to return to the idea that one cannot stick to the character of two different orders of citizens if one wants to understand in what political freedom consists. Indeed, the desire of the people, which is more reliable than that of the dominant stratum, only endures to stand in opposition to the contrary desire; the best Republic not only does not succeed in eliminating, but doesn't even tend to eliminate, command, which always harbors oppression. Where free institutions blossom forth, the great remain; they pursue their own objectives: wealth, power, honors. In their own way, they are free; their appetites nevertheless are contained; law restrains them.

On the other hand, however obstinate may be the people's desire not to be commanded, it never attains its goal. The people cannot become free in the sense that being free would presuppose deliverance [*affranchissement*] from all domination. For us readers, who have known the extraordinary enterprise that, under the name of Communism, gave itself for its end the complete emancipation of the people, Machiavelli's lesson is fully confirmed by History. From the destruction of a dominant class arose not a homogeneous society but a new figure of social division. The latter is not, let us observe, a de facto division; this is why the supposed triumph of the people is accompanied by a new split between a small number who desire to command, to oppress, to possess, and the others. The Republic and its free institutions live only in the gap between the two desires. The fecundity of the law depends on the intensity of their opposition, and, since there is no doubt that the desire of the great, if they encounter no obstacle, does not cease to grow, the intensity of the opposition depends on the vigor of the people's resistance.

I have just recalled the argument that the decision to launch into a policy of conquest didn't suffice to account for the role the people had played in building institutions favoring freedom. Indeed, the fact that Machiavelli erects Rome as a model doesn't mean that he is calling upon the Florentines to launch undertakings comparable to those of the Romans. The main thing is that the idea of the citizen-soldier is to be preserved, and that idea presupposes that those who command understand that the Republic's survival requires the extension of political rights. Nonetheless, it is true that his argument is guided by the conviction that free institutions are necessarily associated with military institutions, which serve either to extend one's territory or to defend it.

In the light of the history of modern democracies, this conviction might find confirmation in a reflection upon some facts that are of another order. Where the desire for power is invested in industrial conquest, it tends to bring about the reign of a new, unbridled form of oppression. Under cover of equality before the law, a split between the great and the many is reproduced. It is not because the great succeed in satisfying their ambition that they moderate themselves and give up the practices characteristic of "unfettered capitalism [*capitalisme sauvage*]." It is quite rather because they run up against the resistance of those of whom they have need in order to preserve and to extend their field of profits. It is also because the principles of political society obtain for the latter the possibility of winning recognition for what they have discovered to be their rights.

The best republic yields no *solution* to the political problem. (Let us understand *the best republic* as the one whose institutions are not condemned to become fixed and settled, with everything serving to prop up an oligarchy; it is the one in which there is "the most life.") It distinguishes itself, rather, by its tacit abandonment of the idea of a solution, by the welcome it extends to division and, under the effect of the latter, to change.

In the same stroke, it is distinguished also by the chances it offers for action. In the other forms of government, there is only one principal actor or a small number of actors. In tyranny, the prince holds the monopoly on action, even though the conspirator may enter on the scene. In oligarchy, the game is more open; its members keep an eye upon one another and may seek to take precedence one over another. In a republic of the Roman type, by way of contrast, a considerable number of citizens are led, in the course of time, to assume responsibilities and to takes initiatives whose effects are decisive for the fate of the regime. The conduct of each one among them, the motives for his conduct, and the results he obtains all call for interpretation and judgment: there is debate about them.

Machiavelli, who, living in a republic, experienced conflicts that mobilized multiple actors and that were also in one way or another activated by these actors, finds in the Roman Republic a sort of laboratory that allows him to detect—always subject to the examination of particular situations—an ample variety of schemes of action. Men concerned with obeying the law make decisions that, under this or that set of circumstances and without knowing it, run the greatest risks for the city. Others, who violate an order of the Senate, manifest thereby an exemplary *virtù,* and their disobedience produces the most happy effects. Still others try to mount a plot against the regime, but their procedures, which would have been effective under different conditions, are catastrophic for them. And mildness or brutality in one's command of the situation proves to be, depending upon the moment, either good or disastrous.

Whence are drawn some conclusions that are general in import but that take into account, each time, the nature of the situation. Certainly, the boundaries of the inquiry are not limited to Rome. Thus, Hannibal's conduct is no less instructive than that of Scipio precisely because their methods and the men over whom their authority was exercised are different. Epaminondas, for his part, offers the example of a most audacious sort of action, guided as it was by the knowledge of historians and philosophers and making its end the liberation of a people. But clearly the Republic prompts reflection upon action because, in the Republic, the experience of time is not occulted. Taken in itself, time doesn't allow itself to be apprehended, the writer suggests, either under the heading of corruption or under that of progress.

In chapter 6 of the *Discourses*—just before concluding that the best model is Rome and that its divisions were beneficial to it—he observes: "All human affairs are in movement and cannot stand still"; and, he adds, the movement itself rises or falls.[52] That is why the best Republic is superior to all other regimes: it lends itself to movement. In the test of instability, it succeeds in obtaining the greatest stability. But in addition, by rendering palpable the indetermination connected with every human establishment, it allows one to discover the role of the individual, a capacity to judge and to act that, whatever may be the motives or motivations, goes beyond the framework of institutions, that of the laws or that of custom.

Thus, when the reader stops at the analyses presented in the *Prince,* they seem to him to testify to the viewpoint of a pure observer detached from his object. Not only does the reader thereby neglect the fact that the *Discourses* grant a still greater role to the study of the most diverse and even contradictory forms of conduct, but he fails to comprehend that only a republican is open to indicating the place of the Subject, the Subject's "freedom," and to investigating action as such. Where monarchy exists by divine right or where peoples have become habituated to submitting themselves to a few whose domination is perceived as natural, it is always possible to complain of the conduct of the master or masters, but power seems organically bound to the society. In contrast, as soon as parties face off against each other, the plurality of possible choices excites one's interest and the idea of fatality stands aside.

Machiavelli is far from yielding to the vertigo of a freedom of action that would open up the Subject, at every moment and in every place, to the entire field of possibilities. He maintains that the political actor, the citizen determined to defend the common good, or the conspirator, or even the prince who is capable of launching into the excessive [*démesurée*] undertaking of creating an entirely new regime, cannot fail to follow the *veritá effetuale,* as we have said, if he wants to succeed. Institutions, he judges, tend to fashion the character of a people as well as of its leaders. But, as Aristotle already observed, they do not sprout up like plants, nor do they reproduce themselves as such. Not only do they bear the imprint of the hand of man at their origin, but they require, in order to endure, the action of individuals — be that action perverted to the point that it induces them to work toward their own servitude. The analysis of the forms of political society therefore leads to the examination of the forms of action, and vice versa. There are two poles of experience and two poles of knowledge, and the gap is irreducible. Or, to say it in a modern language: Reflection on the political and reflection on politics are at once distinct and intertwined.

Everything happens, nevertheless, as if for many people the political was noble and politics trivial. One isn't disturbed to see Aristotle asking by what means a tyranny might succeed in preserving itself, for this search for the appropriate means is situated within a work designed to determine the characteristics of various political regimes as well as of the best one possible. But one becomes indignant at the fact that Machiavelli is studying the most varied actions, including the most repugnant ones, and might want to understand what they reveal about the desire of those who practice them, about their ability to gauge the effects of their decision, or about the humors of the people, given a certain social state, a certain combination of circumstances, and a certain configuration of forces. No one, nonetheless, is scandalized when a historian enumerates the errors committed by Hitler in the course of his career—notably that of having attacked Russia—or else the errors committed by Stalin—notably that of having had faith in his alliance with Hitler. The historian is not, for all that, accused of defending Nazism or Stalinism. In contrast, Machiavelli is deemed diabolical for having laid out the broadest range of figures of political action. Why is it, then? With a dazzling agility—thought itself must lend itself to movement, must always be in movement—he detects what, in one place or another, makes sense or does not make sense. What, in our day, is the worst thing for democracy, in the view of those who love it? That its leaders are ambitious, eager to defend their particular interests, or else that they act like imbeciles? The question, to be truthful, is posed not only by the philosopher; it is often posed by the ordinary citizen—whose point of view is so dear to Leo Strauss. Machiavelli does not place all regimes on the same level; still less does he suggest that terror is one means of government like another. He asks himself under what conditions it can be exercised successfully, taking into account the ends being sought.

I see only one writer who, without naming him and without generalizing his process, has followed Machiavelli along this path: Edgar Quinet. In his *Révolution,* Quinet doesn't fear to demonstrate that the terrorists didn't understand in 1793 what the Terror was, that they mistook the era to which they belonged, for theirs doomed them to failure. Nor does he fear to compose a model of "true terror," as it was practiced in the past in Venice or under the Roman Empire. Quinet got himself insulted for the effort. He thought he had to defend himself in the second edition of his book, explaining the function of his argument and protesting his own attachment to the spirit of tolerance. Other times . . . .

I unhesitatingly believe that, given the opportunity, Machiavelli would not have wanted to justify himself. He wrote for those who would have wanted to understand him and didn't imagine convincing his enemies. Moreover, he combined the desire for knowledge with a taste for humor. That was enough to array against him, across the centuries, a great number of his readers and to lead astray others who wished to make of him a "friend of the people." Nietzsche's judgment on the author of the *Prince* hit the mark. In a passage quite unkind to German philosophers, he wrote (*Beyond Good and Evil* §28):

How could the German language, even in the prose of a Lessing, imitate the *tempo* of Machiavelli, who in his *Principe* [*The Prince*] lets us breathe the dry, refined air of Florence and cannot help presenting the most serious matters in a boisterous *allegrissimo,* perhaps not without a malicious artistic sense of the contrast he risks—long, difficult, hard, dangerous thoughts and the *tempo* of the gallop and the very best, most capricious humor?"[53]

Notes

"Machiavel et la *veritá effetuale*" was originally published in *Écrire,* 141–79.

1   Niccolò Machiavelli, preface to Book 1 of *The Discourses,* ed. and intro. Bernard Crick, trans. Leslie J. Walker (London: Penguin, 1970, 1983): 98. [T/E: Lefort notes: "All texts cited are drawn from the Pléiade edition, *Machiavel, œuvres complètes* (Paris: Gallimard, 1978). The indication of chapter numbers seemed sufficient. I have only on occasion retranslated a phrase or restored words in fidelity to the original." Adding book and chapter references (as well as page numbers in parenthesis), I have generally followed the Walker translation but have deviated therefrom when it differed significantly from the version Lefort offers.]

2   Ibid.

3   Ibid.

4   Ibid.

5   Ibid., (98–99).

6   Ibid., 1.4 (113).

7   Ibid., (114–15).

8   Felix Gilbert, "Florentine Political Assumptions in the Period of Savonarola and Soderini," *Journal of the Warburg and Courtauld Institutes* 20 (1957): 187–214.

9   Niccolò Machiavelli, *The Prince,* ed. and trans. David Wootton (Indianapolis: Hackett, 1995), 3 (11). [T/E: Again, where Lefort cites Gallimard's French translation, sometimes altering it, I cite the English translation, modifying it when necessary, as here, to make it conform to the version Lefort offers.]

10 Ibid.

11 Nicolai Rubinstein, "The Beginning of Political Thought in Florence: A Study in Mediaeval Historiography," *Journal of the Warburg and Courtauld Institutes* 5 (1942): 198–227.

12 Hans Baron, *The Crisis of Early Italian Renaissance: Civic Humanism and Republican Liberty in an Age of Classicism and Tyranny* (Princeton: Princeton University Press, 1955).

13 Lauro Martines, *The Social World of the Florentine Humanists* (London: Routledge and Kegan Paul, 1963).

14 *Discourses,* 3.1 (389).

15 Leo Strauss, "The Three Waves of Modernity," *Political Philosophy: Six Essays* (Indianapolis: Pegasus, 1975), 84.

16 Ibid.

17 *The Prince,* 15 (47–48).

18 Strauss, "The Three Waves," 87.

19 Leo Strauss, *Thoughts on Machiavelli* (Glencoe, Ill.: The Free Press, 1958).

20 Claude Lefort, *Le travail de l'œuvre* (Paris: Gallimard, 1972, 1986).

21 Strauss, "The Three Waves," 85.

22 Ibid.

23 *The Prince,* 24 (76–77).

24 Ibid., 3 (11).

25 Ibid. [T/E: translation altered].

26 Ibid., 18 (55) [T/E: translation altered].

27 *The Prince,* 25 (74).

28 Ibid., 25 (75).

29 Ibid.

30 Ibid., 25 (74).

31 Ibid., 6 (19).

32 Ibid., 6 (18).

33 *Discourses,* 2.29 (372).

34 Ibid., 1.1 (102).

35 Ibid., 1.3 (112).

36 Ibid.

37 Ibid.

38 Ibid., 1.3 (111–12).

39 Ibid., 1.3 (112).

40 *The Prince,* 17 (52).

41 Ibid., 9 (33).

42 Ibid., 10 (35).

43 *The Prince,* 9 (31); cf. *Discourses,* 1.4 (113).

44 Machiavelli, *Florentine Histories,* trans. Laura F. Banfield and Harvey C. Mansfield (Princeton: Princeton University Press, 1988), 7 [T/E: translation altered].

45 *The Prince,* 3 (14).

46 Ibid., 5 (17).

47 Ibid., 5 (18).

48 *Discourses,* 1:5 (115).

49 Ibid., 1.5 (116).

50 Ibid., 1.6 (123).

51 Ibid.

52 Ibid.

53 Friedrich Nietzsche, *Beyond Good and Evil: Prelude to a Philosophy of the Future,* trans. Walter Kaufmann (New York: Random House, 1966; New York: Vintage, 1989), 41, §28.

The Idea of Humanity and the Project of Universal Peace

I N CONTEMPORARY discourse, the affirmation of the *absolute value* of peace tends to serve as the substitute for the ideal of universal peace, which used to be formulated in full. If I am not mistaken, this new formula bears the mark of a new exigency: How is one to maintain the philosophical task of trying to provide a foundation for the idea of peace —which doesn't relate merely to circumstantial considerations (however urgent these may be, since they relate to our knowledge of the danger a new world war would entail for entire populations)—without drifting off into utopia, that is to say, without falling back into the illusions that have nourished projects of perpetual peace? Nevertheless, some of the difficulties to which the present reflection exposes us can be glimpsed in the definition of peace as an absolute value. Furthermore, it seems to me worthwhile to examine it briefly in order to open up for me a path.

Taken in its philosophical acceptation, the concept of *value* pertains to a modern way of thinking. One would search in vain for a trace of it in pre-nineteenth-century philosophy. It implies reference to a subject that, in the absence of an extrinsic guarantee, draws from itself the principle for discriminating between the desirable and the undesirable, the good and the bad, the just and the unjust, the beautiful and the ugly. One is undoubtedly tempted to discover in Kant's doctrine, and the division it establishes between theoretical reason and practical reason, the premises for the modern conception of value. Yet one must agree that it doesn't have a place there, since the Kantian subject finds in its very will the sign of an unconditioned foundation, even as the latter eludes our knowledge. Generally speaking, so long as the idea of a standard of human conduct is affirmed in reference to nature, reason, or God, the notion of value couldn't take on any meaning.

Let us add that it is also alien to philosophies of history, be they of the Hegelian or Marxist type. Whether history might be conceived as the advent of spirit to its own fullness or as the fulfillment of man's social calling at the end of a path of contradictions that are engendered by technological development [*le développement de la technique*] and class divisions, in one case as in the other the positing of knowledge as knowledge emerging from an effectively real process of which it holds the key excludes the arbitrary will of the subject.

It is rather toward Nietzsche that one should turn in order to shed some light on this new disposition to think in terms of value, for his work implies a systematic destruction of every standard. But my purpose here not being to offer a historical account of the concept of value, I shall limit myself to emphasizing that this concept begins to spread during the nineteenth century and spreads much more broadly in the twentieth century, both in philosophy and in the human sciences. It serves to buttress a new conception of existence—one in which experience, within its limits, cannot help but put both sense and non-sense to the test (this conception will belatedly receive the name of existentialism). Second, it will come to provide support for a theory of the historical relativity of visions of the world (which will be named historicism). In the third place, it will undergird a theory of the irreducible plurality of cultures (which culminates in cultural anthropology).

Clearly, no one has better responded to this threefold inspiration—existential, historicist-leaning, and sociologically inclined—than Max Weber, even though the richness of his research goes to show very well that he was sometimes able to escape therefrom. Weber pushed relativism the furthest under all its forms, simultaneously attributing the arbitrariness of values, one after another, to the *individual*—notably to the historian who constructs his object of knowledge on the basis of a reality deemed to be, in itself, formless, a "pure miscellany"; to *each epoch,* which constitutes a unique perspective for thought and action; and to *each culture,* which draws from its own depths the generative symbols of an experience of the visible and the invisible. As a consequence, his studies bear the mark of an obstinate concern to deny any universal criterion for good and evil, the just and the unjust, and even the true and the false—this distinction being valid only upon the condition that it is subordinated to the construction of the object of knowledge, about which we have just said that this construction can be effectuated only in terms of the values of the subject. If I think it's worthwhile mentioning Weber, that is because, while this thinker had, as a man, nothing of the warmonger about him, he nevertheless found in the diversity of values (maintained, as they are, *absolutely* by men, peoples, or cultures) the motive for perpetual war. Humanity would be, to hear him tell it, doomed to tear itself apart because it would be, according to his celebrated formula, the theater for an "inexpiable war of the gods."

If one consults the works of a number of contemporary historians and anthropologists, one can glimpse the fact that Weber's pantragicism has lost its attraction. But it has been lost, unfortunately, to the benefit of a vague relativism that excludes reflection on principles as much as on its own practical consequences. It has long been apparent to me that, outside scholarly circles, this relativism has been giving sustenance to a vulgar discourse in which every opinion, every belief, every judgment is good—provided that they testify to a genuine adherence on the part of those who state them as their values. This discourse can be summarized in the slogan "To each his values."

Now, just as much as respect for the other's identity or the critique of egocentrism, of ethnocentrism—and particularly of Eurocentrism—can be fully justified, and tolerance, consequently, can be erected into a principle, so an unbridled relativism turns out to confer a legitimacy upon all sorts of impostures and, more precisely, upon all systems of oppression that, under cover of an ethic placed in the service of the purity of a race, the integrity of a nation, or the instauration of a classless society, goes around hounding individuals and groups whose characteristics are judged not to be in conformity with the right model. It is trite, no doubt, but always of the essence to recall that tolerance finds its limit in aggressive intolerance of the other. The critique of all forms of totalitarianism would be futile if it were reduced to the statement of a de facto preference for a regime based on liberties. The meaning of the relative does not erase, but rather carries within it, a universal exigency. The Universal Declaration of Human Rights offers powerful testimony to this fundamental conjunction, which is surely difficult to assume but whose parts cannot cancel each other out.

Thus, the idea of peace as absolute value seems to me to go to the heart of the philosophical questions of our time. The word *value* indicates that it is impossible to rely any longer on a guarantor recognized by all (nature, reason, God, History); it indicates a situation in which all figures of transcendence have become blurred. Yet, posited as absolute, the value of peace requires a foundation that is removed from every relativist interpretation. Here then might be our task for reflection: to try to direct our investigation toward this foundation, scrutinizing the signs that allow us to glimpse it, but without evading our situation here and now, which summons us, as a matter of fact, not to rely any longer on the old certainties—certainties that, moreover, have painfully collided against the hard facts [*l'épreuve des faits*].

Although I am fully aware of how futile it can be to make rapid incursions into theories that saw the light of day in a distant past, I am equally certain that, in order to give proper recognition to their originality, one would have to revive, along with them, the intellectual debates out of which they arose and, still more than that, lay out the horizons of the world that was theirs. I would nevertheless venture to mention straight off a work that, I believe, was the first to formulate in secular terms, in political terms, the idea of peace—certainly not as absolute value (the concept didn't yet exist) but as something good for all men. I am talking about Dante's *De Monarchia*. In an age when Florence, and Italy in general, was the theater of incessant conflicts among a multiplicity of factions, Dante undertook to demonstrate the need to instaurate perpetual peace with the help of the establishment of a universal monarchy.

This work has often been reduced to an episode in a discussion, which ran for centuries, about how to evaluate the emperor's and the pope's respective claims to embody divine authority in the temporal order. Dante, it is said, wanted only to mobilize the resources of theology and Greek (basically Aristotelian) philosophy to aid the emperor in putting forth his claims. There is no point in entering into an analysis of this polemic and of the circumstances within which Dante intervened by writing his text. Our interest does not lie there. What matters to us is his attempt to tie the idea of peace to that of humanity or, to say it better, to the idea of the advent and self-revelation of a humanity that had previously developed in dispersion, in ignorance of its identity as a unique body of which each people figures as a member.

Dante is the thinker who both forges the theory of a worldwide form of domination and, at the same time, brings out the notion of a humanity that, through the multiplicity of human establishments, is *one*. This constitutes a strange conjunction between the dream of empire and the foundation of humanism, certainly. If I had the time, I would show what fortune *De Monarchia* experienced later on, the attraction it exerted over the minds of Charles v in Spain, Elizabeth i in England, Henry iii, Henry iv, and Francis i in France, and how, under its inspiration, the phantasm of imperialism and that of a monarchical mission in the service of humanity came to be articulated. But let us stick to the essential: Humanity will know itself as one when it submits to a single authority; it will gain the representation of its own body when the body of its sovereign will deliver to it, as in a mirror, the image of the One.

Such is Dante's argument. It has, of course, a theological basis. The image of the One is that of God. Man has been created in His likeness. There isn't anything here that wouldn't conform to the teachings of the Scriptures. But what is true of the finite creature is also for Dante true of the entirety of men taken over the whole extent of the earth and through successive generations. Let us quote just one brief passage. After having recalled that it has been said, "Let us make man in our image and after our likeness" (Genesis 1.26), and then observed that "the whole universe is nothing but a kind of imprint of the divine goodness," the philosopher adds:

> Therefore, mankind exists at its best when it resembles God as much as it can. But mankind resembles God most when it is most unified, for the true ground of unity exists in Him alone, as is written: "Hear, O Israel, the Lord thy God is one" [Deuteronomy 6.4]. But mankind is then most one when it is unified into a single whole; which is possible only when it submits wholly to a single government.[1]

We noted that the body of the monarch delivers to humanity the image of its unity. It gives rise to this image inasmuch as it is itself God's visible representative. As Ernst Kantorowicz has rightly remarked, Dante's originality can be spotted very clearly in this definition of man, which combines the criterion of intension with that of extension. Man is the human individual and humankind. Now, one should not assume that the domination Dante is imagining implies the uniformity of humankind. He recognizes the singularity of each body: the body of the individual, of the family, of the town, of the city, and of the kingdom. Basing himself on Aristotle, he maintains that each one has its own finality, just like the thumb, the hand, the arm, and the whole man, but they are all ordered for an ultimate, universal end: humankind.

The idea of the mystical body and that of the organic body are brought together to serve the representation of a humanity in harmony with itself, thereby discovering the supreme good, peace. What seems to us no less remarkable, however, is the explanation Dante gives of humanity's embryonic development until his time. In fact, far from presenting universal monarchy as a solution that would have awaited discovery by men, whose error in former times would have been to have lived in ignorance of one another and in conflict, he presents this monarchy as arising from a series of combats that are apparently governed by desire for conquest on the part of the strongest but that are secretly guided by Providence, which made men discover what is ultimately at stake: their unity. The theorist of peace produces peace out of war. It is at the end of a series of *duels* in which the Assyrians, the Egyptians, the Persians, the Macedonians, and, finally, the Romans triumph, one after another, that, thanks to the last of these, one discovers, under the reign of Augustus, the image of a world embracing virtually all men and that Christ can descend upon earth to incarnate man as such.

Let us linger over this rapid evocation, in which it is troubling to glimpse the first signs of a Hegelianism. I would like to accompany it with two commentaries. In the first place, Dante's borrowings from Aristotle (from the *Politics* and from the *Nichomachean Ethics*) only serve to highlight more clearly his break with classical political philosophy. The latter was attached, as one knows, to the representation of a historical cycle; it did not concern itself with imagining the conditions for overcoming war, and it was unaware, beyond the borders of the city, of the existence of humanity as such. These three characteristics, it seems, are interconnected. Without a doubt, the nature of man was supposed to maintain a close affinity with that of the city. But the very notion of nature implied the delimitation of a political body distant from other bodies and the permanence of the image of the foreigner as potential or actual enemy. In fact, if, leaving aside the theses of the philosophers, we observe the style of the wars the Athenians conducted, not against barbarous attackers but against inoffensive Greek cities, it very well must be agreed that they did not hesitate to champion cynically the right of the strongest without fear of incurring the disapproval of other peoples. Thucydides left us a memorable account of their conduct in his narrative of the conquest of Melos. In contrast, Dante inaugurates a reflection that situates the whole political community within the horizons of a humanity in embryo, and, in the same stroke, he makes of the search for peace *the* goal par excellence. In the second place, the relationship he establishes between the imperial monarchy and peace lets one glimpse (however admirable and new may be his conception of a world that, while diversified, is capable of recognizing itself as the same in space and in time) what dangerous backing the humanist project can provide for the ambitions of a great power when it gives itself for its objective a universe delivered from all antagonism.

Whoever considers the efforts accomplished by great jurists since the sixteenth century to define international law [*un droit des gens*] will be tempted to think that Dante's theory was buried by the rise of nation-States. But perhaps that would not be entirely accurate. These efforts continue to testify to a humanist concern, to a will to conceive and to instaurate balanced relationships among political communities. Indeed, I have already alluded to this phenomenon. The new European powers were not content to appeal to a theory of sovereignty in terms of which the prince, having no one above him, calls himself emperor in his own realm; this prince who claims to represent God in the temporal order, to reign on a *sacred land,* to lead a *chosen people* (see the fine studies of Joseph Strayer) is obsessed with the desire to extend his jurisdiction to the ends of the world. This desire risked changing the nature of war, eliminating the boundaries within which it had, de facto, been contained during feudal times.

The inspiration behind the efforts of the jurists can surely best be recognized in the idea that the spirit of war doesn't have to be so alien to the spirit of peace that, in conducting the one, one wouldn't allow any chance of returning to the other. The works of Hugo Grotius, Samuel von Pufendorf, Jean-Jacques Burlamaqui, and Emmerich de Vattel do not only bear the mark of realism — that is to say, a mode of reasoning that takes as a given the state of war and tends to subject it to a minimum of rules — but they also imply that war doesn't have to destroy the conditions for peace, that States in conflict have to know, amid the conflict, that they will have to recognize each other's independence in the future, as they recognized it formerly. One abandons the idea of perpetual peace, therefore, but one does so precisely because one wants to prevent perpetual war.

In a moment I shall have occasion to return to this point: the great legal tradition supports the project of a necessary legalization of war. But what can be detected to lie at the origin of such a project is the awareness of a common good, different from the good of States. It remains the case that, as soon as the sovereignty of the State was fully recognized, the notion of this common good could no longer be made the support for a consistent articulation of law. The theory that founds the idea of sovereignty really seems to forbid that. This, indeed, is what is entailed in the distinction between the state of nature (in which men live in a state of permanent insecurity) and the civil state (in which, thanks to a contract with one of them or to a dual contract of union and submission, someone finds himself erected into a sovereign). This distinction, I say, is such that the State appears with two different faces: instigator or guarantor of the law vis-à-vis its own members and capable, like a great individual, of enjoying vis-à-vis other States a natural independence. To what higher legislative authority might it submit itself, and against what legal limits might its will collide in times of war, if it possesses sovereignty? And how could it not possess this sovereignty if this sovereignty coincides with the very formation and the constant maintenance of the civil state?

Exchanging the ideal of peace for the legalization of war would be realistic only upon the condition that one forget that States obey only their own passions or their own interests and that they do not feel compelled to obey any rule that contradicts these. That is pretty much what Rousseau says. His reflections on peace — stimulated by the *Projet de paix perpétuelle* (Project of perpetual peace) worked out by Charles Irénée Castel, the Abbé de Saint-Pierre — are guided by a conception of the state of nature that is radically opposed to Hobbes's view. Unlike the latter, who, forging the fiction of an originary war of all against all, seems to project onto the natural man the traits of man wrought by present-day society, Rousseau denies that the natural man could find in his condition the motive for wanting to destroy his fellow men [*semblables*]. Even assuming that, occasioned by some rivalry in the pursuit of the same object, a conflict might set him against his neighbor, and even assuming one of them is murdered, the state of conflict ceases as soon as the occasion has disappeared. Thus the philosopher adopts the statement that "there is no war between men. There is war only between states."[2] On the other hand, he observes the unfortunateness of a world wherein the independence of which men have been deprived reappears in States and "takes refuge in societies, and these great bodies, delivered over to their own impulses, produce shocks that become more terrible as their masses take precedence over those of individuals."[3]

As he too is concerned with realism, Rousseau takes note of the natural independence of States, judging that they alone are up to the task of putting an end to the state of war. Repudiating the jurists' attempts to guarantee international law, which could bind sovereigns only to the extent that they consent thereto, his argument rests, on the contrary, on the hypothesis that these rivals together become aware of the danger contained in their inability to set a limit on war. Against the illusion of legalizing war, he opposes the vision of a gaping abyss. Security not being guaranteed, any more than conquest, in a world where for each the adversary will always rise up again, the princes are doomed to an endless expenditure of material resources and human energies that they might otherwise master and invest in order to obtain lasting glory.

Whatever the naïveté that to us seems to enter into the project of a confederation that arises from a sudden and simultaneous agreement to abandon power politics, the questions posed by Rousseau have lost none of their current interest. Why, indeed, would the effort to introduce law into war have any chance of success if respect for such law remained subordinate to the pure arbitrary will of the sovereigns? Let us recall, moreover, that Rousseau concluded his writings on the Abbé de Saint-Pierre's *Projet* with a statement that doesn't testify to any excessive hopes on his part: "The only thing that we have assumed about [sovereigns] is that they are both rational enough to perceive what is useful to them and courageous enough to work toward their own happiness. If, despite all this, the project remains unfulfilled, it is not therefore because it is too idealistic; rather, it is because men are insane and because it is a sort of folly to remain wise in the midst of those who are mad."[4] Let us state further that Rousseau's argument could seem more eccentric in his day than we would judge it in ours. In fact, at the heart of his reasoning lies the hypothesis of a mutual extermination of the protagonists. This was a logical possibility, but the state of the technological development of the means of destruction hardly permitted its conversion into a real possibility; present conditions, however, give his thinking an edge that his contemporaries didn't foresee.

Whatever the case may be, and keeping in mind our mention of Dante, it must be agreed that the connection established between the idea of peace and that of humanity takes on here a new meaning. It is in terms of a reflection on humanity, its passage from the state of nature to the state of civilization, that one can gauge the folly of war and the chance of going beyond it. Nonetheless, Rousseau doesn't let one assume that civilized humanity might become a reality in a political body whose members, across space and time, would be so many little bodies; he brushes aside the image of their integration in the One. The plurality of States remains; their association does not imply their subjection to a higher law. They restrict themselves to internalizing, I would dare say, the effects of a natural necessity, which for this reason is converted into a will to mutual recognition. The civilizing process is doubled with a process of humanization that exists not on the order of incorporation but rather on the order of rationalization.

Following a closely related inspiration, Kant's project for *Perpetual Peace,* it seems to us, marks a considerable theoretical advance. It would, of course, be impossible within the framework of a simple article like the present one to attempt an analysis of it. Let us content ourselves with a few observations useful to our purpose.

In the first section, Kant, in conformity with the legal tradition, formulates six articles whose purpose is to specify the limits within which the exercise of war is to be maintained. "Some level of trust in the enemy's way of thinking," says the sixth article, "must be preserved even in the midst of war, for otherwise no peace can ever be concluded and the hostilities would become a war of extermination (*bellum internecinum*)." Then, deeming that "war is but a sad necessity in the state of nature (where no tribunal empowered to make judgments supported by the power of law exists), one maintains the rights of a nation by mere might," he adds in substance that "neither party can be declared an unjust enemy" and that "the outcome of the conflict . . . determines the side on which justice lies." This declaration is worth highlighting because it contradicts the widespread image of him as a moralist in political matters. And, finally, he returns to denounce the peril of a war of extermination, based on the argument that no protagonist could occupy the de jure position of being superior to another, and thus conduct a war of punishment (*bellum punitivum*); "from this it follows that a war of extermination—where the destruction of both parties along with all rights is the result—would permit perpetual peace to occur only in the vast graveyard of humanity as a whole."[5] Paradoxically, for Kant the state of nature, provided that it is respected, offers the guarantee of a balanced state of war—the worst thing being, in his view, that a belligerent imagines himself to be the possessor of a right that transcends the conflict.

Let us make a second observation: After having declared that the state of right, which does not exist in nature, has to be established, Kant undertakes to demonstrate in the second section that the republican constitution—by which we are to understand: the representative system—is the only one on which an edifice of perpetual peace can be built. Indeed, only that one turns out to respond "to the principles of *freedom* of the members of a society (as men)"—principles that assure "the dependence of everyone on a single common [source of] legislation"[6]—and it alone derives from the idea of an original contract as the foundation of all juridical legislation. In fact, in such a regime the decision to declare war does not pertain to the arbitrary will of the prince but requires the assent of the citizens, and the latter prove capable of evaluating, in full knowledge of the relevant facts [*en connaissance du cause*], the ills they would have to endure.

It is worth lingering over this point. Although history teaches that peoples subject to such a constitution have on several occasions consented to war, showing that they fail to recognize its causes and the stakes involved as well as its consequences, Kant's judgment, it seems to us, hasn't ceased to gain in depth. If the power of public opinion, enlightened by freedom of information and association, does not suffice by itself alone to guarantee a State's will for peace, there is no doubt that its absence, the monopolization of public decision-making by the established power—as one notes in dictatorial regimes and totalitarian ones of all kinds—creates a threat to peace of the first magnitude.

A third observation: The greatest originality of Kant's thesis lies, without a doubt, in the distinction and the connection between two conceptions of peace: as an idea of Reason and as a product of nature's finality. Kant states, on the one hand (in the second article of the second section), that "from the throne of its moral legislative power, reason absolutely condemns war,"[7] and, on the other hand (in the first supplement), that the guarantee of perpetual peace is to be found in "that great artist *nature* (*natura daedala rerum*)" that "permit[s] harmony to emerge among men through their discord, even against their wills."[8] It is tempting to think that this concept of *nature*—which Kant employs, he tells us, to avoid that of Providence—heralds that of *History,* as it will be understood by Hegel. More precisely, it is tempting to think that his theory of natural finality heralds the *Cunning of Reason.*

Disencumbering myself from the details of the argument, I will say that the instauration of peace appears as the result of people's expansion over the entire extent of the earth and of the constitution of a network of relations among them that, although legal to a greater or lesser extent, testify to the necessity of *living together.* Heading in this direction, Kant declares: "In taking care that men *could* live everywhere on earth, nature has also despotically chosen that they *should* live everywhere, even against their inclinations, and without presupposing that this should [*Sollen*] rest on a concept of duty that binds men as a moral law; instead, she has chosen war as a means whereby this purpose is to be fulfilled."⁹

Whatever might be the reservations this theory of nature arouses, let us remark that it allows for an exigency of which Rousseau was unaware. The latter reduced the problem of peace to a constant set of givens as soon as one has exited from the state of nature. And this problem appears solvable only by virtue of a reasonable decision among sovereigns who are concerned about avoiding the madness of permanent insecurity. Kant, by way of contrast, describes the process by which humanity comes to recognize itself as de facto humanity, in a de facto unique space, the earth, and to enter little by little into communication with itself in all its parts. This natural movement, which takes place without the knowledge of individuals, proves in his view to be in the first place constitutive of political societies, in the second place constitutive of the establishment of their relations in war, and, finally, constitutive of a worldwide mode of existence or, if one prefers, a *living together* under the banner of peace, at once in proximity and amid the differences pertaining to each society. Being natural, the movement requires at each stage its reflection in the form of law: civil right, which accompanies the formation of political unities; international right [*droit des gens*], which accompanies wars; and, finally, cosmopolitan right.

Let us highlight once again the distinction, firmly formulated, between what is of the order of nature and what is of the order of morality: "When I say of nature that she *wills* that this or that happen, that does not mean that she sets it out as a duty that we do it (because only practical reason, which is free of constraint, can do that); rather, she does it herself, whether or not we will it" (first supplement to the second section).¹⁰ This language calls for a fresh commentary. Inasmuch as it is worth articulating in a practical project, the idea of peace, if we are to follow Kant, could not be rooted in the unconditional exigency of the subject; it demands to be founded upon the interpretation of the signs of humanity's becoming or, to express it better, of humanity's advent unto itself.

Let us take one further step in order to get at the import of Kant's reflections in his *Perpetual Peace*. Although a number of commentators have rightly emphasized the influence the great legal tradition had exerted over Kant, it seems to us that the philosopher breaks loose from that tradition in the short treatise we are discussing. The notion of cosmopolitan right illustrates this point quite well. Such a right arises from a situation in which the entire earth sees itself occupied by men, and, this occupation being known,

the earth is revealed to be their common abode or their common possession. "Our concern here is not with philanthropy, but with *right,* and in this
context *hospitality* (hospitableness) means the right of an alien not to be
treated as an enemy upon his arrival in another's country." What, then, is
this right? "The *right to visit,* to associate, belongs to all men by virtue of
their common ownership of the earth's surface; for since the earth is a globe,
they cannot scatter themselves infinitely, but must, finally, tolerate living in
close proximity, because originally no one had a greater right to any region of the earth than anyone else."[11] Going on to prosecute the conduct of
civilized States toward foreign peoples and lands, where they are "guests"
(their visits being the same as "conquering" these people, he points out) —
that is to say, in putting colonization on trial — Kant concludes the "third
definitive article" on the following note:

> Because a (narrower or wider) community widely prevails among the
> earth's peoples, a transgression of rights in *one* place in the world is felt
> *everywhere;* consequently, the idea of cosmopolitan right is not fantas-
> tic and exaggerated, but rather an amendment to the unwritten code
> of national and international rights, necessary to the public rights of
> humanity in general. Only such amendment allows us to flatter our-
> selves with the thought that we are making continual progress toward
> perpetual peace.[12]

No more than Hegel does Kant imagine that peace might result from a
fusion of States. Perhaps recalling his Dante, he declares in the first supplement to the second section that the notion of universal monarchy is eminently dangerous: "For laws invariably lose their impact with the expansion
of their domain of governance, and after it has uprooted the soul of good,
a soulless despotism finally degenerates into anarchy."[13] But whereas Hegel
finds, as limit to the absolute sovereignty of States, only a simple fact —
namely, that "States reciprocally recognize each other as States . . . [that
there is] a bond wherein each counts to the rest as existing in itself and for
itself" (last part of the *Philosophy of Right*)[14] — Kant, setting aside all the
while the idea of a higher legislative authority, does indeed identify a universal right that is inscribed in what might be called the development of
sociability on the universal scale. Does not Kant thus inaugurate a path that
is still demanding to be explored?

Raymond Aron, it is true, rightly observes that the First World War
marked a break in the conception of right and of peace. The entire legal tradition had until then tended to legalize war, he notes; thenceforth, the idea
of outlawing it came to the fore. This objective was not what Kant had in
mind. Legal decisionism seems to me to be alien to his project, and the cri-

tique the author of *Peace and War* makes of such decisionism perhaps does not get at what is most interesting in *Perpetual Peace*. Aron rightly judges that the Kellogg-Briand Pact and the League of Nations demonstrated the futility of outlawing war.[15] The attempt collided with the facts: the States remained in their natural independence; some refused to accept the status quo on which the agreement was supposed to rest; the international authority was impotent to use coercive means—which, moreover, it did not have at its disposal—to bring recalcitrant States into line. Furthermore, it is shown to us that the ideology of peace paralyzed the democracies, and in particular France. The members of the League proved incapable of applying sanctions against Hitler and Mussolini when they began to violate international law. As for France, it didn't dare bar Hitler's way when it still disposed of a force superior to that of its adversary. Lastly, France's and England's capitulation at Munich convinced Hitler and his general staff that their conquests would encounter no obstacles.

If one sticks to this analysis, which in itself is convincing, it seems that the lessons to be drawn confirm the thesis of those who, conscious of the inevitable arbitrary might of States, reason as realists, imagining no other solution than a balance of forces to check attempts at aggression and counting only on an obstinate will to exclude from war those means that would risk changing it into a war of extermination. From this standpoint, peace might be considered an absolute value only on the basis of purely moral considerations.

Such reasoning suffers already from an intrinsic defect. Indeed, as soon as right collides against the limit imposed by considering States as the only identifiable actors on the world stage—powers that face off against each other in a state of nature—it is deemed impossible to provide any definition of who is the aggressor. Now, it is not moral conviction but good sense, in the classical acceptation of this term, that brings out the distinction between the aggressor and the aggressed, whereas any traditional legal apparatus is incapable of offering a definition of them. On what would good sense base itself during the Second World War, for example, if not on the idea that Nazism and Fascism were violating the rights of men and of peoples?

Aron's critique of the project of outlawing war generally appears to be well founded, but within the limits of a conceptualization that retains only the following alternative: state of nature/state of right—the latter being understandable only as the civil state. Consequently, as Rousseau saw quite well, the attempts of jurists to legalize war remain artificial contrivances without any theoretical basis. They boil down, in short, to the establishment of rules of the game, which the actors respect so long as these rules seem to them advantageous but which they do not hesitate to violate if that is their interest. Whatever may be their import—and one can certainly deem it useful—these attempts do not go beyond the boundaries of pragmatism. Let us recall that Hegel, although he certainly cannot be counted among the theorists of peace, urges one to go beyond this framework when he speaks of a mutual recognition among States, doing so at the very moment when he makes of the State as such an absolute. This recognition, we said, is posited as a mere fact. But who doesn't see that it cannot be a question of a fact? Either it is the relation of force that at each moment constrains the one to take into account the independence of the other or there really is mutual recognition, that is to say, an internalization by the one of the aim of the other in a necessarily symbolic space that it is fitting to identify.

Now, what could this symbolic space really be if not humanity? Let us not understand by the latter a singular entity that would stand above States as each State stands above men. So long as one doesn't give in to a conception of humanity as a total body, a higher individual encompassing States that are themselves thought of as great individuals encompassing their subjects, no theoretical possibility offers itself for a new conception of right. Pried loose from this fiction, humanity would appear as a field both material and spiritual, always unrealizable, in which is born and toward which are polarized every form of political existence and coexistence. Upon this condition alone, the conjunction of the idea of humanity with that of right can take on some meaning.

Let us remark that the conception of a right of humanity can lean on that of a social right. A great legal tradition is based on the representation of a supposed passage from the state of nature to the social state in order to accredit the thesis that there is right only where the principle of a common submission, embodied in the sovereign, is affirmed. Far from supporting this construction, our anthropological knowledge and, more specifically, sociology on the one hand and phenomenology on the other unveil for us a network of originary relationships; more than that, there is an intricate connection of beings, perceiving, thinking, and acting in their common world, that underlies the symbolic constitution of every community. Under its most primitive forms as well as under its most elaborate ones, social right seems to us already to be irreducible to the classical model—which, if I may risk this expression, takes into account only the vertical dimension of the society-space. As futile as it would be to deny the notion, everywhere present, of a pole of sovereignty, a pole of power and of law, so would one be mistaken in wanting to draw back toward this pole the institution of the social. The sovereign instance of authority is not the full-fledged founder of the social order; that instance is a part of this order, and it arises from that order just as much as it determines that order. Now, granting this point, one should agree that no abyss stretches between the world of States and the world of humanity and that right does not stop at the State's borders since it has never drawn entirely from the State its own origin.

Let not one think that these last remarks are taking us away from our chosen topic. They bring us back to the idea sketched by Kant of a right of emergent humanity, of a humanity revealing itself on the basis of its experience of war and consequent upon the increasing proximity of men on the *finite surface* of the earth. Kant's vision is for us an astonishing anticipation, so much does the world that he had before his eyes seem to us, in comparison to our own, multiform and lacunary. But this power of anticipation is not his. Most of the great thinkers of the early nineteenth century, whatever their beliefs and whether we are talking, for example, about Saint-Simon or Chateaubriand in France or Marx, were perceiving a new rhythm of human history, a tremendous acceleration of that rhythm that coincides with the advent of a finite space, palpable in itself and in each of its parts. And one could say that this anticipation is ever renewed, even into our own age, where the imagination staggers, so much is it always outdistanced by the speed of change. Paul Valéry's words, which, in 1938 (in his *Reflections on the World Today*), seemed so new to his contemporaries, no longer relate to us anything but a mere statement of fact: "The entire habitable globe," he wrote,

> has now been explored, seized, and shared among nations. The age of uncharted areas, of unoccupied territories, of places which nobody owns, and therefore the age of free expansion, is at an end. There is not a rock without its flag, there are no more blanks on the map, no region beyond law and custom, not a tribe whose affairs do not give birth to some dossier and do not depend, through the maleficent powers of the pen, upon various remote humanists in their offices. *The age of the finite world is now beginning.*[16]

He added: "An entirely new, excessive, and instantaneous solidarity between regions and events is already a most marked result of this great development. We must henceforth relate all political phenomena to this new universal condition."[17] He also spoke of an "increasingly close interdependence of human dealings."[18] Valéry, it is true, did not deem this new experience of the world a happy one. He retained the imprint of the Greek spirit, which loves limits. In the same passage, these misgivings of his come through: "There is no prudence, wisdom, or genius but is soon baffled by this complexity of affairs, for there is no recognizable pattern of duration, continuity, or causality in this world of multiplied relationships and contacts."[19]

This judgment cannot be ignored. It is certain that the closer men become, the more they rub up against each other in ways that hurt. But that is only a half-truth. Is it not rather because they are not multiplied enough that relationships and contacts become so dangerous? Is it not because the closer and closer interdependence of human dealings does not find its counterpart in the real spread of human rights, in the institution of a public space on a world scale, so that divisions might find therein another expression than war? Is it not also because the movement of erosion of the old particularisms, which has become in everyone's view irreversible, runs up against tremendous resistances and gives rise, on the part of the established hierarchies, to new methods of self-preservation and also to new forms of exclusion with regard to all those who would, despite their different condition, otherwise risk appearing as fellows [semblables]? Indeed, peace can be based only on the idea that the relationships among men are relationships among fellow men. It follows, then, that this idea is not unconnected with that of freedom. It also follows that it would be hypocritical to countenance, in the name of peace, every form of exploitation of peoples who see themselves, under cover of the laws of the market, deprived of the resources of their territory and subjected to an overt or disguised form of dictatorship: it would be hypocritical, too, to countenance every form of totalitarianism that denies elementary rights to individuals and to minorities.

Mindful not to succumb to utopian thinking and careful to take into account the exigencies of the contemporary world, let us not confuse the cause of peace with an unprincipled pacifism. But, mindful of reality, let us not succumb, either, to the dizzying spectacle of current conflicts. Let us recognize, rather, that the sovereigns do not decide alone the fate of humanity, as Rousseau supposed, and that, far from being futile, the silent work of rapprochement among men, which takes place with the aid of increased mutual knowledge of mores and mentalities, progress in education, the spread of information, and the rise of the idea of human rights, can engender decisive effects of a political order heading in the direction of peace. The question certainly remains: Will these hopes be disappointed? But if they were to be disappointed, rather than concluding, with Rousseau, that it was folly to have wanted to be wise in the midst of fools, it would be better to note soberly, with Freud, that in the incessant struggle that opposes Eros to the death instinct, the latter has decidedly revealed itself to be the more powerful.

Notes

"L'idée d'humanité et le projet de paix universelle" was originally published in *Diogène* 135 (July–September 1986): 14–32 under the title "L'idée de paix et l'idée d'humanité." The text is based on a paper for the International UNESCO Colloquium on "Peace as Absolute Value." Reprinted in *Écrire*, 227–46.

1 Dante Alighieri, *On World-Government or De Monarchia*, trans. Herbert W. Schneider (New York: Liberal Arts Press, 1949), 8–9.

2 Jean-Jacques Rousseau, "Que l'état de la guerre naît de l'état social," *Œuvres complètes* (Paris: Gallimard, 1964), 3:604.

3 Ibid.

4 Jean-Jacques Rousseau, "Rousseau's 'Summary' of the Abbé de Saint-Pierre's *Project for Perpetual Peace*," in *Reading Rousseau in the Nuclear Age*, ed. Grace C. Roosevelt (Philadelphia: Temple University Press, 1990), 220.

5 Immanuel Kant, "To Perpetual Peace: A Philosophical Sketch" (1795), *Perpetual Peace and Other Essays on Politics, History, and Morals*, trans. Ted Humphrey (Indianapolis: Hackett Publishing Company, 1983), 110.

6 Ibid., 112.

7 Ibid., 116.

8 Ibid., 120.

9 Ibid., 122–23.

10 Ibid., 123.

11 Ibid., 118.

12 Ibid., 119 [T/E: translation altered].

13 Ibid., 125.

14 Georg Wilhelm Friedrich Hegel, *Philosophy of Right*, trans. T. M. Knox (Oxford, England: Clarendon Press, 1942, 1962), 215, §338 [T/E: translation altered].

15 T/E: Raymond Aron, *Peace and War: A Theory of International Relations*, trans. Richard Howard and Annette Baker Fox (Garden City, New York: Doubleday, 1966), 113.

16 Paul Valéry, *Reflections on the World Today* (1938), trans. Francis Scarfe (New York: Pantheon, 1948), 21–22.

17 Ibid., 22.

18 Ibid.

19 Ibid., 23.

The Revolution as New Religion

THE IDEA OF a new religion haunted many minds at the beginning of the nineteenth century. To plumb its depths, we would have to investigate Saint-Simon, Auguste Comte, Pierre Leroux, and other, more obscure figures. As for the interpretation of the Revolution, during the same period, as an event willed by Providence or as a new stage in the fulfillment of Christianity — nay, more specifically, of Catholicism — that is a theme that would merit exploration across the various and even opposing versions of Joseph de Maistre, Pierre Simon Ballanche, and Chateaubriand, Pierre Joseph Benjamin Buchez, and Henri François Alphonse Esquiros. The connection between the political and the religious, already highlighted so very well by Paul Bénichou, has not ceased to trouble us. I shall take a brief interest here only in one of its manifestations: the representation of the Revolution as a new religion. This is a representation that testifies undoubtedly to the spirit of the time but is no less specific to it, and it arouses all the more interest as it owes nothing to the attempts made during the Revolution to forge new religious institutions.

That the Revolution might have contained, in the very principle of its existence, a new religion is a conviction shared, as one knows, by Jules Michelet and Edgar Quinet. One is tempted not to take it seriously. But rather than imputing this conviction immediately to their romantic imagination, one would undoubtedly be better advised to ask oneself what was seeking to be said through these words *new religion*. Rather than seeing in them only the sign of a failure to provide a positive explanation and of an unfortunate flight into irrationalism, one would undoubtedly be better advised to try to hear the question these two philosopher-historians were trying to bring forth at the very moment, perhaps, that they were rendering it obscure.

I shall take as my guide a writer whom one would certainly never accuse of making the least concession to irrationalism, Alexis de Tocqueville. His reflections on the Revolution and religion are precious for the very reason that they betray a hesitation on his part; the value of these reflections lies in what about them is discordant, if not contradictory. The subject matters enough to Tocqueville for him to treat it at the very beginning of *The Old Regime and the Revolution* (book 1, chapters 2 and 3) and for him to return to it in the third book (chapter 2) and in the notes he wrote for the fourth book. A comparison of the titles of the two chapters on this subject contained in book 1 speaks eloquently; the first (chapter 2) is entitled "That the Fundamental and Final Objective of the Revolution Was Not, as Has Been Thought, to Destroy Religion and Weaken the State," while the second (chapter 3) is entitled "How the French Revolution Was a Political Revolution Which Acted Like a Religious Revolution, and Why." We can already glimpse an interpretation. But, as the actual reading of Tocqueville often verifies, with his approach some surprises may be in store.

Tocqueville observes in the first place that "among the passions born of the Revolution the first lit and the last extinguished was the passion against religion."[1] But this statement is formulated only to bring us back immediately from appearance to reality. The "war against religions" is revealed to have been only an incident in the Revolution. It marks a "striking but fleeting aspect."[2] The author sees the proof of this in the present state of things: the Church has recovered, and people's minds have calmed. He finds in eighteenth-century philosophy one of the principal causes for the passions set loose during the Revolution. There were two parts to this philosophy that are "both distinct and separable":[3] on the one hand, a critique of all opinions touching upon civil and political society; on the other, a critique of the clergy, its hierarchy, and its institutions, which incited people to want to "tear Christianity up by the roots."[4] Nevertheless, "it was much less as a religious doctrine than as a political institution that Christianity aroused these furious hatreds."[5] And thus it is understood why the struggle against religion ceased after its political objective was attained. This analysis is reinforced by an argument of general import: "To believe that democratic societies are naturally hostile to religion is to commit a great mistake: nothing in Christianity, nothing even in Catholicism, is absolutely contrary to the spirit of democratic societies, and many things are very favorable."[6] To this is added the conviction that the religious instinct has always been rooted in the people.

The interpretation we have just summarized is completed, but also appreciably modified, in the following chapter, which opens with a new observation. "Every political and civil revolution," Tocqueville notes, "has taken place within the borders of a single country."[7] The French Revolution, by way of contrast, has obliterated all the old borders; it has brought people together or divided them, whatever their laws, their traditions, or the features of their language. This revolution has created

> a common intellectual homeland where men of all nations could become citizens. In all history you will not find a single political revolution which has had this character. You will find it only in certain religious revolutions. The French Revolution must be compared to a religious revolution, if you want to find an analogy to help in understanding.[8]

Tocqueville is no longer content merely to state that the Revolution proceeded in the manner of a religious revolution; he even specifies that it has taken on the "look [of] a religious revolution."[9] We learn that, as with the latter, the French Revolution is "widespread" and that it uses the methods of "preaching" and "propaganda."[10] "It is a political revolution which inspires conversions, and which preaches as ardently to foreigners as it acts passionately at home: think what a new sight this is!"[11]

This new spectacle, let us agree, weans us from the judgment that the Revolution's antireligious furors were but an incident, a "striking but fleeting trait." The present calming of passions that our author notes no longer suffices now to expunge an upheaval whose only precedent was the hatreds of the wars of religion. Tocqueville, moreover, does not hesitate to ask whether "this resemblance of effects does not derive from some hidden resemblance in their causes."[12] And his answer is remarkable. He observes, first, that religions were generally designed to reach man himself, without taking into account the traditions and customs of a country. He then rectifies his remark, specifying that such a design became fully formed only with Christianity and that, in short, there was no great religious revolution before its advent. The French Revolution then acquires with regard to Christianity a new dimension that is comparable to Christianity's own. The Revolution considered the citizen in an entirely abstract manner, we are told. Its intention was to set the general duties and rights of men in political matters. It sought to bring everything back from the contingent to the natural. It is precisely because it seemed to tend toward the regeneration of humankind that the Revolution gave rise to propaganda and encouraged proselytism.

At this place in the text, Tocqueville takes one further step, writing that, on account of this immense ambition, the Revolution was able to take on "that appearance of a religious revolution which so astonished its contemporaries."[13] Then, he specifies: "*Or rather, it itself became a new kind of religion,* an incomplete religion, it is true, without God, without ritual, and without a life after death, but one which nevertheless, like Islam, flooded the earth with its soldiers, apostles, and martyrs."[14] There were in the past, even in the Middle Ages, hints of such an undertaking, but people were too different from one another to conceive of "the idea of one law applicable to all."[15] But other times came "when it is enough to show them, as in a glass darkly, the image of such a law, for them to immediately recognize it and run towards it."[16]

The argument, we see, has been modified considerably. Let us reformulate it: What constitutes the essence of a religious revolution—this essence that is fully unveiled in Christianity—is that it claims to sift out from all particular laws the founding law of the human order. Now, the French Revolution pursued this same objective—with the small difference that the founding law is discovered in the political institution of the social.

Let us now proceed to book 3. The chapter that holds our attention is entitled "How Irreligion Was Able to Become a General and Dominant Passion among the French of the Eighteenth Century, and What Kind of Influence This Had on the Character of the Revolution." For Tocqueville it is a matter of showing why France, and France alone, became the theater for a fight against religion. The general scheme of his argument, to be honest, has something in common with the one he had followed at the beginning of book 2, when he asked "Why Feudalism Was Hated by the People in France More Than Anywhere Else." In brief, the general causes are not adequate to account for the violent explosion that ensued. If one goes back into the past, one will agree that unbelief was born in the sixteenth century in the wake of heresy. Nonetheless, for a long time its practice remained confined within narrow circles. If one considers the state of belief in the eighteenth century, one will see "in a general way, that in the eighteenth century Christianity had lost a great part of its power throughout the European continent; but, in the majority of countries, it was more abandoned than violently attacked."[17] The case of France is therefore unique. It appears even more so when one notes that the vices and the abuses of the Church existed to a lesser degree there than anywhere else and that its tolerance was unprecedented and unequaled in the Catholic world. As a consequence, the particular causes must be sought in the state of the society and not in that of religion.

Now, if he develops once again the same thesis—that it is as a political institution that the Church excited hatred—Tocqueville is shedding new light on the authority the Church claimed to exercise over the whole of society and on the function the Church fulfilled in the system of powers. The conflict between the Church and the new opinion leaders does not pertain to an opposition between their competing principles: on the one hand, attachment to tradition, respect for a transcendent authority, the defense of hierarchy; on the other, criticism of past institutions, the affirmation of individual freedom and of the equality of conditions. This conflict was born of the confusion between the religious and the political that was characteristic of the Ancien Régime. For Catholicism to have been able to coexist with the new thinkers, "both sides would have had to recognize that political society and religious society were by nature essentially different, and could not be ordered by similar principles."[18] Lacking such a distinction, the Church seemed to support and did in fact support the regime in all its parts. Tocqueville states this expressly:

> Further, the Church was then itself the leading political power, and the most detested of all, although it was not the most oppressive; for it had come to join itself with the political powers without being forced to do so by its nature and vocation, and often blessed in politics the vices that it condemned elsewhere, covering them with its sacred inviolability, and seeming to want to make them as immortal as itself.[19]

This judgment merits some meditation on our part, for it is not far from the one Edgar Quinet would come to formulate—with the difference that the latter would come to draw an entirely other conclusion therefrom: viz., the need to extirpate Catholicism in order to bring society back to life.

Let us pass over the secondary arguments, in particular the idea that the Church's tolerance made the interferences on the part of its censors more unbearable—in short, the idea, familiar to readers of Tocqueville, that a power becomes all the more odious when it sheds some of its means. The key point lies in his demonstration that unbelief or, more than that, antireligious hatred is the product of the Ancien Régime's political system, since the Catholic religion, though for bad reasons, had become consubstantial with that system. Such unbelief, therefore, cannot entirely be imputed to the extravagant theories of writers who had no sense of political necessities, and it refers not to an accidental phenomenon but to a spectacular though superficial manifestation of the Revolution.

Certainly, Tocqueville still considers irreligion as unfortunate, but he catches sight of the fact that it relates to a positive passion that substituted itself for a failing faith. Let one be the judge of it. After having observed that "without doubt the universal discredit in which all religious beliefs fell at the end of the last century exercised the greatest influence on the whole of our revolution,"[20] he returns to the effects of irreligion to find that "they were much more in disordering minds than in degrading hearts, or even in corrupting mores; that irreligion inclined the people of that time to go to very unusual extremes."[21] He then goes even further, stating: "When religion deserted souls, it did not leave them, as often happens, empty and debilitated; rather *they were briefly filled by feelings and ideas which momentarily took the place of religion,* and which did not let them be depressed."[22] Finally, his thought is carried beyond what it allows itself to concede: "If, with regard to religion the French who made the Revolution were more unbelieving than we, at least there was left them one admirable belief which we lack: they believed in themselves."[23] In themselves? The phrase does not seem right to him, for he goes on to specify immediately:

> They did not doubt the perfectibility, the power of man; they readily became impassioned for his glory, they had faith in his virtue. They put in their own strength the prideful confidence that often leads to error but without which a people is capable of nothing but servitude; they did not doubt in the least that they were called to transform society and to regenerate our species. These feelings and these passions had become *a kind of new religion* for them, which, producing some of the great effects which we have seen religions produce, tore them away from individual egoism, encouraged them to heroism and devotion, and often made them seem insensible to all the petty goods which we possess. I have studied much history, and I dare affirm that I have never met with a revolution where one could see at the start, in so many men, a more sincere patriotism, more disinterest, more true greatness."[24]

True, the chapter to which I am referring does not end quite there. In a few lines the author recalls the immense public evil that irreligion produces. This evil's effects are to be seen in the appearance of "revolutionaries of an unknown species . . . who took boldness to the point of folly. . . . [T]hese new beings . . . have since formed a race which has perpetuated itself, and spread among all civilized parts of the earth. . . . We found them in the world when we were born; they are still with us."[25] Let us note again, in passing, that Tocqueville moves from one point of view to another without worrying about harmonizing them. Thus does he observe, one after another, that his era marks the reconciliation of society with religion, that this society is sinking into mediocrity, and, finally, that it is becoming the theater for a proliferation of revolutionaries.

Tocqueville's interpretation renders Michelet's and Quinet's ideas less strange. Undoubtedly, their inspiration is wholly different. Whereas Tocqueville ends up with the hypothesis of a new religion through a movement that contradicts his initial judgment, Michelet and Quinet find in this religion the very essence of the Revolution. Tocqueville explains that it was to vanish with the end of social and political turmoil; Michelet and Quinet are persuaded that it is on account of its religious failure that the Revolution was unable to attain its goal and that the society of their time continues to require a faith of a new kind. All three, at least, hold in the same contempt the cult of Reason and the worship of the Supreme Being; in their view, that masquerade has nothing to do with religious experience. All three, above all, are of the same mind about celebrating the *heroism* of the revolutionary era, this forgetting of self and this abandonment to supernatural forces, of which there were so many examples and which provides so powerful a contrast with the pettiness of the present. Is this not, ultimately, for Tocqueville the most troubling phenomenon? Nevertheless, heroism does not say it all. And Michelet and Quinet, without quite agreeing with each other completely, are the only ones to seek the *meaning* of the new religion, of a religion that breaks with all former institutions and that, they judge, is still in gestation.

Michelet discovers the greatest sign of the new religion in the spectacle of the people gathered together for the Fête de la Fédération, communing with all of humanity in the expectation of a new world—a spectacle that he also calls France's marriage with France. He sees the Revolution breaking free from History, rendering itself unlocalizable: "It knew neither time nor space," he marvels.[26] This writer also indulges in various formulas that allow him to evoke the passage of Christ, his birth at a time when the emperor had decreed the census of all men in the known world. Michelet's inspirations come to him, one after another, from Saint Paul and Dante. Let us recall the way in which he speaks of the meeting on the Champs-de-Mars, that great rendezvous of the nation: "Such a place seemed destined to receive the states-general of the world."[27] Shortly beforehand, he wrote: "On that day, everything seemed possible. Every kind of dissension had ceased: there was no longer either nobility, bourgeois, or people. The future was present. . . . That is to say, time itself was no more. It was a flash of eternity."[28] For him, the new religion is more than just a formula. He makes it the express theme of four chapters in his *Histoire de la Révolution française:* the last two chapters of book 3, the first of book 4, and the first of book 14. These texts are too well known for us to bother to cite them. Let us recall, at least, how he contrasts religious inspiration with the work of the Jacobin machine and the exalted feelings of those faced with the task of constructing a new world with the fear and vertigo that seize hold of the revolutionaries. "To oppose the vast conspiracy then preparing, it was necessary to invent another conspiracy," he writes near the beginning of book 4.

Let that of the Jacobins now arise, and envelop the whole of France. *Two thousand four hundred* societies, in as many towns or villages affiliated to it in less than two years. A great and terrible machine gives the Revolution an incalculable power, which alone can save it, in the dissolution of public authority; but also it seriously modifies its character, *and changes and alters its primitive inspiration.*[29]

Let us recall, too, how he denounces in the same place the timidity of a bourgeoisie that was wrongly thought of as resolute and radical: "The bourgeoisie trembled in the presence of the revolution that it had made, and recoiled at its own work. It was led astray and ruined by fear far more than by self-interest."[30] This judgment will be reformulated by him in the first chapter of book 14, which he has no fear of entitling "The Revolution Was Worthless without a Religious Revolution." There the full breadth of his interpretation becomes apparent, and his reasons become clear: "The most advanced among them, Saint-Just, does not dare to tackle either religion, education or any fundamental social doctrines. It is hard to discern what he thinks about property. Whether this political and superficial revolution went a long or a little way, whether it went faster or slower as it rushed headlong down its single *track,* it was bound to end up badly."[31] And, he specifies: "To ensure the success of the Revolution, a real religious and social revolution was required to lend it strength and support, to provide a firm foundation."[32] What he reproaches in the revolutionaries is their having remained within the bounds of the philosophy the century had bequeathed to them. He sees in the Girondists and the Jacobins "parties of reason"[33] that had no idea of "the eternal craving of the human soul, which starves and thirsts after God."[34]

Although he has just condemned their failure, their withdrawal within the confines of a debate that didn't matter to the people, Michelet, in a few striking words, suddenly brings to light the connection between the fear of religious renovation and the headlong rush toward Terror: "All the sound and fury of the parties failed to conceal their lifeless doctrines. Fiery and scholastic, eager to proscribe each other they all were: differing but little on fundamentals, the nuances of opinion amongst them could only be resolved by the ultimate *distinguo,* death."[35]

Michelet is decidedly far removed from Tocqueville. He does not only concede the grandeur of the new religion, he exalts it; he affirms that the political is indissociable from the religious and from the social, and he does so exactly at the point where Tocqueville is claiming to keep them apart. Without a doubt, as I have already pointed out, he has the same vision of a heroic form of behavior that exceeds the limits of reason. But he thinks through this heroism in a more subtle way. For him, it does not suffice that men defy death for them to merit the name of *hero*. What counts for him is only the heroism of the mind—to use a formula dear to him that he borrowed from Vico—a heroism that attaches itself to the individual only if it does not cut itself off from the people.

Considering the idea he has of the new religion and of the reasons for its failure, one must grant that Michelet maintains the closest affinity with Quinet. That the social revolution would have been nothing without the religious revolution, that the latter was not to be confused with a social revolution, that the revolutionaries might have been afraid of their own revolution, that those dubbed furious madmen were in fact timid souls, that "*the spiritual emptiness*" of the Revolution came to mask itself beneath the Terror, all these ideas lie equally at the center of Quinet's interpretation. In what way is Quinet nonetheless distinct, and why does he prompt us to investigate more closely the meaning of the religious?

In the first place, Quinet discovers in the fate of the Revolution the indication of an inheritance. What matters to him is to bring to light the tradition of servitude that characterized monarchical, Catholic France. He is not content, as Michelet was, to present Robespierre as a new tyrant— nay, more generally, he isn't content to locate in the established revolutionary power the return of absolutist practices. His thesis is harsher: It is the French themselves—it is, in its depths, the nation that in his view became for centuries, under the spiritual yoke of the Church, accustomed to servitude.

For his part, Michelet in his works never stopped celebrating France, a chosen nation. One need only refer to his *Introduction à l'Histoire universelle* (Introduction to universal History). This writer, who later affirmed that there was no mind less mystical, nor more realistic, than his own, never shrank before a religious metaphor. "[As] the moral world had its word in Christ, son of Judea and of Greece, France shall explain the word of the social world," [36] he wrote then, adding: "It is up to her to detonate this new revelation." [37] In this sense, France held in his view "the pontificate of the new civilization." [38]

Certainly, the author of the *Histoire de la Révolution française* has changed; he no longer thinks that "the name of the priest and the king, representatives of what is most general, that is to say, divine, has given rise to the obscure right of the people as a mystical envelope, in which it has grown up and become stronger." [39] When he speaks of the past, he pleads for the victims of the monarchy who have had to wait so long for the return of justice. But these victims, they have been brought into subjection; they are not themselves servile. Moreover, his critique of Christianity, and in particular of Catholicism, does not prevent him from seizing hold of their symbols in order to glorify the advent of the people. As I have attempted to show on another occasion,[40] his 1868 preface testifies to an extraordinary transferral of the decor of the rites of the king onto the stage of the rites of the people. By way of contrast, for Quinet there is no chosen people. No concession is made to Christian symbolism. The new religion, he affirms, would have destroyed all images had it been able to take form. Idolatry, whatever its object might be, is his target.

Should one think, then, that his new religion is an offspring of Protestantism? Do we find here, in the debate over the connections between the Revolution and the Reformation, where the divide originates between these two historians who gladly called each other *brothers?* Michelet clearly notes in his 1868 preface, "The Revolution, it is said, was wrong. Against the fanaticism of the Vendée and the Catholic reaction, it ought to have armed itself with a credo of the Christian sects, appealing to Luther or to Calvin. My answer: it would have abdicated. It adopted no church. The fact is that it was itself a church."[41] One may doubt, however, that Michelet was referring here to Quinet. Were one to believe so, one would have to agree that he was mistaken. Nowhere does Quinet say or leave it to be understood that, in 1789 or 1793, the French ought to have rallied to the Protestant cause. His judgment is simply that they missed the chance the seventeenth-century Reformation had had and that they didn't know how to act with the same fervor as the English revolutionaries. But in his view, the hour has passed and the tasks have become of another order. The example of image breakers, whether English or Dutch, is recalled, certainly, in order to demonstrate that one does not uproot an established Church without violence and that the prudence of the most radical Montagnards in matters of religion has been revealed to be the most dangerous of errors. Nonetheless, he says no more than that. As for the Reformation itself, he praises it for being at the origin of individual liberty, but he recalls that its side effect was the fabrication of a despotic God. To him, Calvin's doctrine seems hopeless. He resolutely rejects every attempt to remake a religion in the traditional sense of the term. In *The Religious Revolution of the Nineteenth Century,* he eliminates all equivocations concerning his intentions: "This idea of making an universal dogma is nothing but an unhappy legacy of the very church you want to fight" is the statement he launches against his contemporaries who are searching for new cults of worship and new certitudes.[42] He makes fun of those "persons who adjourn all life, all effort, in the expectation of I know not what social Messiah."[43] Those people, he thinks, "seek the impossible, and are quite in opposition to the modern spirit."[44] Finally, let us recall that already in *Le Christianisme et la Révolution française* he went so far as to ask whether it might happen that God Himself might withdraw the Book.[45]

What then does Quinet mean by *new religion?* Perhaps one will catch a better glimpse of it if, without remaining bound to his formulas, one examines closely the connection he establishes between the advent of the individual, that of the people, and that of humanity. This is an essential connection, if one understands it well. He has faith in the individual, but upon the condition that the individual would want to be free, and how would the individual will freedom if he remained captive in a society ruled by the prince and the priest or came to enjoy his independence only in pursuit of his self-interest? The individual — the most noble creation of Modern Times, according to Quinet — can affirm itself only by breaking with individualism and becoming the bearer of a power to raise itself up above itself, to assert a freedom that is felt in contact with others, that seeks at once its guarantee and its meaning in free institutions, which go to make up the true life of a people. Yet one must not make of the people an idol, measuring one's faith by its capacity to will itself to be free, to give expression to humanity, which tends to fulfill itself through the people: "One sacrifices everything to the idea of I do not know what People-Messiah who has need of bloody sacrifices. But all peoples claim to be the Messiah at that price. All want their acts of violence, their iniquities, and their ferocity to be adored as sacred. Let us put an end to this sanguine mysticism."[46] Ultimately, what would one gain by venerating humanity itself when one has converted it into a new deity? Humanity merits our faith only inasmuch as it asks us to answer for it, only inasmuch as it entrusts us with an infinite task. Addressing the advocates of the religion of humanity, Quinet hurls the following: "So, they tell me, adore Humanity. Oh, what a strange fetish! I have seen it too close up. To kneel before he who is on two knees before every triumphant force! To crawl before this crawling beast with a billion feet — that is not my faith. What would I make of that god? Bring me back to the sacred ibises and the ringed serpents of the Nile."[47]

The individual, the people, humanity — these are not empirical beings. If Quinet does not dissociate them, if he invests them with a religious meaning, it is because no positive definition of them can be found; it is because they testify to a transcendence that, when missing, makes democratic society, and democratic man, give way, and turns freedom into an underhanded form of servitude. Upon reflection, the fears and the hopes of Quinet are not alien to those of Tocqueville. The latter, however, retains the idea that democracy finds a somehow external support in the religious sentiments of individuals but that it also possesses its own dynamic, whose mainspring is the equality of conditions, whereas freedom maintains itself therein only though institutions that pertain to an art. Differing from Tocqueville, Quinet seems to tie the existence of democracy to faith in its ends, inasmuch as it brings together the image of the individual, the people, and humanity—a faith that is therefore private, social, and universal. Does this word allow one to respond to the question raised by the notion of a new religion? One may doubt it, but who would say that, as a question, it does not reach all the way to us?

Notes

"La révolution comme religion nouvelle," a contribution to a September 1988 colloquium on "The French Revolution and Modern Political Culture," was originally published in *The Transformation of Political Culture*, vol. 3 of *The French Revolution and the Creation of Political Culture 1789–1848*, ed. François Furet and Mona Ozouf (Oxford: Pergamon Press, 1989), 391–99. Reprinted in *Écrire*, 247–60.

1 *The Old Regime and the Revolution*, ed. François Furet and Françoise Mélonio, trans. Alan S. Kahan (Chicago: University of Chicago Press), 1:96.

2 Ibid.

3 Ibid. [T/E: translation altered].

4 Ibid.

5 Ibid., 97.

6 Ibid.

7 Ibid., 99.

8 Ibid.

9 Ibid.

10 Ibid.

11 Ibid., 99–100.

12 Ibid., 100.

13 Ibid., 101.

14 Ibid. (emphasis added).

15 Ibid.

16 Ibid.

17 Ibid., 203.

18 Ibid., 204.

19 Ibid., 204–5.

20 Ibid., 207.

21 Ibid., 208.

22 Ibid. (emphasis added).

23 Ibid.

24 Ibid. (emphasis added).

25 Ibid., 208–9.

26 Jules Michelet, *Historical View of the French Revolution, from Its Earliest Indications to the Flight of the King in 1791*, trans. C. Cooke (London: Bell, 1908), 3.11 (393). [T/E: This is not a complete translation of Michelet's *Histoire de la Révolution française*. See note 31 for a translation of some of the later books. Here and below I have indicated book and chapter, followed by page number in parentheses.]

27   Ibid., 3.11 (411).

28   Ibid., 4.1 (419–20) [T/E: translation altered].

29   Ibid., 4.1 (416), emphasis added on the last phrase.

30   Ibid., 4.1 (421) [T/E: translation altered].

31   Jules Michelet, *History of the French Revolution,* trans. Keith Botsford (Wynnewood, Pa: Kolokol Press, 1973), 7.1 (13) [T/E: translation slightly altered].

32   Ibid., 7.1 (14).

33   Ibid., 7.1 (13).

34   Ibid., 7.1 (14).

35   Ibid.

36   Jules Michelet, *Introduction à l'Histoire universelle suivi du discours d'ouverture* (Paris: Hachette, 1834), 104.

37   Ibid., 106.

38   Ibid., 107.

39   Ibid., 80.

40   T/E: Claude Lefort, "The Permanence of the Theological Political?" (1981), *Democracy and Political Theory,* trans. David Macey (Minneapolis: University of Minnesota Press, 1988): 213–55.

41   Jules Michelet, Préface (1868), *Histoire de la Révolution française* (Paris: Gallimard, 1952), 1:12.

42   Edgar Quinet, *The Religious Revolution of the Nineteenth Century* (London: Trübner, 1881), 34.

43   Ibid., 31.

44   Ibid.

45   Edgar Quinet, *Le Christianisme et la Révolution française* (Paris: Fayard, 1984), 185: "And how do they know whether one day or another God might not want to withdraw the Book itself in order that the Word, thought, the soul would live on without being tied down by the letter?"

46   Edgar Quinet, *La Révolution* (Paris: Belin, 1987), 505.

47   Ibid., 773.

Three Notes on Leo Strauss

O F ALL THE BOOKS and articles Leo Strauss has written, *Persecution and the Art of Writing* is undoubtedly the one that has contributed the most toward making him famous. His three major essays on Jewish thinkers of the Middle Ages and on Spinoza "all deal," he tells us in his preface, "with one problem: the problem of the relation between philosophy and politics."[1] Strauss sheds light on the general character of this relation in an introduction and in a first essay that provides the work with its title. There he states—in a thesis that he will maintain with a rigor that implies conviction—that one can gain an intelligent understanding of the philosophers who lived in Antiquity, in the Middle Ages, and even beyond, until the period called the Age of Enlightenment, only upon the condition that one is attentive to the exoteric part of their teaching. "The exoteric teaching was needed for protecting philosophy. It was the armor in which philosophy had to appear. It was needed for political reasons. It was the form in which philosophy became visible to the political community. It was the political aspect of philosophy. It was 'political' philosophy."[2]

Strauss would later reformulate this thesis in other writings,[3] drawing one's attention again to the character of political philosophy, which is not distinguished only, nor even principally, by its object—the nature of political things—but by the way in which philosophy proceeds in order to find public expression. For the philosopher, to proceed politically presupposes that one take into account the friend-enemy opposition. Philosophy is always in danger, since it runs up against the upholders of tradition: more specifically, it runs up against people who have faith in the teachings of religion as conveyed by the poets or priests; and, more broadly speaking, it runs up against all those who are instinctively hostile to it, owing to the fact that they are not equipped to understand it. The philosopher is therefore led to address his writings to his real or potential friends, endeavoring to fool [*ruser avec*] his real or potential enemies. He succeeds in doing so either by formulating here and there in his work commonly shared opinions that disarm his adversaries or by committing gross errors, by putting forward contradictory statements, by skipping silently over certain names or certain references in a way that will catch the attention of those who are made to understand him and will leave in a stupor the majority of his readership — not only those in the present but in the future, for it is not so much his own life as a philosopher that the writer is defending but philosophy itself.

It is up to the interpreter therefore to *read between the lines:* "The expression 'writing between the lines' indicates the subject of this article," he notes in the first essay of *Persecution.*[4] This would leave things up to the arbitrariness of reading, had Strauss not set down a rule:

> The context in which a statement occurs, and the literary character of the whole work as well as its plan, must be perfectly understood before an interpretation of the statement can reasonably claim to be adequate or even correct. One is not entitled to delete a passage, nor to emend its text, before one has fully considered all reasonable possibilities of understanding the passage as it stands — one of these possibilities being that the passage may be ironic.[5]

Strauss didn't cease to practice that *art of reading.* Upon an examination of Plato's texts, we may judge that Strauss's method is confirmed, as supported by the hypothesis that in Socrates' death sentence, and the warning philosophy took away from it, there originated a turning point in his teaching. Let us note also that Strauss maintained these same principles of interpretation in his *Thoughts on Machiavelli,* though not without exposing himself to some fresh difficulties, since he recognizes in Machiavelli, beyond the appearance of a new conception of politics as a technique, a project of *divulging* knowledge that boils down to abolishing the distinction between the philosophical life and the nonphilosophical life. But I cannot linger over the problem raised by the Straussian reading of Machiavelli. More important for my present purpose is to bring out, in the essay I have mentioned, all the signs of that *art of writing* Strauss himself practices.

At the very beginning of the essay, Strauss observes that "in a considerable number of countries which, for about a hundred years, have enjoyed a practically complete freedom of public discussion, that freedom is now suppressed and replaced by a compulsion to coordinate speech with such views as the government believes to be expedient, or holds in all seriousness."[6] He goes on to specify that "a large section of the people, probably the great majority of the younger generation, accepts the government-sponsored views as true, if not at once at least after a time."[7] Which ones are these "considerable number of countries"? Who is this "younger generation"? The text refers us to a footnote. We would expect it to shed some light for us on the situation, but it contains only a reference to Plato. In our time, is it a matter of countries subject to a totalitarian government? But who would say that they had previously enjoyed "a practically complete freedom of public discussion"? Is he talking about democratic countries? It seems not: there speech is not compelled to coordinate with views the government believes to be expedient. Nevertheless, a few lines later Strauss declares: "What is called freedom of thought in a large number of cases amounts to—and even for all practical purposes consists of—the ability to choose between two or more different views presented by the small minority of people who are public speakers or writers."[8] This assertion, in turn, refers us to a footnote specifying that " 'Reason is but choosing' is the central thesis of Milton's *Areopagitica*."[9]

Now, where is choice reduced to a single alternative, or else at best to the rallying to one opinion among several? Would this not be in liberal democracy, where conservatives and progressives clash with each other— as we are told in his book *Liberalism Ancient and Modern?* Would it be that Milton is being held up to ridicule, he who pronounced himself in favor of a limitless freedom to express whatever opinions one wants and to print anything one pleases? Does Strauss seriously think that reason is only the faculty of choice? True, he goes on to say in the text that "if this choice is prevented, the only kind of intellectual independence *of which many people are capable* is destroyed, and that is the only freedom of thought which is of political importance."[10] A reassuring phrase for a liberal reader—provided he forgets that people are not in general capable of acceding to philosophy and that politics is not the domain of virtue. After having observed that persecution furnishes "the highest efficiency of what may be called *logica equina*," the author emits the important judgment that in the countries in question—but which countries?—it is impossible to make "all those capable of *truly independent thinking* . . . accept the government-sponsored views."[11] Furthermore, persecution is unable to prevent not only the expression of such thought to "benevolent and trustworthy acquaintances," that is to say, "reasonable friends,"[12] but also public expression, provided that one "moves with circumspection"[13]—which means *that one should write between the lines.*

It is then that Strauss delivers the meaning of this formulation. He illustrates it with the example of a historian in a totalitarian country who, apparently faithful to the party, could avoid suspicion by combining a violent denunciation of liberalism with a statement that would make its greatest advantages known to his readers. Pointing out that all he need do would be to slip into the main body of his presentation "three or four sentences in that terse and lively style which is apt to arrest the attention of young men who love to think," he himself slips in a short phrase: "That central passage would state the case of the adversaries more clearly . . . than it had ever been stated in the heyday of liberalism, for he would silently drop all the foolish excrescences of the liberal creed which were allowed to grow up during the time when liberalism had succeeded and therefore was approaching dormancy."[14] Thus allowing the hasty or distracted reader to assume that the condition of the writer under a totalitarian regime prompts us to understand what was the condition of the writer in periods when his freedom of expression was threatened, he denounces the progress of liberalism, which is leading it to the edge of dormancy.

Still must one forbid oneself from imagining that the author is manifesting any attraction for the "heyday of liberalism." It can happen, let us not forget, that one might take literally a phrase that has an ironic twist. Moreover, the term *liberal creed* ought to alert us. It goes without saying that Strauss would not dream of speaking about the Ancients having a liberal creed. The substantive defense of historical exactitude, whose meaning escapes commentators who at present champion a literal interpretation of texts, is based on the argument that these commentators are unaware of the conditions under which writers have had to blaze a trail in order to escape the dangers of persecution. The passage at the center of the second section is of the utmost importance, but let it not lead one to neglect, on the one hand, the considerations that follow it and, on the other, the reasons that are given for their ignorance. "Modern historical research, which emerged at a time when persecution was a matter of feeble recollection rather than of forceful experience, has," we learn, "counteracted or even destroyed an earlier tendency to read between the lines of the great writers, or to attach more weight to their fundamental design than to those views which they have repeated most often."[15]

This much seems clear: When one is no longer suffering from persecution, one forgets what in other times were its effects. Strauss is drawing from this sort of acknowledgment the legitimacy of his reading criteria: "If it is true that there is a necessary correlation between persecution and writing between the lines, then there is a necessary negative criterion: that the book in question must have been composed in an era of persecution, that is, at a time when some political or other orthodoxy was enforced by law or custom."[16] But he immediately advances a second criterion, one that he calls "positive." This time he is no longer referring to the age when a book was composed but retains only the cleverness an author seems to display when we see him surreptitiously contradicting this or that aspect of an orthodoxy that he upholds everywhere else. He concludes this section by warning that one will not be able to recognize the signs of his design, still less understand it, "so long as we confine ourselves to the view of persecution and the attitude toward freedom of speech and candor which have become prevalent during the last three hundred years."[17]

These last arguments become half clear in the third section. There one learns, first, that the term *persecution* covers a variety of phenomena, from the cruelest type, as exemplified by the Spanish Inquisition, to the mildest, social ostracism. What is social ostracism? Strauss does not tell us; at least—we cannot doubt it—it does not fit into the category of visible forms of persecution, as practiced by political or religious authority. Strauss notes that there are periods when several religions were accepted and where, in spite of the freedom of choice, "free inquiry was not."[18] This reference to the past does not stop one from thinking of the world today . . . and more particularly of the United States, the country that tolerates several religions, dozens if not hundreds of denominations, but where, according to Tocqueville, there reigns in general *less independence of mind* and genuine freedom of discussion than anywhere else. "The majority raises formidable barriers around the liberty of opinion; within these barriers an author may write what he pleases, but woe to him if he goes beyond them."[19] Here social ostracism is depicted quite well. Tocqueville becomes still more specific: "The master no longer says: 'You shall think as I do or you shall die'; but he says: 'You are free to think differently from me and to retain your life, your property, and all that you possess; but you are henceforth a stranger among your people.'"[20] And from this sad picture he draws the following conclusion:

> The Inquisition has never been able to prevent a vast number of anti-religious books from circulating in Spain. The empire of the majority succeeds much better in the United States, since it actually removes the wish to publish them. Unbelievers are to be met with in America, but there is no public organ of infidelity.[21]

One will perhaps judge that my commentary on Strauss's silence is arbitrary, but I am following his rule for reading. In the present instance, the reader whose complicity he expects to have is a cultured person who cannot be unaware of *Democracy in America*.

Strauss notes, in what follows, that a great change took place around the middle of the seventeenth century: "What attitude people adopt toward freedom of public discussion, depends decisively on what they think about popular education." In brief, "an ever increasing number of heterodox philosophers" began to combat persecution openly, with the intention not only of communicating their thought but of abolishing all persecution and with the conviction that "the kingdom of general darkness could be replaced by the republic of universal light."[22] Thus, we are led to understand that if one no longer knows how to read between the lines, it is because one has wedded the *liberal creed;* it is because one has yielded to the illusion that each person can say everything and can understand everything; it is because one has eliminated the distinction, constitutive of classical culture, between the few and the many.

What does this event signify, if not the debasement or the abandonment of political philosophy? It appears at present that persecution is, at its most profound, the work of people who, it would be senseless to deny, are by nature rebellious against philosophy. In contrast to the "heterodox philosophers" who dreamed of the people's emancipation, previous writers thought that the abyss separating "the wise" from "the vulgar" was a basic fact of human nature that no "progress in popular education" could change.

> They were convinced that philosophy as such was suspect to, and hated by, the majority of men. Even if they had had nothing to fear on the part of any particular political quarter, those who started from that assumption would have been driven to the conclusion that public communication of the philosophic or scientific truth was impossible or undesirable, *not only for the time being but for all times.*[23]

Whence follows some consequences that, it seems to me, are not formulated. The first is that the wellspring of political philosophy, if not of philosophy—in the sense in which the latter is, as Strauss very rightly says elsewhere, not a teaching, a body of principles, but a way of life—is persecution. He who ignores that proves impotent to communicate the love of truth. The second consequence is that, by their concern to eliminate persecution, the "heterodox philosophers" have created a new orthodoxy, that of freedom of discussion—which is not at all genuine discussion—against which the very few have to defend themselves, keeping in mind the works of the Ancients. Persecution is now exerted in connection with the socially dominant imperative of disclosure [*divulgation*]. The third one, which goes without saying, is that the loss of the art of reading proceeds from the loss of the art of writing.

I maintain that we are touching here the heart of Strauss's thought. It may be that Socrates' sentence by the Athenian court sheds light on the strategy Plato adopted; likewise, the power exercised in Holland by Judaism and, more dangerously still, by the Protestant denominations sheds light on Spinoza's strategy. But the main point is that the communication of philosophical truth is *never possible or desirable*. Why water down Strauss's thought? In order to try to make him into a philosopher who prudently puts us on guard against the effects of modern liberalism's degeneration? His design is otherwise *subversive*. I borrow this last term from him. He applies it to Machiavelli's project. To hear him tell it, the latter's real target was the Bible and, beyond the Bible, the principles of the classics. Would not his own target be the principles of liberal thought?

It will be said, however, that Strauss is not asking us to return to the principles that guided the Athenians' "way of life," still less those of the Spartans. He even says expressly in several spots that such a return is impossible, since modern political philosophy and modern science have fashioned a world the Ancients could not have imagined. Certainly, that is so. Shouldn't one perhaps answer him by saying that he is attacking liberalism and agreeing to philosophize in a world ruled by diabolic principles? Perhaps he would respond as Nietzsche did. Anticipating the objections of his adversaries, the latter wrote (*Beyond Good and Evil* §37): "What? Doesn't this mean, to speak with the vulgar: God is refuted, but the devil is not? On the contrary! On the contrary, my friends. And, the devil—who forces you to speak with the vulgar?"[24] Is not Strauss suggesting that the Moderns are incapable of showing any interest in anything other than life in the city? Why then shut him up in some vulgar alternative? Philosophy remains what it is everywhere and always. As for thinking what the time in which one lives holds, it may be that it is good to preserve that for its own sake.

A note from the essay on "Persecution" intrigues me. It is supposed to shed light on the passage where it is said that the modern philosophers, the *heterodox philosophers*, "looked forward to a time when . . . *no one would suffer any harm* from hearing any truth."[25] In this note, Strauss quotes the phrase of an author who, I admit, is unknown to me, Archibald MacLeish: "Perhaps the luxury of the complete confession, of the uttermost despair, of the farthest doubts should be denied themselves by writers living in any but the most orderly and settled times. I do not know."[26] Let us recall only that Strauss warned that a prudent writer sometimes delivers in a mere note remarks that, in a text, would risk being taken as being in bad taste.

II

Most of Strauss's writings are devoted to the study of philosophical—or, to express it better, philosophical-political—works, classical works or premodern ones or those standing at the origin of modernity that still bear the trace of the principles they are intending to refute (notably those by

Machiavelli and Hobbes). The task is to restitute the design of their authors, as these authors themselves conceived it. This task is guided by the conviction that their thought has been smothered under the weight of the tradition that has been grafted onto it and that it is misrecognized by modern commentators who have become incapable of challenging the presuppositions of their time. There are other writings, whose intention is apparently didactic. I am thinking of the ones in which he proposes to deliver, in a condensed form, the teachings of classical political philosophy, bringing out the kinship that exists among Plato, Aristotle, and Xenophon. Some other ones, finally, preferably placed at the head of a collection of scholarly articles, tend to bring out the character of modernity, or certain peculiar aspects of modernity, and cling to "the crisis of our time." The essays of the second kind are those that apparently pose the least problems for reading. This does not mean that they would be entirely limpid. The writings of the first kind are addressed to a small number of rather curious, enlightened, and patient readers in order to put them to the test of deciphering texts that testify to an *art of writing* of extreme refinement—a test, therefore, that I would not call unpleasant, since the subtlety of the interpreter often elicits a sense of enchantment, but difficult enough to discourage a public generally more disposed to pass judgments than to ask questions. According to Strauss, these texts are guided by the idea that there exist truths that are valid in all places and at all times, and they impose on us the exigency that we discover these truths or at least face up to some permanent alternatives. His posture is therefore not that of a historian of ideas but that of a philosopher-interpreter. There is every reason to suppose that this philosopher-interpreter best offers us his thinking when he shows himself to be questing after truths or permanent alternatives, and that he also communicates to us a teaching about our time since in our time we are led to challenge the idea of permanence in general; but this teaching then remains implicit. The writings of the third kind apparently do not spare the most widely shared opinions; they even intentionally leave room for polemics. Also, they set partisans and adversaries in motion. Nothing is less certain, however, than the idea that the oppositions they stir up are most often well founded. These writings, like the other ones, are exoteric, as must also be the entire oeuvre of political philosophy. In a sense, they seem to me to be even more exoteric, for the public to which they are addressed is larger and the art of dissimulation in the communication of his thoughts is here more necessary.

To justify this impression, I shall limit myself to offering a brief exploration of the three texts that open the collection entitled *Liberalism Ancient and Modern:* the preface, "What Is Liberal Education?" and "Liberal Education and Responsibility."[27] Strauss's language being extremely controlled, a serious study would require a much more extended treatment. But a few castings of the lead may be profitable for sounding the depths and may serve to shed doubt on two images that seem to proceed from an insufficiently attentive reading. According to the first one, Strauss's political philosophy would be inspired by conservatism or might lead to conservatism. According to the second, it would in practice tend, in response to the "crisis of our time," to persuade the most enlightened of the need to go against the current that is more and more making modern liberalism deviate from its initial direction, to assess the dangers modern liberalism harbors when it abandons classical liberalism, and, finally, to reform it, for its vices ought not to distract one from the defense of its virtues.

Since I wish to be brief, I shall have recourse to what I would willingly call the *sampling process* of which Strauss so often makes use, not without drawing attention to his silences or to what seem to me to be signs of deliberate simplification. Let us consider the preface. From the start, Strauss inquires about the nature of liberalism. It is through opposition to conservatism, he notes, that it "is understood here"[28]—that is to say, in America. So be it, people may prove to be liberals on some points and conservatives on others. What remains, it seems, is the distinction between two ideal types. In fact, we know that the author hardly relishes concepts forged by Max Weber. He feigns to give the terms some consistency by referring to the common opinion, which provides him, like Aristotle, with a point of departure. Thus does he observe that the then-present criterion for opinion was the Vietnam War and the War on Poverty. However, he breaks with opinion in order to observe that liberalism and conservatism have a common basis; they both define themselves in opposition to Communism. The opposition between the two therefore does not seem fundamental. Yet soon a parallel is established between liberalism and Communism: they pursue the same ultimate end, it is said, even though they disagree over the means; the ultimate end is "a classless society or, to use the correction proposed by Kojève, the universal and homogeneous State, of which every adult human being is a full member."[29]

One can ask oneself whether Strauss is not exploiting Kojève to advance what is at first sight a crude and untenable version of liberalism. Who could seriously confuse it with Marxism? Speaking manifestly of liberalism "here and now," Strauss silently passes over one of the fundamental criticisms lodged against it, namely that it has, with positivism, engendered a generalized relativism, that it attributes equal value, in the world, to the most varied cultures, and that, in the context of America, it opens onto the belief that each person has a right to live as he pleases and to believe what he pleases. From that angle, doesn't it appear radically alien to Communism?

Is Strauss then treating liberalism in the same way that a conservative blinded by partisanship does? Some readers may be tempted to judge him in this way, noting the portrait of conservatives that immediately follows. Adversaries of "the universal and homogeneous State," the latter think such a State is "both undesirable and impossible." Of course, they do not fear envisaging the creation of larger political units, but they "look with greater sympathy than liberals on the particular or particularist and the heterogeneous."[30] Strauss, and there is no doubt on this subject, thinks that politics is, by nature, concerned with the "being and well-being of this or that particular society."[31] Nonetheless, I observe that the concept of heterogeneity is hardly one familiar to him. After having noted that conservatives are accused of discrediting the idea of the unity of reason—a reproach he does not make his own—the author takes a new step: to "remain closer to the surface," conservatism could be said to be distinguished by its "distrust of change," while liberalism would best be defined as "progressivism."[32]

Nevertheless, hardly has this remark been advanced when it seems in effect to be superficial. "The conservativism [sic] of our age," we learn,

> is identical with what originally was liberalism, more or less modified by changes in the direction of present-day liberalism [a strange turn of phrase—C. L.]. One could go further and say that much of what goes now by the name of conservativism has in the last analysis a common root with present-day liberalism and even with Communism.[33]

That would appear quite evident "if one were to go back to the origin of modernity, to the break with the premodern tradition that took place in the seventeenth century, or to the quarrel between the ancients and the moderns."[34] Let us halt here our examination of the preface. One must admit that at the end of a winding path, it is discovered that modern liberalism is inconsistent and that, despite appearances, conservatism offers only a variant thereof.

Let us cast a glance now on the essay "What Is Liberal Education?" This question is not unconnected with the one posed in the preface: What is liberalism? Strauss shows first how difficult it is to come by teachers who are capable of instructing their pupils, since one's capacity as a teacher depends on the education received and since the latter, from generation to generation, requires an understanding of the only true teachers, "the great minds,"[35] who do not agree with one another. It follows therefrom that education "cannot be simply indoctrination."[36] If one recognizes at least that it is an education in culture, one must confront another difficulty. Is it possible that liberalism is concerned only with the Western tradition when what it wants is to give the diversity of cultures its due? After having asked himself where the discovery of this diversity leads and having pointed out that the very notion of culture is becoming less and less definable, since it covers any and all "pattern of conduct common to any human group" ("culture of suburbia or . . . the culture of juvenile gangs, both nondelinquent and delinquent," nay even that of "inmates of lunatic asylums"), Strauss, following a customary procedure, suddenly abandons his question in order to return to the traditional idea that liberal culture is "some sort of education in letters or through letters." [37] This idea being at the basis of modern democracy, he arrives at the question: What is modern democracy? which is thus substituted for the initial one: What is liberalism?

Here we have arrived, it seems, at the heart of the matter. According to some, modern democracy is the regime in which all men would give some proof of virtue and wisdom; it would be the model of "*the* rational society." [38] This opinion permits him to introduce the concept of aristocracy, which is soon going to push the discussion in a new direction: "Democracy, in a word, is meant to be an aristocracy which has broadened into a universal aristocracy." [39] Who has lent support to this thesis? Strauss does not specify. The least that can be said is that once again he evokes an extreme opinion, one liable to awaken in the reader a sense of absurdity, in order to examine another opinion from which he will bring out equally absurd consequences. This opinion, which in turn he characterizes as extreme, is the one that predominates in political science. In a word, the ideal of democracy is denounced as an illusion: far from aspiring to becoming a universal aristocracy, democracy can only claim the title of a government of the masses; but in fact, the masses not being capable of governing, it could only be a government of elites and, for such a kind of government to be practiced efficiently, the most desirable thing is that the masses not get themselves mixed up in public affairs. Such is the condition for the "smooth working of democracy": its "virtue" depends on "electoral apathy, viz., lack of public spirit." [40] Putting forward the term *elite,* Strauss sticks on it the following label: a government "of men who for whatever reason are on top or have a fair chance to arrive at the top." [41] He thus is suggesting that another illusion is to see in the leaders wise men or even simply competent ones. There may be some of those; that isn't impossible. But elites are composed only of those who have already "arrive[d]," or "arrivistes," as one says in French.

Is it not clear that Strauss is going after one aspect of conservatism? We know that the language of a portion of conservatives is that of order and stability—as distinct from that of the "progressives"—and that the former willingly invoke virtue rather than liberty and equality. Now, it turns out that this language proves to be a cover-up for cynicism: order proceeds from the absence of public spirit. To hear him tell it, "those citizens who read nothing except the sports page and the comic section" are "not indeed the salt of the earth, but the salt of modern democracy."[42] Cynicism, moreover, as we already announced, is allied with dormancy. On the one hand, mass culture itself requires "new ideas" and "creative minds"—or at least what are labeled thus—within mediocrity itself; it is impossible, let us understand, to erect a barrier against change. On the other hand, "democracy, even if it is only regarded as the hard shell which protects the soft mass culture, requires in the long run qualities of an entirely different kind: qualities of dedication, of concentration, of breadth, and of depth."[43]

This second objection is troubling. The image of the *hard shell*—here I permit myself a literal translation into French, *cage dure*—does it not evoke the one, forged by Max Weber at the very end of his essay on *The Protestant Ethic and the Spirit of Capitalism,* of a capitalism liberated from the Puritan ethic? I believe so all the more as Strauss adds almost immediately: "Liberal education is the counterpoison to mass culture, to the corroding effects of mass culture, to its inherent tendency to produce nothing but 'specialists without spirit or vision and voluptuaries without heart.'" Now, the unmentioned author of this expression is, as a matter of fact, Weber himself. No doubt, it is one familiar to his audience; "What Is Liberal Education?" is the text of a lecture given at the University of Chicago. The quotation is taken from a passage precisely where the cage image is introduced. Following Strauss's reading method, let us restore Weber's text:

> No one knows who will live in this cage in the future, or whether at the end of this tremendous development entirely new prophets will arise, or there will be a great rebirth of old ideas and ideals, or, if neither, mechanized petrification, embellished with a sort of convulsive self-importance. For of the "last men" of this cultural development, it might well be truly said: "Specialists without spirit, sensualists without heart; this nullity imagines that it has attained a level of civilization never before achieved."[44]

Weber himself, it must be pointed out, is quoting, without mentioning him, Nietzsche, a writer who came to exert upon Strauss an extraordinary attraction. Finally, let us not fail to point out that, before formulating his question, Weber had just referred to the United States, a country in which "the pursuit of wealth, stripped of its religious and ethical meaning, tends to become associated with purely mundane passions, which often actually give it the character of *sport*."[45] It is worthwhile to observe that Strauss is substituting for the problem of capitalism that of mass culture—judging highly significant the passion for sport that guides the newspaper reader—and of democracy: the *last man* is, for him, as for Nietzsche, the democratic man, the man of the herd. And likewise, it is worthwhile observing that he envisages neither an appearance of new prophets nor a powerful renaissance of old ideals; solely the defense of liberal education as "counterpoison to mass culture" suffices for him.

My commentary may seem heavy-handed, but it invites one to look closely at Strauss's design. From the formula "Liberal culture is the counterpoison to mass culture," he glides to another one: "Liberal education is the ladder by which we try to ascend from mass democracy to democracy as originally meant."[46] Then, to still another one: "Liberal education is the necessary endeavor to found an aristocracy within democratic mass society."[47] These last two phrases struck the imagination of his audience —and of his readers—so much so that he was invited to be more specific about what he meant—a request that offered him the opportunity to present a new lecture (which forms the substance of the following essay, "Liberal Education and Responsibility"). Clearly, those who pressed him to explain himself thought that he was delivering here his most important message. They hadn't paid attention to the following phrase that, in the text, closes the paragraph: "Liberal education reminds those members of a mass democracy who have ears to hear, of human greatness."[48] Now, it might be that the pleasant phrase relating to the qualities always required to maintain the "cage" or "shell" of democracy are only the first rung, which would allow one to ascend from the idea of safeguarding democracy to the only idea that counts, that of safeguarding "human greatness." It might be that returning to the signification of democracy as originally meant is in no way Strauss's concern, if it was carrying the germ of mass democracy and was already championing the principles that would have brought about the loss of meaning for classical political philosophy and the liberal education that was associated with it. It might be, finally, that the notion of an aristocracy within democracy is a decoy [*un leurre*].

This hypothesis, it seems to me, is confirmed by a reading of "Liberal Education and Responsibility." The final part of this essay allows one to glimpse only a faint part of Strauss's thought. There, Strauss offers one sterling remark after another, all of them designed to win sympathy from a "humanist" public. Asking himself, "What are the prospects for the liberally educated to become again a power in democracy?", he declares: "We are not permitted to be flatterers of democracy precisely because we are friends and allies of democracy."[49] (This is a phrase of which Straussians will make great use.) He is not forgetting that, "by giving freedom to all, democracy also gives freedom to those who care for human excellence."[50] He does not hesitate to rejoice that "no one prevents us from cultivating our garden [as if this formula did not seem to him execrable—C. L.] or from setting up outposts which may come to be regarded by many citizens as salutary to the republic."[51] Warning that such "exertion[s]" are a necessary but not sufficient condition for success, he quotes the following maxim: "Men can always hope and never need to give up, in whatever fortune and in whatever travail they find themselves."[52] That the author of this phrase is Machiavelli, an eminently "subversive" thinker whose project was to undermine the teachings of the Bible and the classics, is something he takes care not to specify. It is up to his complicitous audience to comprehend the ruse. He insinuates that one can doubt the good political effects of modern liberal education since "Karl Marx, the father of communism, and Friedrich Nietzsche, the stepfather of fascism [an opinion that isn't his—C. L.], were liberally educated on a level to which we cannot even hope to aspire."[53] But this is to say that one is to draw a lesson from "their grandiose failures," to understand anew that "wisdom cannot be separated from moderation . . . and . . . that wisdom requires unhesitating loyalty to a decent constitution and even to the cause of constitutionalism."[54] For the rest, the critique of scientists' present confinement within specialities as well as the praise of humanists, of "the spirit of perceptivity and delicacy," and of "the reading in common of the Great Books" have the best effect.[55] But one would search in vain for the signs of Strauss's true thought in his supposed conclusion. Previously, he described at length what, according to the Ancients, a city governed by gentlemen was, in what their education (the cultivation of character) and their way of life (a certain idleness that prompted them to reading, to conversations among discriminating men, and to reflection on the common good) consisted; he showed why, even though they didn't understand the meaning of philosophy (a search for truth that is indifferent to conventions), their political virtue was like a reflection of the virtue of the philosophers, why they didn't have to feel *responsible* before the vulgar, and why the philosophers didn't have to feel responsible before them.

Is not an aristocracy within modern democracy then chimerical? How is one to imagine it after this picture has been painted? It is true that a fully aristocratic regime undoubtedly never existed in Greece itself and that, according to the philosophers, the formula best adapted to reality is that of a *mixed government.* Now, isn't there an affinity between modern republicanism and mixed government? The answer, immediately announced, is that the modern doctrine is distinguished by its affirmation of a natural equality among men and that of a sovereignty of the people that is supposed to be in harmony with the guarantee of the natural rights of individuals.

Without entering into the detail of the argument, let us underscore a few points. Strauss agrees then that the government of gentlemen does not necessarily conform to the presentation he has made of it, but he specifies that the latter contains in its very principle a refutation of democracy: "Roughly speaking, democracy is the regime in which the *majority of free adult males* in a city rules, but only a minority of them are educated."[56] On the other hand, democracy is guided not by the idea of virtue but by that of liberty, which is understood as the right of each citizen to live in his own way. In Strauss's mind, this refutation is aimed not only at ancient democracy but much more still at modern democracy.

The opposition between virtue and liberty, it seems to me, is at the center of his reflections. Virtue does not consist in cultivating one's garden but in seeking the good. In this regard, political virtue is not alien to philosophical virtue, though the former is inferior to the latter. In a city that obeys the principle of virtue, the relations among men are ordered in terms of an end: common happiness. In a city that obeys the principle of liberty, the dominant concern is to permit each to live as he pleases, provided that he does not harm others. The political thinkers who defend this principle maintain a faith in reason, for in their judgment each can discover through use the utility of respecting the law, which is conceived as a rule of the game and without which no order would be possible. No need for an *idea* of the common good; the latter seems to come out of each person's pursuit of his enlightened self-interest. Gentlemen, let us repeat, do not know the highest virtue, but at least they have some notion of virtue.

Strauss does not say it expressly here, but that is very much what he thinks: Gentlemen have not lost the sense of a fundamental distinction between what is noble and what isn't. It is through this distinction that their political virtue proves to be a reflection of philosophical virtue and that the existence of philosophy is itself profitable for the city, for it testifies to a detachment from all the goods of this world that men covet as well as to an aspiration to excellence. In this sense, even in a regime that rests on a certain compromise between the desire of gentlemen and the desire of the people to participate in public affairs and to demand of those who possess authority to account for their actions—that is to say, even in a mixed regime—a separation is maintained between the cultivated minority and the greater number. But this is possible only upon the condition, as a matter of fact, that the minority acquire an education that disposes it to conduct itself in a disinterested way. Thus does it continue to stamp its style on the city. Let us say quite simply that the gentlemen are respected and that those who are inferior to them know or believe that these gentlemen legitimately stand above them — were this only on account of their belonging to old and distinguished families. What else Strauss does not say expressly, but which emerges from his comparison between the Ancients and the Moderns, is that *the majority of free adult males* are distinguished from unfree men and that this majority therefore possesses, despite its lack of cultivation, the notion of a natural inequality. By way of contrast, modern republicanism, although it might recognize the merits of a mixed regime, rests, we have said, on the entirely new doctrine of the natural equality of men.

What becomes of democracy under such conditions? It is a form of society in which one has obliterated the image a minority might give itself and might give others regarding its legitimate superiority. The loss of this image goes hand in hand with the disappearance of a kind of education that would tend toward the cultivation of character. Remarkable is the fact that in the essay with which we are concerned, although there is passing mention of the effect the rise of commerce and industry had on the very early stages of the American Republic, and although the misdeeds associated with the new scientific spirit governing the training of specialists are denounced, Strauss brings the main force of his critique of modernity to bear on the principles of liberalism or of the "original democracy."

First, he is seen mentioning sympathetically Hamilton's efforts to preserve something of the spirit of the classics. Hamilton and his colleagues, indeed, signed their articles in the *Federalist Papers* with the single name of Publius, eloquent testimony to their attachment to Antiquity. Conscious of "the difference between business and government,"[57] they wished to delimit, at a distance from groups moved by their interests (mechanics and manufacturers, themselves subordinated to merchants, on the one hand, and landlords, on the other), a category, that of the learned professions, which, having no distinct interests, would be best suited to perform leadership roles with a concern for the public good.

But Hamilton is mentioned as an authority only to highlight the difficulties the American Republic faced at the time of its foundation. How could the new elite receive an education fit for gentlemen — a liberal education — since the doctrine has destroyed their image? In fact, this new elite was composed mainly of lawyers, that is to say, of men whose training was limited to specialized knowledge of law. In passing, I observe that Hamilton, unlike Madison who dreaded this expression, defined the new regime as a "representative democracy." Strauss undoubtedly isn't unaware of that fact.

Likewise, Strauss wraps himself in Burke, who, despite the respect he shows for lawyers, emphasized that "to speak 'legally and constitutionally' is not the same as to speak 'prudently' "; thus did he restore an appreciation for the task of the legislator and held as a *single rule* "the great principles of reason and equity, and the general sense of mankind."[58] Now, cannot one also doubt the credit granted to this writer, for his ideas become the object of a thorough analysis in the last chapter of *Natural Right and History*,[59] which tends to show that, despite his vehement condemnation of the principles of the French Revolution, he no less broke with classical political philosophy?

The work of John Stuart Mill, which has the merit of having defended liberal education, is equally invoked as a source for the critique of the vices of representative government. But, in the first place, all he did was imagine a reform of legislation, thanks to the establishment of proportional representation, and this remedy, it rapidly became apparent, was "insufficient, not to say worthless."[60] Then, abandoning the idea that the method of recruitment for assemblies might ever allow "a selection of the great political minds of the country,"[61] he placed his hopes on the transformation of the bureaucracy into a body of functionaries devoted to their tasks, a genuine "civil service."[62]

Of course, Strauss is not challenging this noble project, but his silence about its chances of success is significant. A few lines further on, he deems it "more modest, more pertinent, and more practical to give thought to some necessary reforms of the teaching in the Departments of Political Science and perhaps also in Law Schools."[63] Allow me to leave matters here without pursuing them further; I have said enough to be able to conclude that Strauss is closing off all the exits for the modern republic. The possible remedies change nothing in its essence.

This conclusion does not prompt one to give up on philosophy. Although we might not be able to be philosophers, "we can love philosophy; we can try to philosophize."[64] To understand what this last formulation means, one must refer back to the last part of the previous essay. "Liberal education," he tells us there, "consists in listening to the conversation among the greatest minds."[65] Far from being easy, this task faces an "overwhelming difficulty."[66] Strauss presents it in admirable terms that show how mistaken his adversaries are when they condemn him for dogmatism. In short, it may be said that "listening to the conversation among the greatest minds" does not exactly account for our task, for this conversation takes place only thanks to us;[67] it is we who instigate it. "The greatest minds utter monologues. We must transform their monologues into a dialogue, their 'side by side' into a 'together.' "[68] Of course, Plato himself wrote dialogues, but these were pseudodialogues: a superior man conversed with interlocutors who were inferior to him. "We must then do something which the greatest minds were unable to do,"[69] that is to say, we must establish a dialogue between superior beings. And as they disagree with one another, we still must judge, even though, on account of our inferiority, we wouldn't be competent to judge. And we are concealing this difficulty from ourselves when we imagine that with time we have obtained a superior standpoint. In succumbing to this illusion—Strauss does not say it, but let us say it in his place—we would have to set them on a ladder, from the top of which we would measure how high they have risen. But it doesn't suffice to "face our awesome situation"; we still must know its "cause."[70] Now, to this question Strauss provides a political answer:

> As it seems to me, the cause of this situation is that we have lost all simply authoritative traditions in which we could trust, the *nomos* which gave us authoritative guidance, because our immediate teachers and teachers' teachers believed in the possibility of a simply rational society. Each of us here is compelled to find his bearings by his own powers, however defective they may be.[71]

And, he adds, "We have no comfort than that inherent in this activity."[72]

This argument is enigmatic, not because he admits that philosophical activity is without an extrinsic guarantee, that it discovers its "truth" only in its own movement—such is, it seems to me, the unsurpassable mystery of faith in reason—but because, in the formulation Strauss provides, he is urging one to, by turns, condemn and honor democracy. He seems to honor it, for it is really from the situation in which it places us, from the obligation it imposes upon us to go forward without guideposts, that the possibility is opened—not, as Strauss says elsewhere, for us to give in to relativism, to obtain our good where it pleases us, but to establish (at our own risk, certainly) a dialogue among the philosophers, to bring into existence a *community of philosophers*. Husserl says nothing else in the *Krisis* (although Strauss does not do justice to Husserl when he retains only Husserl's project of a "rigorous science"). There is no need to point out that democracy no longer appears, in this light, as that amiable and inconsistent regime that permits each to "cultivat[e his own] garden," including his philosopher's garden, but very much rather as that regime which is generative of a search for truth, of a test of freedom in which what is proper to philosophy is recognized. Wouldn't one have to admit, in the same stroke, that people's lives in democratic society bear the stamp of a philosophical restlessness? Nevertheless, from another point of view the argument seems to be discrediting philosophy, since belief in the possibility of a rational society and the illusions of universalism are allegedly making us lose the meaning of proportion, the confidence in a reason that is always faced with its limit.

Strange, nonetheless, is the conjunction of two statements, as Strauss is not unaware that they have quite different significations: "We have lost all simply authoritative traditions"; and we have lost "the *nomos* which gave us authoritative guidance." Did he not himself on several occasions draw attention to the fact that political philosophy was born in Greece from a shaking of traditions? I do not know how to follow Strauss's thought here. His oscillation reminds me nonetheless of Nietzsche's, in his famous aphorism on the historical sense (*Beyond Good and Evil* §224), between the enchantment the aristocratic desire for the beautiful and for the perfected work procures for him and the enchantment the modern desire for everything unknown and for the infinite procures for him. And I recall not only Strauss's attraction to Nietzsche but also his attraction to Machiavelli, two "diabolic" minds. While Strauss may be judging that the classical notion of virtue has disappeared or is in the process of disappearing in our world, it is certain that his hypothesis of an aristocracy within democracy is a fiction. But perhaps he is preserving the idea that there is some *virtù* in defending virtue. Upon second reading, the tiny phrase I found both anodyne and cunning could very well be faithful to his thought: "Men can always hope and never need to give up, in whatever fortune and in whatever travail they find themselves."

III

Of all the exoteric texts Strauss has devoted to modernity, one of the most instructive, it seems to me, is the article "The Crisis of Our Time," published in 1964.[73] It must be believed that he prized it particularly, since one finds an almost completely identical passage in the introduction to *The City and Man* and numerous traces of it in "An Epilogue" from *Political Philosophy: Six Essays*.[74] Let us freely summarize the argument of the first section, the only one that matters to us. The diagnosis is formulated at the start: "The crisis of our time" resides in the doubt raised by what we can call "the Modern Project."[75] This project has garnered a broad success since it has led to the formation of an unprecedented type of society. But it is generally granted at present that it has become inadequate, and we are also compelled to reinterrogate its principles. The concept of *project* alerts the reader. Strauss sheds light on it by declaring quite clearly that it proceeds from a new political philosophy that emerged in the sixteenth and seventeenth centuries. And he boldly points out that the ultimate consequence has been "the disintegration of the very idea of political philosophy."[76] For most political scientists, it no longer seems like anything more than ideology or myth. The task would therefore be "the restoration of political philosophy," and, to do this, one would have to "go back to the point where the destruction of political philosophy began," that is to say, the destruction of "the political philosophy originated by Socrates and elaborated above all by Aristotle." [77]

It would thus be fitting to reopen *the quarrel of the Ancients and the Moderns,* whose stakes are not literary but philosophical. As for the diagnosis, the author judges that these stakes were formulated by Spengler in the aftermath of World War I. Western culture, according to the latter, didn't belong only to the small collection of higher cultures; this was the culture that had conquered the globe, had opened itself to all the others, and thought of itself as culture *as such.* In fact, there is room to doubt that Spengler is an authority for Strauss. Indeed, Strauss notes in passing that the notion of culture, thus understood, presupposes the abandonment of the classical conception of culture as the molding of the mind. He silently skips over the name of Nietzsche, that is to say, the only thinker whose merit he recognizes for having attacked the bases of modernity. Spengler's work is only a vulgar by-product of the grandiose work of Nietzsche. The latter never judged that the decline of the West meant the decline of the most elevated culture or of culture as such. Likewise, let us observe that authority ironically devolves upon science ultimately to refute Spengler and the thesis that, at present, "the highest possibilities of man are exhausted." [78] That "our highest authority, natural science, considers itself susceptible of infinite progress" seems, in effect, to demonstrate that the ultimate questions, *the riddles* confronting man are still not resolved. [79] Every reader of Strauss has learned that science is unaware of the ultimate questions, that it has established the reign of positivism—or else that it is the consequence thereof—and that one must therefore not expect from it a "culture of the human mind." [80]

Why, then, this curious manner of proceeding? Strauss sets out the guideposts familiar to his reader in order to lead the reader to follow him upon dangerous ground. The crisis of our time, we are to understand, is something quite other than what is called the *crisis of culture,* and it is certainly not in science that one can place one's hope, if hope there is. Strauss therefore returns to his first statement, modifying it slightly, as if he has spoken too abruptly: "The crisis of the West consists in the West having become uncertain of its purpose." [81] What was this purpose? That of uniting all men. "The West . . . had a clear vision of its future as the future of mankind." [82] Here, we tell ourselves, we have a formula that accounts rather well for the ideal of the American republicans, or certain ones among them, in 1776. According to Strauss, the loss of hope in the future is an eloquent sign of the *degradation of the West.* Nevertheless, he specifies immediately, we do not have to suppose that a society would have to pursue a universal purpose in order to be healthy. A tribal society can very well be so. A nice remark intended for readers who are respectful of the customs of savages. But let us emphasize that the criterion of health is not to be confused with that of the good, and that the authority of cultural anthropology does not count any more than that of natural science. What matters is to convince one that "a society which was accustomed to understand itself in terms of a universal purpose cannot lose faith in that purpose without becoming completely bewildered."[83] The grand declarations of statesmen during the two last world wars still testified to this conviction. They did nothing more than reflect the spirit modern political philosophy had at its origin. Yet, even while invoking classical principles, modern political philosophy broke with them, claiming to lay down the bases for a society that would be superior to the one to which the Ancients had aspired. At this stage, a question comes to us: Do Strauss's reflections bear upon the crisis of our time? And must one worry about the loss of hope in the future, about the degradation of the West? Isn't the essential thing rather to examine the crisis that opens at the birth of modern political philosophy and to worry about the degradation, if not the disappearance, of classical political philosophy, which is not *another* political philosophy but political philosophy as such?

Finally, we get a description of the modern project: Philosophy or science has ceased to be understood as "essentially contemplative" so as to become "active."[84] Let us remark that Strauss says *philosophy* and no longer *political philosophy*. Why? Because political philosophy was for the classics only philosophy turned toward human things, toward the life of man in the city. By adopting a political mode of communication, philosophy showed itself to be concerned with prudence in its public expression, carefully brushing aside, through a certain art of writing, the mass of readers who, by nature, cannot rise to the knowledge of the true and the just—a knowledge that destroys all prejudices. In challenging the ideal of the contemplative life, the new philosophers have no other goal but to change man's condition. Their thought is no longer guided by the idea of a nature proper to the human being and to all things nonhuman, of a nature to which the relationships among all beings conform. The goal is henceforth to make of science an intellectual activity that manifests man's all-powerfulness, to "become the master and the owner of nature."[85] The adventure of modern science is a philosophical adventure—if that can be said, since in a sense the new philosophy signifies a break with philosophy as such. At the origin of modernity, notes Strauss, philosophy and science intermingled. They proceeded from a conversion of the mind. In the same movement, the mind ceased to aspire to what is higher and, being concerned only with the reality of the senses, claimed mastery over what is.

Without pausing over the mediations his argument would require, Strauss bundles under the same "Modern Project" label the idea of natural science, that of "progress toward an ever greater prosperity," that of the "natural right of everyone to comfortable self-preservation," that of the harmonious development of everyone's faculties, that of "an ever greater freedom and justice," and that of the universal league of all nations, won over little by little to the cause of freedom and equality.[86] The project turns out to be the same on the level of knowledge, the economy, social life, and the history of humanity—with the latter no longer understood in its intension but in its extension: the set of men populating the earth. How, in the final analysis, is this project to be characterized? It is that of democracy. The objective is to make of each society a democratic society and to dissolve all societies into a single democratic society. And it finds its primary justification not in a faith in universal rationality but in its conformity to the shared wishes of the large majority of men. Much more than the changes introduced by modern science, Strauss places the accent here on the *irresistible* movement (as Tocqueville named it) that is triggered by the upsurge of the masses. In a certain sense of the word, his interpretation is political. And were we still to doubt it, the remarks he makes afterward about Communism would end up persuading us of that fact. "The experience of Communism has provided the Western movement with a twofold lesson: a political lesson, a lesson regarding what to expect and what to do in the foreseeable future, and a lesson regarding the principle of politics."[87]

In short, the democracies' conflict with Communism, which conducts a policy of conquest, has rendered futile the faith in a universal State. Even supposing a federation of democratic nations were to be established under threat of thermonuclear war, one would have to agree that the political hasn't rid itself of "particularism." Thus, "for the foreseeable future political society will remain what it always has been: a partial or particular society whose most urgent and primary task is its self-preservation and whose highest task is its self-improvement."[88] As for the character of this self-improvement, Strauss quickly observes that the West has begun to doubt its belief in the virtues of an affluent society at the same time that hope in a world society is slipping away. Nevertheless, he is not satisfied with these considerations inspired by the experience of Communism. His critique of the modern project suddenly highlights the vice of liberal democracy's constitution; this vice is such that it hardly lets one think—assuming that the present need to resist its enemy is leading it to give up its universalist principles—that it would have any chance of devoting itself to "the highest task." In abandoning the principles of classical political philosophy, it has engendered a split between that which pertains to the operation of political and economic institutions and that which pertains to education (understood as the cultivation of character); a split between that which pertains to the law and that which pertains to morality and also between that which pertains to a purely theoretical knowledge and a knowledge ruled by ends that would involve a sense of responsibility on the part of enlightened citizens.

Strauss develops at this point an argument that lay at the center of his essays on liberal education but, in addition, he attacks head-on the modern idea of a system of representation. Liberal democracy presents itself as a regime in which the government would be responsible to the governed, whereas the governed would be responsible to itself. Now, when one examines this system more closely, one observes that the consequence of the rigorous distinction between the public domain and the private domain is that not only do laws assure the protection of individuals but they have been removing the private domain from public jurisdiction. They are there to protect the sphere in which each can act and think as he pleases, in which each can be as arbitrary and as prejudiced as he pleases. In reality, things certainly happen otherwise. But there is, at least, one situation where the individual is placed in an inviolable spot, the voting booth. The exercise of sovereignty is set up in such a way that this exercise is recognized as belonging to a set of individuals who are not responsible to anyone and whose morality cannot in any way be assessed. "The voting booth is the home of homes, the seat of sovereignty, the seat of secrecy." [89]

The reader glimpses again that, under cover of examining the crisis of our time, Strauss is attacking the very bases of democracy. Of course, at its origin liberal democracy implied the notion of an individual conscious of his duties, whereas at present, in the absence of a citizen education, it has been transformed into a "permissive egalitarianism." [90] At the same time, however, Strauss shows that it was always impossible to set a legal definition of the responsible citizen—whatever the criterion retained: "property qualifications, literacy tests, and the like." [91] As soon as one trusted in the popular suffrage, nothing could oppose the vices of egalitarianism. The author observes, it is true, that awareness of one's duties or, as one likes to say, a sense of responsibility can be maintained only through moral education and that no measures have been taken to develop it. But, while failing to state it frankly, he is suggesting that no one in a democracy can have authority to decide about what the norms of education are to be, since the governors enjoy legitimacy only by being responsible to irresponsible people. Besides, individuals were no more conscious of their duty in times past except thanks to the survival of traditional beliefs and, more precisely, of religious ones.

I leave aside the critique of positivism's reign in the social and political sciences and of the relativism to which belief in the irreducible diversity of cultures gives rise, for that critique is well known. Positivism is the offspring of modern liberalism, since the latter renounces the idea of a general norm for life in the city; relativism is an offspring of positivism, since, once the separation of facts and values has been affirmed, the latter slip free of all criteria that would allow for their hierarchization. My question bears on the following twofold proposition: Political philosophy has disintegrated; what matters is to restore it.

Now, is such a restoration possible? Strauss rightly indicates that the political scientists and sociologists who treat classical political philosophy as an ideology and claim to be conforming to the rules of exact knowledge prove indifferent to the conditions under which the new scientific spirit emerged. Thus does he cleverly place himself upon their terrain: science should be concerned with accounting for its own formation; if it is faithful to its principles, it has to return to the doctrines that marked a break with premodern political philosophy, examining the teachings of Machiavelli, Hobbes, and, more generally, the theory of modern natural right. Moreover, if it wants to understand the meaning of this break, it also must examine the classical doctrine, from which modern thought detached itself (and more than that: of which it was the target). But what may be called the classical doctrine can be discovered only by reading authors who, despite their divergences, contributed toward its elaboration. One must therefore patiently take up again the texts of Plato, Aristotle, Xenophon, and Cicero and apply oneself to the task of understanding these authors, as they understood themselves, that is to say, by ridding oneself of the prejudices of one's own time.

Of course, no one would object to this recommendation. Strauss formulates it with carefully calculated precautions in his introduction to *The City and Man:*

> The return to classical philosophy is both necessary and tentative or experimental. Not in spite of but because of its tentative character, it must be carried out seriously, *i.e.* without squinting at our present predicament. There is no danger that we can ever become oblivious of this predicament since it is the incentive to our whole concern with the classics.[92]

"We cannot reasonably expect," he adds, "that a fresh understanding of classical political philosophy will supply us with recipes for today's use. For the relative success of modern political philosophy has brought into being a kind of society wholly unknown to the classics."[93] Here we have another passage on which some of his disciples improperly rely. And yet, the seduction operation is rather conspicuous. The modern idea of experimentation is alien to Strauss. Indeed, he does not abstain from affirming on various occasions that classical political philosophy alone has devoted itself to the knowledge of nature and of things political—not to say that it possesses this knowledge, since it is doubtful that knowledge could ever be possessed.

I retain, however, only the remark that the situation in which we find ourselves might serve to provoke in us an interest for the classics. What is its distinctive trait? Uncertainty. In the present combination of circumstances, all traditions have been shaken. Now, let us recall that classical political philosophy itself arises in a similar situation. Here, certainly, is something that brings us to a better understanding of men who drew from the conditions of their social life a new strength to ask questions and also leads us to seek to instruct ourselves at their side. Still, we would also need to recall that traditions have been shaken more than once. To mention only some authors to whom Strauss was particularly attached—Machiavelli, Hobbes, Spinoza, Nietzsche—these writers, deemed eminently subversive, have also benefited from the "chance" to live in turbulent times, ones in which beliefs were crumbling and conflicting opinions collided against each other. Do they not help us to ask ourselves questions about our time, without our having to seek recipes in their works? Can it be judged that today's political and social sciences, while not knowing it, proceed from their work? As for the natural sciences of our day, despite considerable changes they remain conscious of the continuity of an undertaking that was inaugurated in the seventeenth century. Whence does it come that so deep a fracture might have occurred between modern political philosophy and what at present is called political science? Can one account for this event within the limits of political philosophy and maintain that it has dug its own grave?

Let us nonetheless disregard once again this observation and this question. Classical political philosophy seems to be situated at the opposite pole from political science, in the sense that it combines the study of forms of political society and of types of political behavior with a search that bears on the ultimate ends of the city and of man. Unlike modern science, it is not detached from that which it is trying to know. When the contemporary scientist reasons in terms of the distinction between facts and values, he is challenging the viewpoint of the citizen, for the latter does not stop judging that there are good and bad things, just and unjust things; likewise does he judge that there are true and false things and also factual truths as well as lies or illusions. The scientist is unaware of the fact that his knowledge presupposes a prescientific understanding of social and political life. Different is the attitude of the philosopher who takes as his point of departure the experience of the citizen or of the leader. I will add that he finds this point of departure not only in frequenting other men but in himself, since he is not born to philosophy without knowing anything about society and politics. He gains knowledge, therefore, by virtue of a reflection on opinions, which are diverse and often contradictory but always proceed from a primary power of discrimination that renders possible the labor of discernment.

It matters little that the language we employ here would not exactly be that of Strauss; I do not think I am betraying his thought. On the other hand, I cannot or I know not how to follow him when he declares, at the end of the first section of his essay on "The Crisis of Our Time," that if we want to rest on this primary layer that is that of the prescientific comprehension of the political in order to shed light on the source of our knowledge, we must return to Aristotle. Why is this return deemed necessary? He said so already at the end of the chapter of *Natural Right and History* that is devoted to Weber: We are immersed in a world wrought by science that strips away the fundamental experience of the political.[94] Now, let us grant that faith in the authority of science might have been substituted for the faith one previously placed in religion; it could not abolish the *natural* disposition to judge. When Strauss asks in what liberalism consists, he begins by searching for what the word *liberal* and the word *conservative* signify for ordinary citizens. His first reference, moreover, is to the Vietnam War. Now, if some approved of the war while others were against it, was this not because they had the notion of what is or is not a just or necessary war, or one good for the nation? He adopts a point of departure here in order to advance in his search for the nature of liberalism. This search leads him to judge that liberalism is a doctrine that dissimulates the essence of political things. The declarations of Wilson and Roosevelt at the time of the two world wars seem to him to testify to a misrecognition of politics. But it is certain, he points out, that we are still living today in a political situation.[95] This is a way of saying that the universalist discourse does not take this situation into account. Were that true, Strauss could not ignore the fact that the discourse and the practice do not coincide. After all, the Americans made war and have not stopped defending their particular interests in the times that followed. The least that can be said is that their concern with promoting democracy in the so-called underdeveloped countries has hardly ever manifested itself. Upon numerous occasions, they supported dictators and barred the way to democratic aspirations. Were it again true that their rulers went astray in imagining that the League of Nations or the United Nations might become organs capable of imposing a world order, this judgment would not require knowledge of the classical teachings; it can be based, and it has been based in fact on an analysis of the present state of the world.

Strauss uses a wholly different argument when he attacks the bases of democratic society. In affirming that the men who hold authority are responsible only to irresponsible individuals, he is insinuating that this authority is no longer a political society. It is one thing to admit that there always exists a political situation—that is to say, a situation in which there exist cities, empires, and nations requiring self-preservation, nay even "self-improvement" (which can simply mean that they are occupied with better assuring the conditions of their existence)—it is another thing to grant the permanence of societies that could be defined chiefly by their political character. Wherever permissive egalitarianism reigns, wherever there exists only an agglomeration of individuals, which keeps itself going with techniques of all sorts that answer to their needs and that tend toward "improvement" through the increase of these needs, is the notion of the political preserved? Strauss encourages us, at the very least, to doubt it. Now, if I am not mistaken, one would then have to doubt the permanence of the nature of the city and of the nature of man. According to the classical teachings, the most corrupt regime, tyranny, at least contains the possibility of a return to some other regime that is more in conformity with nature. By way of contrast, it very well seems that nothing would allow one to expect from modern democracy a substantial change. The Nietzschean image of the "last man" is sketched in the portrait of the irresponsible individual, even as the myth of the superman is set aside. Whence the question: What can "the restoration of political philosophy" signify in a society that is no longer political? Might political philosophy no longer exist then except in books?

At the heart of the Straussian critique of contemporary democracy and of the original (modern) democracy is found his critique of freedom. What, according to our author, is political freedom? Certainly, we do not doubt for a single moment that he was determined to defend it against the threat of despotism of the totalitarian kind. Nevertheless, he is suggesting that it is superficial, and he is confusing it with the set of liberties granted to private individuals who are lacking a moral education and a sense of responsibility. Strauss is not far from reducing liberalism to the utilitarian view that limits modern liberty to the commercial sphere. Of course, modern republics have always been in collusion with the commercial mind-set—as a number of philosophers have remarked—and this form of republic that is the regime of democracy has proved indissociable therefrom.

Nevertheless, there is another form of commerce that Strauss deliberately ignores. I am speaking here of *commerce* in the sense in which the word designates — in a vocabulary that has today fallen into disuse — all the relations men establish [*nouer*] with one another, as soon as the barriers separating their conditions fall. He is ignoring the virtue of a kind of sociability that escapes the grips of government and, likewise, the unfolding of a public space within which conflicts between interests, opinions, beliefs, and ways of living come to manifest themselves and also to regulate themselves, owing to the sole fact that individuals, encouraged to speak and to listen [*entendre*], can *understand and get along with one another* [*s'entendre*]. The latter doesn't mean agreeing harmoniously about everything [*s'accorder*] but making movement together, in the overlap and interconnection of their aspirations, their representations, even their myths, and putting in check the raw desire for the death of the other.

There is no need to insist upon it: opinions are divided, in part, as a function of the pressure exerted by the particular interests of certain social categories and, in part too, as a function of their dependence upon various more or less powerful, more or less enduring authorities — political authorities, religious authorities, scientific authorities, authorities connected with institutions and persons (and eventually movie stars and sports figures). Of course, the public space is not the theater for a charming debate between reasonable individuals. Political freedoms, which are at the origin of this space and maintain it, are not made to create a community of enlightened citizens, conscious of their duties. On the other hand, what they do tend to do is spread the right to judge, a right that presupposes that there exists no site from which the Law might be enunciated.

Strauss targets liberalism's alleged project of instituting a universal aristocracy. In doing so, he is aiming only at an ideology — not without simplifying it, moreover. He allows the "effective truth" it halfway covers over to escape. How much closer to this truth is Montesquieu's formula:

> In a free nation it is very often a matter of indifference whether individuals reason well or ill; it is sufficient that they do reason; hence springs that liberty which is a security from the effects of these reasonings. But in a despotic government, it is equally pernicious whether they reason well or ill; their reasoning is alone sufficient to shock the principle of that government.[96]

Tocqueville is following Montesquieu when he shows what, alongside and connected with its vices, is the virtue of the American democracy. But, it will be said, doesn't this word *virtue* then have a meaning entirely different from the one Strauss gives to it? Undoubtedly so. Nonetheless, is there not virtue in facing the unknown as one lives among others, in expecting something from the process whereby everyone relates to everyone else [*la mise en rapport de tous avec tous*]? Of course, it is futile to assume that the good derives from a system that requires each to adjust his interest to that of the others. Nevertheless, a system is not born from the institution of political freedoms. This institution involves an ethic, for there is no doubt that such freedoms last only so long as one might want them, as one might take them to be true, and as one might be inclined to mobilize in their defense.

If political freedoms are not to be reduced to guarantees offered to individuals to live as they please, neither can they be dissociated from these individuals' aptitude for a certain kind of conduct, from the formation of a sort of character whose distinctive trait seems to be revulsion against servitude. Let anyone who doubts that simply observe how difficult it is, for a people accustomed to living under a despotic regime, to regain the will to be free. A change in institutions does not suffice to achieve it. It is Strauss's judgment that the modern philosophers' presuppositions are amoral, but these philosophers have made this difficulty a primary object of their reflection. How can a corrupt people change its character? Is this even possible? Would the question of corruption have mattered so much to Machiavelli, Spinoza, Montesquieu, or Rousseau if they hadn't had an idea of what conforms to the truth of the political and what pertains to ignorance and lies?

Now, isn't this question of burning importance today, in circumstances where the power of Communism has collapsed in the Soviet Union and in Eastern Europe? Here one discovers that a reform of political and economic institutions doesn't suffice, that their success depends on a change in mores, on the capacity of the many once again to give proof of a sense of the law, of a sense of *responsibility*. Here one discovers that labor in industry or in administration and the practice of commerce require these tiny invisible things that lie at the heart of life in a democracy. If he could have witnessed recent events, would Strauss have been able to maintain his diagnosis of the "crisis of our time" and limit himself to condemning a regime based on the irresponsibility of all? I don't know. The fact is that he mentions Communism in the essay with which we are concerned only to point out that the merit of its antagonism with democracy was to inspire the latter with a political concern to preserve itself. He doesn't fear to maintain, as I recalled, that liberalism and communism tend toward the same end, "the universal and homogeneous State," and differ only over the means.

These remarks are so extraordinary that one can hardly take them seriously. If the author had limited himself to observing that the Communist enterprise is conceivable only against the background of the revolution that arose in the seventeenth or eighteenth century, no one could have contradicted him. But how can one overlook the fact that the goal of Communism is the creation of a society whose every domain of activity, whose every mode of conduct in public or private life, is subject to the same norms, norms decreed by the established power and broadcast by a single party? In contrast—and this is, moreover, the primary motivation behind the critique he addresses to it—liberal democracy seems to institute a society without norms, one pulverized or in danger of being so on account of the modern principle of freedom.

I am in no way insinuating that Strauss is indifferent to the opposition between totalitarianism and democracy. The latter is assuredly preferable, were it only because it permits the exercise of philosophy and—I recall his expression—"the only kind of intellectual independence of which many people are capable." Neither am I forgetting that, for want of being ruled by general norms, democratic society ends up being leveled out more and more on account of shared beliefs in equality, resemblance of the needs of individuals, and technological expansion [*l'expansion de la technique*]. Nonetheless, Strauss is blind to the effects of dissociating power, law, and knowledge, which produce and maintain an irreducible gap between what is of the order of politics, law, religion, education, art, and knowledge (which is itself divided into many branches). If, on the one hand, liberal democracy experiences an increasing process of homogenization, on the other, it generates by its very principle a constant heterogeneity. And if one objected that the "universal and homogeneous State" signifies, for Strauss "the world State," I would note that this image implies that of the homogeneity of its parts and that, in addition, it is still less credible inasmuch as national sentiment has remained lively in people's minds and inasmuch as the principle of noninterference in affairs pertaining to the sovereignty of a particular State has proved immutable as a matter of Right, despite its sometimes evil consequences and its hypocrisy.

The Straussian critique of modernity has the defect of bearing on only one side of things. The other side it neglects or conceals. Perhaps this is out of a concern to appear provocative. But it is not certain that, in arousing in the reader a feeling of "terror"—as one knows, terror works in the service of foundation—one will pry loose the reader from his prejudices and provide him with the distance he requires to understand the society in which he is immersed—nor is it clear that this will bring the reader back from his enslavement to the possessions of this world to the exigency of philosophy. The idea of the crisis of modernity is born with modernity; it is the ingredient modernity can never do without. This crisis is always formulated in such a way that the present-day world seems encompassed by a single view, taken from an observatory that theoretically frees us from its reaches. But from there, one face of the world offers itself while the reverse side is removed from our sight.

May a few final questions suffice to give one a glimpse of what escapes the view of this overlook from the heights of classical philosophy. With unmatched acuity, Strauss has discerned certain traits of our intellectual landscape: positivism, relativism (the most striking expression of which proves to be historicism, but which also spreads forth under the banner of culturalism), and, finally, universalism (which, despite its contrast with relativism, remains stuck to it). He brings into full light the contradictions each of these positions and their combination harbor. To conclude, however, that the principles of liberal democracy are fully unveiled in this constellation would require of him much audacity—and the abandonment of the classical ideal of moderation, which he champions.

The critique of positivism is fully justified. But whence comes this perverse propensity to dissociate facts from values in the political and social sciences? Is it not stirred up by the distinction between spheres of knowledge and, consequently, the proliferation of these scientists of a new kind who are specialists? Does not this phenomenon, which is not alien to that of the division of labor in industrial society, proceed from the "constitution" of a political society in which knowledge has to seek its own rules in its very activity, in the absence of an extrinsic norm? As soon as the theological-political sphere has disintegrated, as soon as there no longer is some ultimate referent for the activity of the scientist, a path opens up, at the end of which authority displays itself in the proof seemingly furnished by the "rational" arrangement of facts. This is certainly an illusion.

And in our day, it happens that things are reversed; historians, for example, take pleasure in saying that truth is futile [*un leurre*]. We should understand at least that the illusion proceeds from the historian's undeniable right—fully asserted at the beginning of the nineteenth century—not to *serve,* his right to extract himself from political or religious authority; it also proceeds from a will to reject the idea of an edifying history or the conviction that History cannot but be intrinsically edifying. Here is what is written at the base of modern knowledge: Let the historian's work suffice unto itself. How can one avoid observing that there is a close affinity between these dispositions toward a self-regulating knowledge and the dispositions of the writer, of the painter, of any artist who claims a right to literature, to painting, to the art to which he is devoted and who challenges the supposed "laws of genre"? Positivism is a perversion, but there is something better to do here than contrast it with the exigencies of a moral education.

Strauss's critique of historicism is no less ambiguous. Under this label, he places both the Hegelian or Marxist philosophy of history and the one that, as a consequence of its failure, comes to affirm that there are only "visions of the world" that are formed within the confines of an age and that are mutually irreducible. The second version of historicism countenances relativism, but, like the first, and, in a certain way, more rigorously, it results from the birth of the "historical sense" that is characteristic of the new spirit of modernity. For Strauss, as for Nietzsche, this event testifies at best to a break with all previous principles. But, remaining within the strict framework of theory, it does not take into account a nevertheless unchallengeable prephilosophical experience, that of the *irreversible*. Clearly, he affirms, no return to the letter of the classical teachings is possible, since the shape of the world in which we live is unprecedented. But there is not only a de facto irreversibility of the flow of time that forbids one from imagining that one might draw recipes from the teachings of the classics. Thought itself is put to the test of the irreversible. We can understand the meaning of the way of life of idle gentlemen who, on account of their leisure, have an education and breeding that separates them from the vulgar. But their condition presupposed a "natural" division between masters and slaves. Now, this division that was thinkable has become unthinkable. Every critique of the "historical sense" runs up against this rock. The return to the quarrel between the Ancients and the Moderns, as important as it might be, will never be able to deprive us of the sense of the irreversible.

Similarly, denouncing the excesses of sociology, cultural anthropology, or psychology is legitimate only if the target is a discourse that closes out the investigation instigated by the exploration of the depths and variety of those unknown continents that are the psyche of a people or the psyche of the individual who, under a variety of shapes, is always revealed to be a member of this immense species that is the human species. It seems to Strauss that the idea of humanity, in its modern acceptation, the idea of a single world, one in which all the changes that take place in one spot resound throughout its expanse, has to destroy the signification of the political. Paradoxically, this thinker so concerned with connecting political philosophy to the point of view of the citizen and to the point of view of the statesman forbids himself from taking on the tension, inhabiting each, that exists between his experience as a citizen, as an individual, and as a man. He who, better than anyone else, denounces the imposture of positivism, ends up, in order to reach his targets (relativism, historicism, culturalism, universalism, and positivism itself), giving them a full consistency and confers upon them a positivity they do not have.

Notes

"Trois notes sur Leo Strauss" originally appeared in *Écrire*, 261–301.

1 Leo Strauss, preface to *Persecution and the Art of Writing* (Glencoe, Ill.: Free Press, 1952; reprint Westport, Conn.: Greenwood Press, 1976), 5.
2 Ibid., introduction, 18.
3 Leo Strauss, *What Is Political Philosophy?* (Glencoe, Ill.: Free Press, 1959; reprint Westport, Conn.: Greenwood Press, 1973, 1976), 93–94.
4 Leo Strauss, "Persecution and the Art of Writing," *Persecution and the Art of Writing*, 24.
5 Ibid., 30.
6 Ibid., 22.
7 Ibid.
8 Ibid., 23.
9 Ibid., 23n3.
10 Ibid., 23 (emphasis added).
11 Ibid. (emphasis added).
12 Ibid.
13 Ibid., 24.
14 Ibid., 24–25.
15 Ibid., 31–32.
16 Ibid., 32.
17 Ibid.
18 Ibid., 33.
19 Alexis de Tocqueville, *Democracy in America*, trans. Henry Reeve, revised by Francis Bowen, corrected and edited by Phillips Bradley, intro. Daniel J. Boorstin (New York: Vintage, 1990), 1:264.
20 Ibid.
21 Ibid., 1:265.
22 "Persecution and the Art of Writing," 33.
23 Ibid., 34 (emphasis added).
24 Friedrich Nietzsche, *Beyond Good and Evil: Prelude to a Philosophy of the Future*, trans. Walter Kaufmann (New York: Random House, 1966; New York: Vintage, 1989), 48.
25 "Persecution and the Art of Writing," 34 (emphasis added).
26 Ibid., 34n14.
27 Leo Strauss, *Liberalism Ancient and Modern* (New York: Basic Books, 1968).
28 Ibid., preface, v.
29 Ibid.
30 Ibid., vi.
31 Leo Strauss, *Studies in Platonic Political Philosophy* (Chicago: University of Chicago Press, 1983), 29.
32 Preface to *Liberalism Ancient and Modern*, vii.
33 Ibid.
34 Ibid.
35 "What Is Liberal Education?" *Liberalism Ancient and Modern*, 3.
36 Ibid., 4.
37 Ibid.
38 Ibid.
39 Ibid.

40 Ibid., 5.

41 Ibid.

42 Ibid.

43 Ibid.

44 T/E: Max Weber, *The Protestant Ethic and the Spirit of Capitalism,* trans. Talcott Parsons (New York: Charles Scribner's Sons, 1976), 182. I have followed Talcott Parsons's standard translation, which differs from Strauss's. However, and quite significantly, Parsons's translation of Weber's unattributed reference to Nietzsche's "*letzten Menschen*" appears as the "last stage" instead of the "last men," which I restore along with its quotation marks. One wonders whether Parsons, the distinguished proponent of an American sociology, totally missed the obvious Nietzschean reference here or deliberately excised it from Weber's text, substituting a bland replacement phrase.

45 Ibid. (emphasis added).

46 "What Is Liberal Education?" 5.

47 Ibid.

48 Ibid.

49 "Liberal Education and Responsibility," *Liberalism Ancient and Modern,* 24.

50 Ibid.

51 Ibid.

52 Ibid. [T/E: "Travail" appears in the French as "épreuves"; the source is Machiavelli's *Discourses on the First Ten Books of Titus Livius,* 2.29].

53 Ibid.

54 Ibid.

55 Ibid.

56 Ibid., 12 (emphasis added).

57 Ibid., 16.

58 Burke, quoted in ibid., 17.

59 Leo Strauss, "The Crisis of Modern Natural Right," *Natural Right and History* (Chicago: University of Chicago Press, 1950, 1953): 252–323.

60 "Liberal Education and Responsibility," 18.

61 Mill quoted in ibid.

62 Ibid.

63 Ibid., 19.

64 "What Is Liberal Education?" 7.

65 Ibid.

66 Ibid.

67 Ibid.

68 Ibid.

69 Ibid.

70 Ibid., 8.

71 Ibid.

72 Ibid.

73 Leo Strauss, "The Crisis of Our Time," *The Predicament of Modern Politics,* ed. Howard J. Spaeth (Detroit: University of Detroit Press, 1964).

74 Leo Strauss, introduction to *The City and Man* (Chicago: Rand McNally, 1964), 5, and "An Epilogue," *Political Philosophy: Six Essays,* ed. Hilail Gildin (Indianapolis: Pegasus, 1975).

75 Ibid., 41.

76 Ibid.

77 Ibid., 41–42.

78 Ibid., 43.

79 Ibid.

80 Ibid.

81 Ibid., 44.

82 Ibid.

83 Ibid.

84 Ibid.

85 Ibid.

86 Ibid., 45.

87 Ibid., 46. This passage is reproduced in its entirety in *The City and Man*, 5.

88 Ibid., 47.

89 Ibid., 48.

90 Ibid.

91 Ibid.

92 *The City and Man*, 11.

93 Ibid.

94 T/E: "Natural Right and the Distinction between Facts and Values," *Natural Right and History*, 35–80.

95 "The Crisis of Our Time," 47.

96 Montesquieu, *The Spirit of the Laws*, vol. 38 of *Great Books of the Western World*, ed. Robert Maynard Hutchins (Chicago: Encyclopaedia Britannica, 1952), 19.27 (145).

Dialogue with Pierre Clastres

SHORTLY AFTER Pierre Clastres's death, Maurice Luciani, who undoubtedly was his closest friend, as he was mine, wrote in the name of the editorial staff of the Paris review *Libre* a few sober and true lines — lines that are all the more moving to reread now as he was soon to die in turn, carried away by an extremely cruel illness, and because the quick portrait he then sketched brings back his presence no less than that of his comrade:

> The work is there, and it will make its way. But to keep Pierre living among us is also for us to recall what this work was based on and what made us love him: his disdain for big shots and big talkers, as well as the attention he paid to any straight talk; his perpetual jesting, but also his sudden bursts of anger against oppression and imposture; the aloofness of his irony and the laconic presence of his friendship; his indifference to the spirit of the times, his contempt for derivative thinking, his solitary bearing.

Luciani added: "We shall often see again on street corners this bantering and discreet stroller."[1] This last phrase has often come back to me in memory, as Luciani was himself a singular stroller, and we, Clastres and I, loved to talk about it. Luciani, however, didn't leave behind him an oeuvre bearing his mark. In Clastres's oeuvre, by way of contrast, those who didn't know him can still discover something of his character — the disdain for the big shots and the big talkers, the anger against imposture joined with the jesting and irony — if they read, for example, his ferocious and witty pamphlet, "Les Marxistes et leur anthropologie" (The Marxists and their anthropology), which was printed, after his death, in the third issue of *Libre* (1978);[2] they will also discover the attention he paid to straight talk and the laconic presence of friendship, if they can make out the personality of the narrator in his *Chronicle of the Guayaki Indians.*

It is this work that best reveals his sense of friendship, taken in the old meaning of the term: the ability to discover in another a fellow [*semblable*] and to make of thought something to be shared. In a death notice I wrote for him a few years ago, I already expressed my feelings about the author of the *Chronicle;* I noted the precociousness of his vision, which was "already formed before he began his voyages."[3] Permit me to quote therefrom, for I do not know at present how to find any better words:

> It would be futile to suspect that he either could or would see only what fit his expectations. When one is reading him, one marvels, on the contrary, at an encounter with the *other* that was prefigured in himself. True, Clastres discovered the Indians in books before discovering them in the tropical forest, and he drew his inspiration from the narratives of old travelers and missionaries. Nonetheless, if he was able to decipher so quickly what the latter allowed only a glimpse of, without naming it, and sometimes while hiding it, that is without any doubt because, before devoting himself to ethnology, he bore within himself the figure of this other; it is because he was made to recognize this other on the outside, to reveal the other's identity and let him speak.[4]

Clastres's concern in writing a chronicle—and especially the way he brought it off, removing all the artifices that may tempt an author who wishes to ingratiate himself (or, to borrow once again Luciani's words: *his manifest indifference to the spirit of the times*)—reveals the quality of his attachment to the Indians whose life he had shared, his willingness to make himself their witness, and even something more, a sort of piety due a proud people, doomed to disappear. No bombast when mentioning the tragedy that was reaching its end, the soon-to-be-finished work of a world that had been proclaimed to be "new"; he then leaves it to Montaigne to speak a few words. No self-complacency, but only the simple concern, when speaking in the first person, not to conceal the presence of the narrator in relationship to what he discovers. Nothing that would betray the vain desire to believe in the goodness of the victim people, for he spares us in our sensitivity as readers no detail that revolts him: there is solely the constant effort to understand other men.

If I mention first the *Chronicle,* it is because this work bears witness to his extraordinary gift of seeing and hearing. Let it suffice to evoke the first few pages, which relate the crucial event of a child's birth. "Every birth," he notes, "is experienced dramatically by the group as a whole. It is not simply the addition of an individual to one family, but a cause of imbalance between the world of men and the universe of invisible forces; it subverts an order that ritual must attempt to reestablish."[5] He was not unaware of this before he attended the delivery of an Indian girl and followed the episodes of the rite that unfolds after the "fall" of the child. Likewise did he already know, before his stay among the Guayaki, the principal myths of their culture. But his *observational* and *descriptive* faculties, which are never subservient to theory, are only more remarkable as a result.

And not even these words are fitting, for it is not only a matter of observation. Clastres's gift for hearing and seeing is best exercised when he grasps what does not seem worth grasping: a fleeting gesture, a snatch of conversation—as if the most precious thing resided not so much in the ability to concentrate one's attention but in that of allowing oneself to be taken in by the spectacle, to pick up some signs at the edge of the visible, the audible; for example, at the moment of birth, perceiving the strangeness of the silence. And, similarly, it is not so much a matter of description, either. The narrative ceaselessly intertwines with an investigation into the social being of the Guayaki, which also opens onto their history. At the very time he is endeavoring to depict a scene, for example that of the delivery, noting with surprising precision the mother's posture at the end of her labor, the gestures of the characters appointed to greet the newborn, and then, on the day after the event, the father's departure to go hunting—vested, as he is for a moment, with exceptional powers and marked by a no less exceptional vulnerability—Clastres does not confine himself to making his reader see what he sees; he renders present what the actors see and, beyond what the latter see, in the forest that surrounds them, the invisible beings who watch over them or await them.

Clastres has distinguished himself, as one knows, on account of his conception of primitive society: an eminently singular political society, he affirmed, a "society against the State." Some embraced this conception enthusiastically, finding therein a justification for their condemnation of our present-day social organization, whereas others turned it into an object of ridicule. But it is worthwhile to recall, first of all, that this conception—however it might have arisen in his mind—took on form in contact with experience, in response to questions Western travelers' "good sense" prohibited them from answering.

This experience not only put the observer's categories off track; the encounter with the absurd contained a challenge, as the *Chronicle* shows quite well. At one point in this book, he relates to the reader the apparently unintelligible behavior of the chief of a tribe that lived for two years under the authority of a Paraguayan. Whereas the latter, each time he made a decision concerning the collectivity, communicated it publicly, so that everyone was aware of it, the Indian chief then made it his duty to inform each family about it, personally, as if those families knew nothing. Even better, Clastres notes: "As they listened to [their chief, Jyvukugi], the Indians seemed to know nothing about what he was saying: this was a strange comedy, in which the people paid close attention and pretended to be surprised, even though he was obviously not fooled."[6] This is a precious example of the encounter with the absurd. But we see how it can yield to an interpretation that breaks with the tangible evidence. "What was the secret behind this game? What rule had they all agreed to obey? Why did Jyvukugi have to repeat what they already knew?" Clastres answers: "The Indians . . . did not feel that they had really been informed until they heard the news from Jyvukugi's own mouth; it was as though only his word could guarantee the value and truth of any other speech."[7] And he then adds:

> What this represented was the essence of political power among the Indians and the real relationship between the tribe and its chief. In his role as leader of the Atchei, Jyvukugi *was obliged to speak;* this was expected of him. . . . For the first time, I was able to observe directly—for it was working transparently before my eyes—the political institution of the Indians.[8]

This episode, let us note, is not only of a nature to reveal the difference between two types of power. Clastres's shrewdness consists in discovering, in the fact of their coexistence in the same spot, that one testifies to the negation of the other. This is a symbolic negation, certainly, since the Indian chief can only repeat and comment the orders given by the Paraguayan chief, but, in this very sense, it is fully effective, since the power of the first, in doubling that of the second, challenges the legitimacy of command as such. As the author states specifically, we thus can see how the Guayaki, without working out "a theory behind their concept of political power[,] . . . simply create and maintain a relationship that is built into the very structure of their society and found in all Indian tribes."[9] Generally speaking, "these 'savage' societies *refuse,* by a sociological act and therefore unconsciously, to let their power become coercive."[10]

In response to a suggestion from Miguel Abensour, I would like to say now why the work of Clastres has mattered so much to me and also to impart some of the questions it raised for me and raises for me still. A brief bit of backtracking consequently seems to me to be necessary. Smitten by ethnological literature in my youth, I soon acquired the conviction that the phenomenon of so-called primitive societies eluded the principles of the philosophy of History—that of Hegel and of Marx and what still bears the mark of this philosophy in the last writings of Husserl. At the same time, it required a philosophical reflection, no trace of which is, despite their fecundity, contained in the work of the Structuralists. So, I tried to broach a reflection of this sort in a 1952 article entitled "Société sans histoire et historicité" (Society without history and historicity).[11] There, I brought out the difficulties involved in a theory that claimed to exclude from the course of History societies which are apparently closed upon themselves, and therefore showing no sign of evolution, and that nevertheless could not bring itself to define them as *natural*, since this theory did indeed have to see in them an initial figure of humanity. These difficulties, it seemed to me, were indications of an abstract conception of History; it was my judgment that one couldn't dissociate a mode or style of becoming from a mode or style of social life and that one therefore had to grant that primitive societies fit together in such a way as to preserve their organization, to maintain themselves lastingly in existence while conjuring away the threat of the new. "Ethnology," I said at the time, "could allow one to resume reflection upon History in new terms, provided that one seeks therein not an access to some primitive forms of human evolution but, rather, the elements for a confrontation between types of becoming."[12]

Without going back into the details of my argument, I think it is worthwhile to indicate its main lines. In the first place, I was noting that, once one has abandoned the illusion of rudimentary social organisms, whose functions could be deduced from natural imperatives of subsistence, and once one has recognized, in institutions, practices, and primitive beliefs articulated wholes that bear traces of a human form of logic, it didn't suffice to elucidate the underlying rules of social life. We still had to understand how these rules involve a *setting into form* [*une mise en forme*] of the people's lived mutual relations and toward what this "setting into form" was tending. In other words, without ignoring the problem that bears on the conditions of possibility for culture in general, or for this or that cultural system in particular—a question that is at the center of the Structuralist school of thought—I was formulating an entirely different one: What intention (a tacit one, certainly) is manifested in primitive societies that attests in particular to a "singular manner of being in Time"?[13] Leaning on a certain number of facts that indicated, in one place or another, an insufficient correlation [*inadéquation*] between behavior and rules or conflicts among rules or the existence of institutions whose apparent purpose is to defuse the effects of these conflicts, I was seeking to detect in every culture the signs of a genesis, a dimension of *advent,* an internal play of questions and answers.

In the second place, I was challenging an interpretation that, while neglecting the meaning of a sociocultural elaboration of a unique type, claimed it could, in the last resort, attribute the course of History either to the concatenation of changes in the forces of production or to the march of Spirit in quest of itself. I was endeavoring at the same time not to set aside but to reformulate the idea of a break between what Hegel had named "societies without history" and "historical" societies—what, for my part, I called *stagnant societies* (undoubtedly not a very satisfactory expression, which I had introduced to translate the term Gregory Bateson had introduced: *steady-state*) and *progressive societies* (assuredly a maladroit expression, that one, since it was being applied to a number of societies that were unaware of the idea of "progress," even though it was intended to bring out that these latter societies had been laid out in such a way that cumulative changes were becoming possible). In trying to conceive this break, I asked myself about the signification *the event* acquires in a world where there is an apprehension of the distinction between a human past, present, and future, a legitimation of action by historical precedents, a vision of an articulated time that maintains continuity with itself. I also called for a similar questioning about primitive society:

> Just as it is a matter of situating oneself at the heart of historical society in order to apprehend the movement of meaning, the plurality of possibilities, ever open debate, so it would be advisable to try to understand how primitive society shuts out the future, becomes without being conscious of transforming itself and, in some sort, constitutes itself in terms of its reproduction. In short, one would have to search for what kind of historicity stagnant society reveals.[14]

In the third place, I was extracting from Bateson's description of social life in Bali a schema whose import, in my view, went far beyond the confines of his study. In people's mode of insertion in space and in time (an always concrete, singular space, defined in terms of habitation and distances traveled, and a no less concrete time, circumscribed in terms of sociobiological or sociosupernatural events), in the constitution of a rigorous network of social relations, and in the representation of a closed universe from which every neutral relation and every sign of the unknown find themselves banished, it seemed to me that one could decipher the signs of a collective, deliberate practice that, arranging itself under the representation of man's proximity to man, was endeavoring, in the face of latent or declared conflicts, to set aside the threat that their effects would bring to bear on the stability of the community.

Finally, far from lingering over the idea of a radical difference between "societies without history" and "historical societies," I called attention to a series of characteristics within the first group that were not alien to the configuration of the second; and, in these latter ones, I brought out the ever persistent signs of a resistance to change, an ever reiterated tendency toward a closure within the limits of the already attained. Thus was I able to conclude that the terms of the question formulated at the outset in the modern theory of history had to be reversed: "If one grants that history . . . is not given with coexistence, one must comprehend how a coexistence makes itself history."[15] It is no longer, then, primitive society that is paradoxical; we have to think history as an adventure arising upon a base of human relations that do not necessarily call for it.

To summarize my point as briefly as possible, I would say that the Structuralist view and the evolutionist view seem to me, though to differing degrees, similarly flimsy. On one side, it was forgotten that a society defines itself, relates itself to itself, through a singular experience of being and of time. On the other, it was forgotten that the events in which one sought the cause for changes (whether they be of a technical, economic, or demographic order or else consist in the encounter or collision between different peoples) acquired meaning only within the framework of a given culture and that their effects depended on the way in which they were greeted or interpreted. Thus was it necessary to abandon the idea of a History in itself and for itself, within which social formations would link up with each other, as if each one were creating by its own development the conditions for its overcoming. The nature of primitive societies testified at best to a rejection of history, as that of modern Western societies to a consenting to history. What we name *history* cannot be detached from a singular mode of institution of the social.

I have taken the liberty of mentioning this old study (certain themes of which I was later to rework) because it formulated questions that are certainly not foreign to those Clastres raised later. My education [*culture*], in the domain into which I was venturing, was, it is true, purely book-learned and full of gaps; I was providing only a glimpse of what ethnology could contribute to a new reflection upon History. Also, Clastres appeared to me, when I discovered his first writings, to be this anthropologist I was calling for. Drawing on an intimate knowledge of savage societies (which was acquired during a long stay in Paraguay and then in Brazil), he was overturning the self-evident truths of evolutionism and detecting the inadequacies of Structuralism. Better than anyone else, he was showing what in the primitive world could not be reduced to the categories of thought of Western man, who is dependent upon the modern experience of History; he was showing how such a humanity—which, in the judgment of some, had vegetated and which others thought had deployed all the resources of a savage knowledge while awaiting the throw of the dice that would give rise to progress—had closed off the paths of a change, the dangers of which it had a presentiment; that is to say, it had methodically defended itself against any excesses [*tout démesure*] that might destroy its unity.

Clastres, moreover, opened a path along which I had not advanced. It was not the rejection of history, or that of social conflict, that he judged to be at the basis of the primitive community but, rather, the refusal of a power liable to detach itself from this community, the rejection of an internal division that in the end rendered possible the advent of the State. The question he was articulating—or, to say it better, discovering—at the heart of primitive society was the question of the political. As he was to state with vigor, primitive society is a political society, for, whatever might be the mechanisms [*mécanismes*] that assure that humanity is constituted beyond the reign of animality, there exists, under one form or another, only political society. In this sense, the first task he assigned to himself was to understand how primitive peoples achieved and perceived their political existence, forging institutions and having recourse to practices that can put in check every attempt to erect a power above the community.

His general thesis was based on a series of convergent analyses:

—that of chieftainship, which unveils the prohibition against anyone installed in a preeminent position exercising any sort of command;

—that of the initiation ritual, where, by means apparently akin to torture, the elders imprint upon the bodies of the adolescents the law of the community (a law that, they will know forever, dictates that each one remain the equal of the others);

—that of the production of the goods that assure subsistence, which is proportionate [*mesurée*] to the maintenance of the group in the present and the near future and is always guided by the deliberate rejection of any accumulation of wealth that would risk upsetting the group's equilibrium.

There is also his analysis of:

—the incessant wars savage tribes indulge in, the function of which seems to be to maintain the integrity of each tribe through its struggle against the outsider, or, more generally, to preserve the configuration of a diversified world, which is rebellious against all intrusions from a conciliatory and unifying power.

Clastres brought together facts that a number of ethnologists had described without relating them to each other, and he shed light on them, showing, beyond the singularity of various behaviors or institutions, an intention common to all primitive societies, a political intention.

I was all the more attentive to his design as the conviction had grown in me, since the mid-1950s, that only intelligence of the political could get us out of the positivist rut in which Marxist theory as well as the social sciences were keeping us. Via an entirely different path than the one Clastres was to follow, little by little I had been led to think that society was in its essence a political society, that one type of society was to be distinguished from another by the way it "set into form" its relations among people, classes, or groups, and that the principle behind this "setting into form" was connected to the way in which power is generated and represented.

My itinerary doesn't matter. I shall simply point out that I acquired this conviction in part because of the need to conceive the change that took place at the origin of totalitarianism and, in another part, by being in contact with the work of Machiavelli, to which I devoted a long study.[16] The formation of the regime of the USSR seemed to me to require an analysis that went beyond the economic and social fields: neither the rise of the bureaucracy nor the process of capital concentration in the modern world were sufficient to account for the birth of a new State that, as a consequence of one-party rule, was working persistently to destroy the articulations of civil society and to cover over all division. As for my reading of Machiavelli, it persuaded me that class antagonisms or, more generally, the differentiation of social forces acquired a determinate meaning only through the position the established power occupied and, what is the same thing, through the representation both the prince or his agents and the collectivity subject to him forged of it. Thus was forced on me the idea of an originary division, one constitutive of society as such, the sign of which could always be spotted in the figuration of power—a symbolic instance of authority that was, properly speaking, neither external nor internal to the space upon which it conferred its identity but furnished it simultaneously with an *inside* and an *outside*.

Far from judging them to be in contradiction with mine, Clastres's analyses prompted me to deepen my reflection on the political. Thus were some mistaken in thinking that behind our agreement lurked an opposition; these people argued that while he spoke of an "indivision" of primitive society, I was advancing the idea of an irreducible social division. To say that was to have not understood him and to have seized upon a word he had indeed employed—imprudently, I believe—so as to ignore the essential part of his interpretation. Clastres was not affirming that there existed societies without power, ones therefore that were unaware of division. That conception was dependent upon a traditional viewpoint that he had criticized. It was his judgment—which is something entirely different—that primitive society had been built up as a *society against the State,* that it had mounted a system of defenses in order to make it impossible to form a power that, detached from the community, would have the freedom to turn around against it and enslave its members to a chief. There is hardly any need to insist upon this, for such an idea presupposed that society didn't coincide de facto with itself and that it was confronted with a division whose effects it was endeavoring to cancel out. Our respective labors had simply followed different directions. Clastres recognized, as I did, that the origin of social division cannot be grasped in the realm of the real, that power cannot be summed up in its empirical operations, however these might be defined. And in his view, as in mine, sociological knowledge was not to be split off from philosophical interrogation for the simple reason that social life already implied, for those who had been caught up therein, an interrogation concerning man and the world.

It is nevertheless true that our affinities were accompanied by certain divergences that it is important for me to point out. They bear in the first place on the thesis of a radical opposition between primitive society, conceived as a society against the State—free, egalitarian society—and all other societies, ones including a State, which supposedly are established and maintained to benefit a complicitous relationship between the desire for oppression and the desire for servitude. As we shall see, this thesis challenges the very idea one has of the political. Still, I must avert one misunderstanding straight off. One cannot reasonably attribute to Clastres the thesis that primitive society would offer us the image of the "good society," that it might furnish us with a model to which our contemporaries ought to become attached in order to deliver themselves from the perversity of modern institutions. A few readers certainly believed that they had found in *Society against the State* some reasons to adopt such a thesis, and they seized upon it to become its partisans. They were mistaken. Clastres was not unaware of the phenomenon, and I heard him speak of it with his usual humor. But my testimony matters little. If one wants to know his thinking on this point, the best thing to do is to reread the few lines where he describes La Boétie's design:

> Just this easy and slight slippage from history to logic, just this gaping hole in what is most naturally evident, just this breach in the general conviction that one couldn't think society without its division between dominators and dominated. Wondering about that, the young man La Boétie transcends all of known history to say: Something else is possible. Not at all, certainly, as a program to be realized; La Boétie is not a partisan. In a sense, the people's fate matters little to him, so long as the people do not revolt; that is why, author of the *Discourse on Volun-*

tary Servitude, he can at the same time be a functionary of the monarchical State. (Whence the buffoonery of making him into a people's classic.) [17]

Nonetheless, there is room to question the argument that the existence of the State—which arose in the aftermath of the formation of a power detached from the community—could, by itself alone, be the indication of a fracture in the History of humanity, a fracture by which we would, in discovering it, gain a complete understanding of History, since History would be, up until a certain moment, the history of struggle against the State and, from that moment on, the history of a struggle that fosters a continual expansion of the State.

In the essay he wrote about La Boétie (in the very passage we just mentioned), Clastres, borrowing a term from this thinker, names *misfortune* [*malencontre*] the moment of rupture, and he accompanies it with the following commentary: "Misfortune: tragic accident, inaugural mishap, whose effects do not stop expanding to the point that the memory of what went before is abolished, to the point that the love of servitude has been substituted for the desire of freedom." [18] No doubt, he shares here the opinion attributed to La Boétie, since he judges him straight off to be "more than anyone else clairvoyant." Let us observe already that the "slippage from history to logic" involves a slippage to morality. But the troubling point does not lie there: political philosophy has never stayed within the limits of objective knowledge. I am astonished only at the haughtiness of the judgment, at the will to embrace the past in its totality in order to locate therein the dividing line between the age of freedom and the age of servitude. Certainly, we ought once again to forbid ourselves from indulging in oversimplification. Clastres never claimed that, since the State's formation, all political regimes have been the theater of one and the same oppression. He even challenged this judgment expressly in the same essay:

> It naturally goes without saying that the universal essence of the State does not manifest itself uniformly in every statist formation, whose variety is taught to us by history as we know it. It is only in relation to primitive societies, to societies without the State, that all others are revealed to be equivalent . . . ; there is a hierarchy of the worst, and the totalitarian State, under its various contemporary configurations, is there to remind us that, however profound might be the loss of freedom, it is never lost enough; one never finishes losing it.[19]

But his prudent way of condemning statist formations doesn't cancel out the audacity of someone who wants to get to the root of the evil and cut.

Thinking a form of servitude that is voluntary seems to me to be a fruitful exercise; indeed, I believe that it opens a "breach in the general conviction that one couldn't think society without its division between dominators and dominated" and that it leads one to take a new look at our own institutions. Yet, the following four propositions seem to me unjustifiable:

1. that the regimes of statist societies are to be distinguished solely by the degree of oppression exercised or the intensity of servitude;
2. that the effects of misfortune "do not stop expanding";
3. that the nature of the State can be summed up by the exercise of coercion;

and, finally:

4. that social life, in the cases where the State exists, remains completely in its grip.

The first of these propositions leads one to forget in particular the classical distinction between arbitrary power and power ruled by laws, but also the distinction that in our time we have been taught to recognize between a power incorporated in the person of a master or in a group, which makes itself the holder of the principle of law and of the knowledge of the ultimate ends of society, and a power that is shielded from being appropriated by the repositories of authority and is, in the same stroke, impotent to subjugate law and knowledge. The second proposition refers to a new version of the historical fiction that owes its seductive power to the theories of Hegel and Marx. These theories cannot resist an in-depth examination as to how societies develop, since there is nothing linear about that development. The third one reduces all of the characteristics of the State to that of coercion, for the sole reason that coercion is always found to be present, whereas one couldn't conclude from this that coercion offers the key to the State's formation and still less to its transformations, or to its evolution within a given civilization. The fourth, finally, neglects all the modes of sociability that escape the control of state power, as much during the centuries when the bureaucracy's means of intervention in the life of rural communities or cities remained narrowly circumscribed as in the modern era, when civil society enjoys a recognized autonomy, even if that autonomy remains relative.

Perhaps it is worthwhile pointing out in passing that Clastres sometimes reorients La Boétie's thinking in a direction his text doesn't seem to warrant. He attributes to La Boétie the idea that voluntary servitude is "the constant common to all societies, mine, but also those I learn about in books," conceding only parenthetically "with the exception, perhaps rhetorical, of Roman Antiquity."[20] Now, the author of the *Discourse* does not confine himself to celebrating Rome; he invokes the examples of Athens, Sparta, and the Renaissance cities, specifically Venice. The fact is that he does not pause to describe what free institutions are, but nothing suggests that he is hurling the republics into the dark abyss of the State. Besides, the question of the State isn't his. He is investigating voluntary servitude, whose striking sign he finds in loving submission to the prince, in the transport that, all at once, makes men lose the sense of their own identity, attaches them to the imaginary body of a master, and includes them therein as if they were its members. He is investigating the attraction exerted by the *One*.

Let us not seek to explore here La Boétie's own thought. I mention his work only because Clastres offers a reading of it that prompts one to ask oneself what place he himself can make, in his interpretation, for the struggles that have mobilized men against tyranny—or, more generally, against monarchy—in Antiquity or in the age of the Renaissance, as well as in Modern Times. What place, too, we may ask, can Clastres make for a political tradition that is held together by the conviction that power belongs to no one and that strictly opposes to the love of the good master the meaning of the law (which guarantees in principle an equality for all)? Indeed, one reads at the end of his study on La Boétie:

> Denaturation is expressed both in the contempt necessarily felt by he who commands for those who obey and in the love of the subjects for the prince, in the worship the people devote to the person of the tyrant. Now, this flow of love which unceasingly springs up from below to gush ever higher, this love of subjects for the master equally denatures the relationships among subjects. Exclusive of all freedom, these relationships dictate the new law that rules society: One must love the tyrant.[21]

But the strange thing is that he doesn't glimpse the fact that this language is quite precisely that of political humanism—not only the language of La Boétie, which might have been informed by the discovery of free and equal Indians in the New World, nor his very own, but the language the Florentine citizens at the very beginning of the fifteenth century were already speaking and the one still spoken by the English revolutionaries in the seventeenth century and by the French or American revolutionaries in the eighteenth century, or, in the nineteenth century, by all those who condemned at once the monarchy of the Ancien Régime, Bonapartism, and Jacobinism. Perhaps more must be said. Isn't it because he is connected with such a tradition that Clastres is capable of discovering in savage societies something other than the absence of a coercive power, an affirmation of the humanity of man in the will to put into check the desire for submission?

One would be mistaken to believe that the objections I have just formulated have no bearing upon the interpretation of primitive social organization, that the idea of a radical rupture in the History of humanity is altogether secondary in Clastres's work. It seems to me that this idea is tied to a conception of power that merits a reexamination in the very field where it was worked out.

On several occasions, Clastres denies the reality of power in Indian society. He writes, for example: "Power is exactly what these societies intended it to be. And as power is—to put it schematically—nothing, the group thereby reveals its radical rejection of authority, an utter negation of power."[22] Or again: "The power relation realizes an absolute capacity for the division of society. It is under this heading the very essence of the statist institution, the minimal figure of the State. . . . Every society-machine that functions according to the absence of the power relation will be determined as a primitive society."[23]

Nonetheless, these formulations do not yield us his own thought, which is much more subtle. His analysis of chieftainship rests on the idea that a separate power is conceived as a "resurgence of nature" within culture,[24] or, in other terms, that power's transcendency harbors for the group a deadly risk. Listening to him carefully, we understand that the power relation is not absent; it is fully recognized and transcribed in the institution of chieftainship in such a way that its pernicious effects are rendered harmless: "Indian societies," he notes, "were able to create a means for neutralizing the virulence of political authority. They chose themselves to be the founders of that authority, but in such a manner as to let power appear only as a negativity that is immediately subdued."[25] As Clastres describes him, the chief sees himself forbidden from exercising command; he is under "the obligation to exhibit at every moment the innocence of his office."[26]

We really ought to be persuaded therefore that each time he speaks of the power relation, Clastres is designating a relation between the community and an organ that, be it as reduced as possible, claims the right, and disposes of the means, to obtain obedience. But his argument doesn't halt there. He is affirming, in addition, that effective power turns out to be held by the group as such. This is a basic proposition, and it is accompanied by a repeated critique of the thesis that society's functioning might result from a spontaneous sort of social control, from a consensus based on custom. Clastres in no way wants to dissolve the unity of the social into a myriad of relationships that would regulate themselves by virtue of a sort of homeostasis of practices and beliefs. He speak of a *choice,* of an *intention,* of a *decision*— unconscious, certainly, but general. The choice is signified in the rejection of a separate power as well as in the affirmation of a communitarian power. Now, the latter power is, according to him, exercised in a rigorous and ongoing way. As much as he contests the reality of the chief's power—"Holding power is to exercise it: a power that is not exercised is not a power; it is only an appearance"[27]—so much so does he also insist on the might of communitarian power:

> The essential feature (that is, relating to the essence) of primitive society is its exercise of absolute and complete power over all the elements of which it is composed; the fact that it prevents any one of the sub-groups that constitute it from becoming autonomous; that it holds all the internal movements—conscious and unconscious—that maintain social life to the limits and directions prescribed by the society.[28]

These two moments of analysis cannot be dissociated. To hear Clastres tell it, there is a simulation of a separate power in the institution of chieftainship so as to conjure away the threat that this power would imply and, in the same stroke, to make manifest the active sovereignty of the group.

How could a reader, however superficial he might be, fail to ask: Isn't this power coercive? The answer, which can be glimpsed, seems to me to be as follows: Certainly, there is coercion, and it can even at certain moments border on terror, but it has no other function than to ensure that equality reigns among men. No one benefits at the expense of others; no one can, in taking part in its exercise, increase his own strength. Thus, the power of the chief is hollow, but that of the group is full. Or, to say it schematically, the first is nothing, but the second is everything: it does not allow of any degree. No dynamic therefore is indicated within society that would render change possible. Power does not cease to remake itself as it was made on the first day.

Let us take a closer look at it. Clastres describes an essential moment of the action of communitarian power in a quite beautiful passage devoted to rituals of initiation. Not hesitating to label *torture* the ordeals that are inflicted, he shows us what their goal is: "*Society imprints its mark on the body* of the young people."[29] And he specifies the meaning of this mark, an index of writing on the body: "Society *dictates its laws* to its members. It inscribes the text of the law on the surface of their bodies. No one is supposed to forget the law on which the social life of the tribe is based."[30] And, finally, he gives us the lesson of this law at the same time as the reason why it could not be divulged but only imprinted on the body:

> The law they [the young people] come to know in pain is the law of primitive society, which says to everyone: *You are worth no more than anyone else; you are worth no less than anyone else.* The law, inscribed on bodies, expresses primitive society's refusal to run the risk of divi-

sion, the risk of a power separate from society itself, *a power that would escape its control.*[31]

The interpretation becomes more specific later on: "That non-separate law can only have for its inscription a space that is not separate: that space is the body itself."[32] Nonetheless, the answer we were seeking refers us to another question. It is not, in effect, an accident if the only text, we believe, in which Clastres describes one of the modes of exercising communitarian power introduces the notion of the law and clings to the unfolding of a ritual. Let us add that he introduces in the same stroke the notion of knowledge: "Why," he asks,

> can the secret only be communicated by means of the *social* enactment of the rite on the *body* of the young people? The body mediates the acquisition of a knowledge; that knowledge is inscribed on the body. The significance of initiation is contained in the answer to the twofold question concerning the nature of the knowledge transmitted by the rite, and the function of the body in the performance of the rite.[33]

As I have already suggested, comprehension of the political could not be limited to determining the site of power and the way in which authority is exercised from this site. In a sense, Clastres is quite conscious of that fact in the text we are mentioning: the nature and exercise of communitarian power implies a singular relationship to the law and to knowledge. He is recognizing in the same stroke that where a particular site of power comes to be circumscribed, this separate power is accompanied by a different relationship to the law—although it would have to be remarked, on the one hand, that the latter appears to him as the "separate, distant, despotic law of the State"[34] and, on the other hand, that he holds back, except in a brief passage relating to writing, from speaking of a *knowledge* both separate and despotic, for this final qualification would discredit any effort to attain knowledge, including his own.

Let us put into parentheses for a moment the critique of the law and possibly of knowledge, such as they would be determined with the advent of the State. From his argument one can draw two entirely different conclusions. One seems to conform to the letter of his text. The law of primitive society would be purely social; it would boil down to the formula (it matters little that this formula is called *unconscious*) of its constitution as a community rigorously subjugating "all the elements of which it is composed"[35] and thus maintaining its members in a position of strict equality. Or, to put it in other terms, the law would boil down to the expression of the collective will to nonseparation. As for ritual—at least the one that concerns the life of the community—it would be of the order of artifice (it matters little that it too, in turn, might have been unconscious), and it would be, with the aid of a mark on the body, destined to give rise to a process of complete and irreversible internalization of the law by those who are liable to initiation.

This conclusion, it must be emphasized, would appear to be Durkheimian in inspiration, even though it was established on the basis of political premises. Clastres, no doubt, might be tempted to endorse it. The very last lines of his essay on the initiation ritual persuade us of that. After having observed that a nonseparate law can only be inscribed in a nonseparate space, he marvels at the Indians' skill [*science*]: "It is proof of their admirable depth of mind that the Savages knew all that *ahead of time,* and took care, at the cost of a terrible cruelty, to prevent the advent of a more terrifying cruelty: *the law written on the body is an unforgettable memory.*"[36]

The other conclusion, which I make my own, and to which I am going to return, would be that it is impossible to dissociate the religious (the religious among savages) and the political in order to bring the first back within the orbit of the second. That is to say, it is impossible to dissociate the experience the primitives have of the order of the world—that of their insertion in natural and supernatural life—from their elaboration of the communitarian order. This conclusion would lead one to judge that it is then no less impossible to conceive the change that marks the collapse of primitive society as the unique passage from one type of power to another, from the noncoercive to the coercive.

But before heading in this direction, which seems to take us away from Clastres's position, it is worth pointing out that Clastres himself is not unaware of the phenomena that exceed the limits of his thesis. Let us still stick to his analysis of the rite of initiation. Before reducing the statement of the primitive law to the commandment "*You are worth no more than anyone else; you are worth no less than anyone else,*" he gave it a broader signification:

> You are one of us. Each one of you is like [*semblable aux*] us; each one of you is like the others. You are called by the same name, and you will not change your name. Each one of you occupies the same space and the same place among us: you will keep them. None of you is less than us; none of you is more than us. *And you will never be able to forget it.*[37]

In its first part, this version allows us to hear something other than the imposition of equality. It encourages us to recognize an incorporation of the being of the group by those liable to initiation, called upon as they are to become alike [*semblables*] (which does not necessarily signify *equals*), and their incorporation in the being of nature, which fixes each at his place and with his name. Clastres nonetheless abstains from scrutinizing the terms he employs and halts at a commentary that neglects the fact that there is a violent intrusion of the law into the body. Of course, he talks about the terrifying cruelty of the rite, whose virtue would be to inscribe the nonseparate law in a nonseparate space, that of the body. But he doesn't note that this mode of inscription presupposes the primary idea of a law that lies at a distance from men, so that it swoops down upon them from the outside.

Now, this law is in principle removed from all interrogating speech; it leaves no margin for the will, for initiative, for the mobility of those who are subjected to it. Far from the writing of the law on the body making itself the sign of a consubstantiality of the one with the other, there is an interiority that bears on its flip side an absolute exteriority. The very notion of a writing on the body, which seems to Clastres to be the index of a nonseparate and, in a sense, egalitarian primitive law, is introduced moreover in opposition to writing as it arises in historical society, an index, as far as it is concerned, of a separate and, in the same stroke, despotic law. But one can ask oneself whether, quite to the contrary, this latter sort of writing does not establish a gap in relation to the law. One can ask oneself whether it does not include, in the same stroke, a virtual interpretation, owing to the fact that it is no longer imprinted on the seeing body and that the gaze, and the thought the seeing body harbors, detach themselves from what is signified to the seeing body — whereas primitive writing buries in each and seals a commandment that will never be thinkable and cannot even be apprehended as a commandment.

Furthermore, despite his efforts to place in the very principle of primitive society the rejection of separate power — and to articulate with this rejection a refusal of a separate law and a separate knowledge — Clastres makes us glimpse in the phenomenon of the ritual the sign of a relationship to the real that is indissolubly of a social and a religious order. Not only does his *Chronicle of the Guayaki Indians* persuade us that ritual yields for us the essence of primitive social life, but he affirms this expressly in his final essay, where he accuses the Structuralist school of having lost interest therein and of thus ignoring the being-society of society. Now, as he presents it, ritual does indeed reveal in a sense the individual's tight insertion within the social world and the natural world; in this way, it lends itself to an interpretation in terms of nonseparation. Witness of the Guayaki, Clastres speaks of "text and image."[38] One reads a gesture as one hears a speech. And his observations suggest no less the complementary relation: *one hears a speech as one perceives an action.* However, the nonseparation is then that of speech or of thought and of practice. Now, no one would risk saying that this regime of speech or of thought might be the effect of a decision, of a refusal of separation, and, in addition, that this refusal might be ruled by the rejection of a separate power. At the very most, one can presume that the conception of social organization is worked out within the horizons of a primordial experience of the world, the singular manifestation of which is ritual.

But one must still draw out another inference from the observation of the ritual. It does not only attest to nonseparation; upon it is read an ordeal of alterity. Let us say therefore that if the ritual seems to us to be constitutive of the identity of the social, of communitarian life or of the life of individuals as members of a group, there is a chiasm between the movement that binds the agent or the patient to the group or relates the group to itself and the movement that opens them to what is "other." Ritual rests, in effect, on belief in the power of invisible beings, on the belief that men are in constant commerce with them, nay, that they are inhabited by them or shot through with forces that are *other*. Generally speaking, the meticulous sequencing of the ritual's operations testifies to belief in a knowledge that hangs over and looks down upon the actors, one that has been transmitted to them by their ancestors and draws its origin from a past that lies beyond the frontiers of the time in which men move.

Let us now ask: Is it not the phenomenon of this belief that allows one to pose in the right way the question of social division and to set aside resolutely the unfortunate image of "indivision" to which Clastres sometimes had recourse? The full affirmation of the community, and the way in which it forbids the chief from exercising a particular power, cannot, in effect, be dissociated from the assignment of its order and of the origin of its institution to a site that is *else*where [*un lieu autre*].

I was already thinking of Clastres when, in an old article from 1973— "L'ère de l'idéologie" (The era of ideology)—I made a distinction between formations in which the institution of the social is supposed to be engendered from the very site of society in which it is conceived, and formations that are supposed to be engendered from a site that is *else*where. In reference to the latter social formations—in particular, to savage societies—I observed that the "real . . . proves to be determinable only inasmuch as it is supposed, by virtue of a mythic or religious form of speech, to be determined; it testifies to a knowledge whose basis cannot be challenged by the effective movement of knowing, technical inventions, or the interpretation of the visible."[39] Nevertheless, I did not draw out the inference that, with the aid of such a distinction, one might, if not account for the great change to which Clastres is pointing, at least grasp a radical difference between the primitive type of society and all other types of society. The little we have glimpsed of the Indians' beliefs in the wake of Clastres's analyses ought to suffice to turn us away from a crass use of the religious. The savage rituals, notably those involving initiation, that occupy such a great place in his argument testify to a relationship with the other [*autre*] world, with the invisible, which reveals both a tight subjection of men to a knowledge, and to a law, upon which they have no grasp, and a constant intertwining between the world down here and the other world, between the visible and the invisible. In other words, it needn't escape us that if the notion of "alterity" is revealed to be omnipresent, this alterity remains unlocalizable; it does not refer back to a definite instance of authority; it never makes itself the sign of the presence of a "great Other." To speak like Clastres does, the *other* is not *One.*

Let us note in passing that his interpretation of the primitive law as a writing on the body not only does not take into account the initial exteriority of the law, as we have said, but also neglects the fact that the incision and the mark signify an opening of the body to the *other,* the fact that each person's own body does not belong to himself; that, being a natural body, it is simultaneously a supernatural body; that, being a suffering, mortal body, it finds itself inhabited by, shot through with forces that have their seat outside it. In this sense, one must agree that there is no split between the visible and the invisible and that this split arises only in historical society (and rather belatedly) with the aid of a religious experience of an entirely new type.

I thus come back to a proposition advanced shortly beforehand: It is futile to pretend to bring the religious back within the orbit of the political. Still, it must be added at this point: if, at least, one conceives the political as the system that would fit together solely as a function of the determination (indissociable from its representation) of the site of power. This last stipulation requires explanation. In formulating it, I wish to emphasize once again that the site of power is designated in relation to a certain aim of knowledge and of the law. We could undoubtedly say—and such is in a sense my conviction—that the nature of a political society, the very nature of the political, is delivered to us in this relation. But this language is legitimate only upon the condition that it is recognized that the political—thus identified with the institution of the social, with the generative principles of its "form"—doesn't allow itself to be reduced to a pure choice made by men (be it deemed an unconscious one), that is to say, that it testifies at once to an *elaboration* and to a *test* of the human condition under given circumstances.

If that is really how things are, the critique to which Marxism gives rise can be reformulated in other terms for theorists who dispute these categories. As I have attempted to show elsewhere, Marx gives in to the temptation to project social division *into* society (in order to determine the moment of its appearance and the moment of its suppression); he wants to discover for it a *real* basis and, in the same stroke, to define all knowable figures of power, law, and knowledge as the products of an empirical process (the development of the forces of production and the accompanying transformations in the relations of production).[40] Against this myth — more generally, against every form of economism, sociologism, and historicism — it is fitting to reestablish the primacy of the symbolic order. Nevertheless, such a requirement is immediately perverted if we treat the symbolic as we do the real, with the same concern for scientific objectification. Now, that is very much the case when, manipulating with the casualness characteristic of Structuralist thought the categories of power, law, and knowledge, those of the visible and the invisible, and those of the social world and the other world, one limits oneself to spotting in each historical formation a symbolic mechanism [*dispositif*] (an expression I myself employed without suspecting the possible equivocations) and, ultimately, when one claims to discern two general types of mechanisms, one belonging to societies without a State, the other common to all societies including a State. Within such a perspective, one only transfers onto the symbolic register an idea of functionality, and even of instrumentality, that was previously formulated on the register of realism.

In short, the primitives' "choice" consists then in fixing the *other,* the invisible, the origin of power, law, and knowledge in a site absolutely distant from their own living space, from their own time, with the intention of banishing all division within the limits of the social, whereas, after the collapse of this mechanism, all the figures of the *other* see themselves, by virtue of a new choice, brought back within these limits and condensed into that of the State; the division first instaurated between the other world and this world down here appears to be resolutely inscribed within the latter, the intention being to assure for it mastery over its institution. That the choice is said to be unconscious doesn't matter. Not only would such an interpretation fail to recognize the singularity of primitive practices and beliefs (which can't be reduced to the separation of the invisible from the visible), and not only would it identify the essence of religious belief with that of the primitives and make of the great historical religions transitory by-products of the building up of the State, but — and this is the point that to us seems decisive — it would take away all signification from the very notion of the *other.*

Either this notion merely designates the effect of a process of alienation, and this version is tenable only upon the condition that an end point be assigned to this process (according to a Hegelian or Feuerbachian-Marxist argument that at present no one seems to be defending), or it must be agreed, as I wrote again in "L'ère de l'idéologie," that it is futile "to think the social within the boundaries of the social, History within the boundaries of History, man on the basis of and in view of man" and to ignore the enigma of the institution, the signs of a question that goes beyond every given response and remains ever implicated in each one.[41]

This brings us back to the problem of the great change of which Clastres speaks (and, in a more general way, to the problem of discontinuity in History). I intimated in passing some reticences his interpretation of La Boétie inspires in me. At least, the notion of *misfortune* allows him to point to an *inconceivable* event, the reason for which could not be found on the factual level. In contrast, in *Society against the State* he does not dismiss the possibility of finding an explanation for it, and he then runs up against difficulties that are worth mentioning because they are significant.

After having noted that the mystery of the origin was only "perhaps a temporary one,"[42] he takes an interest in the transformations that affected the social organization of the Tupi-Guarani on the eve of the discovery of the New World. The increase in population and the enlargement of the dimensions of the local groups seem to him to have brought about a disturbance in the structure of primitive society—founded as it always was on the scattered nature and numerical weakness of communities—and in particular to have favored the reinforcement of chieftainship by giving rise to chiefs who, without becoming despots, "were not altogether powerless chiefs either."[43] Hardly has Clastres formulated this hypothesis when he contests the idea that the change could have led to a statist formation, for this change seems to have provoked a salutary reaction, the appearance of prophets calling for the tribes to abandon the "evil land" and rejoin the country of the gods, the "Land Without Evil." Then, interpreting this movement as a response to the danger created by the advances of chieftainship, as "the heroic attempt of a primitive society to put an end to unhappiness by means of a radical refusal of the One, as the universal essence of the State,"[44] he comes to ask himself whether prophetic speech, because of the fact that it suddenly succeeded in unifying in migration the various tribes, might not have had an effect contrary to the one it was intending, whether the entirely new power it was harboring was not opening the way to acceptance of command and obedience, that would later take on political signification. Thus does he conclude: "Prophetic speech, the power of that speech: might this be where power *tout court* originated, the beginning of the State in the Word?"[45]

As fruitful as it seems to me to articulate the signs of a change that occurs on several registers at once—expansion and concentration of the population, increase in the chiefs' role, new religious experience—this hypothesis of the origin of the State still seems to me to be a disappointing one. Who doesn't see, indeed, that the control over its conditions of existence which Clastres imputes to primitive society is so rigorous, so deliberate, that the sudden intrusion of the demographic accident could not have occurred there? The author of *Society against the State* has placed us in the presence of a system so closed that no event seems capable of unsettling it.

Should it therefore merely be offered in opposition to this that the facts are missing? I would say, rather, that it is the very attempt to search for an explanation in the facts that signals, to use Merleau-Ponty's term, the vanity of a high-altitude viewpoint [*un point de vue de survol*] of History. Instead of detecting the causes for the passage from one formation to another, don't we have to maintain—without ever forgetting that our interpretation is laid out within the horizons of our own culture and reminding ourselves what our questions owe to our own experience of the social—the exigency of thinking History when faced with the test of what I called the enigma of the institution?

This exigency does not condemn one just to take cognizance of the variety of types of society, and still less does it force one to embrace the thesis that each type would proceed from an unmotivated human choice. One can, on the contrary, justifiably ask oneself whether one cannot spot in each, whatever might be the site to which the investigation is carried, the traces of a legacy, the signs of a reshuffling of previous cultural social relations, of a reinvestment, within a new experience of the world, of former practices and beliefs. One can ask oneself, finally, whether the notion we have forged of "primitive society" is not connected to the fact that the depths of history vanish therein. In other terms, recognizing discontinuity in no way forbids one from deciphering that which *arises* [advient] in time, nor does it forbid one from perceiving in History a dimension of *revelation*—if, nonetheless, we maintain ourselves in the opening of the interrogation that is born of the present and we refuse to give in to an overall theory of progress or regression.

These last remarks would call for a long series of developments that would take us away from the problem posed by Clastres. But they can receive an initial confirmation if we consider first the figure of the chief as Clastres has described him. This figure seems to Clastres, as was said, strictly tied to the definition of a nonseparate power. Now, the phenomenon of sacred kingship, to which a small number of anthropologists have devoted their studies since James George Frazer, offers traits analogous to those he deemed specific to primitive chieftainship.

Let us confine ourselves to mentioning Arthur Maurice Hocart's effort, because it exhibits singular affinities with Clastres's undertaking, even though Clastres was undoubtedly unaware of Hocart, since, to my knowledge, Clastres makes no mention of him. Hocart was already opening a path to political anthropology. He had the idea that every society is in its essence a political society, though he does not state this expressly, since he thought that all governmental functions existed among peoples without government, that is to say, in the absence of an instance of authority regulating social relationships as a whole. His concern was to understand how a power comes to be circumscribed within society, how it comes to exercise and, at the very same time, to win recognition for an authority over everyone.

Undoubtedly, the schema he develops is evolutionist in orientation and is borrowed directly from the natural sciences. But, far from sharing the prejudices of a school, he invokes neither necessity nor progress. His point of departure is very much rather a critique of his contemporaries' ethnocentrism. Our usual way of governing is such, he tells us in substance, that the fact passes for being natural; the philosophers limit themselves, when examining it, to searching for the basis of this constraint: "Had they had, like us, information from all over the globe, they would have heard of numerous societies that have no government, and yet are functioning quite well." [46]

Not content to halt at this statement, Hocart thinks that it prompts a reexamination of the place the State holds in our time, and he wants to bring back out everything that lies beyond its grasp in the operation of social life. He does not speak, it is true, as Clastres does, of society *against* the State, but he denies that the absence of the State would be a sign of a lack. Societies unfamiliar with government are in his view complete societies, ones capable of satisfying men's needs fully. Without being able to follow here the details of his argument or to restitute its principal articulations, I will underscore only that the passage from a society without government to a governed society results, according to him, from an always localizable combination of transformations that are simultaneously of a physical, social, and religious order.

The first fact to be taken into account is the increase in volume and density of the population, which requires hitherto unknown tasks of coordination. Nevertheless, the meaning of the process of change is to be discovered in the centralization of ritual. In fact, ritual has always been, our author affirms, the wellspring of communitarian existence: it condenses all the "life-giving methods" [47] that constitute the basic preoccupation of societies, at the very least until a recent epoch. It is through ritual that men determine in what object life resides and into what objects it can pass, and that they seek to attain their goal: "to increase the supply of food and wealth, . . . to ensure progeny, to ward off illness and untimely death, to thwart enemies."[48]

Now, the comparative study of societies situated in Asia and in Africa yields one and the same lesson. From an initial dispersion of rituals, carried out as they were within the framework of family or tribe (families and tribes coexisting under the banner of equality), one has passed to an overall set of rituals, which implies a principal officiant and a differentiation of the functions to which secondary personalities are assigned. The former sees himself granted the prerogatives of the chief or king, while the others become subaltern chiefs or vassals. At the end of this evolutionary process, a few examples of which persuade us that the general direction is not subject to doubt, it appears that the supreme chief or the king ceases to be the *primus inter pares* and comes to incorporate in his person the attributes of the other chiefs, who, after having been his auxiliaries, become his dependents and are distinguished by the role they fulfill in his service, that is to say, by the responsibility they hold in certain offices.

In the same stroke, the god with which he had been identified condenses in itself the properties of divinity belonging to the various particular groups. Thus is centralization revealed at the moment when the central character—by virtue of an identification with each element of the ritual, which is rigorously defined in correlation with an element of the universe—takes on the figure of a microcosm that "corresponds point for point with the macrocosm."[49] There is no doubt, according to Hocart, that this "logic of ritual" controls the transformation of religious beliefs; he even ventures to seek in this transformation the explanation for the passage from polytheism to monotheism. Nonetheless, his interpretation doesn't allow one to hold to this thesis, for he strives to show, via comparative studies, that only a small number of symbols are liable to attach themselves to the function of royalty, that the duality of Earth and Sky seems to be recognized everywhere, and that, again everywhere, the worship of the Sun or of the Sky ends up becoming dominant while the idea of *one* world, whose principle the king personifies, is affirmed. Thus does he make us perceive in connection with the "logic of ritual" a "logic of belief."

The emergence of the figure of the chief or king, onto which is imprinted the force of instituting, maintaining, and increasing the life of society, becomes the object of Hocart's inquiry as well as of his reflection. He states his question clearly at one point: "Of families formerly coequal one has become supreme. What has led to this predominance?"[50] And on one point at the very least his answer is unequivocal: The historian is mistaken who tries to "consult his records and to pick out some accident, such as the personal ascendency of some masterful man, as the cause of this rise."[51] The concordance of changes of a religious order across distinct cultural areas forbids one from imputing to chance the formation of kingship.

The question is reformulated in different terms in another passage: The existence of the king being given, do we, he asks, have to interpret the fact that "one god devour[s] all the rest" as "a roundabout way of centralizing government," an expression of the king's symbolic desire to concentrate in his hands all powers by using a sort of subterfuge?[52] His answer is again negative and is based on an argument that bring us back to the problem with which we had started. The idea of such a subterfuge, he observes, will occur "only to those who are still possessed by the idea that the primary function of a king is to govern, to be the head of the administration. We shall see that he is nothing of the kind. He is the repository of the gods, that is of the life of the group."[53]

This argument is abundantly developed throughout the work to which I have been referring. The break introduced by the advent of the king in societies formerly based on equality in no way signifies that the king has a command over men. Mentioning the most varied examples, Hocart keeps bringing out the unique qualities of the king: he is a mediator between the gods and men; he is in his essence liberal; he is the man of the good word and of the just action; his function answers to a demand coming from society—a demand so manifest that, in a number of instances, the man sought to incarnate this function does everything he can to back out of it and that, in exercising this function, he sees himself caught in a network of obligations that make him at least as much a prisoner of the community as its master, if not more so.

In considering this phenomenon, a new question therefore is posed: How is the passage effected from a form of kingship that does not involve governance of a State (understanding by the latter a system of power that includes an administration and coercive means)? The least that could be said is that Hocart hesitates in his response. He happens to insist upon a change of a religious order: the substitution for materialistic rites of "ethical" rites that make of the king the "repository of all power,"[54] that is to say, if we understand well, ones that guarantee the king a command in the image of an all-powerful god. He also happens to suppose that this command is born in the shadow of the royal function and that some dignitaries seize hold of it, taking advantage of the impotence of the divinized man, paralyzed as he is by all the etiquette and ceremony. Nevertheless, the answer that most often seems to win out combines the idea of a proliferation and hierarchization of responsibilities, as required by the development of the royal function, with the idea of a growing complexity of the tasks involved in coordinating social activities, which permits the exercise of some real authority to be grafted onto services that are at first symbolic.[55]

Our intention is not to discuss this interpretation. One can ask oneself whether Hocart is simply displacing the difficulty Clastres runs up against, i.e., whether, once placed at the end of the symbolic kingship of the first type (dispensing prosperity), the change that marks the advent of the State really becomes clear or whether one remains instead in the presence of changes that escape objective knowledge. In fact, by challenging the hypothesis that society might desire a master and that the king might desire to govern, Hocart, like Clastres, renders dubious any recourse to events that would shatter such a rigorously worked out system. At least, our brief incursion into the domain he has explored obtains for us a few precious indications.

In a sense, Clastres's thinking is confirmed on one key point: over a very long duration and over the expanse of the globe, societies have existed that ordered themselves while doing without a coercive power, and yet these are no less political societies. Nevertheless, as soon as he comes to base his thinking on the case of formations that make room for a king and set at a distance from the community the seat of social power—or, to say it better, of the institution of the social—this confirmation prohibits one from conceiving a radical discontinuity between primitive societies and all other societies, between the time of the struggle against the State and the time of the struggle for the State. In addition, Hocart's analysis prompts us still more to interrogate history by paying attention to how the political and the religious are articulated and thus to pursue the exploration of societies that will come to order themselves under the aegis of the State, doing so with the conviction that their own development doesn't become clear solely in light of the enterprise of man's domination over man, or even of man's domination over nature.

Notes

"L'œuvre de Clastres" was originally published in a collection of texts written in honor of Pierre Clastres, *L'esprit des lois sauvages,* ed. Miguel Abensour (Paris: Éditions du Seuil, 1987), 183–209. Reprinted as "Dialogue avec Pierre Clastres" in *Écrire,* 303–35.

1 Unsigned editorial for *Libre* 2 (1977): 3.

2 Pierre Clastres, "Les Marxistes et leur anthropologie," *Libre* 3 (1978): 135–49.

3 Claude Lefort, "Pierre Clastres," *Libre* 4 (1978): 51.

4 Ibid.

5 Pierre Clastres, "Birth," *Chronicle of the Guayaki Indians,* trans. Paul Auster (New York: Zone Books, 1998 [1972]), 16. [T/E: Auster's dramatic and moving Translator's Note is worth reading in its own right.]

6   Ibid., 105.

7   Ibid.

8   Ibid., 105–6.

9   Ibid., 107.

10 Ibid.

11 "Société sans histoire et historicité," *Cahiers internationaux de sociologie* 12 (1952): 91–114; reprinted in *Les formes de l'histoire* (Paris: Gallimard, 1978), 30–43.

12 Ibid., 32.

13 Ibid., 33.

14 Ibid., 40.

15 Ibid., 47.

16 T/E: Claude Lefort, *Le Travail de l'œuvre Machiavel* (Paris: Gallimard, 1972).

17 Pierre Clastres, "Liberté, malencontre, innommable," postface to the reprint edition of Étienne de La Boétie's *Discours de la servitude volontaire* (Paris: Payot, 1976), 230.

18 Ibid., 230–31.

19 Ibid., 234–35.

20 Ibid., 230.

21 Ibid., 245–46.

22 Pierre Clastres, *Society against the State: The Leader as Servant and the Humane Uses of Power among the Indians of the Americas,* trans. Robert Hurley (New York: Urizen Books, 1977), 34.

23 Pierre Clastres, "Liberté, malencontre, innommable," 234.

24 *Society against the State,* 34.

25 Ibid., 35.

26 Ibid.

27 Pierre Clastres, "Liberté, malencontre, innommable," 234.

28 *Society against the State,* 179–80.

29 Ibid., 154.

30 Ibid., 156.

31 Ibid.

32 Ibid., 158.

33 Ibid., 151 [T/E: emphasis restored on *social*].

34 Ibid., 157.

35 Ibid., 179.

36 Ibid., 158.

37 Ibid., 155–56.

38 *Chronicle of the Guayaki Indians,* 17.

39 Claude Lefort, "L'ère de l'idéologie," *Les formes de l'histoire,* 293. This text was originally published in the *Encyclopaedia Universalis.*

40 Ibid., 289.

41 Ibid., 291.

42 Ibid., 173.

43 *Society against the State,* 181.

44 Ibid., 184.

45 Ibid., 185.

46 Arthur Maurice Hocart, *Kings and Councillors: An Essay in the Comparative Anatomy of Human Society,* ed. and introd. by Rodney Needham, foreword by E. E. Evans-Pritchard (Chicago: University of Chicago Press, 1970), 128.

47 Ibid., 34.
48 Ibid., 62.
49 Ibid., 64.
50 Ibid., 96.
51 Ibid.
52 Ibid., 98.
53 Ibid., 98–99.
54 Ibid., 82.
55 Ibid., 293.

Philosopher?

SOMEONE ASKED me recently, "How did you become a philosopher?" An apparently harmless question. It wasn't the first time I had heard it posed. Indeed, everyone, no matter what he might do, has heard himself called upon to answer a question of that sort. But that day I felt particularly perplexed, and I had the feeling, not so much of having sidestepped the answer as having fled before another question. After the fact, this minuscule event inspired me to engage in a few reflections that led me rather far afield from my point of departure. As I was questioning myself, for some time, about the nature of my contribution to a volume on the state of philosophy in France, I imagined that these reflections might provide me with the appropriate subject matter.

How did I become a philosopher? The question had embarrassed me. Why? Undoubtedly because it took for granted something that didn't go without saying. The answer would imply that I had assumed the identity of a philosopher. True, it didn't leave a particularly good taste in my mouth when people talked about me as a sociologist or political scientist, under the pretext that my reflections bear mainly upon social and political facts. I sometimes have had to shield myself from such labels. Still less could I introduce myself as a historian, though I have often sought support in historical works. Generally speaking, it has always been important for me to specify that my endeavors did not pertain to the so-called human sciences. But to classify me among the philosophers has never been something easy for me to take.

On that occasion, the word aroused in me a new feeling of resistance that surprised me. It seemed easier for me to fall back on my profession. I therefore told of how I decided to turn toward teaching. I don't take enormous pride in being a professor; that kind far from enchants me. The image I had of this profession, even before becoming part of it—that is to say, as a pupil, then as a student—wasn't very exalted. Of course, there were, it seemed to me, a number of exceptions, and I like to imagine myself as one of them. Nevertheless, as I cannot take note of my exceptional qualities without looking ridiculous, I really must fit under the rule of the common representation. It remains the case that this is my trade. One cannot get around that fact. Furthermore, of all the characteristics that go together [*s'entrecroisent*] to define me, that one, I want to persuade myself, is the least necessary. After all, I have always been, and I remain, free to change my career, though this freedom diminishes over time. On the other hand, accepting the title of *philosopher* creates in me a growing problem. My reticences, I tell myself, do not pertain to the unpleasant experience of seeing myself labeled: I ought rather to fear usurping a title that I am not sure I merit and that becomes more and more reckless to claim.

In Socrates' time, as everyone knows, the word, with the full force of its original meaning, designated the love of wisdom—something that has become difficult to translate but that combined the search for truth and the search for a life lived in conformity with the nature of man. In Socrates himself, philosophy blended with the modesty of a disposition to ask questions, placing one's confidence solely in reason. That constituted a break with the previous assurance, nay arrogance, of those who didn't doubt that, by virtue of tradition—that is to say, with the aid of the religious teachings handed down by their ancestors—they possessed the principles of correct judgment. The debasement of the original sense of the term is such that philosophy has to an increasing degree allowed itself to be conceived as a discipline that would have jurisdiction over the principles of all knowledge—a particular discipline, even if it be a science of the universal, whose progress would be measured by how highly systematized its conceptual operations have become.

I was never fond of this definition of philosophy. Still, we are talking about the past. In our day, philosophy has lost the credit this ambition had won for it and, simultaneously, its place in the architecture of academic knowledge. But in the same stroke, it tends to lose all credit. From all sides one hears talk about its disappearance. In France, at least, some mediocre minds, for whom university diplomas take the place of authority, dispute among themselves over the date of the end of philosophy—which is sometimes associated with Hegel or with Fichte, sometimes with Husserl, and sometimes with Heidegger, who, however, had himself begun to put metaphysics in the dock.

Just as I have never espoused the view of philosophy as the ultimate system—a representation which, while it lies at the heart of the great classical works and of German Idealism, has been turned into a caricature with the rise of the academic discipline known as "the history of philosophy"—so am I loath to join the chorus of philosophy's destroyers. I find it a bit funny, moreover, to see that it is often the same people who pat themselves on the back for having provided a whirlwind tour of Hegel's alleged system in just a few pages and who proclaim that it marks the end of philosophy. But, as a paradoxical consequence of this attitude, let us note that to declare oneself a philosopher under present conditions is, it seems to me, to take on an immoderate ambition. Claiming that it is possible to undertake an interrogation that emancipates itself no longer from the authority of religion but from that of the sciences, and in particular the human sciences, trying to restore meaning to what on all sides is denounced as an illusory and outdated undertaking, one loses the modesty of its initial inspiration and finds oneself raising one's voice a notch or two.

The image of myself as a professor, I concluded, suited me because it appeared to place me *beneath* myself. In agreeing to accept this title, I without a doubt was sustaining the hope that I might surpass the definition. The word *philosopher* troubled me because it seemed to place me *above* myself.

Wasn't this a double mistake? Would I not do better to lower the position of professor less and raise less that of philosopher, too? Ought I not, moreover, to pay close attention to the way they intersect [*leur entrecroisement*]? Can philosophy, indeed, be completely dissociated from teaching? Here, I told myself again, is something that would be worthy of examination. Failing to undertake that examination, I had the following morose reflection: Perhaps my embarrassment resulted from the widely shared feeling that one runs less risks in donning a trivial image than in aspiring to a sublime one.

Yet I've known for a long time that we wrongly call upon psychological considerations while forgetting how we are inscribed in a culture. My initial reflection thus seemed to me a new way of fleeing before the unexpected question that the innocent one posed by my interlocutor had insinuated into me. Wasn't it better to think that the professor-philosopher duality had been imposed upon me as the offspring of a duality, characteristic of modern Western man, as he is shaped by the Christian tradition? Hadn't the idea of a division between temporal life and eternal life, between a natural, functional, mortal pole and a supernatural, mystical one, secretly informed my representation—and this even though, from the end of my childhood years, I haven't espoused, at least consciously, any religious belief? At first I asked myself the question only half seriously. But, in questioning myself in this way, I felt my reference to Socrates, so cherished, begin to waver. My reluctance to call myself a philosopher pointed me in a new direction.

Why had my thinking made this digression? It was the words *beneath* and *above* myself that had provoked the turn. They reminded me, indeed, of a book I had read a few years ago: Ernst Kantorowicz's *The King's Two Bodies*. This work had aroused my interest to the point that I devoted a yearlong seminar to it. In fact, before discovering it I had begun to take an interest in the representation of the body as body politic in the ideology of totalitarianism. It seemed to me that this representation was formed in a reaction against democracy, against a type of society in which the idea of an organic unity of the social is dissolved, and, in the same stroke, the hitherto established conjunction between the mystical unity of the people and the closed figure of a body whose members are like functionally inter-articulated organs comes undone. For me, Kantorowicz shed unexpected light on the genesis of the image of the body politic during the Middle Ages and the Renaissance, and, more particularly, on that of the king's body, a double body, natural and supernatural, functional and mystical, which had itself leaned on the representation of the nature of Christ.

Now, one formula he knowledgeably analyzed had struck me most vividly. Applied to the Christian emperor, in the *Liber Augustalis* (written under the reign of Frederick II and dedicated to him), it described him as *major et minor se ipso*. There one could detect a key representation of the modern prince, who is both subject to the law and unbound by laws. The historian was teaching us to recognize the efficacy of this representation in Dante's description of the universal monarch and in the tragedy of Richard II.

This recollection inspired me to new reflections. If my associations had been guided by a psychoanalytic concern, I would have been alerted by my identification with a royal figure, but since I was seeking only to elucidate my relationship with philosophy, I confined myself to observing that, even while reactivating perhaps a thought inscribed in the womb of our culture, I was developing a silent opposition to the image of the philosopher as sub-stitute for the priest-king or to that of philosophy as the philosophers' mys-tical body. To call myself or to allow myself to be called a philosopher would pose a problem for me not because I might fear placing myself above myself but because there could be in my view no philosophy in the sense intended by those who fully affirm its substance or by those who are claiming to be destroying it — that is to say, as a mode of transcendence.

At bottom, I concluded, there is at present a way of pronouncing the death of philosophy, or of placing oneself back under its law, that recalls the quarrel between theology and atheism. And as there was a way of putting God to death that proved to be a way of confirming Him, and as there was a futility to atheism as a response to the certitude of the theologian who, based on revelation, claimed to give reality to a site that is elsewhere, so is there a futile quarrel between philosophy and nonphilosophy. I added: The third option, which, in the wake of Marxism, consists in heralding the fulfillment of philosophy in life and in history through its very destruction reproduces no less vainly the belief, so lively at the beginning of the nineteenth century, that God had vested Himself in humanity or that Christianity, qua separate religion, had become invested in social institutions. Didn't I finally have to recognize that if a contradiction was living inside me, I was refusing to materialize its terms in a *near side* or a *beyond*, even if these terms were apparently liberated from religious discourse?

Why had this train of thought led me to evoke *major et minor se ipso?* The answer came to me along with the question. In fact, it was a much more recent reading than my reading of Kantorowicz that had guided me. A few weeks before the aforementioned conversation, I did indeed think that I had found an avatar of this theological-political formula, though one that served a quite new intention, in a rather lovely text by Edgar Quinet. This historian, who was Jules Michelet's contemporary and his friend, a poet and author of political and philosophical essays to whom we owe, in particular, one of the most audacious and penetrating works on the French Revolution, is a writer who has inexplicably fallen into oblivion.

An avid follower of his work, I came across a preface he wrote in 1853 for his epic drama, *Les esclaves* (The slaves). The spectacle of ancient slavery and the slave revolts, and foremost that of Spartacus, had, he declared in substance, prompted him to stage the universal drama of humanity, torn, as it seemed to him, by a twofold movement that lowers it beneath or raises it above itself. Turning to the volume I had in my hands, I immediately found again two passages I had underlined. The first one read:

> Do you want to have the spectacle of the fall of man? Look at this spirit which, at the height of its revolt, doesn't even dream of freeing itself; in each outward emancipation, it finds a new way to limit and bind itself. Ingeniously deducing servitude in the very midst of freedom, we see it return home by night along the path that guides others to the light. Rubble upon ruin, it overturns slavery without glimpsing the fact that it carries it within itself and recreates it with each breath.[1]

The second passage read:

> I thought it would add a new element to the drama to take man where one hadn't looked for him before, beneath humanity, deformed, denatured, annihilated from within by slavery; then, after having brought him back to life, restoring him through heroism.[2]

Exploiting all along the theme of man's tornness [*déchirement*], Quinet had thus seemed to me to be offering a reformulation of this theme: he was summing up, in a tension between servitude and heroism, the paradox of man's condition.

What did he mean by servitude? What La Boétie called *voluntary servitude*. Indeed, he employed this quite enigmatic expression himself on other occasions, notably in the last chapter of his *Révolution française,* without citing his source. That I knew because I had been smitten by La Boétie and had written an essay a few years ago as a postface to a new edition of his famous *Discourse on Voluntary Servitude.*[3] Furthermore, I had trod the path leading to the idea of voluntary servitude in my works on ideology and totalitarianism. In discovering La Boétie, I had been struck to see this idea associated with that of an attraction for the *body* of the tyrant, or more generally of the king, of the master in whom is found to be incarnated the fiction of the social body. And I was no less struck to see it combined with the idea of an "enchantment [*charme*]" emanating from the name of *One,* which delivers Subjects from the fear of division, from the ordeal of the plural, and, finally, from the enigma of the human institution of society. In short, I had found in La Boétie an extraordinary anticipation of what I had attempted for a long time to formulate in examining the totalitarian phantasm. Still more: This thought, which was surging up from the past, enlightened me and exerted an attraction upon me as if I had to rejoin it, as if it were dangling before my own thought.

And what about heroism? In what way did this concept speak to me? What did Quinet intend by it? It was exactly what his friend Michelet called during the same period the "heroism of the mind," thereby translating and making his own the phrase of Vico, "*mente heroica.*" Although one knows how prudent are his remarks and how diligent he was never to stray from Catholic orthodoxy, the formula of this Neapolitan thinker applied best to the philosopher of Modern Times. It was formulated to celebrate the risk involved in a search that lacks any model and is emancipated from the authority of established knowledge; it was formulated to defend the exorbitance [*démesure*] of a desire to think, beyond the separation of different disciplines of knowledge, in quest of the truth. But it is also true that, in the usage Quinet or Michelet made of it, this formula was of such a kind as to awaken or reawaken in me a confused aspiration not to allow myself to be closed up within the boundaries of what is conventionally called philosophy. I tried to explain to myself the reasons for this. At bottom, they came together in the fact that the heroic movement by which thought eludes the already traced out and separate paths of knowledge wouldn't allow itself to be defined: the risk of thinking had no name, be it even that of philosophy.

I had been, in the first place, responsive to the connection established between heroism and servitude. The latter, for Quinet, was not the sign of a state, produced by de facto conditions: it bore the mark of a desire. These words had remained imprinted on my memory: "Look at this spirit . . . ingeniously deducing servitude in the very midst of freedom." They seem to come straight out of La Boétie's work. Both left it understood that the same desire prompted an indeterminate demand for independence and knowledge and, turning itself upside down, placed men in subjection to a master, in whom was embodied the omnipotence of belief.

For his part, La Boétie was suggesting that the desire to be free, or the desire to know, was freedom in actuality, knowledge in actuality; in short, he was suggesting that neither freedom nor knowledge constituted an object of desire, whereas, in contrast, servitude clung to the desire for something — an indescribable something [*un "je ne sais quoi"*] that would gratify it, both materializing it and wearing it out, as, in a phantasm, a pseudo-visible "object" comes to fill up and extinguish vision. This *"je ne sais quoi"* offered itself through the image of the master, or the singular charm of the name of One, or some substitute for this form of enchantment. La Boétie was also suggesting that through this image, this name, this charm, serf-men gained the illusion of their own unity, their own identity; they took pleasure in the very suffering of being delivered from the image of separation. He suggested, as well, that servitude was held together, for this very reason, by an identification of each person with the master — and this, at all levels of the hierarchy.

Quinet's reasoning followed the same inspiration. It guided, after all, his critique of the French Revolution, his analysis of Robespierre's and the Jacobins' reestablishment of despotism and servitude in the aftermath of the institution of freedom. What was then, in his view, this conversion of the Revolution into a counterrevolution if not the result of an effort to reconstitute a despotic power that embodies a phantasmatic unity and pulverizes the rights heroically proclaimed just shortly beforehand? But what seemed to me had made his thinking unique is that it was liberating itself from the still classical opposition between a natural freedom and a servitude that would be "against nature." This he did in order to describe the contradiction of man beneath and above himself. Of course, he spoke of a servitude that was being deduced "in the very midst of freedom," but he also declared he had wanted to "take man where one hadn't looked for him before, beneath humanity." No doubt, too, he called this man "denatured," but Quinet didn't seek so much to restore to him his nature as to make him be reborn through heroism.

I therefore repeated the question: What does heroism signify? Was it not—according to an idea that, it seems to me, was shared by a new generation of thinkers at the beginning of the nineteenth century—the power to assume a *right* that has no guarantee in nature and that finds its truth in its very exercise? Or, in other words, was it not the attempt to conquer or to win back desire from the grip of servitude, with no other support than the work [*œuvre*] of its own self-accomplishment?

It would take too long to retrace the path that led me to scrutinize this notion of a heroism of the mind. Let it suffice for me to point out that, having decided to devote several years of my main seminar to the birth of democratic society and of the democratic sensibility in early nineteenth-century France, I became interested in writers of various political convictions who seemed to me equally haunted by this "impossible" task: to unveil what is—the being of history, of society, of man—and to create, to bring forth, through the exercise of a dizzying right to think and to speak, that work in which meaning arises. Far from espousing the criticisms of certain contemporaries who denounce, under the name of romanticism, the twin phantasm of *revelation* and *creation,* I believed I saw taking shape in the nineteenth century the enigma with which we are still confronted today, one that lies at the very heart of our modernity and that removes us from the classical tradition. This enigma is best expressed by a thinker who is still quite close to us. It was Maurice Merleau-Ponty who, it seemed to me, had formulated it best: "Being is what requires of us creation for us to experience it." [4]

Thus, when I observed that the words that had come to my mind—*beneath myself, above myself*—had made me waver in my reference to Socrates, I had simply glimpsed that the test of an internal contradiction between the lapse or the relapse of desire, attracted by the figure of the One, and the conquest or reconquest of desire, in the exorbitance of freedom, of thought, in the unknowable exercise of the work—that this test cuts us off from every guarantee of human nature. This, I told myself, is what didn't stop me from finding in Socrates, or for example in La Boétie, exemplary figures of the heroism of the mind—but upon the condition, at least, that their task be conceived in another way than they themselves conceived it. This was what didn't induce me, either, to decree vainly, as some contemporaries have done, that reason or nature or man "doesn't exist"—though it does impel one to decipher the signs of what is, of what arises, only in the interminable risk of thought, of speech, or of action. Becoming aware of this risk, I felt I was justified in asking myself whether it was legitimate to relate to it the definition of philosophy.

This question returned to me by another path. Quinet's remarks, which had led me back to those of La Boétie, testified to a tie between the exigency of philosophy and the political exigency; between an exigency of thought, which takes responsibility for asking about the very essence of thinking, and an exigency to intervene in public life (through speech or by action, it little matters which), which might take responsibility for our relationship with what was formerly called *the city*. This tie, I would add, seemed to me unbreakable.

Quinet's hero, in the aforementioned preface, was Spartacus. The latter provided him with the figure of a combatant-philosopher. It had seemed to me earlier on, when reading Machiavelli, that, as Leo Strauss had seen quite clearly, Machiavelli's hero was Epaminondas—who, in a much more explicit way, and in conformity with a solidly established tradition, represented the type of the captain-philosopher. Didn't I have to recognize that my own heroes were thinkers who had put all their energy into trying to analyze and to change the conditions of the political regime in their times: Machiavelli, to whom I devoted a work that occupied me for so long that I dare not tell the amount of time, La Boétie, Spinoza, and since then, for a few years, a few French writers who fought fearlessly for the cause of democracy or socialism, in the first rank of which are Michelet and Quinet?

I was going to omit Marx. A strange oversight, since no other work but his, except for Machiavelli's, or that of a contemporary whose student I was and who was himself haunted by politics, Merleau-Ponty, has cleared the path for me into my own questions. This omission, however, is not accidental, for at the time when I thought myself a Marxist, I was concealing from myself, at least partially, the problem that philosophy's relationship to politics was later to pose for me. Now, it is really this problem with which I found myself more and more confronted: my refusal to make a definite place for philosophy, but no less, as I said, to erase it in favor of politics.

Of course, my talk of heroes may elicit a smile or two. This word even upset me. The fact is simply that in recalling the works that had exerted over me the most powerful attraction, I observed that they were all *hybrids* and that some of them would not even be recognized to have a philosophical status, according to academic criteria. Besides, why mention only my attachment to a certain type of thinker? I never cut off my labor of interpreting works of the past from the interpretative labor that forced itself upon me either when examining contemporary events (for example, in the French context, the Indochinese War, the Algerian War, the rise of Gaullism, the creation of the Union of the Left, and, especially in the European context, the revolts that shook the Eastern-bloc countries back in the mid-1950s and more recently, or the de-Stalinization process inaugurated by Khrushchev) or, more generally, when I investigated the principles of modern democracy and totalitarianism. There never was, in my view, a specific place for "works of thought" and another one for "sociohistorical reality." I never analyzed Machiavelli's work and that of Marx, for example, in order to extract therefrom a system of thought—or, to use the formula of a historian of philosophy, to bring out an "order of reasons"—and still less to catch them in the trap of their own contradictions. Such a disposition, in one case as well as in the other, would have led me to lose interest in the writing of the work so as to reconstruct a hypothetical body of assertions. I have endeavored, on the contrary, to restore both what is deliberate, controlled, in the thought of the writer and what for him proves to be unmasterable, what constantly carries him along toward or carries him outside the "positions" he has adopted. I am speaking, in short, of what constitutes the adventures of thought in writing, to which the writer consents; I am speaking of what summons him to lose sight of himself so as to place himself in the work.

Now, these adventures, these tests, in connecting me as closely as possible with someone's writing, became the sign for me of the site, and of the time, in which the work takes shape, of an experience of the world from which the experience extracts itself and that gives rise to this experience. It is the sensitivity to these adventures, to these tests that, both at once, made me read in the work the questions it took on and allowed me to hear or to reformulate the questions our own time bears. On the other hand, I never conceived of studying modern democracy or totalitarianism from the objectivist standpoint of the sociologist or the political scientist who endeavors to define systems of institutions and to compare them; I was attempting to comprehend what the totalitarian enterprise—whether of the Fascist type or of the Communist type—was intending, beyond the destruction of bourgeois democracy. Convinced [since the late 1950s] that it is not starting from the transformations in the mode of production that the advent of the totalitarian regime is to be explained, I had endeavored to bring out a symbolic mutation.

Now, how could I have tried to gauge, to take the measure of what was meant by totalitarianism's denial of social division—denial of the division between the State and civil society, of class division, of the division of sectors of activity—its denial, too, of the difference between the order of power, the order of law, and the order of knowledge (a difference that is constitutive of democracy) without seeming to legitimate, without fearing to see myself legitimate, the de facto divisions that characterize the established democratic regimes in which we live? How was I to provide a glimpse of the deadly finality of totalitarianism without justifying the conditions of oppression and inequality belonging to our own regimes? How, too, was I to carry out a critique of Marxism, which reveals everything that has fed the phantasm of totalitarianism, without erasing what constituted the truth of

Marx's critique of the society of his time? To give readers a feeling for the dynamic of democracy, the experience of an ultimate indetermination at the bases of the social order and of an unending debate over right and law, I had to try to shake up not only their convictions but their intimate relationship with knowledge; I had to try to reawaken in them a sense of the kind of questioning that would induce them to undertake the necessary mourning of "the good society" and, at the same time, I had to escape from the illusion that what seems real here and now is to be confused with the rational. Is this undertaking philosophical or political? I wouldn't know how to answer. What is certain is that this task, which little by little had taken shape inside me, had driven me to a method of reading that I had never decided to adopt. It is one that merges with my way of being and that is not normally associated with philosophy.

At this stage in my reflection, I had to agree that my doubts about the possibility of defining the scope of philosophy were not only provoked by the idea of a political exigency that forbids it from closing upon itself. My interest in certain nineteenth-century French thinkers is not only philosophical and political. Will it be said that Michelet's *The People* is a political work? That his *French Revolution* is a work of a historian? That his *Origines du droit en France* (Origins of law in France) is that of an anthropologist? That *La sorcière* (The witch) is that of a sociologist? Will it also be said that Michelet belongs above all to the world of literature? The truth is that these distinctions are deceiving. And in fact, historiographical criticism and literary criticism — even when conducted by Roland Barthes (or especially by him, for, less than anyone else, Barthes doesn't ask himself what makes Michelet think or what he makes of thought) — testify to the futility of the approaches of a number of our contemporaries.

Michelet has a sense of time, as creation-destruction. He had a sense of universal life and of death, a sense of right as the expression of human establishment and as a "savage" demand lodged against every established institution. He had a sense of unity and of fragmentation. He is the thinker of roots, the thinker of identity — hasn't it been said enough? — but no less is he the thinker of the barbarian, nomadic, undomesticatable spirit. He allies the idea of a humanity that makes itself — that communicates with itself through the variety of its works — with that of the impossibility of humanity ever closing upon itself. One would search in vain through his works for a theory of all that. But what I called the adventure of thought, as it is lived and as it is delivered in his writing, is imprinted on his reader by means that, while not being those of philosophy, are no less effective; they are so in another way, and similarly they awaken the reader to the question: *What is thinking?* As I do not see any question that would be more originary, I am more and more subject to the following doubt: In order to sustain such a question, must it be *named?* Or even, if it is to be so, is it not in life, in the mode of engendering thought, that it finds its greatest strength?

Philosophy, nonphilosophy? What is the boundary to be traced between them? I wasn't the first person, of course, to ask myself those questions. But it seemed to me inadequate to respond that there can be more philosophy in a history book, in a political work, in a novel, or in a poem than in a treatise bearing the name of philosophy. This answer leaves in the dark what it ought to shed light on: What is to be understood by philosophy? So long as one believed that one could define philosophy by the way in which it was distinguished from theology in the treatment of ultimate questions, perhaps one possessed a criterion. Speaking only of Modern Times, it seemed possible, as Leo Strauss has suggested, to make belief in revelation the criterion of religion and to make free inquiry into the foundations of knowledge and human conduct, placing one's confidence in reason, the criterion of philosophy.

But the tie between philosophy and theology has come undone to the point where one can doubt that philosophy might allow itself to be conceived as an appropriation of the ultimate questions over which theology used to extend its jurisdiction. Nor is the relationship that has been established between philosophy and science of a nature to enlighten us on this question. To say that philosophy seeks the conditions of possibilities for new scientific approaches would be to reduce it to the limits of epistemology. To say that it seeks to formulate questions that are engendered by burgeoning scientific approaches does not necessarily mean that these questions would be ultimate ones, that they would have a privilege of some sort, that they would be more pertinent than the questions engendered by changes affecting art or literature, or one's conception of history or one's feeling for history, or political reflection, or, generally speaking, people's relationships to politics. It will be agreed, furthermore, that the disintegration of philosophy into philosophy of the sciences, political philosophy, philosophy of art, etc., only ratifies a failure to think philosophy as such.

What remains, then, of the exigency of philosophy if it cannot be related to some object? What remains that prompts one indeed to declare that it can manifest itself in writings that do not know that they are philosophical?

I still couldn't find an answer to a question like that. But it doesn't seem to me to be a futile one because it leaves me disarmed. As I have already said, it is the discourse about the disappearance of philosophy that I deem to be futile. But that very discourse isn't motiveless. Its only error is to convert an interrogation into an affirmation — that is to say, in the present circumstance, into a negation. I shall add that this interrogation is all the more insistent as it doesn't concern only philosophy and as it even gained recognition for itself earlier in other areas, notably in literature and in art (painting, music). It is trite to say that the painter has for a long time, and to an ever increasing degree, been confronted with the question "What is painting?", as the idea of an essence of painting and that to which it corresponds, an essence of vision, has slipped away from it. Likewise, the writer yields to the dizziness of the question, "What is writing?" The essence of literature and that to which it corresponds, the essence of language, has slipped away from it, while assurance as to what the novel or poetry would be was vanishing.

In an essay, "Indirect Language and the Voices of Silence" (which is in fact a chapter the author had excerpted, in altering it, from an unfinished book, *The Prose of the World*),[5] Merleau-Ponty had already offered an enlightening comparison between the adventure of painting and of literature and that of philosophy. His concern was to show in particular that the classical writer was haunted by the phantom of a pure language but also that we allow ourselves to be taken in by his illusion when we forget that, in his actual practice, such a writer was already dedicating himself to a labor of expression, a creative labor, that found no guarantees in the nature of language. Generally speaking, what Merleau-Ponty observed was that the classical writer or painter was, unknowingly, conducting research about that which gives itself out to be said or to be seen and about writing or painting, which later proved ever more expressly to be his goal.

In the wake of these interpretations, I had asked myself whether philosophy had not been, over a longer period still, haunted by the phantom of pure thought. And agreeing, along the lines of this same inspiration, that in his practice the philosopher had always been dedicated to a labor of expression, to the production of an oeuvre, one in which thought was seeking itself through writing, both unveiling itself and inventing itself, there never having been a self-transparency of thought and this notion of self-transparency not accounting for philosophy's own approach, I concluded that this research, this question, "*What is thinking?*", connected as it was to the question of writing, was becoming, in our time, ever more characteristic of philosophy.

Now, didn't I have to draw two conclusions from this reflection? The first would be that the philosopher finds that he is led to welcome, instead of deny, his vocation as a writer and to recognize that which unites philosophy with literature. The second would be that if the question that makes him unique, as philosopher, very much is "What is thinking?", this question could not be circumscribed, defined in the traditional sense, as a question of knowledge, a question that places a subject in view of its object, a question that would invite one to reascend toward an origin so as to deploy and to master the articulations of a field of consciousness. It would be a matter of an unlocalizable and indeterminable question that accompanies all experience of the world—whether it would arise from the most palpable or most general relationships, inscribed in the organs of our body (our body, which both opens it to others and to things and imprints these others and things on it), or from those relationships that are set up in us owing to our involvement in a culture and, beyond that, in a history of humanity. In this sense, what we called the exigency of philosophy would be born, wholly reborn, and what would rule it would, for the philosopher-writer, be only the call of the work, wherein the question remains in quest of itself, retracing its steps from all the places where its singular desire has led it.

I already have cited Merleau-Ponty's formula, "Being is what requires of us creation for us to experience it." But ought we to preserve this singular form (being)? We can still give that toward which the word is pointing the force of a name if, as the same author once wrote (indicating here a reservation with regard to Heidegger), there is no ontology but an *indirect* one, in the deciphering of beings [*étants*] and in the adventure of expression. And if, in order to relate to what makes us think and speak, we must allow ourselves to be carried away by thought and speech, if the same movement uproots us and implants us, doesn't someone who knows the attraction of philosophy have to champion this wandering, deliberately welcome this nomadic life, wrap himself in the whirlwind that for each person already, without his knowing it, institutes and blurs unceasingly the boundaries of the here and now, of the inside and the outside?

I was going to stop there when I remembered the answer by which I had eluded the question of my interlocutor: "How did you become a philosopher?" I had rushed immediately to relate the circumstances of my encounter, at the end of my secondary-school studies, with a teacher who, it had seemed to me, was extraordinary and whose influence almost immediately determined my future orientation. His name was Maurice Merleau-Ponty. Furthermore, as the references to his work that I have made in these pages suggest, I have not ceased to be guided by his inspiration. After all, I was to devote to him a number of essays that a few years ago were gathered together in a volume.[6]

I could certainly have said more about my interlocutor, about this encounter. The questions with which Merleau-Ponty was dealing gave me the feeling that they were living inside me before I discovered them. And he himself had a unique way of asking questions. He seemed to invent his thought while speaking rather than teaching us what he already knew. That was a strange and troubling spectacle. Though I would have been temperamentally too rebellious at the time to formulate it in this way, I had found for the first time a master teacher [*maître*] in this person who knew how to avoid the position of mastery [*maîtrise*].

As one can see, had I taken note of this experience I would have been led to consider closely the relationship between teaching and philosophy. But I glimpsed that, in my embarrassment in assuming the name of philosopher, I had made an even more significant omission. In fact, my choice didn't result solely from this encounter, as decisive as it was. Well before taking that high school philosophy course, I was possessed by a desire: I wished to be a writer. Since my early adolescence, this desire was my secret. Like many other young people who had similar feelings, I didn't know what I wanted to write; my desire was objectless, in expectation of an object. Philosophy just fixed that desire by metamorphosing it. Abandoning literature—without, moreover, that being a decision I ever truly settled upon—I experienced the attraction of a form of writing that retained the imprint of my first desire.

This recollection prompted in me a final question: Has what I owe to my personal history led me to misrecognize "the essence of philosophy," or have I gained therein some ability to fathom philosophy's relationship with writing? For the moment, that is the question to which I cannot respond. As I observed at the start, my reflections had carried me quite far from my precarious point of departure. Where they had finally led me, I could only stand aside when faced with [*m'effacer devant*] the other's point of view. Perhaps this justifies the fact that these reflections might have come along to summon up a reader.

Notes

"Philosophe?" was originally published in *Poésie* 37 (1985): 124–34 and, in an English translation by Lorna Scott Fox, as "'How Did You Become a Philosopher?'" in *Philosophy in France Today*, ed. Alan Montefiore (Cambridge, England: Cambridge University Press, 1983), 82–99. Reprinted in *Écrire*, 337–55. [T/E: I have on occasion consulted this previous English-language translation. I myself have supplied all the notes for the present chapter.]

1 Edgar Quinet, preface, *Les esclaves* (Brussels: Ch. Vanderauwera, 1853), ix–x.

2 Ibid., xi.

3 Claude Lefort, "Le nom d'Un," postface to the reprint edition of Étienne de La Boétie's *Discours de la servitude volontaire* (Paris: Payot, 1976), 247–307.

4 Maurice Merleau-Ponty, *The Visible and the Invisible* (1964), trans. Alphonso Lingis (Evanston: Northwestern University Press, 1968), 197 [T/E: translation slightly altered].

5 Maurice Merleau-Ponty, "Indirect Language and the Voices of Silence," *Signs* (1960), trans. Richard C. McClearly (Evanston, Ill.: Northwestern University Press, 1964), 39–83; cf. Maurice Merleau-Ponty, "The Indirect Language," *The Prose of the World* (1969), ed. Claude Lefort, trans. John O'Neill (Evanston, Ill.: Northwestern University Press, 1973), 47–113.

6 Claude Lefort, *Sur une colonne absente. Écrits autour de Merleau-Ponty* (Paris: Gallimard, 1978).

Reflections on the Present

Decomposition of Totalitarianism

WHAT'S THE STATE *of totalitarianism at the present time* [July 1989]? The decomposition of the totalitarian State is underway. Its appearance was the major event of the first half of the century. If it should come to founder decisively in the coming years, that will be the major event of the end of the century. No one can foresee, it is true, the rhythm of the process. Its bastions are still solid in Eastern Europe, Asia, and Cuba. But in those very places where the intimidation, even, in certain cases, the bludgeoning with slogans, has not let up, the faith has vanished. The Party, once glorious, is now a body without an idea whose principal preoccupation has ever more clearly become its self-preservation. The Chinese people have been struck with a tremendous repression and the image haunts us, but we cannot forget for all that the explosion of democracy in Beijing. These final orgies of the Chinese bureaucracy emit the odor of its putrefaction. The Terror that once infiltrated their souls and claimed to be chiseling the Chinese of the future was of an entirely other kind. At present, there is nothing but the hammered lie, with no recourse to idols, and the exhibition of heads bent beneath the hands of policemen.

But elsewhere, a movement is taking shape that gives us a glimpse of a change occurring; the field of the possible is expanding at the same time that memory is returning. Everyone knows that what is happening in Poland and in Hungary is new. Above all, there is the commotion taking place in the Soviet Union, for there could not be a lasting change at the periphery of the totalitarian world so long as the dominant power remains intact at its center. Since 1956, with the crushing of the Budapest insurrection, the lesson was drawn: the fate of totalitarianism would play itself out at Moscow. Now, should perestroika continue and broaden, whatever its ups and downs might be, one can assume that nothing of the totalitarian universe will resist in the long run, for, despite its diversity and even its divisions, everything holds together there, by virtue of the model's attraction.

In other times, Trotskyism wagered on the logic of "combined development" to herald economically backward countries' passage to the stage of socialism. This scenario, which was fictional, could very well become true — when applied to the process of democratization. It is not unthinkable that at a certain moment Czechoslovakia might cross over in one bound the stages through which Poland and Hungary have passed, nor is it unthinkable that China, which is apparently in a petrified state, might suddenly go further than the USSR on the path of democracy.

Was what is happening in the USSR foreseeable? In my view, yes and no. Since the collapse of the myth of socialism, another widespread illusion has taken over. The totalitarian State seemed so thoroughly bolted down that it was deemed invulnerable. For some, it was a matter of resigning oneself to the current division of the world and making the necessary compromises with the adversary. For others, the sole task was to condemn a monstrous system and to defend the values of the West, expressing solidarity with the dissidents — some of whom, including, more than anyone else, Alexander Zinoviev, were encouraging a deep-seated pessimism.

A curious thing: a vision of the soviet regime as all-mighty was allied with the vision of an economy that was in perpetual disorder and a population forever condemned to live in poverty. Khrushchev's failure made one forget his evaluation of the contradictions of the bureaucracy and of a management style bordering on the unlivable. Finally, the information that, these past years, has continually been confirming and amplifying this evaluation — concerning administrative incompetence, production waste, Party parasitism — was garnering less attention than the indications of the USSR's military might. How could one believe, I asked myself, that such a disparity between the archaic social state and the most modern technical resources might continue on indefinitely?

A greater acumen, I now tell myself, would have made less surprising the whirlwind in which the bureaucracy finds itself caught. What to me seems extraordinary, what I didn't imagine, is that this whirlwind might be produced at the instigation of the general secretary of the Party. Yuri Andropov's brief reign had already suggested that a new generation of engineers, technocrats, and university-educated KGB cadres might be won over to a new sense of realism, but those men didn't constitute a social force; they didn't contain a level of violence capable of shaking the established power. Where then might such violence come from, if not from below, in order to force the most enlightened section of the elite to stir to action? I admit my error: the violence came from on high. Someone who had been raised to the summit is responsible for initiating a break with the reigning conventions of the bureaucratic order. I speak of violence, for this violence is implicated in the political imagination.

Gorbachev's role calls for some reflections, ones that are all the more necessary as he is the target of criticisms, most often ones coming from early and clairvoyant analysts of totalitarianism who persist in saying that nothing has changed in the reality of soviet society. Let us summarize their argument: Gorbachev's policy is a political spectacle, and the naive are caught in the trap of his seduction. As a reformer, he's a mere juggler: he leans on the advocates of change to intimidate the conservatives, and vice versa. Undoubtedly, he wants to remedy the bureaucracy's inertia, but he is not the first bureaucrat to benefit from putting the bureaucracy on trial. How can one believe that he might be working for the democratization of the regime when one sees him concentrating all the power in his hands? Finally, we are told, it is foolish to imagine that one individual might be able to change the course of History.

A political spectacle? This appreciation of the situation fails to recognize the nature of the totalitarian world. In this world, everything is symbolic. Everything has to be made a sign of social cohesion; every reference to reality — past and present events, disappeared or living persons — is intolerable and must be prohibited if it harms the image of what *had to be* and of what *has to be,* if it unsettles the idea of an irreversible order.

Thus, when Gorbachev decided to liberate Andrei Sakharov, this gesture was not just for show [*spectaculaire*]; it was a violent gesture, one that made the ruling bureaucracy's image of its own authority waver. This first event convinced me that Gorbachev was inaugurating a policy whose inspiration was truly new. I saw the naïveté of those who, in the name of good sense, stated that Sakharov was no more dangerous set free than under house arrest and that it was just a maneuver meant to please international public opinion. When Gorbachev decided to allow free rein for debates among the intelligentsia, this too was much more than mere artifice. Those who then thought that debates and articles affecting only a thin layer of the public remained harmless were forgetting the status of speech in the USSR and were testifying, in general, to a failure to recognize the efficacy of speech. One only needs to reread Tocqueville's pages on the role men of letters played in preparing the Revolution.

The events that followed have shown, moreover, that freedom of expression, contained at first within a limited circuit, has spread to the press. The latter is now broadcasting information and analyses previously deemed inconceivable. When Gorbachev decides to rehabilitate revolutionaries whose name had for a long time been taboo, he is precipitating and legitimating a demand for knowledge of the past that had already been formulated in a few debates and a few journals reserved for intellectuals. Here suddenly the right to memory is being recognized at the very moment when calls are being made for change. And this right is soon going to find its most vehement expression in the publication of *The Gulag Archipelago*.

A tactic designed to maintain power? It is true that Gorbachev's policy is disquieting. Hardly has he made one step in the direction of the reformers than he makes a compromise with the conservatives. One shift to the right, one shift to the left: Isn't this the well-known sign of the tactics of a politician who exploits opposing forces in order to maintain himself in the position of arbiter? But were it true that he yields only to necessity and that he could act more resolutely, there would also remain the fact that it is he, Gorbachev, who unleashed the turmoil, who brought about the public appearance of *division* by organizing elections and by setting up a parliament whose debates are broadcast on television. It is therefore in the very midst of this turmoil, of which he is the instigator, that he behaves like a tactician.

Suddenly, any comparison with the ruses of a politician from a democracy proves to be absurd. Again, one says that Gorbachev decides everything. He has, indeed, succeeded in the exploit of getting himself elected as head of both the Party and the State. But how can one not see that, owing to this very fact, he is depriving the Party of its prerogatives. He takes half away from this Party, and that suffices for it no longer to be a compact body and for it to start to become dismembered. One is mistaken, then, to think that the established power remains unchanged. The apparently extraordinary authority Gorbachev holds is of another nature than that of his predecessors. He is wielding it, moreover, in a new way. He doesn't stop talking, he doesn't stop showing himself. This is not exhibitionism. The established power is thus rendered visible, identifiable, liable to evaluation, to judgment in terms of the reality of an individual—one who doesn't hesitate to say "I."

Might an exceptional man change the course of History? I suspect that the distrust Gorbachev's policy provokes comes from a strong reluctance to attribute to one man a creativity that can be found only in social forces. But, beyond the fact that appreciating the importance of Gorbachev's initiatives in no way means that one would be losing sight of a situation whose interpreter he is, isn't it important to recognize that we are brought back before a question, and a case, that is far from new?

Let us refer back to Machiavelli and his question: How can a people long accustomed to living in servitude become free? Isn't the answer that, where the meaning of the law, of equality before the law, has little by little been obliterated, only a man whose ambition and talent are out of the ordinary is capable of restoring it through his own authority, which is no longer in step with the ruling stratum? Successes are rare, certainly, but up till now Gorbachev's talent is clear and the breadth of the crisis of totalitarianism reinforces our hopes.

Rebirth of Democracy?

Communist regimes long seemed immutable. A large — quite large, need we recall? — number of people who didn't want to know anything about the cruel oppression these regimes harbored believed that they were seeing established the model of a planned, organized, harmonious society, one that was freeing itself from the old capitalist world, itself condemned to ruin. The reality, of course, didn't exactly measure up to the ideal. History, they thought, was giving birth to Communism, slowly but surely. The image faded little by little and gave way to feelings of repulsion. What one discovered was a power completely preoccupied with extending its might, peoples enslaved and ravaged by unchecked domination or else harshly brought to heel as soon as they stood up again. There was the quickly crushed East Berlin insurrection of 1953 — which troubled few minds, it is true — then the invasion of Hungary and the reestablishment of order in Poland in 1956, followed by the invasion of Czechoslovakia in 1968. There was the failure of the Khrushchev reforms, but also the revelations of his famous report on Stalinist-era terror and his inventory of the vices of the bureaucracy. Finally, and especially, the testimony of those who returned from the camps and of the dissidents upset public opinion.

Nevertheless, having become evil, the model remained no less fascinating. Totalitarianism, it was said, couldn't be uprooted because it concentrated in itself all the evils of politics, because there the might of the State had reached its final stage. Zinoviev's perverse argument enchanted a number of his readers, even here, and made them forget about Solzhenitsyn. The soviet people had adopted the cynicism of their rulers; they had no notion of law and, even in misery, rivaled one another in the art of shifting for themselves [*débrouillardise*]. They loved corruption; they loved their regime. The system was proving to be perfectly well bolted shut on high as well as down below.

As for Eastern Europe, everyone knew that it was riveted to Russia. The heroic effort of Solidarnosc couldn't fail to run up against a power that was incapable of conceding anything. In Hungary, the loosening of economic constraints and toleration for private initiative had, with progress on the consumer front, given rise to unbridled individualism; the depoliticization of society was going hand in hand with the maintenance of the Party's monopoly. In short, realism dictated its own conclusion: Europe had been divided once and for all, the soviet power had mastery over its empire, and it itself was proving to be unshakable. On the Western side, all that remained for the intellectuals to do was to condemn the violations of human rights in the East, and for the politicians all that remained was to speculate about the virtues of commerce and about how the needs of their economy might inspire Kremlin leaders to adopt a moderate stance.

Now, here we see the Communist regimes caught in the torment. Whence comes this torment? From the fatherland of socialism. What one was refusing to imagine is taking place at an ever increasing pace. The Polish rulers are beating their retreat before the reformers' drive; Solidarnosc is imposing its formula for a new government. In Hungary, the Communist Party is abdicating; it is repudiating its ideology; the People's Democracy is changing into a republic. That bastion, the Democratic Republic of Germany, is cracking apart; the most arrogant party is becoming aware of its troubles and its leader is resigning as demonstrators by the tens, then hundreds of thousands, clamor for freedom. It is doubtful that Czechoslovakia will long resist the tremor spreading from one country to another.

Little by little, totalitarianism is decomposing. We are not witnesses to a revolution in the strict sense of the term: nowhere, at least until this day, has there been a mass uprising, a direct confrontation between the established power and some insurgents, an explosion similar to the one Budapest experienced. Simply, the winds of History are passing through.

Isn't there some danger that one is becoming accustomed here to events, however extraordinary they may be; that one might be losing the faculty of astonishment; that, instead of gauging the breadth of the change taking place before our eyes, the West's leaders are parsimoniously calculating how much in the way of credits a successful democratic policy in the East would require? One hears it said, for example, that the Polish government or the Hungarian government has to give proof of its effectiveness before it is to be granted all the aid it desires.

But the first proof they must give is the one the population is awaiting. Let us turn the saying around: People do not live on hope alone. The new democratic institutions have a chance to become fully legitimate only upon the condition that they change the social situation, that they satisfy in some way basic needs. Nonetheless, signs of inurement are becoming manifest not only here but there, too. I am not referring to the skepticism of a segment of the population that may tire of free speech, whose effects change nothing about the extant poverty. Among those very people who are enjoying this freedom, there are, if one believes the testimony coming from the Soviet Union, some who seem to set little value on the changes underway.

I have sensed this impression personally in listening to Soviet intellectuals talk about perestroika before a large audience in Geneva. Through their remarks, one could guess at the turbulence of a population that not so long ago was paralyzed by fear and the agitation of minds not only among the intelligentsia but within the most varied circles. One could also glimpse the effects brought on by the spread of information being peddled not only by the major press outlets and television stations but also by a hundred little journals hawked on Moscow street corners, as well as a profusion of leaflets and pamphlets. Finally, one could get an idea of the debacle of Communist ideology. But, with the exception of a euphoric and resolute Latvian deputy, these men expressed themselves in cool or disabused or disrespectful tones. Their distrust of Gorbachev's policy perhaps was justified. But one couldn't fail to find disquieting the distant attitude they displayed toward the reforms. They complained of enjoying only "conceded liberties," as if their own speech didn't testify to a wholly new independence with regard to the authorities and a wholly new sense of security. They said nothing of the road traveled these very last few years. Listening to them, I thought of Nadezha Mandelstam, Kouznetzov, and Solzhenitsyn, along with many others, and of the overpowering stories I used to read, my throat all twisted in knots.

This was a strange spectacle, both reassuring and troubling. These conceded liberties, they added, were they not still at the mercy of the new master, who might, with a wave of the hand, decree their elimination? No one can exclude that hypothesis, but were not these free men betraying how they were still marked by the phantasm of totalitarianism when they imagined that a power might give away freedom and take it back at will? All Gorbachev had to do was lift the censorship restrictions for debate to become possible, so be it! But people seized the occasion to speak. Does one believe that speech could be rationed as one rations potatoes? Quite recently, it was learned that Gorbachev had severely scolded some journalists and asked one of them to resign. If I am not mistaken, until this day that journalist has not complied. This fact speaks volumes. Doesn't one remember the times of silence and fear?

In the view of various Sovietologists, the Soviet State has for quite some time now no longer been a totalitarian State. To look at what is happening now by referring to the Stalinist era would therefore be meaningless. The regime would be sliding simply from one method of bureaucratic management to another, the excess of authoritarianism proving incompatible with the requirements of production. In this way, after having been largely denied during the era when Stalin reigned, totalitarianism sees itself finally being identified post-mortem.

Another thesis also has its backers: Totalitarianism would be a concept lacking all scientific relevance. One would therefore be still more mistaken to speak of its decomposition. On what arguments is this theoretical criticism based? To be brief: Society never was homogeneous; it was, already under Stalin, the theater of many conflicts; the ruling circles themselves experienced dissensions; far from reigning above everyone, the supreme guide maintained his position via a consummate art of maneuvering and by cunning. To halt at this affirmation, however, would be to condemn oneself to confusing principle with fact.

Yet even these terms are unsatisfactory, for the principle is inscribed in reality. By *principle* I mean the ideas that are generative of the constitution of the social [*le social*]. Now, there is in my view no doubt that society is conceived in this instance as a society without internal division, every sign of division being imputed to the action of foreign powers or to elements remaining from the old regime, the supposed kulaks or the bourgeois, or both at once. It cannot escape the notice of an analyst not blinded by ideology that in reality society might not be homogeneous, that there might be in society diverse interests that not only set the bureaucracy and the masses in opposition to each other but that also can be spotted even within the bureaucracy itself and throughout the population, and that there are, furthermore, aspirations based on local and ethnic traditions, an entire set of tiers of differences. It remains no less true that these divisions, and this heterogeneity, are not *recognized* and that the conflicts to which they necessarily give rise can be expressed only indirectly and can emerge within the ruling circles only at the price of a series of major distortions after having been filtered through the many dependents of the Party's petty tyrants, who themselves make up the clientele of this or that one of the regime's top men.

Is one referring to ideology when speaking of the principle for the constitution of the social? One can answer in the affirmative, but upon the condition that one admits that ideology is not to be confused with the propaganda that feeds on Marxism (although the latter isn't exploited just by accident). There is no public space in totalitarian society; there cannot be any as soon as free speech is stifled, as soon as conflict sees itself denied. But the official discourse does not reject it. It is simply that the established power makes it its own private domain. Free speech is not impugned; each person has the right and the duty to speak; everyone is even noisily encouraged to engage in criticism and self-criticism. It is simply that the right and the duty are to speak "truly," that is to say, in conformity with the desires of one's governors, with their statement of the truth at a given moment. The official discourse does not state that the law is a fiction invented by the bourgeoisie. It is simply that the law finds itself placed in the hands of the established power, so that the positive laws have no value in themselves and officials exploit or violate them according to the instructions they receive or the idea they form of the summit's intentions. The concept of totalitarianism does indeed designate the following twofold phenomenon: a society without division; a power that condenses in itself might, knowledge, and the founding law of the social order. It becomes fully relevant when one notices that the entire system rests on a logic of identification: there is no conceivable gap between the people, the Party, the Politburo, and the Egocrat; they add up to one, spiritually speaking, if I dare advance this expression.

For such a system to be established, a mobilization of the masses and a rather widespread collective faith in shared ends are needed, and terror is also required. But the ebbing of belief, disenchantment when faced with the test of reality—the reasons for which I see no need to enumerate—and coercion without terror in no way signify the end of totalitarianism. When the matrix was in place, Brezhnev exercised the same kind of power as his predecessors, by other methods. Generally speaking, one cannot provide the definition of a political, economic, or sociological concept (monarchy, despotism, democracy, totalitarianism or feudalism, capitalism or nobility, bourgeoisie, bureaucracy, etc.) without taking into account the data of History. Their signification changes over time.

What seems ridiculous is the attempt to compare the totalitarian model or its latest version to that of a military-bureaucratic dictatorship. Distinct from all kinds of dictatorships that present themselves as legitimate under particular circumstances, claim to be saving the country, or even begin an open-ended reign, totalitarian power arrogates unto itself an absolute legitimacy and instaurates an order that claims to be *irreversible*. It sets up a society within unsurpassable horizons. The possible is ruled out. A voice from on high, speaking at first in lyrical tones, announces: *Here is the new world, the new man;* later, the voice intones: *Whatever you desire, you won't ever get out.*

Doubts about the future assail us from all sides. What are the limits of Gorbachev's power? What are his intentions? Up to what point is he ready to head down the path of reform? Perhaps these questions, to which we cannot avoid harking back when examining the events now taking place, are also without answers. He seems to be of that breed of politicians who know what it is from which they must break, but, once the adventure has begun, bargain with Fortune. For him, in any case, the imperative of movement and that of retaining power cannot be separated. That is what clarifies his oscillations and heralds many ups and downs. But, whatever interpretation one might make of his policy, at least one must recognize what is unprecedented in his action: he has shattered the image of the irreversible.

There is another extraordinary phenomenon that merits investigation, one which, it is discovered, is indissociable from the decomposition of totalitarianism: the reawakening of democratic aspirations. This phenomenon has been observed for years, it is true, in Latin America, in countries long subject to a military dictatorship supported by the technocracy. One and the same language has made itself heard in Buenos Aires, São Paolo, or Santiago, and in Budapest and Warsaw. The key phrase, in one place as in another, is that of the "democratic transition." But this is not a mere coincidence. The Marxist ideology that once mobilized opposition groups in Argentina, Brazil, and Chile disintegrated while the Soviet model, and then the Chinese model, have lost their force of attraction. As people have become aware of the fact of totalitarianism, this awareness has fostered the conviction that the struggle against dictatorship passes by way of the defense of human rights.

Paradoxically, what must very well be called the *renaissance of democracy* has barely stirred minds over here, in the very place where civil and political freedoms are enjoyed. Of course, all politicians declare themselves to be democrats, from the National Front's Jean-Marie Le Pen to the Communists' Georges Marchais. But this consensus is hardly instructive and doesn't prompt one to conceive the virtues of a regime that nevertheless seems so precious to those who have known only the vices of totalitarian power or of dictatorship. There is a singular contrast between the sympathy shown toward opponents in the East or reform currents and the reservations their attraction for Western societies inspires.

This contrast seemed particularly palpable to me when tens of thousands of East Germans fled toward the Federal Republic. In a homage to Václav Havel, portions of which were published in the 13 October 1989 *Le Monde*, André Glucksman observes quite rightly that this exodus is not being provoked by poverty, and he adopts as his own the formula: "The refugees are voting with their feet." His judgment is convincing, in part: "All the individuals and peoples are carrying out the most difficult choice, that of risk. They don't know what the near and distant future holds in store for them. They are not embarking for Cythera; they no longer believe in paradise, even the liberal one." Glucksman deems it appropriate to add, however: "They are motivated solely by the thought of what they are fleeing. If they enter into our history, if they come to join us, it is, in some sort of way, by going forth backwards [*à reculons*]."

By going forth backwards? Is that the right image? Of course, as Glucksman says, liberating oneself from totalitarianism is to reject the lie or, as Havel puts it, it is to want not to "die an idiot." But isn't it more than that? Glucksman declares again, commenting Havel: "To leave Communism is to enter back into history and not to leap from one system to another. One never begins to escape from Communism; perhaps one never finishes doing so either."

I leave aside the second proposition, which is, to say the least, murky. But, sticking to the first one, I ask myself what is designated here by *system*. The fact is that Glucksman refrains from uttering the word *democracy*. What a strange silence when the word is being shouted everywhere. Now, if it is true—as I myself have written for a long time—that the Communist regime, under cover of building a new world and a new man, has brought about a closure of History, has denied that anything whatsoever might arise that could put the Party's dogma into question, it seems to me no less certain that democracy is the regime that, in welcoming conflict, social and political debate, makes room for the possible, for the new, doing so on all levels, and exposes itself to the unknown. It is, in short, essentially *historical society*.

I would not have employed the term *rebirth* [*renaissance*] if I didn't think that democracy had arisen at a certain time, that it had won out by breaking with an orderly, hierarchized world subject to supposedly natural principles, and that those who at present are attempting to free themselves from totalitarianism are dedicating themselves anew to a labor of creation. Western societies are not to be summed up as the establishment of a neutral space within whose borders individuals would find the chance to breathe and not to die idiots; such societies are distinguished by their institutions and notably by their system of representation. In these societies, individual liberties would soon die out, as Tocqueville already observed, if political freedoms were lacking, if universal suffrage as well as open and public political debate found themselves abolished.

Democratic aspirations in the countries of the East would be less astonishing if one reexamined the origins of totalitarianism. I am not identifying Nazism or Fascism with Communism. Beyond the fact that they are based on irreconcilable principles, it is a fact that one of the mainsprings of Nazi or Fascist ideology was anti-Communism and that, starting in the 1930s, one of the mainsprings of Communist propaganda was anti-Fascism. But the existence of this antagonism doesn't make us forget that in these two versions the totalitarian power's target was the democratic regime, a type of constitution and a mode of existence.

Fascism and Communism participated in one and the same counterrevolution; they undertook to overturn the course of the "democratic revolution." The characterization of Nazism as the agent of Big Capital is no longer worth the effort of refutation. At least one can say that it usefully served to hide from the eyes of countless Left militants the relationship this movement maintained with its rival as well as its political project, that is to say, the attempt to subject all social activities to shared norms and to create a power capable of embodying the people-as-one. Hitler's target was democratic anarchy and, more profoundly, the "monstrous" heterogeneity of a world of which he would make the Jew both the symbol and the diabolic agent. What would have remained of Marxist science if the Communists hadn't assigned to the Nazis the function of saving capitalism? How would they have still justified their devotion to Stalin's power if they had gauged the extent of the transformation wrought simultaneously in Germany's power structure and in its social structure?

Anyone, moreover, who considers the way in which totalitarianism was implanted in the Soviet Union would have to agree that this form of totalitarianism was sketched out well before the mode of ownership had been entirely modified and that the bureaucracy flourished thanks to the resources it was able to draw from its management of the economy. Lenin undoubtedly wanted to instaurate socialism. But that didn't prevent him from being fascinated by the model of German industry or from making a compromise with the market system when he deemed it necessary.

On the other hand, he didn't tolerate the idea of public debate, of a right of the majority to decide. He destroyed representative institutions, not only the parliament but the soviets. He couldn't bear the image of social divisions, that of organs, whatever kind they might be, or of centers of thought that demonstrated any independence. He wanted society itself to be completely orderly. He treated intellectuals in general, all those who demanded free speech, as demagogues and parasites. As one knows, it was he who created the first camps in Russia in order to lock up there all suspect elements.

It therefore ought not to come as a surprise that the rebirth of democracy is taking place at the same time that totalitarianism is decomposing. What is astonishing is that a few of the most lucid intellectuals, who knew how to take the measure of Nazism and Stalinism at their birth, found in the events no motive to reflect upon the essence of the regime that aroused the hatred of the new masters of Germany and Russia and that alone offered chances of a free life. One would search in vain for this sort of reflection from Boris Souvarine or Simone Weil, or even from Theodor Adorno, Max Horkheimer, or Hannah Arendt. They sought much too quickly to detect in Western societies the prolegomena of totalitarianism. And this disposition continues.

The questions that pass for being the sole fundamental ones do not bear on the character of our political societies, on their capacity to maintain themselves by making room for social, economic, and technical change or for changes in mores. They bear on *modernity*, and more particularly on "the crisis of our time," which is deemed to be revelatory of modernity, nay, revelatory of the break that occurs with modernity—which is sometimes called the entry into postmodernity. This, as if the antagonism between democracy and totalitarianism was only secondary with regard to the major tendencies of History. These questions, which pass for being the sole fundamental ones, concern capitalism—though the term might hardly ever be employed any longer, on account of the decline of Marxism—the might of technology [*la puissance de la technique*], the rise of the Welfare State, mass culture, and individualism. That such questions are not alien to that of democracy is beyond doubt, but, as formulated, they make one lose trace of it or, in the best of cases, they render it unrecognizable.

There is certainly one way of taking exception to the paradox of which we are speaking. Some deem that, under cover of looking for democracy, those who try to reform the totalitarian regime or to escape from it are seeking to rationalize the economy, to appropriate the technological resources, to establish an efficient management of a State that has been dismantled by bureaucratic practice. Or they judge that those people have no other concern than that of gaining free access to business and to the enjoyment of the consumer goods from which a great number of people in the West benefit. This interpretation is nonetheless incapable of helping us understand why Gorbachev finds himself obliged to have recourse to the "myth" of democratization; why he must mobilize the intelligentsia; why, too, he has to create a forum in which public debates have inflamed the imagination of tens of millions of citizens (who previously had the dogmas of Marxism-Leninism pounded into their heads); why, finally, he endeavored to split state power from the power of the Party (whose unity was required by the system), and why, then, he needed to play out this "comedy" if he was acting only to restore the rational management of the economy, technology, and public administration.

If one were to assume that Glasnost, rendering speech public, is only the means for ensuring modernization, one would still have to inquire about this necessary detour via political reform. Such an interpretation is no less futile if one considers how vigorous are the demands in favor of political pluralism, the demand that rulers account for the acts of extortion committed in the past in the name of Communism, the will to rehabilitate the victims of terror, and that of giving memory its due. Furthermore, is it not true that the search for democracy is by its nature tied to the desire for an improvement in the material conditions of existence? And isn't it true that this desire in no way obliterates the value of political freedoms? How would one remove from democracy the social question and therefore that of economic organization, if not by joining up with the most reactionary form of free-market liberalism?

All the same, let's not oversimplify: the regime under which we live does not exert unreserved attraction in Russia. I am not speaking of the hostility borne by Party conservatives but that of its opponents whom we admire. We already knew that dissidents had expressed their disappointment, nay even a certain repugnance, at a civilization in which everything is granted indifferently and therefore nothing is truly respected and respectable. Some of those who were able to flee or to benefit from exile take care to live together, to remove themselves as far as possible from the setting in which fortune has placed them, and to defend themselves against what they feel is an assault on their integrity, doing so to the point of refusing to learn the language of the country that has welcomed them. They have no doubts about what they have rejected, but they have a keen sense of what they have lost. What they have lost, beyond their country that they don't confuse with the regime that was enslaving them, is a certain quality of the social bond — a religiosity that was often, but not always, nourished by a belief in God and that was expressed in their sense of community.

This community was not visible, but it had a virtual existence: it was that of the persecuted, that of resistants, be they reduced to impotency, and, more broadly speaking, that of men and women who carry within themselves a memory, not so much the memory of particular events as that of a culture, of a sensitivity to things, to others, to time, that of the mores that the reign of dogmatism, brutality, cynicism, and lies was dead set on burying. It was possible for them, before exile, to share thoughts, recollections, the flavors of life, forbidden tastes. But another motive helped to keep this religiosity alive. The persecuted or the silent resistants could in their own country very well claim to be cutting themselves off, if not in fact at least in thought, from a society perverted by mutual mistrust, denunciations, lies, and corruption; they felt themselves immersed within a people that suffered daily from poverty. The vices of those who merely subsist are not the same as the vices of those who dominate, even if the former resemble the latter and ultimately lend them their support. Poverty has other effects than to make each a stranger to the other; in contradictory fashion, poverty makes itself the sign of a shared fate.

In response to the aspirations now dawning in the East and to the kinds of resistance to which these aspirations are giving rise, are we doomed to fall back on a cramped position, limiting ourselves to Isaiah Berlin's notion of "negative liberties"? Isn't the task before us to conceive democracy as a form of political society, a regime in which we have an experience of our humanity, rid of the myths that conceal the complexity of History? This regime, like all others, is characterized by a constitution and a way of life. Still, one must not take the term *constitution* in its purely legal meaning or treat its way of life as a simple fact. Democracy does not allow itself to be reduced to a set of institutions and rules of behavior for which one could provide a positive definition by means of a comparison with other known regimes. It requires people's adherence. And this adherence, or approval, isn't necessarily formulated in strictly political terms. Someone who exercises some public responsibility is under no obligation to take an oath of faithfulness to the constitution. It is perfectly possible for this or that person to flaunt his contempt for elections, for the decisions of the majority, for the demagogy of parties, and at the same time to display a desire for independence, a freedom of thought and speech, a sensitivity to the other, an investigation of the self, a curiosity for foreign or former cultures. All of these displays bear the mark of the democratic spirit.

In order to appreciate the limits of a sociological interpretation, let us go back to the lectures of Raymond Aron published under the title *Democracy and Totalitarianism*. The author defines democracy as the pluralist constitutional regime and totalitarianism as the regime of the monopolistic party. His intent is to show that democracy is to be distinguished by its willingness to accept competition and to organize it by subjecting it to rules. In vain would one try to erect freedom into its principle, for that would be to choose among philosophical conceptions, each of which is debatable. Democracy's merit is to adapt itself to a differentiated and conflictual society and to arrange the conditions for a peaceful competition among groups aspiring to exercise power and, by way of consequence, the conditions for a peaceful settlement of conflicts within society. Aron endeavors to underscore that democracy is imperfect, that it includes oligarchies and lends itself to the demagogy of parties, and that it is exposed to the double threat of anarchy and tyranny. But he deems these to be de facto imperfections. By way of contrast, the imperfection of totalitarian power seems to him to be basic, since, in championing the notion of a homogeneous society, it deprives itself of the means to justify its own existence and since, in admitting that it is not yet so, it can present itself only in a deceitful way as the expression of the entire people.

Now, doesn't this way of defining democracy and totalitarianism encourage one to dissolve their antagonism in the element of the legal-political? Doesn't one's appreciation of their imperfections lead one to conclude that both regimes are variants of one and the same society, industrial society? In fact, according to Aron, democracy's superiority becomes clear in observing that it is the one that expresses best, on the superstructural level, the characteristics of the infrastructure. Thus, this highly lucid thinker who is so attentive to the mystifications of the socialist State ends up declaring among his conclusions:

> The societies which see each other as the greatest enemies, that is the Soviet and Western societies [let us note that the words *democracy* and *totalitarianism* are avoided here—C. L.] differ less from one another in that they are developed industrially, than they both differ from societies which are only starting along the path of industrialization.[1]

Shortly beforehand, he was declaring: "I do not think that the contrast between the two kinds of regimes is a contrast between two fundamentally different ideas."[2] And a little later, when mentioning the variety of modern societies, he specifies: "Let us ... confine ourselves to stating ... that, in this diversity, ideological conflicts are partly conflicts of myths and that these myths can for a long time withstand the facts."[3]

Nevertheless, observation of the constants of industrial society does not suffice. To account for the advent of a competitive society, Aron has to have recourse to an argument he formulates only once, as if in passing, in his conclusion: Competition or "rivalry is inevitable because there are no more rulers by divine right or by tradition."[4] But is that a simple statement of fact? Has the rejection of an authority requiring unconditional obedience nothing to do with people's representation of what is just and unjust, true and false, or, again, of what conforms or not to the human condition? Aron himself, in the passage we are citing, deems essential "the potential participation of all the citizens" in public life,[5] then he notes again that "another essential factor in a multi-party system is the right to debate what should be done and what is the best constitution for the city."[6] He even goes further, adding: "It seems to me to be in conformity with the essence of our societies and in conformity, too, with the *human vocation* [my emphasis— C. L.] that all men who want to should take part in the debate."[7] This is to recognize that, beyond the rules for competition and, more generally, the constitutional works, democracy requires a mutation that has philosophical import. Although he refuses to decide among conceptions of freedom, the author tacitly rallies to the spirit of human rights. But why, one then asks oneself, isn't the question of legitimacy at the center of his reflection?

Let us come back to this mutation. Democracy instituted itself by challenging the notion of an ultimate referent. This implies that power has ceased to incorporate the law and the ultimate knowledge of the social order. This implies, too, an irreducible gap between the idea of law and positive laws as well as between the idea of truth and the effective development of various forms of knowledge. In the same stroke, it also implies a profound change that takes place throughout social life.

The exigency of legitimation becomes imperative in the very movement of action and thought. Men are condemned to interpret events, behaviors, and institutions without being able to rely on the authority of a preeminent judge. The fact that those who govern and the designated representatives find themselves in a position where they must gain recognition for their competency, their fitness to respond to collective expectations and to regulate public affairs, could not make one forget that this need to gain recognition becomes all the more imperative when the certitudes of reason and moral certitudes that have been substituted for the certitude of faith start to waver. All figures of authority are assailed in civil society. The latter—which, as has so often been observed, achieves some independence as the old hierarchies connected with the political, religious, and economic spheres are dismantled—little by little becomes the theater for an upheaval in mores and an erosion of the ultimate bearings for people's conduct.

Such a revolution has to be taken into account when one inquires about the dissociation of the political [*le politique*] from the nonpolitical that is essentially characteristic of democracy. We are using this term *political* at present in its everyday acceptation in order to designate the set of activities whose end is the regulation of public affairs. In this sense, politics [*la politique*] runs up against a *limit*. Those who govern have no right to transgress it, since they are not the repositories of law and knowledge. They cannot set the norms for the functioning of the economy. They have to respect the independence of justice. They could not prescribe to scientists, historians, or sociologists the conclusions deemed useful for society, or subject information to censorship, or infringe upon the freedom of writers or artists.

Are these just regulations? But when they are violated, it is the democratic ethic that is injured. The dissociation of that which is political from that which is nonpolitical does not relate to some artifice for guaranteeing the operation of a society deprived of an ultimate referent. It expresses a new understanding [*appréhension*] of law and of freedom, of their connection that is made and remade in each site of the social sphere [*le social*] and transforms the meaning of right for the individual as well as for the collectivity. What characterizes the democratic experience is that a question is being posed and that an answer is being sought, here and now, in one area of action or of thought and that these are removed from any common denominator that might be formulated.

Should one then accept the image of a shattered society? Sometimes the formation of a neutral State, for example, is denounced as it implies the destruction of the community; one complains about an educational system incapable of molding citizens or about the decomposition of an art form that no longer fits in a shared space. But what we must understand is that the limit with which thought and action are confronted cannot be projected into the real. For, democracy proves to be a political society; the fragmentation of which we were speaking is the sign of a singular constitution. The "indivision" of the social gives way to the test of alterity. In other terms, the world gives itself as such from each unique site. Although impossible to encompass, it requires debate about the legitimate and the illegitimate and, in each person, an incessant effort in order to judge.

Aron, I recalled, distinguishes the de facto imperfections of democracy from the basic imperfection of totalitarianism. In this way, he observes that democracy makes room for oligarchies that can take on disproportionate strength; that it lends itself to the demagogy of parties, when these parties find themselves obliged to seek the favors of the electorate; that it harms governmental efficiency and sees itself threatened by anarchy; that this very threat, by a rebound effect, bears the threat of tyranny. Fair remarks all. Nonetheless, they concern only the strictly political aspects of the regime and thus allow one to ignore the danger of a laceration [*déchirure*] that comes from the destruction of old networks of dependence or, what boils down to the same thing, from the affirmation of the absolute principle of freedom.

It is rather in the wake of Tocqueville—although he largely neglected the economic transformations and technological changes taking shape in his time—that we can detect this laceration or what we might also call the turning points where freedom reverts into its opposite. Tocqueville, as one knows, was worried less about the perils of oligarchy, demagogy, and anarchy than about the strength of public opinion and about the birth of a despotism of a new kind, appearing under cover of the tutelary State. It seems to me that the key idea, which he only sketches out, is that the shared will *not* to obey *anyone* leads to enslavement from an *impersonal* power, which is to be feared all the more as it is invisible.

I would risk saying that Tocqueville glimpsed a new form of "voluntary servitude." Whereas it seemed to La Boétie that voluntary servitude is born of the attraction for the name of One, it is from the absence of a name that for Tocqueville this kind of servitude is engendered. No one is raised in democratic society above all others in order to steal everyone's glances [*regards*], in order to give shape to a body of which each person, not knowing himself as an individual, imagines himself to be a member; but an anonymous power, "social power" swallows up men who believe themselves to be free. Is not this social power, which Tocqueville ultimately attributes to the State, the one that, following a similar pattern, Marx would soon attribute to Capital and that was later to be vested in technology? In all three cases, domination is not the product of one will but bends beneath it all wills, those of its agents as well as those who only submit to it.

Of course, neither the State, nor capitalism, nor science, nor technology is the invention of democracy. But one cannot hide from oneself the fact that democracy liberates them from the impediments that were braking their expansion. At this point the drawback of my rapid analysis becomes apparent. The regime of democracy does not only bring about the institution of a symbolically differentiated field, such that all practice and every mode of knowledge—and, through them, every experience of the world—find themselves faced with their limit; it also gives rise to the image of a reality in itself. The negativity operative in the rejection of a power that enjoys an absolute legitimacy goes hand in hand with the affirmation of a wholly positive being over which men have no grasp. Thus comes to the fore at the same time the idea of a necessity that is foreign to the order of law. But as important as it is to observe how democracy lends itself to the representation of the all-mightiness of the State, of capitalism, or, as is said at the present time, of the market, and of technology, so should one also resist the temptation of attributing to them this omnipotence in reality and recognize that it is, as a matter of fact, held in check by the dissociation of the political from the nonpolitical and by the irreducible divisions of civil society.

What works against the full expansion of the State is both the fact that it is cut off from the source of public authority and that its administration, in each of its departments, is subject to the demands of many categories of people that the representatives are obliged to take into account. If the state bureaucracies cannot fuse together, it is because they are themselves caught in a turbulent society that makes it impossible for positive laws and for regulations to become petrified. And it is still worth pointing out that, where the reign of the bureaucracy arises, in a totalitarian system, its efficiency sees itself conspicuously reduced; the State as such sees itself becoming dismantled as the Party intrudes into all areas of social life. What works against the all-mightiness of capitalism is that capitalism must deal more and more with the demands of wage earners who benefit from rights that are guaranteed by the Constitution and imprinted on mores — right of association, right to strike, multiple social rights — and who have acquired, by universal suffrage, the opportunity to put their interests forward on the political stage. What also works against it is a more-difficult-to-define resistance, which at present is based on the refusal to allow oneself to be determined wholly by one's condition as a laborer or on the desire to open up multiple spaces for living — a refusal, a desire, one of whose remarkable consequences is disaffection from union activism. The unfettered capitalism that continues in some major countries of South America, where democracy has never succeeded in implanting itself deeply, would suffice to convince us that the mode of production doesn't have a dynamic of its own [*en soi*], that is to say, independent of political institutions, independent of the way in which social conflicts are expressed, and independent of the state of mores.

Finally, what works against the omnipotence of technology is that it cannot be subjected to ends decided by those who govern, not only because it is disseminated in the most varied domains — for, from this fact alone one can immediately draw the conclusion that it is omnipresent — but also, and here is the essential point, because it finds that it is assimilated by an eminently heterogeneous society, which gives various modes of existence, modes of thought, and discordant beliefs their due and because, as a consequence, it is not wholly subservient to those who hold the means of production, the means of administration, and the means of information. It procures for individuals new capacities for initiative. It participates in the extraordinary adventure that is constituted on a multiplicity of levels by the exploration of unknown continents — what the "wise" foolishly reduce to the project of man's domination of nature. Nothing better instructs one about the phantasm of a world entirely ruled by technology than the argument advanced by Martin Heidegger, who shows his disdain for any attempt to distinguish its centers, its uses, and its effects, and who, in order to respond to what he calls its "challenge," joins with Nazism, that is, a totalitarian formation that wanted to rivet everyone to his particular post and to destroy every sign of independence in society — to achieve, in short, under cover of a moral revolution, that strict integration of men and things that was being imputed to the artificialist philosophy of the West.

Is it so difficult to hold two ideas at once? Can't one recognize that the history of democracy cannot undo the histories of the State, of capitalism, and of technology, and that it is ruled by principles that are its own? When we said that democracy is a form of society, that doesn't mean that in democracy the signification of everything that comes to pass and shapes the life of a people is neatly wrapped up in it. If one examined, for example, the phenomenon of *the nation,* one would also have to agree that it, too, is irreducible and yet closely interconnected with the development of democracy, that there exists a tension between identification with the nation and the democratic ethic, one that becomes all the more lively when the nation finds itself less and less capable of closing back upon itself.

Undoubtedly, the critique of mass society, on the one hand, and of the progress of individualism, on the other, sometimes uses another method of argumentation, although it might easily connect up with that of the misdeeds of the market economy, the inflated growth of the products of technology, and the reign of consumerism. Tocqueville, it turns out, provides the obligatory reference. Is it not, one says, the equality of conditions that engenders in each the attraction of resemblance, that leaves no other criterion for judgment than the decrees of the majority, and that doesn't cease to accentuate the uniformity of opinions, tastes, and forms of behavior? Is it not the same process that deprives the individual of the sense of his roots, of his insertion in the space and the duration of the institution (whether we are talking about the family or the city), and no longer allows him even to distinguish his own desire from the needs this or that milieu imprints on him? It is beyond my purpose here to return to the analyses offered by Tocqueville. It should at least be recalled, however, that he never lowered democracy to the level of the equality of conditions. He endeavored to decipher the opposite effects to which it gave rise. He explicitly challenged the thesis that democracy might be able to hold on in the absence of civil and political freedoms, after having insinuated just that. Finally, if one grants that he deemed the "democratic revolution" irresistible, one would no less have to agree that the contradictions to which it gave rise required in his view incessant invention — an "art," he said — for such contradictions were bound to the essence of democracy.

To put mass culture or individualism in the dock without understanding that these phenomena are themselves irresistible, without trying to discern what the counterpart of their vices is, to decide, for example, that the spread of information, the discovery of foreign lands, the curiosity for shows [*spectacles*] and for works previously reserved for the few, and the considerable enlargement of the public space have no other consequences than to bring into broad daylight the stupidity of modern man is to give proof of an arrogance that is itself not exempt from stupidity. Is it not remarkable that the intellectual talk incessantly being spread about the leveling of our society is itself busy leveling everything, busy ruling out all signs of the doubt that haunts the life of the individual, the relationship of the one with the other, the operation of the institution? Is it not remarkable that the commonplaces with which we are assailed daily are duplicated in the commonplaces of an intellectual aristocracy?

There is nothing to hide about the ambiguities of democracy. Criticism is healthy. Still, such criticism must not sink to the ridiculous level of putting reason or unreason on trial. It must know how to denounce relativism without abandoning the sense of relativity that the totalitarian system sought to destroy.

The Test of Truth

Last Monday, the announcement of the coup d'état in Moscow alarmed me. Like many others, I was convinced that totalitarianism would not be reborn from its ashes. It doesn't matter: the idea of the irreversible doesn't chase out that of a monstrous power of repetition at work anew in History. A moment later, a thought came to me: Wouldn't now be the test of truth? Isn't the event going to render visible, finally decipherable, the reality of this society that has remained so opaque, despite the celebration of the reign of transparency? Who can do what in the Soviet Union? Such really was the question long posed, not only by Western leaders or mere observers, but first of all by the Russians and, over the whole extent of the Russian Empire, by the principal political actors themselves. At present the putsch has failed, the situation has become clear. But to what extent? Has the USSR experienced its test of truth? Or, as considerable as its import may be, does the failure of the neo-Stalinists constitute only one episode? Does the future remain uncertain?

One often fears letting oneself get caught in the trap of appearances. One shouldn't shun them either. Muscovites, in great numbers, rushed into the street to defend their parliament and shout: "Fascism won't pass!" Soldiers joined them. Leningrad offered the spectacle of tremendous resolution. Leaders, Yeltsin up front, have enlivened the resistance with a remarkable sense of cool composure. They spoke the language of freedom and the language of law at the same time. This is not only admirable; it harbors a profound political signification. Still, one must observe — sticking, at least, to the information that has come our way — that the mass mobilization remained restricted to a few zones. Apparently, the call for a general strike launched by Yeltsin wasn't followed very widely. Yet it is true that the rapidity of the course of events doesn't allow one to judge its chances for further development. But looking in the opposite direction, one has more reasons to be astonished that, according to numerous witnesses, the majority of the population in Moscow seemed to have greeted with indifference the news of this *coup de force*. If the information is accurate, this fact would merit being weighed carefully.

On the other hand, what is striking at first sight is how feeble the conspirators were. This trait has quite rightly been underscored: the burlesque beat out the tragic. What is this junta that doesn't respect the elementary rules of a putsch, doesn't seize its principal adversaries by night, holds a press conference without presenting a program, puts up with questions that are an outrage to its dignity, sends tanks out into the public square without giving the officers instructions? These tacticians of intimidation show that they are themselves timid. Their incoherence seems to provide the proof that the enemies of the reforms, so feared, were lacking in firmness.

Nevertheless, what goes for our relationship to appearance also goes for our relationship to rationality. As convinced as we may be, in general, that the conduct of the men in power is not necessarily rational, let us not too hastily conclude that such conduct can be purely irrational. I find tempting the hypothesis advanced by some keen observers that the conspirators had to rush their coup and that they believed they had to act before the signing of the pact that sealed the new Union. This hypothesis neglects, however, the fact that the agreement between Yeltsin and Gorbachev was established weeks earlier and that the pact itself was a semifailure. More convincing, it seems to me, is this other hypothesis, that the putsch leaders overestimated the effects of Gorbachev's unpopularity and underestimated the attachment of a part of the population to the fundamental freedoms acquired not so long ago. So be it! But it doesn't satisfy me fully. How can one believe that they had no good reasons to count on the cooperation, a bit everywhere, of their supporters in various sectors of the *nomenklatura,* beginning with those who were directly under their authority?

Now, this support was lacking. If it is significant that a large part of the population has remained indifferent, how is it more significant than the fact that the mass of bureaucrats who are hostile to the regime, worried about their future, and engaged, in part, in sabotaging the reforms wouldn't mobilize themselves? Was it misplaced to expect the formation of hundreds of small committees, ready to serve the great "Committee for the State of Emergency"? Did the putsch leaders know that the administration, the army, and the KGB were divided? Certainly they did. But they had to think that, when the moment came, the upholders of conservatism would pass into action. The events suggest that these people were afraid to appear in broad daylight.

What is extraordinary is the Party's absence in the course of these last few days. People have spoken of its decomposition, which has been accelerating for a year. The picture one gets of it is no doubt accurate. But the numbers in the Party rank and file, as reduced as they might be, remain considerable. There isn't any doubt that a host of militants are in disarray, ideologically disarmed, and simply remain riveted to their posts for fear of no longer being anything at all! But one must distinguish between passive Communists and active Communists. The latter might have become a minority, but it is inconceivable that they would have lost their sense of organization. What would remain for them? The Party's essence is organization. As stunted as it was, it survived through its networks. Now, these networks have not functioned, and their branches extending into the underworld or into the high administration have remained invisible.

One minor fact, moreover, holds our attention: the sudden influx, into state stores, of products that are basic necessities but were previously unfindable; these products had therefore been stocked clandestinely in expectation of the great occasion. What level of complicity must have been required for such an undertaking! If it is therefore our judgment that the elements on which the junta was banking for support have slipped away, let us not hastily deduce from this that they were previously lacking in firmness, either, or that they have been definitively disbanded with the rout of the commando group's coup. A doubt persists about the breadth and the might of those who are opposed to the reforms, for these people haven't revealed themselves.

We should rejoice at their fearfulness; it has reduced the plot to a laughable action. Were they to have supported the junta, perhaps the junta would have turned into an effective dictatorship for a time, or perhaps it would have been defeated only at the cost of a brutal civil war. But it isn't enough to express one's satisfaction at its rapid failure. It seems to me hazardous to maintain that the adventurism of the putsch's architects demonstrates the fictive character of the might attributed to the conservative current. The KGB boss, the minister of defense, the interior minister, members of the government formed by Gorbachev have been unmasked: some are in prison, another has committed suicide, and the rest of the band is in flight. Circumstances being what they are, what better thing could one dream of? But it might be that the failure of the small number of people who have so imprudently unmasked themselves allows a greater number to remain in the shadows.

This last reflection calls for another one bearing on Gorbachev's policy. That policy lends itself to several interpretations. Gorbachev himself placed the future putsch leaders at the head of the State. That was an error or a fault. He agreed with that assessment during his first postcoup press conference. But wouldn't it have been desirable for him to give the reasons for his strange choice? He did not do so. This is a new error or a new fault. In failing to explain his conduct, he risks losing the small amount of credibility that remains for him among the population. What need did he have, anyway, to declare himself faithful to Communism, doing so under a set of circumstances in which he was benefiting from new support that had been brought to him as chief of State and guarantor of the law, and in no way as Communist chief? Either he deemed it still dangerous to detach himself from the Party or he hasn't stopped seeing himself as a Communist; either way, his clumsiness has been patently obvious under the circumstances.

Gorbachev's behavior still seems equivocal. At the very least it is disconcerting. This man has not only acted with a remarkable sense of realism by reestablishing ties with the West and by deciding to withdraw Soviet troops from Afghanistan; he has not only shown great ingenuity in his negotiations with Germany and with the United States; he has known how to display extraordinary imagination and extraordinary intellectual courage within the miserable universe of the bureaucracy in which he had been raised. To him are owed the initiatives that are at the origin of the collapse of totalitarianism in the Soviet Union and in Eastern Europe. Nothing can wipe out his merits, however much one has to deplore his opportunism, his possible trickery, or, who knows, his obstinate belief in the future of Communism.

Do the recent events signal his failure? Perhaps. But in light of them the obscurity of his motives has not dissipated. The evaluation of his policy would go one way if the strength of those, "at the heart of society," whom he called, literally, *reactionaries* was in reality quite small, if he invoked that strength in order to hinder the rise of the reformers, if he enhanced it considerably by placing in key posts notorious adversaries of perestroika. The evaluation would be quite different if the role of the old regime's bureaucrats had remained considerable in all sectors of society, at all echelons of the hierarchy, and if he estimated that the possible was to be gauged at every moment in terms of the resistances being aroused—despite the Party's diminished situation—not only by the rewriting of the Constitution but also by the reform of the administration and of the system of production.

Is it over methods or over principles that the followers of Gorbachev and the radicals have faced off against each other? How is one to settle the question? The methods, moreover, brought the principles into play. And it can be said that the current facts prove Gorbachev wrong. There is no doubt, as far as I'm concerned, that if I were Russian, I would have a long time ago taken sides against Gorbachev's "step by step" policy, if only because, in the absence of the radicals, the path of the possible would have been closed off.

But why then did these radicals wait so long before forming a movement? Why, then, if the choices left no doubt? I add a deliberately provocative argument. It is argued, perhaps rightly, that in handing over the highest offices to the reactionaries, Gorbachev was giving them, without his knowing it, the means to seize power or, worse, was inciting them to do so. Can't one ask oneself whether he was not applying an old recipe that has never proved unavailing: leaning on one's enemies rather than on one's friends in order to win passage for a policy that they would have combated head on, had these enemies been in the opposition. In that case, it will be said, the deceiver was deceived. But let us consider the result: it couldn't be better. At the summit of the State, these men have put their cards on the table and have finally appeared as traitors and imbeciles. May one be reassured: I am not attributing to Gorbachev a divine gift of cunning. I'm just asking.

There is a shadowy area in Gorbachev's policy, but also in the action of various political leaders in the course of these last few years. Now, this obscurity is accompanied by another one that relates to the social state of Russia and, more generally, of the Soviet Union — with the exception of the Baltic countries and of Armenia, where, on one point at least, no doubt is allowed: in those places, the will to independence is quite striking. But how is one to evaluate the changes that have affected, not one's material fate, but the mentality of the people or peoples being delivered from the totalitarian power? How can one know to what extent the desire for freedom, the desire for truth, and the sense of law have been awakened; to what extent are these being expressed in actual attitudes, feelings, and forms of conduct?

To lay all the weight of perestroika on the shoulders of Gorbachev or of a few leaders, or else again to lay all the weight of conservatism on a few notorious Communists, a few influential people from the army and the KGB or from the famous military-industrial complex seems to me to be a mistake. This perestroika effort is tied by a thousand invisible threads to the social fabric, which is made up of millions of beings who evaluate what is real and what is possible, what is permitted and what is forbidden, the lesser evil and the greater evil, and who never cease evaluating one another, divided as they are between suspicion and hope. Who would in good faith deny it: for thousands, tens of thousands of soviet people, whatever judgment they may make about perestroika, the latter has brought them the good fortune of escaping from their condition of silence, of asserting their rights to know, to express themselves in all areas, to judge, each where he is. This phenomenon, by itself alone, shows how ridiculous are the sententious defenders of Western culture who flail at the Russians' eternal barbarism!

But where are they at, these millions, these tens of millions, who populate a society and on whom the fate of the political regime ultimately depends? We don't know. We observe simply a terrible habit to submit. The people's passive attitude toward the worsening food shortage disconcerts us. No collective initiative, no rebellion, no resupply committees to take it upon themselves to search for provisions; the shops reserved for the privileged still with impunity give to those who are deprived the spectacle of a small number of people who have everything at their disposal. The passivity is the same in the face of the housing shortage. And many other facts send us warning signs: one still sees most of those who made the law in Brezhnev's time running various institutions. Up till now, the people have not budged.

Yes, perestroika has constituted a revolution. But, a very astonishing thing, this was a revolution without a revolution—by which I mean: without the characteristics of modern revolutions, which involved a popular uprising, the spontaneous combustion of a thousand burning hearths of collective energy. The absence of violence, until these last few days, is certainly something to rejoice about, in a sense. It is no less true that a reform of institutions, of mores, and of social life so broad that it proves to be revolutionary has, it seems, run up against the following terrible obstacle: the inability to disentangle the old from the new regime. Solzhenitsyn, in a superb passage from his *Gulag Archipelago,* waxed indignant about the impunity enjoyed by great and small former Stalinist tyrants: "They must all be judged," he wrote. "How many are they? More than 250,000, perhaps," he added. Since then, in his short book, *Rebuilding Russia,*[8] he took up this theme again, in a less heated fashion, one more conscious of the constraints of reality. It is not only moral indignation that was guiding him; it was a political concern. For him, a purge, great public trials brought against those officials responsible for tremendous oppression, had a symbolic function: they alone could have brought before the eyes of all the break between past and present. Failing that, one acted as if yesterday's masters, and the executioners under their orders, were victims of the system just as much as those who had been locked up in the camps or in the psychiatric hospitals. Now, what is a democracy, whatever its inequalities and its blemishes, if not a regime in which each person and, in the first place, those who hold authority are duty bound to account for their acts?

Hardly had I written these lines when I heard a report about the session of the Soviet Parliament on this twenty-third day of August 1991, announcing that those guilty of leading the coup d'état and their accomplices are to appear before a court, that the activities of the Russian Communist Party have been suspended, and that its archives, which contain a wealth of information about the role of its officials, have been confiscated. And I learn, too, of the breadth of the Muscovites' demonstration. Might the moment have arrived when the genuine liquidation of the old regime would be starting and when, more profoundly liberated from their fear, the Russians and the peoples still called "Soviet" would be prompted to believe in justice and would thus rid themselves of the bitter taste of fatality? If such were the case, this putsch really would have been a test of truth.

—23/24 August 1991

Notes

"Réflexions sur le présent," *Écrire*, 357–90. The first part, "Décomposition du totalitarisme," was originally published in *Libération*, 10 July 1989, and reprinted in *Écrire*, 357–62. The second part, "Renaissance de la démocratie?" was originally published in *Écrire*, 362–82. The third part, "L'épreuve de vérité?" was originally published in *Libération*, 28 August 1991, and reprinted in *Écrire*, 383–90.

1 *Democracy and Totalitarianism: A Theory of Political Systems* (1965), ed. Roy Pierce (London: George Weidenfeld and Nicolson, 1968; Ann Arbor: Ann Arbor Paperback, 1990), 253.
2 Ibid., 244–45.
3 Ibid., 254.
4 Ibid., 241.
5 Ibid.
6 Ibid.
7 Ibid. [T/E: translation altered].
8 Alexander Solzhenitsyn, *Rebuilding Russia. Reflections and Tentative Proposals* (1990), trans. Alexis Klimoff (London: Harvill, 1991).

Index

Abensour, Miguel, 210

Absolute(s), 15, 18, 51, 101, 104, 109, 142–45, 151, 153–55, 220–21, 224, 227, 260, 269–70; and absolutism, 28, 32, 51, 68, 119, 167

Abstractions, 20, 36, 51, 161, 211

Absurdity, the absurd, 46, 79–80, 86, 98, 104, 182, 209–10

Abuses, 62

Abysses, 55, 71, 81, 83, 87, 106, 149, 156, 177, 219

Academics, 71, 237–38, 244

Accidents, 50; and essence, 53

Action, 26, 37, 47, 57, 73, 88, 94, 111, 113–15, 118, 126, 137–39, 189, 201–202, 212, 243–44, 254, 261, 268–69, 275, 279; administrative, 48; chances for, 137; collective, 47; common, 43; intellectual, 192; just, 232; of knowledge, 202; of lawyers, 41; and passivity, 94, 97; philosophical, 189; "restless" (Tocqueville), 35, 40; risk of, 243; Sade's, 67; schemes of, 137; of the scientist, 202; sectors of, 245; social, 233, 263; society's, 94; voluntary and enlightened, 42. See also Political action

Activation, 137, and reactivation, 239

Active life, 94–95, 97, 100, 118–20, 192, 221, 275

Actors, 54, 113, 137, 154, 209; multiple, 137; as performers, 71; political, 87, 89, 273

Administration, 41, 45, 56–59, 61, 89–90, 94, 200, 232, 270–71, 275; Chinese, 252; public,

56, 265; removal of nobility from, 50, 54; of State, 48

Adorno, Theodor, 264

Adultery, 77, 79

Advent, 20, 39, 42, 117, 211, 229, 232; of a competitive society, 267; of a finite space, 156; of humanity, 145, 152; of the individual, 169; of the people, 167; of the Spirit, 143; of the State, 214, 222, 233; of the totalitarian regime, 245

Adventures, 4, 6, 17–18, 28, 33, 213, 261, 271; of expression, 249; of literature, 248; of modern science, 192; of painting, 248; of philosophy, 192, 248; of thought in writing, 245–46

Aesthetics, 110

Agents, 270; diabolic, 263; social, 43, 95; of the State, 56–57

Aggressiveness, 127, 144, 154

Alamanni, Luigi, 114

Alberti, Leon Battista, 126

Algerian War, 244

Alienation, 227; liberation from, 6

Aliens, 153. See also Foreigners, foreign countries

All-powerfulness. See Omnipotence

Alterity, 225–26, 269. See also Other, the; Otherness

Ambiguity, 37, 48, 202, 273

Ambition, 67, 112–13, 122, 139, 237–38, 256; of the great, 129, 136; of great nations, 147

America, 21, 37, 39, 42, 46–48, 105, 180–81, 198–99. *See also* United States
American Republic and republicans, 105, 187, 191
American Revolution (1776), 48, 68, 191, 219
Anarchy, 85, 153, 267, 269–70
Ancestors, 225, 237
Ancien Régime, Old Regime, 37, 50, 52–61, 63, 88, 91–92, 94, 96, 106, 119, 133, 163, 219
Ancients, xli, 39, 46, 74, 109, 172, 175; as model, 109, 111, 116, 118, 134, 187; and the Moderns, 37, 39, 53, 110, 113–14, 178, 181, 185, 191–92, 203, 219; and their politics, 111; Roman, 218
Andropov, Yuri, 253–54
Antagonism, 147, 200; of classes, 215
Anthropology, 144, 155, 207, 246; cultural, 143, 192, 203; political, 230
Anticipation, 49, 156, 241
Antihumanism, 29, 34
Antiquity. *See* Ancients
Apostles, 162
Appearances, 13, 16, 50, 96–97, 129, 133, 160, 173, 221, 227, 273–74
Arbitrariness, 57, 62, 68, 129, 143, 149, 151, 173, 194, 218
Arendt, Hannah, 2, 264
Areopagitica (Milton), 174
Aristocracy, 34, 36, 39, 44, 50–51, 54, 59, 79, 86, 98, 100, 111, 113, 128, 182, 184, 190; in Greece, 185; intellectual, 273; and legal temper, 41; open, 59; pseudo- and real, 62; universal, 182, 199
Aristotelianism, xl, 145
Aristotle, 21, 68, 116, 130, 138, 146–47, 179–80, 195; on man, 20; return to, 197
Aron, Raymond, 153–54, 266, 269
Arrivistes, 183
Arrogance, 60, 237, 257
Art, 42, 47–48, 91, 201, 247, 269, 272; of contrasts, 37, 40; of dissimulation, 180; of institutions, 170; of maneuvering, 259; political, 121–22, 131; of political action, 111; of reading, 71, 173, 178; of the theater, 76; of war, 121; of writing, xli, 35, 40, 46, 48, 124, 172–73, 178–79, 192
Artificial, 28, 208, 223, 254

Artificialism, 94, 272
Artistry, 1, 7, 9–10
Artists, 109, 202, 269
Asia, 42, 45, 252
Aspirations, 91–92, 99, 102, 120, 186, 198, 238, 241, 259, 261, 263, 266
Assassination, 25; of the Duc de Berry, 90
Association, 46–48, 62; in America, 46–48; civil, 47; local, 47; political, 47–48; science of, 48; theory of, 47
Assyrians, 146
Atchei, 210
Atheism, 239
Athens, Athenians, 130, 218; their conduct of wars, 147; their way of life, 178
Athens, Duke of, 118
Attraction, 7–8, 10, 13, 18, 55, 63, 134, 219, 241, 244, 249, 253, 272
Audacity, 36, 109, 124, 137, 240; of Clastres, 217; of Fabius, 114; of Machiavelli, 134; of Strauss, 202
Audible, the, 209
Augustin the gardener (character), 69–70, 74, 79
Augustus, 146
Authoritarianism, 259
Authority, 34, 43–44, 50–51, 86, 95, 113, 119, 137, 189, 191–92, 198–99, 202, 218, 230, 237, 254–56, 268, 274; to decide, 51, 133, 194; divine, 145; emancipation from, 43; of established knowledge, 241; exercise of, 222; higher, 153; and independence, 49; institutional, 199; political, xlii, 24, 50, 174, 199, 202, 220; public, 270; quasiroyal, 132; real, 233; rejection of, 220; religious, xlii, 24, 32, 174, 199, 202, 238; scientific, 197, 199, 238; social, 44; sports, 199; of tradition, 103; transcendent, 163
Authors. *See* Writers
Autonomy: local, 58–59; of the political sphere, 95; recognized, 218; relative, 218

Backward countries. *See* Underdeveloped countries
Ballanche, Pierre Simon, 159
Barbarians, 147, 246, 278
Barthes, Roland, 246
Bateson, Gregory, 212

Beauty, 29, 190; and ugliness, 29, 142

Becoming, 36; mode/style of, 211; types of, 211

Being, 49, 124, 249; of the group, 223; "is what requires of us creation" (Merleau-Ponty), 243, 249; of nature, 224; social, 209; -society, 224; and time, 213; in Time, 211; and well-being, 181

Beings, 192, 249; empirical, 169; hierarchy of, 122; invisible, 209, 225; perceiving, thinking, and acting, 155; positive, 270; specific difference of, 123; and things, 29

Beliefs, xli, 24, 31, 33–34, 37, 43, 101, 124, 144, 181, 199, 220, 225, 229, 242, 265, 276; collective, 32; common, 43; discordant, 271; dogmatic, 87; and doubt, 25; ebbing of, 260; in hierarchy, 122; in immortality, 13; of the Indians, 226; primitive, 211, 227; religious, 195, 227, 231, 238; shared, 201; traditional, 195; and unbelief, 27, 29–30, 32, 50, 162–64, 176

Beneath and above oneself, 238–40, 242–43

Berlin, Isaiah, 266

Berry, Duc de, 90

Beyond Good and Evil (Nietzsche), 139, 178, 190

Bible, the, 122–23, 145, 178

Big Brother, 1–3, 11–13, 17–18; love of, 3, 15

Birth, 43, 52, 56, 59, 118; of Christ, 165; of Communism, 256; of a child, described by Clastres, 208–209; of democratic society, 243; of Florence, 118; of the "historical sense," 203; of modern political philoso-phy, 192; of Nazism and Stalinism, 264; of a new kind of despotism, 270; of a new religion, 134; of a new State, 215; of power, 102; rebirth, 183, 256, 262, 264; of sociology, 20

Blanchot, Maurice, 69, 72, 76, 80

Blasphemy, 22

Body, bodies, 6, 11–14, 16–17, 63, 73, 78, 82, 101, 104, 145, 147, 155, 177, 214, 222–23, 239, 245, 249, 270; amorous, 16; attraction of, 13; of Big Brother, 17; of Christ, 96; as closed figure, 239; collective, 18; compact, 255; destruction of, 11, 17; dismembering of, 255; double, 239; electoral, 90; enigma of, 13; functional, 96, 239; human,

96; image of, 12, 16; imaginary, 219; interposition of, 15–18; of the king, 239, 241; marking/imprinting/inscription on, 221–24, 226; of the master, 219, 241; meta-phor of, 96; of the monarch, 146; mystical, 96, 106, 146, 239; natural and supernatu-ral, 226, 239; opening of, 226; organic, 106, 146; of others, 13–14, 226; ownership of, 23; political, 51, 115, 147, 150; protective, 18; seeing, 224; social, 43, 57, 96, 101, 241; of the sovereign, 145; suffering of, 226; of the tyrant, 241; without ideas, 70, 252; writing on, 221, 226

Body politic, 239

Bombay, 28–29

Bonaparte. *See* Napoleon Bonaparte

Books: Great, 185; religious, 176

Borgia, Cesare, 125

Boudoir, 73–75, 78; and the city, 67–68, 70; space of, 70

Bourgeoisie, 21, 55, 57, 59–60, 62, 91, 99, 116, 119–20, 165, 245, 259–60; enrichment of, 55; revolutionary timidity of, 166

Brezhnev, Leonid, 260, 278

Brotherhood, 3, 7

Bruni, Leonardo, 117–19

Brutality, 265

Brutus, Marcus Junius, 114, 119

Buchez, Joseph Benjamin, 159

Buondelmonti, Zanobi, 114

Bureaucracy, 188, 215, 218, 253–54, 256, 259–60, 263–64, 271, 274, 276; Chinese, 252; contradictions of, 253; inertia of, 254

Burke, Edmund, 21, 59, 188

Burlamaqui, Jean-Jacques, 148

Burlesque, 27

Caesar, 116–19; and Caesarism, 133

Calculation, 116, 123, 125

Calvin, John, 168

Camps, 256, 264, 278

Capital, 270; Big, 263; and capitalism, 183–84, 256, 260, 263–64, 270–71; concen-tration of, 215; and unfettered capitalism, 136, 271

Captains, 114, 118

Castes, 50, 59

Catholicism, 36, 159–60, 162–63, 167–68

Closure, 211–13, 229, 239, 241, 246, 262, 272

Coercion, 93, 99, 154, 210, 218–19, 221, 223, 232–33, 260; and the noncoercive, 223

Coexistence, 133, 155, 213

Collectivity, 11, 13, 18, 32, 47, 92, 120, 209, 215, 260, 269, 278

Colonization, 27, 153

Comedy. *See* Humor

Command, 93, 113, 127, 129, 133, 135, 210, 214, 220, 232; and obedience, 81, 113, 219, 228; and oppression, 113, 129, 134–35

Commandments, 223–24; divine, 123

Commerce, 187, 198–200, 225, 257

Commoners, 59, 61

Common good, 123, 133, 138, 148, 185–86

Communes, 40, 119; and communalism, 32

Communication: ideal, 30; political, 192; public, 209

Communism, 85, 136, 193, 200–1, 256–57, 262–63, 265, 275–77; and liberalism, 180–81, 185, 200; as a type of totalitarianism, 245

Communist Manifesto, 85

Communitarianism, 22

Community, 22, 59, 81, 96–97, 106, 155, 212, 214, 216, 220, 222–23, 225, 228, 232–33, 269; of enlightened citizens, 199; of philosophers, 189; rural, 218; sense of, 265. *See also* Political community

Competency, 1, 41, 105, 182, 189, 268

Competition, 60, 163, 266–67; peaceful, 267

Complexity, 37, 93, 110, 126, 157; of History, 266; of tasks, 232

Compromise, 115, 253, 255, 263

Comte, Auguste, 159

Concentration, 119; of capital, 215; of powers, 232, 254

Concord, 113, 116, 120

Conditions, 60, 199; change of, 244; de facto, 242; of existence, 198; material, 265; of possibility, 53, 211, 247. *See also* Equality: of conditions; Human condition, the

Conflict, 27, 129, 131, 145–46, 148–50, 163, 196, 199, 211, 259–60, 266–67; in Florence, 119, 137; ideological, 267; latent or declared, 212; in Rome, 111–12; social, 214; welcoming of, 32, 112, 262. *See also* Class conflict

Conformity with nature, 74, 130, 192, 198, 237

Connotation and denotation, 21

Conquest, 112, 123, 131, 136, 146, 149, 153–54; industrial, 136

Consciousness, 7; deluded, 12; field of, 249; of finitude, 17; of mortality, 17; in revolt, 12; self-, 13, 16, 18

Conservatives, conservatism, 29, 36, 85–88, 115, 125, 180–83, 254–55, 265, 275, 277; and liberalism, 180–81, 197; and progressives/progressivism, 174, 181, 183

Conspiracies, 2, 6, 112, 114, 137–38, 165, 274–75

Constant, Benjamin, 89

Constitutions, 88–90, 100, 105, 111, 130, 133, 202, 259, 263, 266, 276; best, 268; and constitutionalism, constitutionalists, 90, 185; decent, 185; liberal-democratic, 193; monarchical, 63; republican, 45, 151

Constraints, 55, 79, 93, 128, 152, 278; economic, 257

Consulte and *pratiche,* 115

Contemplative life, 110, 120; and active life, 192

Context, 124, 127, 129, 173

Contingency, the contingent, 114, 161

Contracts, 148, 151

Contradictions, xli, 48, 51, 76–77, 110, 130, 143, 160, 173, 202, 243, 245, 272

Contraries, contrary properties, 48, 58

Contrasts: in Tocqueville, 35, 37, 39–40, 46, 51

Convention (France), 105

Conventional, 26, 29, 31, 74, 78, 185, 241, 254

Conversions, 161; of the mind, 193

Convictions, 32, 36, 45, 47, 76, 90, 92–94, 110–11, 122, 130, 136, 159, 172, 192, 219, 246, 261

Convivo (Dante), 117

Corruption, 67–68, 70, 73, 75, 77–79, 82–83, 111, 117, 124, 132, 137, 164, 198, 200, 257, 266

Council of State (France), 90

Coup d'état in Moscow, 273–76, 279

Courage, 129, 149; intellectual, 276

Courts: of justice, 41; special, 56

Creation, 26, 34, 169, 243, 248–49, 262; and creativity, 183, 256; and destruction, 246; literary, 29; re-, 29; and revelation, 243

Credos, creeds: of civic humanism, 118; liberal, 175, 177; popular, 98

Crisis: of culture, 191; of modernity, 201; of our time, 29, 179, 190–92, 194, 200, 264; of totalitarianism, 256; of the West, 191

"Crisis of our Time, The" (Strauss), 190, 197

Critics, 3; of Sade, 67, 70, 72

Critique, criticism, 28, 51, 57, 91, 100, 111, 153, 160, 163, 168, 181, 243, 254, 273; of American democracy, 41; of corruption, 68; ethnocentrism of, 230; of freedom, 198; of the French Revolution, 242; of historicism, 202; historiographical, 246; of the imagination, 133–34; of law, 222; literary, 246; of Marxism, 226, 245; Marx's, 246; of mass society, 272; of modernity, 187; of the modern project, 193; of morality, 74; of positivism, 195, 202; of the possibility of knowledge, 222; Puritan, 68; and self-criticism, 260; of specialization, 185; theoretical, 259; of totalitarianism, 144

Cruelty, 67–68, 72, 223–24, 256

Cuba, 252

Cultivation, 47, 186; of character, 185, 187, 194; of one's own garden, 185–86, 189

Culture, cultural, 20, 24, 28, 59, 68, 181–82, 191, 209, 211–12, 229, 232, 238, 249; and culturalism, 202–3; diversity of, 182, 195; foreign or former, 266; higher/elevated, 191; liberal, 182; mass, 183–84, 264, 272; plurality of, 143; Western, 191, 278

Cunning, 121, 190, 259, 277

Curiosity, 69, 266, 273; philosophical, 69

Custom(s), 74, 138, 161, 176, 220

Cynicism, 115, 183, 256, 265; political, 3

Cythera, 262

Czechoslovakia, 253, 256–57

Dante Alighieri, 117, 145–47, 150, 153, 165, 239; and his break with classical political philosophy, 147; and his originality, 146

Danton, Georges-Jacques, 30

Death, 3, 6–7, 9, 13, 17–18, 30, 162, 231, 239, 246, and death instinct, 157. See also Death sentences; Mortality

Death sentence(s), 22, 77; of Socrates, 173, 178

Debate, 24–25, 31, 67, 106, 145, 199, 246, 254–55, 258, 268–69; open, 212, 263; political,

89, 263; public, 95, 263–64; social and political, 262

Decazes, Duke Elie, 90

Decision-making, 51, 104, 133, 137, 194, 220, 225; and decisionism, 153–54; of the majority, 263, 266; public, 151; reasonable, 152

Declaration of the Rights of Man and of the Citizen, 20–21. See also Universal Declaration of Human Rights

Declarations: of statesmen, 192; of Wilson and Roosevelt, 197

Decline of the West, 191–92

Definition, 22, 71, 237–38, 241; positive, 169

Delegates and delegation, 80

Demagogy, 266–67, 269–70

Demands: democratic, 119; indeterminate, 242; for knowledge of the past, 255; of people, 132; for political pluralism, 265; "savage," 246; of wage earners, 271

Democracy, 21–22, 24, 28, 31, 35–43, 45–49, 54, 85–86, 88, 100–101, 104–7, 115, 119, 139, 154, 160, 169–70, 174, 182–87, 189, 193, 198, 243–46, 252–73, 278; ambiguities of, 273; American, 36, 41, 199; ancient, 186; and aristocracy, 37, 39–41, 86, 182, 184–85, 190; and the art of writing, 35–66; bourgeois, 245; and Communism, 200, 245; contemporary, 198; and democratization, 253–54, 264; essence of, 268, 272; "flatterers"/"friends and allies of" (Strauss), 185; as a form of political society, 266; as a form of society, 272; as imperfect, 267; liberal, 174, 193–94, 201–2; mass, 184; modern, 42, 104, 136, 182–83, 186, 198, 244–45; "original" (Strauss), 184, 187, 198; as a political society, 269; rebirth/renaissance of, 256, 261–62, 264; reduced to a social state, 46; refutation of, 186; representative, 187; and totalitarianism, 201, 244–45, 264, 266–67, 269; virtues and vices of, 37, 199

Democracy and Totalitarianism (Aron), 266–69

Democracy in America (Tocqueville), 35, 46, 50, 57, 176–77

Democracy in France (Guizot), 85, 88, 90, 105

Democratic Republic of Germany, 257

Division (*continued*)
command and obedience, 113; between dominators and dominated, 216–17; between the State and civil society, 245; between temporal life and eternal life, 238; of branches of knowledge, 201; of civil society, 270; class, 55, 59, 61, 143, 245; constitutive, 130; covering over of, 215; de facto, 245; denial of, 245; of Europe, 257; fear of, 241; internal, 48, 62, 214, 259; of labor, 202; of the land, 54; "natural," 203; not de facto, 130, 134, 136; originary, 215; public appearance of, 255; of sectors of activity, 245; universal, 130; of the world, 253. *See also* Division of society; Indivision

Division of society, 131, 134, 136, 215–16, 220, 225–26, 263; denial of, by totalitarianism, 245; and projection *into* society, 226

Divulging. *See* Disclosure

Doctrinaires, 90

Doctrine, xli, 187, 195; of Calvin, 168; classical, 195; of Kant, 142; of liberalism, 197; lifeless, 166; modern, 186; religious, 160; social, 166; and theories, xl, xlii, 97–98

Dogmas, 24, 98, 262, 265; and dogmatism, 24, 33, 74, 87, 188, 265; universal, 168

Dolmancé (character), 68–70, 74–75, 78–79, 81

Domination, 30, 57, 79, 82, 99, 116, 123–24, 131, 135, 138, 145, 216–17, 253, 256, 270; of man over man, 233; of man over nature, 233, 271

Doublethink, 2

Doubt, 1, 3, 25, 33–34, 246–47, 261, 273, 275

Drama, 69; epic, 240; universal, of humanity, 240

Dreams, 8–9, 12, 14, 26, 33, 98, 134

Drives, 11, 16, 28, 73, 78

Du gouvernement de France depuis la Restauration (Guizot), 89–90

Duration, 82, 272

Durkheim, Émile, 223

Dutch, the, 168

Duty, 152, 161, 194–95, 199, 260

Dynamics, 271; of democracy, 48, 246; in society, 221

East, the, 27, 30, 257, 261, 263, 266

East Berlin: insurrection of 1953, 256

Eastern bloc, 244

Eastern Europe, 200, 252, 257, 276

East Germans, 262

Economy, the, 193–94, 213, 215, 257, 260, 263–65, 268, 272; and economic institutions, 200; and economism, 227

Education, 59, 69, 72, 157, 166, 177, 182, 187, 194, 201; and corruption, 73; in culture, 182; is not indoctrination, 182; in literature, 182; moral, 194, 198, 202; norms of, 194; public, 89. *See also* Liberal education

Egalitarianism, 86, 216, 224; permissive, 194, 198; vices of, 194. *See also* Equality

Egocrat, the, 260

Egoism, 62; individual, 164

Egypt, Egyptians, 42, 146

Elections, 90, 95, 98, 255; and the electorate, 104, 106, 269

Elites, 91, 182, 187; enlightened, 254

Elizabeth I (England), 145

Elusiveness, 123–24

Emancipation. *See* Liberation

Embarrassment, 236, 238, 250

Embodiment, 3, 14, 63, 97, 104, 106, 146, 155, 232, 241–42, 263

Emperors, 145, 147; Christian, 239

Empire, 198; French, 56; Russian, 273; soviet, 257

Enchantment, 179, 190, 241–42

Encounters, 29–30, 249–50; with the absurd, 209–10; with the other, 208

End(s), 77, 99, 125, 133, 186, 194, 196, 200, 271; "contained in the beginning," 7, 18; of democracy, 170; shared, 260; ultimate, 133, 146, 196, 218

Enemies, 18, 172, 193, 231, 267, 277; identification of, 121; potential/actual or real, 80, 147, 173; unjust, 150

England, the English, 21–23, 28, 46, 68, 85, 145, 154, 219; comparison with France, 59, 61, 89, 168

Enigmas, 1, 6, 13, 83, 189, 228–29, 241, 243

Enlightenment, 69–70, 75, 123, 128, 172, 186, 199, 254

Envy, 80, 113, 119; and pride, 60

Epaminondas, 115, 137, 244
Equality, 36, 38, 44–46, 51, 54, 73, 85, 98–
  99, 131, 201, 219, 221–22, 231; before the
  law, 118, 131, 136, 256; civil, 90, 106; of
  conditions, 37, 40–41, 44, 46, 50, 58, 163,
  169, 272; de jure, 120; in Europe, 42; and
  freedom/liberty, 37, 42–43, 46, 51, 73, 75,
  81, 90, 106, 183, 193; and hierarchy, 49; imposition, 223; natural, 186; of opportunity,
  99; semblance of, 129; as social fact, 42.
  See also Egalitarianism; Inequality: and
  equality
Equal rights: to happiness, 86
Equals, 98, 223
Equity, 188
Eroticism, 82; and Eros, 157
Esclaves, Les (Quinet), 240
Esquiros, Henri François Alphonse, 159
Essence, 49, 53, 162, 217, 264, 275; and the
  anecdotal, 4; and appearance, 133; of
  History, 90; of language, 248; of paint-
  ing, 248; of philosophy, 250; of political
  things, 197; of our societies, 268; of
  totalitarianism, 17; universal, 228
Estates general, states general, 59, 165
Eternity, eternal, 87–88, 91, 165, 166, 238
Ethics, 72, 144, 184, 200; Christian, 113;
  democratic, 269, 272; new political, 119
Ethnocentrism, 144, 230
Ethnology, 208, 210–11, 213–14
Etruscans, 117, 127
Eugénie (character), 68–70, 73–74, 78, 81
Europe, European, 37, 42, 50, 89, 119, 147,
  162, 244, 257; and Eurocentrism, 144. See
  also Eastern Europe
Events, xli–xlii, 8, 10, 11, 13, 16–17, 28, 86, 111–
  12, 120, 126, 159, 209, 212–13, 229, 233, 236,
  252, 255, 268, 273–74; contemporary, 244;
  inconceivable, 228; influence of, 89; particular, 265; past and present, 254; recent,
  200; revolutionary, 52; sociobiological
  and sociosupernatural, 212
"Everything holds together," 96, 253
Evil, 29, 54, 69, 73, 129, 217, 256; lesser and
  greater, 277; not done voluntarily, 72;
  public, 164. See also Goodness: and evil
Evolution, 211, 213, 231; and evolutionism,
  213, 230; human, 211

Excellence: aspiration to, 186; human, 185
Excess, 76, 112, 138, 156, 203, 214, 241, 259.
  See also Proportion
Exclusion, 27, 31, 70
Exemptions: from public responsibilities,
  60; from taxation, 59–60
Exile, 265–66
Existence, 143; and coexistence, 21, 155;
  modes of, 264, 271; personal, 3; political,
  155; virtual, 265
Existentialism, 143
Exoteric: teaching, 172; texts, 190, writing,
  179–80
Expectations, 3, 58, 73, 165, 200, 208, 250, 268
Experience, 20, 27, 29, 49, 156, 209, 249; of
  being through creation, 243; of being
  and time, 213; of citizens, 197; as citizens, as individuals, and as men, 203; of
  Communism, 193; communitarian, 230;
  democratic, 269; of history, 25, 213; of
  humanity, 266; of leaders, 197; modern,
  213; "mute," 49; of the political, 197; prephilosophical, 203; of the present, 53;
  primordial, 225; of reading, xl; religious,
  165, 226, 228; of the social, 229; of time,
  137; of totalitarianism, 2; transcendent,
  33; of the world, 23, 26, 225, 229, 245, 249,
  270
Experimentation, 195–96
Explanation, 228–29, 231
Exploration, xxxiv, xlii, 2, 26, 35, 46, 48–49,
  53, 95, 111, 153, 159, 180, 203, 219, 233, 271
Expression, 26–27, 30, 98, 246, 248–49; literary, 25; of a people, 267; public, 172,
  175, 192; pure, 49. See also Freedom: of
  expression
Extermination: mutual, 149–50, 154

Fabius, 114
Fabric. See Tissue, fabric
Factions, 116, 127
Facts, 2, 37, 121, 155, 228–29, 259, 266–67;
  falsification of, 25; of the past, 2; of the
  past and present, 110, 132; political and
  social, 86, 236; and their separation from
  values, 196, 202; social, 42; unwanted, 126
Faith, 22, 24, 30, 165, 169–70, 173, 192, 252,
  268; in the authority of science, 197; bad,

38; individual, 21, 31, 38, 163, 168–69, 262–63; of information, 151; "is slavery," 2; of *jouissance,* 69; and law, 132, 269; limitless, 174; loss of, 217; modern, 54, 198, 201; municipal, 56; to offend, 31; of opinion, 176; political, 21, 31, 46–47, 105, 133–35, 200, 263, 265; and power, 90; of the press, 90, 95; principle of, 201, 269; public, 61; of public discussion, 174, 177; restoration of, 115; reverting to its opposite, 270; and servitude, 18, 31, 42, 44–45, 49, 62, 169, 200, 217, 240, 242, 256; of speech, 176, 266; of thought, 174, 266; and truth, 21; of writers and artists, 269. *See also* Free inquiry; Free institutions; "Negative liberties" (Berlin)

Free inquiry, 43, 176, 247; and free speech, 35, 258, 260, 264. *See also* Freedom: of speech

Free institutions, 42, 47, 51, 117, 120, 135–36, 169, 219

French, the, 21, 50, 58, 61, 86, 130, 244, 246. *See also* Empire: French

French Radicals, 85

French Revolution (February 1848), 85, 87

French Revolution (July 1830), 86–87, 89, 105

French Revolution (1789) and revolutionaries, 30, 50–56, 58, 61, 68, 70, 79, 87, 90, 92, 97–100, 104–6, 116, 159–71, 188, 219, 240, 242, 254; is/is not over, 67, 75, 87, 91–92, 98; as less innovative than thought, 50; and the Reformation, 168

Freud, Sigmund, 157

Friend, friendship, 185, 207–8; and enemies, 172, 277; "of the people," 139; real or potential, 173; reasonable, 175

Functions, 96, 238–39; political, 47; symbolic, 278

Future, the, xli, 7, 30, 53, 82, 90, 114, 165, 191–92, 214, 261–62, 274, 276; control of, 2; and humans, 212; uncertainty of, xlii, 273; writing for, 4

Gaps, 136, 138, 149, 201, 213, 216, 224, 260; between ideal and existing republics, 133; between speaking and hearing, 31; between thought and being, 124; irreducible, 268

Gas chambers: denial of the existence of, 25

Gaullism, 244

Genesis, 49, 89, 211, 239

Genocide: denial of, 25

Gentlemen, 185–87, 203

German Idealism, 238

Germans, Germany, 126, 139, 256, 257, 262, 263–64, 276

Gestures, 8–12, 209, 224; fleeting, 209; gratuitous, 10, 12; of Jewish woman, 8, 10; O'Brien's, 12; useless, 8, 10; violent, 254; of Winston Smith's mother, 8–10

Gilbert, Felix, 115

Girondists, 166

Glasnost, 265

Glass ball. *See* Paperweight

Glory, 27, 63, 104, 118, 122, 149, 252

Glucksman, André, 262

God, 23, 29, 32–33, 101, 116–17, 123, 126, 142, 144–47, 166, 169, 240, 265; absence of, 33, 162; death of, 239; and gods, 20, 81, 228, 231, 232; refutation of, 178

Goldstein (character), 3, 11, 16, 18

Goodness, 33, 111, 113, 124, 130, 134, 144, 186, 189, 192, 197, 200, 278; and the ancestral, 118; of the city, 113; divine, 146; and evil, 29, 38, 125–26, 142–43, 196; and the good life, 133; and the good regime, 111; and good sense, 154, 209; inherent, 116; natural, 77; of subsistence, 214; supreme, 146. *See also* Common good; "Good society"; Public good

"Good society," 83, 216; mourning of, 246

Gorbachev, Mikhail, 254–56, 258, 261, 264, 274–77

Government, 40, 45, 47, 69, 80–81, 100, 102–4, 106, 132, 153, 174, 187, 194, 199, 230, 232, 257, 269; absolute, 51; arbitrary, 129; of the best, 111, 133; centralizing of, 232; democratic, 40; despotic, 199; of elites, 182; French, 51, 56–58, 61, 88, 90, 93; by gentlemen, 185; and the governed, 103, 194; Hungarian, 257; of the masses, 182; mixed, 186; and mores, 69, 75; participation in, 46; people without, 230; Polish, 257; popular, 128; of a prince, 131; republican, 80; revolutionary, 52, 56; of a State,

History of Florence (Machiavelli), 130
History of the Origins of Representative
Government in Europe (Guizot), 89, 100
Hitler, Adolf, 139, 154
Hobbes, Thomas, 77, 148, 179, 196; design of,
179; teachings of, 195
Hocart, Arthur Maurice, 229–33; reflection
of, 231
Homogeneity, 136, 180–81, 200–1, 259, 267
Honor, 80, 100, 106, 118; and honors, 135
Hopes, 157, 169, 185, 190, 192, 256, 258, 277
Horizons: cultural, 229; of humanity, 22,
147; of time, xli; unsurpassable, 260; of the
world, 53, 225
Horkheimer, Max, 264
Horror, 6, 16–17, 29, 32
Hospitality, 153
Housing shortages, 278
Howe, Irving, 4
Human condition, the, 226, 267; and
humanism, 115, 117, 119–20, 126, 147, 185;
and republican humanism, 77, 117, 185. See
also Antihumanism; Civic humanism
Humanity, 7, 21–23, 26–28, 37–38, 82–83, 86,
106, 117, 142–43, 145–47, 150, 152–53, 155–
57, 165, 169–70, 188, 191, 203, 211, 213, 217,
220, 240, 242, 249, 266; affirmation of,
219; and animality, 214; its becoming/in
embryo/emergent, 36, 147, 152, 156; civilization, 150; taken connotatively and
denotatively, 21, 23, 146, 193; and humanization, 150; and human nature, 21, 73, 83,
122, 129, 132, 177, 192, 243; making itself,
246; regeneration of, 161; unity of, 38. See
also Man
Human sciences, 143, 236, 238
Humor, 72, 78, 125, 130, 139–40, 207, 216
Humors, 129, 139
Hungary, 252–53, 257; invasion of, 256
Husserl, Edmund, 49, 189, 237; and philosophy of history, 211; project of, 189
Hybridity, 28, 32, 34, 244

Ideal, 30; of democracy, 182; old, 183; of
peace, 148; and reality, 133; republican, 119
Idealism, 149; and idealization, 83, 116, 127.
See also German Idealism
Ideas, xl, 21, 26, 31, 50–51, 55, 57, 70, 73, 75–

78, 87, 92, 96, 112, 130, 179, 259, 268; clash
of, 86; of the common good, 186; eternal,
87; general, 36, 49; held in common, 43;
of humanity, 142, 145, 150, 155, 203; of the
irreversible, 273; modern, 68; of necessity,
130; new, 97, 183; noble, 73; of peace, 142,
145, 148, 150, 152; of right, 155; systems of,
xl; of virtue, 186
Identification, 116, 239, 242, 260, 272
Identity, 21–22, 26–28, 106, 110, 114, 144, 215,
231, 242, 246; loss of, 219; national, 21–22;
other's, 208; of the social, 225
Ideology, xli, 21, 25, 32, 74, 83, 99, 134, 154,
191, 195, 199, 225, 239, 241, 257, 258–59, 261,
263, 267
Idleness, 110, 128, 185, 203
Idols and idolatry, 31, 81, 101, 104, 107,
168–69, 252; self-, 86
Ignorance, 200; half-, 7, 9, 175; "is
strength," 2
Illusions, 43–44, 48–49, 86, 92–94, 104, 116,
142, 149, 182, 189–90, 197, 202, 211, 238,
242, 246, 248, 253
Images, 10, 12, 16, 55, 187, 198, 224–25, 237–
38, 254, 256, 261–63; of an all-powerful
god, 232; of the body politic, 239; destruction of, 168; of the dissolution of the
social, 88; of humanity, 82; of man, 20; of
the master, 242; of the One, 145; of reality
in itself, 270; of society, 39; of the tyrant,
117; of unity of humanity, 146
Imaginary, the, 26, 33, 219; efficacy of, 61
Imagination, xli, 33, 69, 82, 87, 101, 121, 133–
34, 156, 159, 258, 264, 270, 276; political,
254
Imitation: of the Ancients, 109–10; of the
Etruscans, 117; of the Romans, 120
"Immense being" (Tocqueville), 40, 43, 57
Immorality, 79–80
Immortality, 10, 13, 36–37, 97, 163; of Big
Brother, 17; of the Party, 13–14
Imperialism, 145, 147; Milanese, 118
Impostures, 7, 16, 144, 203, 207
Improvement, 198, 265. See also Self-
improvement
Improvisation, 120
Impurity, 28, 30, 32
Incest, 74, 77, 79

Irreducibility, irreducible, 124, 143, 195, 201, 215, 268, 270, 272
Irreligion, antireligion, 26, 52, 163–64
Irresistibility, 20, 38, 42, 193, 272
Irresponsibility, 194–95, 198, 200
Irreversibility, 17, 38, 99, 157, 203, 223, 254, 260–61, 273
Islam, 22–23, 32, 162. *See also* Muslims
Isolation, 42–44, 46–47, 51, 55, 57, 59, 63
Italy, 116–17, 145; oppression of, 112, 127

Jacobinism, 67, 165–66, 219, 242
Jewish woman (character), 8, 10
Jews, Judaism, xlii, 22, 172, 263; genocide of, 25; and Judea, 167
Jouissance, 67–68, 72–73, 75, 82; metaphysical, 78. *See also* Orgasm
Judgment, 29, 37, 44, 53, 93, 107, 144, 161, 165, 179, 189, 196–99, 237, 255, 268–69, 272, 274, 277–78; Last, 88
Julia (character), 2–3, 5–6, 8, 10–14, 16–17
July regime. *See* French Revolution (July 1830)
Junta in Moscow, 274–75
Juries, 41, 95; and jurists, 109; popular, 41
Justice, the just, 39, 41, 98, 103–4, 107, 122, 167, 192–93, 232, 268, 279; and the unjust, 29, 107, 142–43, 196, 267
Jyvukugi, 210

Kant, Immanuel, 142, 150–53, 156; originality of, 151
Kantorowicz, Ernst, 146, 239–40
Kellogg-Briand Pact, 154
KGB, 254, 275
Khomeini (Imam), 22–24
Khrushchev, Nikita, 244, 253, 256
Kings, kingdoms, 39, 61, 128, 167, 231–32, 239; French, 51, 56, 61–63, 104, 109, 146, 168; and leveling process, 42; sacred, 229; symbolic, 233. *See also* Monarchy
King's Two Bodies, The (Kantorowicz), 239
Knowledge, 6, 17, 74, 110–11, 115, 118, 125, 134, 138, 142–43, 157, 193, 197, 201–2, 213–14, 218, 221–27, 237, 242, 245–46, 248, 260, 270; academic, 237; in actuality, 242; ancestral, 225; of the classics, 198; of common good, 133; division into branches

of, 201–2; divulging of, 173; drive for, 73; established, 241; foundations of, 346, 247; of history, 110, 115; is not a possession, 196; of the law, 187; mode of, xlix–xl, 26, 29; modern, 202; of nature, 67, 196; of necessity, 122, 126–27; and not knowing, 2, objective, 217, 233; of the past, 54, 110, 255; of the Revolution, 53; ruled by ends, 194; scientific, 118; self-, 17; self-regulating, 202; separate and despotic, 222; separation of, 224, 241; shared, 17; of society's ultimate ends, 218; sociological, 216; theoretical, 120, 194; of things political, 196; of the true and the just, 192; ultimate, 268. *See also* Desire: for knowledge
Kojève, Alexandre, 180
Kouznetsov, Victor, 258
Krisis des europaischen Menschentums und die Philosophie, Die (Husserl), 189

La Boétie, Étienne de, 101, 217, 219, 228, 241–44, 270; and his design, 216; interpretation of, 219; thinking of, 218–19; work of, 242
Labor, 86, 200; creative, 248, 262; of expression, 248; individual, 118; of interpretation, 244
Land, 86, 101; division of, 54; foreign, 153; reform, 92; sacred, 147
Landowners, 59, 61, 100, 187; small/peasant, 51, 54
"Land without Evil," 228
Language, 25–27, 29–32, 87, 161, 248, 265; conventional, 31; and experience, 49; of freedom, 274; and ideas, xl; of law, 41, 273; legitimate, 226; Machiavellian, 80; pure, 248; Rushdie's, 23; shrinking of, 1–2; of Strauss, 180; of virtue, 75
"Last man," (Nietzsche), 183–84, 198
Law, 33, 41–42, 63, 77, 86, 98, 101–5, 115, 128–29, 131–32, 135–36, 152, 155, 162, 176, 187, 194, 201, 218–24, 226–27, 239, 245–46, 260, 268–70, 274, 276, 278; and the body, 221–24; of the community, 214; constitutional, 89; effective, 91; enunciation of, 199; idea of, 57, 112, 222, 256, 268; initial exteriority of, 226; internalization of, 223; meaning of, 219, 256; nature of, 101; nonseparate,

Law (*continued*)
222–24; origin of, 132; primitive, 223–24, 226; of primitive society, 221–22; reign of, 132; repository of, 129; respect for, 186; schools, 188; sense of, 200, 277; separate, 224. *See also* Equality: before the law; International law

Laws, 23, 57, 86, 112, 128, 138, 153, 161, 194, 221, 239; best, 128; defective, 51; "of genre," 202; good, 128; of government, 100; higher, 150; of the market, 157; necessary, 51; particular, 162; positive, 102, 131, 260, 268, 271; respect for, 113; rule by, 130

Laws of nature. *See* Natural law

Lawyers, legal profession, 41, 100, 187–88

Leaders, leadership, 51, 63, 95, 116, 138, 182, 187, 197, 257, 277, 279; Kremlin, 257; of opinion, 163; political, 90, 94, 277; putsch, 276; religious, 33; Western, 257, 273

League of Nations, 154, 198; universal, 193

Learned: interpretations, 71, 74; society, 74; professions, 187

Le Brun, Annie, 70, 72

Legislation, 104, 151, 153; reform of, 188; uniform, 57; wise, 111

Legislators, 134, 188; American, 47; classical, 111; Greek, 79–80

Legislatures, 41, 94, 104, 188. *See also* "Incomparable chamber" (*chambre introuvable*)

Legitimacy, 2, 77, 98, 100–5, 120, 176, 187, 203, 212, 226, 243, 245, 258, 268; absolute, 102, 260, 270; of command, 210; full, 91; and the illegitimate, 102, 269; relative, 40

Lély, Gilbert, 68, 70

Lenin, V. I., 263

Le Pen, Jean-Marie, 261

Leroux, Pierre, 159

Lessing, Gotthold Ephraim, 140

Lessons, 193; of 1830, 87; of the law, 221; of Sade, 72; of Tocqueville, 51

Leveling, 42, 45, 201, 273

Leys, Simon, 4

Liberal education, 183–88, 194; modern, 185

Liberalism, xl, 23–25, 88, 94, 106–7, 174–75, 177–78, 180–81, 197–201, 262, 265; alleged project of, 199; classical, 180; defensive, 88; degeneration of, 178; "dormancy"

of, 175, 183; French, 87–88, 90, 104; heyday of, 175; modern, 178, 195; nature of, 197; polemical, 85; present-day, 181; triumphant, 88

Liberalism Ancient and Modern, 174, 180

Liberation, 6, 18, 31, 33, 43, 72, 75, 238, 240–41, 262, 270; complete, 136; from the land, 51; of a people, 137, of the people, 177

Liber Augustalis, 239

Liberties. *See* Freedom

Libre (Paris review), 207

Licence, 24, 75, 77, 112, 128, 133

Lies, 21, 33, 120, 197, 200, 262, 265–66

Life, 58, 95, 99, 240, 247; after death, 162; among others, 200; civil, 132; in the city, 178; of the community, 222–23, 225; and death, 246; flavors of, 266; good, 133; of individuals/of the individual, 225, 273; more, in a Republic, 131, 135–36. *See also* Active life; Contemplative life; Natural: life; Political life; Private life; Public life; Society, social life; Ways of life

Limits, xli, 17, 21, 25, 58, 62, 99, 132, 143–44, 148–50, 153–54, 156, 166, 174, 190, 213, 217, 227–28, 240–41, 247, 261, 266, 268, 270

Listening. *See* Hearing

Literature, 2, 4, 25–30, 32, 71, 173, 182, 191, 202, 246–48, 250; ethnological, 210; of libertinism, 72; and philosophy, xl; and political philosophy, xlix

Livy, 109–12, 115, 127

Local, the, 39, 47, 58, 259

Logic, 37, 77, 94, 211, 216–17; of being, 49; democratic, 45; of "combined development," 253; of identification, 260; of ritual/belief, 231

Logica equina, 174

Logos, 123

Looks, 10–12, 17–18, 54, 224, 270

Louis XII, 130–31

Louis XIV, 36

Louis XVIII, 90

Love, 3, 12, 14, 16–18, 78, 125; of corruption, 257; gratuitous, 10; of the master, 219; of the prince, 129, 219; of servitude, 217; of truth, 177; of the tyrant, 219; of wisdom, 237

Loyalty, 11; to constitutionalism, 185

Luciani, Maurice, 207–8
Luther, Martin, 168

Macedonians, 146
Machiavelli, Niccolò, xli, 38, 68, 77, 80, 109–
41, 173, 178–79, 196, 200, 244, 256; alleged
contradictions of, 110; and the Ancients,
113; argument of, 110, 120, 124; audacity of,
134; and his break with Christian thought,
114, 178, 185; and his break with classical
philosophy, 114, 121, 185; and his break
with classical tradition, 123, 178; and his
break with humanism, 120; convictions
of, 111, 130; claim to originality of, 109;
design of, 113, 131, 179; as diabolic, 139,
190; on hope, 185, 190; intention of, 109,
121–23, 132; motivations of, 123; in his own
name, 112, 129; plan of, 124; project of,
178; subversiveness of, 178, 185; teaching
of, 195; work of, 77, 121, 215; writing of,
110; and his art of writing, 124
MacLeish, Archibald, 178
Madison, James, 187
Maistre, Joseph de, 159
Major et minor se ipse, 239–40. *See also*
Beneath and above oneself
Majority, 105–6, 176, 193, 263, 266, 272, 274;
of free adult males, 186; omnipotence of,
41; power of, 41; tyranny of, 41, 49
Man, 20–23, 30, 74, 81, 123–24, 126, 143, 145–
47, 198, 212, 228, 233; being of, 243; in the
city, 192; condition of, 192, 241; definition
of, 146; democratic, 184; denaturing of,
242; ends of, 125, 196; fall of, 240; fate of,
120; highest possibilities of, 191; as "measure of all things," 123; modern, 34, 273;
modern Western, 238; in movement, 27,
30; natural, 148; natural goodness of, 77;
nature of, 237; new, 261–62; perfectibility
of, 38; potential of, 123; as social being,
101; and society, 36; tornness of, 241;
Western, 213; and the world, 216. *See also*
Humanity; Rights of Man
Management, 253; bureaucratic, 259; of the
economy, 263, 265; rational, 265
Mandelstam, Nadezha, 258
Many, the, 100, 112, 119, 122, 136, 177, 200–201
Marchais, George, 261

Market economy, 157, 263, 270, 272
Martines, Lauro, 119
Marxism, 215, 226–27, 240, 244–45, 260–
61, 263–64; and liberalism, Marxism-
Leninism, 265, 181; and philosophy of
history, 143, 203, 210
"Marxistes et leur anthropologie, Les"
(Clastres), 207
Marx, Karl, 40, 85, 156, 185, 218, 226–27,
244–46, 270
Mass culture, 183–84, 264, 272
Masses, the, 28, 34, 44, 51, 60, 95, 104, 182,
184, 193, 257, 259–60, 274; "dealing with"
(Guizot), 87, 95. *See also* Mass culture
Masters, 44, 52, 80, 85, 132, 138, 176, 218–19,
232–33, 242; fallen, 101; good, 219; new,
258, 264; and slaves, 203; and workmen, 86
Mastery, 37, 116, 125, 249–50, 257; autho-
rial, 82; of nature, 192; over what is, 193;
over the institution, 227; of speech, xli; of
time, 2
Matter, 94, 96, 155, 242, 277; good and
corrupt, 124
Meaning, 26, 185, 203, 219, 238; genesis of,
49; legal, 266; religious and ethical, 184
Means, 26, 125; of destruction, 149; and
ends, 200; of government, 93–95, 139; of
production, 271
Medici, Cosimo de' (Cardinal), 114, 117
Medici, Lorenzo de' (the Magnificent), 115,
118, 125
Medicis, 115; fall of, 119
Mediocrity, 183, 237
Mélange, 28
Melos, 147
Members, 96, 145, 219, 239, 270; and
dismembering, 255
Memory, 1, 8, 11, 13, 17–18, 27, 239, 250,
255, 265; and childhood, 5, 8, 12; lost, 10;
return of, 252
Mente heroica. See Heroes: and heroism of
the mind
Merchants, 100, 118, 187
Merleau-Ponty, Maurice, xl, 48, 97, 229,
243–44, 248–49
Messiah: People-, 169; social, 168
Metamorphosis, 27–28, 250
Metaphor, 27, 96; religious, 167

Metaphysics, 29, 78, 237
Metternich, 85
Michelet, Jules, xl, 159, 164–68, 240–41, 244, 246; realism of, 167; romanticism of, 159
Middle Ages, 27, 162, 172, 239
Middle classes, 59, 86, 91, 119
Might, 31, 41, 45, 128, 131, 150, 154, 221, 253, 264, 275
Migration, 27–28
Milieux, settings, 272; differentiated, 48
Militants, 3, 12, 263, 275
Military-industrial complex, 277
Military institutions, 127, 136, 253, 260
Mill, John Stuart, 188
Milton, John, 174
Minds, 3, 12, 26, 167, 176, 191, 193; agitation of, 258; creative, 183; diabolic, 190; greatest, 18–89; and matter, 94; mediocre, 237
Ministry: of Love, 6–7, 14, 15, 18; of Peace, 18; of Plenty, 18; of Truth, 3, 18
Minorities, 157, 186, 275; cultivated, 186–87
Misery. See Poverty
Misfortune, 217–18, 228
Mixed: government, 186; regime, 134, 186
Mobilization, 25, 68, 137, 200, 219, 260–61, 264, 274
Models, 1, 29, 58, 75, 89, 102, 109, 111, 113, 116, 118, 134–37, 187, 241, 253, 256, 260–61
Moderation, 90, 100, 115, 120, 132, 185, 202, 257; and immoderation, 238
Modernity, xlii, 25, 28–29, 33–35, 37–39, 42–43, 53–54, 68, 77, 88–89, 102, 104, 110, 113, 119, 124, 136, 142, 168, 175, 178–79, 181–82, 186–88, 190–96, 198, 200–203, 213, 215–16, 218–19, 239, 241, 243–45, 247, 253, 264, 267, 273; and modernization, 265. See also "Modern project" (Strauss)
"Modern project" (Strauss), 125, 190, 192–93
Mohammed, 27
Molière, 71
Monarchy, 46, 58, 61, 63, 96, 100–101, 104–106, 131–32, 138, 145, 167, 217, 260; of the Ancien Régime, 219; imperial, 147; July (1830), 86, 89; people as, 106; rise of, 89; struggle against, 219; ultra-, 45; universal, 145–46, 239, 153; world, 117

Mongrelization, 28–29, 32, 34
Monopolization: by the Party, 257, 266; of power, 98, 120, 132
Montaigne, 80, 100, 208
Montesquieu, 199–200
Moralism, 83, 150
Morality, 29, 43, 49, 73–74, 76, 78–80, 111, 113, 121–24, 133, 152, 154, 194, 198, 202, 268, 272, 278; and spirituality, 29, 32, 38
Mores, 24, 57, 59, 69, 75–76, 110, 157, 164, 200, 264–65, 268, 271, 278; corruption of, 68; softening of, 51, 55
Mortality, 17, 238. See also Death
Moscow, Muscovites, 253, 258, 273–74, 279
Motives, motivations, 5, 21, 75, 94, 98, 101, 137–38, 262, 266; of Gorbachev, 276; of Guizot, 91, 104; of Machiavelli, 123; and motivelessness, 229, 247, 264, of the prince, 122; of Strauss, 201; theoretical, 104; of Tocqueville, 50; ultimate, 7; for war, 143, 148
Movement, xli, 27, 30, 45, 49, 52, 57, 86, 137, 164, 189, 199, 224–25, 240, 249, 252, 261, 277; of action, 268; of bodies, 73, 82; of discourse, 78; heroic, 241; of History, 88; intellectual, 35; irresistible, 193; of knowing, 225; of one's regard, 54; of organs, 73; of things, 126; of thought, xlix, 35, 40, 58, 73, 139, 268; together, 199; Western, 193; of writing, xl. See also Social mobility
Munich, capitulation at, 154
Murder, 24, 74, 149. See also Assassination
Muslims, 22, 24, 29, 32–33. See also Islam
Mussolini, Benito, 154
Mystery: of faith in reason, 189; of the origin, 228
Mysticism, 32–33, 96, 106, 146, 167, 238, 239; and mystifications, 267
Myths, 117, 191, 198, 209, 225, 253, 264, 266–67

Naming, names, 27, 101, 223–24, 247, 250; absence of, 270; of One, 241–42, 270; proper, 130
Napoleon Bonaparte, 91; and Bonapartism, 219, One Hundred Days of, 89
Narratives, 27, 117; of old travelers and missionaries, 208

Nations, 20–22, 37, 68, 106, 132, 144, 197–98, 201, 272; chosen, 167; democratic, 45, 193; free, 199

Nation-States, 149

Natural: life, 223; order, 87, 102; right, xl, 186, 195; sciences, 124, 191–93, 196, 230

Natural law, 73, 75, 77

Natural Right and History (Strauss), 188, 197

Nature, xlix, 41–43, 45, 50, 58, 67, 77, 81, 82, 124, 128, 130, 142, 147–52, 154, 181, 186, 197, 203, 211, 223–24, 226, 230, 233, 238, 243, 262; according to, 38, 99, 131, 163, 177, 181, 192; "against," 242; and art, 48; of Christ, 239; of the city, 129–30, 147, 198; and the contingent, 161; and convention, 74; and corruption, 83; domination of, 123–24, 271; idealization of, 83; of man, 147, 198; masters and owners of, 192; nearly, 39; and its resurgence within society, 220; and the supernatural, 223, 226. *See also* Conformity with nature; Humanity: and human nature; Natural: order; State of nature

Nazism, 154, 263–64, 271

Necessity, 99, 116, 122, 126, 128, 130, 132, 230, 270; enlightened, 123, 128, natural, 130, 150

Needs, 123, 198, 272; basic, 258, 275; increase of, 198; new, 56; of the many, 122; satisfaction of, 82

"Negative liberties" (Berlin), 266

Neutrality, xl, 24, 130, 135, 212, 262, 269

New France, 55, 91, 93

"New historical school," 88

Newness, new things, xl, 17, 24, 28–29, 31, 34, 36, 39–41, 45, 48–51, 53–56, 58–59, 63, 69, 75, 79, 83, 86–93, 97–101, 104, 106–107, 109, 117–19, 123, 125–27, 129, 129, 132–34, 136, 138, 142–43, 147, 150, 155–70, 173, 177, 183–84, 187, 190, 192, 195–96, 202–203, 211, 213, 215, 218–19, 226–27, 229, 232, 236, 238–40, 243, 247, 252, 254–58, 260–62, 264, 269–71, 274, 276, 278. *See also* "New society" (Tocqueville); New World

"New society" (Tocqueville), 50, 53–55, 58, 61

Newspapers. *See* Press, the

Newspeak, 1–2

New World, 208, 219, 228. *See also* World, the: new

Nichomachean Ethics (Aristotle), 147

Nietzsche, Friedrich, 139, 178, 183–85, 190, 196, 198, 203; as diabolic, 190; and Rushdie, 34; on values, 143; work of, 143

Nihilism, 30

Nineteen Eighty-Four, xlix, 1–19; design of, 2

Nobility, 12, 33, 50–62, 83, 90, 112, 116, 135, 165, 186, 260; in England and France, 59; impoverishment of, in Rome, 128

Nomenklatura, 274

Nomos, 189–90

Noninterference, 23, 201

Nonseparation, 7, 16, 40, 71, 112, 124, 222–25, 229, 261

Norms, 73, 79, 111, 122, 132, 194, 201; shared, 263; supreme, 124

Novels, novelists, xlix, 2, 4, 25–27, 32–33, 69, 247–48

Number, 98, 104–6; greater, 186

Obedience, 81, 94, 113, 120, 131, 132, 137, 219–20; blind, 7; unconditional, 267

Objectification, 111; scientific, 227

Objectivity, xl, 217, 233; and objectivist standpoint, 245

Objects, 242, 250; pseudovisible, 242. *See also* Subject, the: and object

O'Brien (character), 3, 6–7, 11–14, 16–18

Observation, observers, 121, 209, 273–74; neutral, 135; pure, 138

Offices, 59, 220; public, 62, 118, 120; responsibility for, 94; sale of, 60–62; sharing of, 118, 120

Old Regime and the Revolution (Tocqueville), 46, 50, 160

Oligarchy, 100, 115–16, 119, 136, 267, 269

Omnipotence, 3, 41, 62, 72, 134, 192, 232, 242, 253, 270–71

Omnipresence, 226

One, the, 145, 150, 219, 226, 228, 241–42, 270

Ontology, 16; indirect, 249

Opacity, 273

Opening: of the body, 226; to what is "other," 225

Opinion, 24, 43–44, 49, 74, 104, 112, 114–15, 122, 127, 129–30, 144, 160, 163, 173–74, 176,

Perfectibility, 38, 164
Permanence, 37, 179
Perpetual peace, 142, 145, 148, 150–51, 153
Perpetual peace (Kant), 150, 152
Persecution, xlii, 22, 24, 173–78, 265–66;
elimination of, 177
Persecution and the Art of Writing (Strauss), 172
Personification, 36, 101, 231
Perspective: changes of, 40, 48, 56–57, 61, 63
Perversion, 72, 75, 83, 202, 256, 266
Phantasms, 15, 101, 145, 241–43, 245, 258, 271
Phenomena, 49, 272; secondary, 100; and phenomenology, 49, 155, 261
Philosophes, 51, 71
Philosophers, xli, 34, 134, 139, 147, 149, 173, 188–89, 197–98, 230, 237–40, 248, 250; ancient, 134, 172; becoming, 236, 249; captain-, 244; classical, 121; combatant-, 244; German, 139; heterodox, 177–78; -historians, 49, 159; and historians, 113, 118, 137; as interpreters, 179; modern, 178, 200, 241; new, 192; and their practice, 248; as professors, 238; as substitutes for priest-kings, 239; and theologians, 121; and the vulgar, 185; as writers, 249; as writer-thinkers, xl. *See also* Philosophy; Political philosophy
"Philosophie politique" (Guizot), 100–101
Philosophy, 25, 69, 71, 75–80, 82, 94, 124, 133, 142–43, 172, 174, 177–79, 186, 188, 191–92, 201–203, 236–41, 243–50, 266, 268; Aristotelian, 145; of art, 247; artificial-ist, 272; in the boudoir, 70, 74, 78; break with (classical), 192, 195; of the city, 70; classical, 83, 114, 123, 195–96, 202; death of, 239; definition of, 237, 241, 243, 246–47; destruction of, 238–40; disappearance of, 237, 247; eighteenth-century, 160, 166; end of, 237–38; "essence" of, 250; exercise of, 201; in France, 236–37; fulfillment in life and in history of, 240; Greek, 145; of history, 143, 203, 210–11; intention of, xl; and literature, 248, 250; modern, 83; nineteenth-century, 142; and nonphiloso-phy, 173, 240, 247; project of, 123; and science, 192, 247; of the sciences, 247; and teaching, 250; and theology, 247; traves-

tying of, 77; as ultimate system, 237–38; and writing, 250. *See also* Philosophers; Political philosophy
Philosophy of Right (Hegel), 153
Physical, the, 44, 73, 125
Place, 223–24; and time, 21
Plato, 68, 77, 83, 101, 134, 173–74, 179, 188, 195; strategy of, 178
Platonism, xl
Pleasure, 16, 28, 70, 72–73, 77, 81–82, 242
Plebs: and Senate, 111–12, 119, 128, 135; and nobles, 112
Plot, 2, 4, 10
Pluralism, 32, 266; political, 265
Plurality, 143, 212, 241
Plutarch, 77, 127
Poetry, poets, 35, 173, 240, 247–48
Poland, 252–53, 256
Polemics, 85, 89, 145, 179
Police, 85, 252; secret, 4; thought, 7
Policy, 92, 94, 112, 120, 123, 136; demo-cratic, 257; of Gorbachev, 254–55, 258, 261, 276–77
Political, the, xlix, xlii, 81, 138, 166, 193, 197, 214–16, 222, 226, 268; autonomy of, 95; and destruction of its meaning, 203; and its dissociation from the nonpolitical, 268–70; hermeneutics of, 54; modern conception of, 88; nature of, 226; and personal existence, 3; and the religious, 32, 46, 159, 163, 174, 223, 226, 233; and the social, 40, 48, 50, 86–87, 93–94, 104–5; truth of, 200
Political action, 7, 40, 93, 109, 111, 139; readability of, 112
Political community, 20, 147, 172
Political institutions, 37, 40, 50, 52, 160, 162, 200, 271; of the Indians, 210; and the social state, 37, 46
Political life, xlix, 83, 197
Political philosophy, xlix–xli, 68, 70, 75, 89, 172, 179–80, 192, 196, 198, 203, 217, 247; abandonment of, 177, 194; ancient, 133, 178; of Aristotle, 191; classical, 122, 134, 147, 179, 184, 188, 192, 194–95; dis-integration of, 190–91; founders of, 134; in Greece, 190; history of, xl; modern, 121, 124, 178, 192, 196; object of, 172; pre-

86, 111; classical, 192; of classical philosophy, 130, 179; of correct judgment, 237; democratic, 86, 244; of equality, 45, 132; ethical, 72; and facts, 259; false, 72, 78; of fear, honor, moderation, and virtue, 80, 100; of freedom, 151, 186, 201; generative, 49, 94, 104, 226; of a government, 199; of interpretation, 173; irreconcilable, 263; of law, 218; liberal, 25; of liberal democracy, 202; of liberalism, 187; and methods, 276–77; modern, 201; of morality, 73, 124, 133; of movement, 86; of noninterference, 201; of order, 86; of "original democracy," 187; of political society, 136; of politics, 193; of primitive society, 224; of religion, 133; republican, 119, 132; statements of, 37; supposedly natural, 262; universalist, 193–94; untouchable, 24; of virtue, 186

Private life, 2, 25, 27, 59, 62–63, 77, 98, 119, 170, 194, 198, 201, 257, 260

Privileges, 50, 54, 59–60, 62–63, 247

Production: forces of, 212; means of, 271; modes of, 245, 271; of an œuvre, 248; relations of, 227; requirements of, 259; and social reproduction, 20; of subsistence goods, 214; waste of, 253

Progress, 38, 56, 58, 137, 193, 212, 214, 229–30, 237, 272; infinite, 191; material, 68; and regressions, 37, 229

Progressiveness, progressives, 174, 181, 183, 212

Proletarians, 5–6, 11, 16

Proletarian woman (character), 13

Proofs, 3, 37, 50, 55, 58, 59, 258, 274; of legitimacy, 103; philosophical, 78

Propaganda, 2, 161, 259, 263

Property, 97, 166, 176; qualifications, 194. *See also* Ownership

Prophets, 32–33, 228; new, 183; unarmed, 127

Proportion, 112, 190, 214. *See also* Excess

Proselytism, 161

Prose of the World, The (Merleau-Ponty), 248

Prosperity, 193, 233

Prostitution, 33, 79

Protestant Ethic and the Spirit of Capitalism, The (Weber), 183

Protestantism, Protestants, 168, 178

Providence, 38, 58, 99, 116–17, 123, 126, 146, 151, 159

Provocation, 29–31, 33

Proximity, 27, 152–53, 156, 212

Prudence, 33, 115, 125, 132, 156, 168, 178, 188, 192, 217, 241; and imprudence, 68, 215, 276

Psyche, 203

Psychiatric hospitals in the Soviet Union, 278

Psychoanalysis, 33, 239

Psychology, xlii, 3, 203, 238

Public, the, xli, 25, 44, 60–62, 95, 98, 107, 114, 118, 120, 133, 151, 153, 164, 166, 172, 174–77, 179–80, 182–83, 192, 194, 209, 244, 254–55, 263–66, 268, 270, 274, 278; humanist, 185; indeterminate, 23; and the private, 25, 194, 201; and the sacred, 25

Public affairs, 51, 57, 92, 100, 109, 119, 133, 135, 182, 186, 268

Public good, 51, 118, 187

Public life, 57, 244, 268

Public opinion, 51, 78, 151, 256, 270; international, 254. *See also* Opinion

Public space, 24, 199, 260; enlargement of, 273; institution of, 157

Publius, 187

Pufendorf, Samuel von, 148

Puritanism, 46, 183; and its critique of corruption, 68

Purity, xl, 31, 248; and impurity, 28, 30, 32; of a race, 144

Putsch in Moscow. *See* Coup d'état in Moscow

Quarrels: between ancients and moderns, 181, 191, 203; between nobles and plebs, 112; between philosophy and nonphilosophy, 240; between theology and atheism, 239

Question(s), 6, 30, 33–34, 40, 54, 71, 104, 179, 196, 212–13, 224, 229, 233, 236–38, 244–50, 256, 262; and answers, 211, 228, 236, 240, 256, 261, 269; of authority, 43; fundamental, 264; hearing of, 159; innocent, 238; of knowledge, 248–49; of legitimacy, 268; little, 70; of a new religion, 170; of the past, 6; permanent, 113; philosophical, 144, 216; of the political, 214; in quest

Question(s) (*continued*)
of itself, 249; social, 265; of social division, 225; of society, 35; of the State, 219; ultimate, xlii, 191, 247; of writing, 248
Quinet, Edgar, 139, 159, 163–65, 167–70, 240–44; intention of, 168, 240; thought of, 242; work of, 240

Race, 144; racism, 25
Racine, 71
Rape, 11, 16, 70, 74, 77, 79
Ratio, 124
Rationalism, 33, 115; neo-, 34
Rationality, 149, 182, 189, 202, 246, 265, 274; universal, 193
Rationalization, 150; of the economy, 264
Rats, 15, 17–18
Reaction, reactionary, 92, 119, 265, 276; Catholic, 168; against democracy, 239; Thermidorean, 67
Readers, readership, xl–xlii, 5, 10, 14–15, 25, 27, 37, 40, 50–51, 54–55, 61, 63, 70–73, 75, 78, 82–83, 89, 110–11, 114, 124, 135, 138–39, 173–75, 182, 191–92, 201, 209, 221, 246, 250
Reading, xl, 35, 52, 71, 74, 110, 112, 124, 160, 173, 178, 183, 246; attentive, 180, 185, 208, 219, 240; between the lines, 173, 175–79; and interpretation, 71; re-, 71; proper, 71
Real estate and personal estate, 86
Realism, 22, 99, 121, 148–49, 154, 167, 227, 254, 276
Reality, 13, 22, 26, 33, 55, 96, 133, 157, 185, 216, 225, 227, 240, 254–55, 259–60, 269–70, 273, 277–78; of the body, 13; and the chimerical, 57; and the image, 55; and the imaginary, 26, 33, 160; of the past, 13; and the rational, 246; return to, 20; of the senses, 193; "sociohistorical," 245; of soviet society, 254; *sui generis,* 40; and the symbolic, 102, 227
Reason, 29, 76, 98, 102–105, 107, 123, 142, 144, 151, 175, 186, 188–90, 199, 237, 243, 247, 268; as choosing (Milton), 174; cult, 165; limits of, 166, 190; Quinet's, 242; parties of, 166; theoretical and practical, 142, 152; unity of, 181; and unreason, 273
Rebellion, 114, 278
Rebuilding Russia (Solzhenitsyn), 278

Recipes, 196, 203, 277
Recognition, 14, 21, 23, 25, 30–31, 39–40, 46, 52, 58, 60, 62, 71, 73, 75, 86, 88, 89, 93, 97–98, 101, 103, 105–106, 113, 128, 130–31, 133, 136, 144–48, 150, 152–53, 155, 197, 218, 220, 227, 230–31, 248, 250, 254–55, 259, 268
Referents: ultimate, 268–69
Reflections, xl, 22, 28, 32, 35, 39, 46, 88, 92, 105, 117, 125, 136, 144, 236, 238–39, 246, 248, 250, 254, 264, 268, 276; on action, 137; on the common good, 185; on history, 213; on humanity, 150; labor of, 16; on opinions, 197; philosophical, 211; political, 247; on the political, 32, 89, 138, 215; on principles, 144
Reformers, 51, 57, 254–55, 257, 276
Reforms, 120, 132, 188, 256, 258, 261, 264; electoral, 90; land, 92; opposition to, 274–75; political, 93, 265; of political and economic institutions, 200; and reformation, 168
Refusal, xlix, 154, 229, 240, 244, 257, 265, 268, 271; of coercive power, 210; of detached power, 214; of division, 221; of the One, 229; to be oppressed, 112; of separation, 224–5
Regeneration, 161, 164
Relativity, 21, 24, 144, 273
Relativism, 23, 25, 30, 143–44, 181, 189, 195, 202–3, 273
Religion, xlii, 22–24, 26, 28–33, 36, 49, 51, 67, 69, 74–76, 79, 86, 117, 120, 123, 133, 159–64, 176, 184, 197, 224–32, 238, 247, 265; historical, 227; of humanity, 169; new, 134, 159, 162, 164–70; separate, 240
Religious, the, 159, 163, 166, 223, 226, 226, 233, 268
Religious Revolution of the Nineteenth Century, The (Quinet), 168
Renaissance, 218–19, 239, 261–62
Repositories, 44; of authority, 44; of the law, 129; of law and knowledge, 268
Representation, 96, 102, 105, 145, 147, 263; proportional, 188. *See also* Representative government; Representatives; Representative system
Representations, 57, 96, 118, 212, 215, 226, 238–39, 270; of the body, 239; common,

Roosevelt, Franklin Delano, 197
Roots, 246, 272
Rosanvallon, Pierre, 89, 99
Rousseau, Jean-Jacques, xli, 77, 148–50, 152, 154, 157, 200
Royal Council (France), 56
Royalty. *See* Kings, kingdoms
Rubenstein, Nicolai, 116
Rucellai, Bernardo, 115
Rucellai, Cosimo, 114
Rulers, 198, 256, 265, 267
Rules, 104, 148, 210–11, 266; of conduct, 121; of the game, 154, 186; of reading, 124; rigid, 57, 62
Rushdie, Salman, 20–34; design of, 25–27; and satanic verses, 33. See also *Satanic Verses*
Russia, Russians, 139, 257, 264–65, 273, 277–79. *See also* Soviet Union

Sacred, the, 24–25, 147, 163, 169, 229
Sade, Marquis de, 67–84; contradictions of, 76–77; critics of, 67, 70, 72; design of, 68, 78; lightness of, 67–68; philosophical saraband of, 79, 82; playfulness of, 76; political and revolutionary writings of, 67; reason of, 76; seriousness of, 67, 72, 77; thought of, 68; work of, 67
"Sages of our time" (Machiavelli), 115, 125
Saint-Ange, Mme de (character), 68–70, 72–75, 78; project of, 72
Saint-Just, Louis-Antoine-Léon, 166; fall of, 67; "intransigence" of, 72
Saint-Pierre, Abbé de (Charles Irénée Castel), 148–49
Saint-Simon, 156, 159
Sakharov, Andrei, 254
Salutati, Coluccio, 119
Satanic Verses, 22–23, 25–28
Satire, 31, 67
Savage, 192, 223, 226; knowledge, 213–14; societies, 210, 213, 219, 225
Scala, Martino della, 118
Science, xl, 118, 177, 185, 187, 191–93, 195, 197, 227, 238, 247, 268, 270; administrative, 89; Marxist, 263; modern, 124, 178, 192–93; modern historical, 89; new, 123, 202;

"rigorous" (Husserl), 189; and the pre-scientific, 197; sure, 122; of the universal, 237. *See also* Human sciences; Natural sciences; Political science, political scientists; Social sciences
Scripture. *See* Bible, the
Search, 7, 25–26, 69, 101, 103–104, 138, 196–97, 212, 229, 241, 249; for democracy, 265; for legitimacy, 103–104; for peace, 147, for political truth, 11; for truth, 17, 185, 189, 237, 241; for virtue, 118
Secrecy, secrets, 3, 4, 6–7, 15, 74–75, 126, 194, 222, 250
Secularism, 30, 32, 145
Security, 51, 120, 122, 132–33, 149, 258
Seduction, 10, 12, 72, 254
Seeing, 224; and hearing, 208
Seigneury, 40, 59
Self, 13–14, 82, 266
Self-improvement, 193, 198
Self-interest, 166; enlightened, 186; selfishness, 60; self-preservation, 135, 157, 193, 198, 200, 252
Sensitivity: to self, 48; to the other, 266; to things, others, time, and mores, 265
Sentiments, 50, 53; legitimate, 98; national, 201; religious, 169
Separate: power, 220–22, 225; religion, 240
Separation, xlix, 4, 37, 46, 48, 58–60, 62, 74, 93, 96, 99, 106, 177, 185–86, 195, 199, 203, 220–22, 224–25, 227, 241–42. *See also* Nonseparation
Servitude, 18, 31, 42, 44–45, 49, 57, 62–63, 68, 164, 167, 169, 200, 216–18, 240–42, 256; as "against nature," 242
Setting into form, 211, 215
Settings. *See* Milieux, settings
Sexuality, 2, 12, 16, 18, 73
Signs, 13, 29, 33–34, 36, 38, 40, 46, 52, 56, 60–61, 64, 70, 75, 80, 87, 94, 112, 118, 122, 130–31, 134, 142, 144, 146, 152, 159, 165, 173, 176, 180, 185, 192, 209, 211–13, 215, 219, 224, 226, 228–30, 242–43, 245, 254–55, 258–59, 266, 269, 272–73, 278
Silence, 13, 89, 93, 111, 157, 173, 175, 177, 180–81, 188, 191, 209, 239, 258, 262, 266
Similarity. *See* Resemblance

Sites, 245, 269; absolutely distant, 227; that are elsewhere, 225, 240; of power, 133, 222, 226; of society, 225

Situations, xli, 144, 196, 256, 273; awesome, 189; extreme, 122; particular, 137; political, 197–98

Skepticism, 34, 258

Slavery, 81, 117, 203, 256, 265, 270; ancient, 240; Greek, 39; revolts, 240

Sociability, 83, 153, 199, 218

Social sphere, the, 35, 39–40, 44, 48, 93–97, 99, 104–105, 162, 220, 225, 227–28, 269; constitution of, 259; dissolution of, 88, 239; and the religious, 166, 225. *See also* Institution of the social

Social bond, 20, 22–23, 25, 28, 31–32, 265

Socialism, xl, 85, 244, 253, 257, 263, 267

Social life. *See* Society, social life

Social mobility, 60, 102

Social order, 156, 246, 268; founding law of, 260; and religious order, 224

Social ostracism, 176

Social sciences, 195–96, 202, 215

Social state, 37–38, 41, 43, 46, 106, 139, 155, 253; of Russia, 277

Social war, 86, 87, 90

Society, social life, 20, 35, 38, 40, 42, 47, 49, 56, 58, 61, 63, 92–96, 99–102, 104, 106, 138, 152, 162–64, 192–93, 196–98, 201, 213–22, 230–33, 245, 263, 268, 271–73, 276, 278; affluent, 193; against the State, 209, 215–16, 230; American, 42; aristocratic, 42, 44, 52; Balinese, 212; being of, 243; being-society of, 224; of the boudoir, 74; classless, 144, 180; closed, 211; competitive, 267; democratic, 42, 160, 169, 184, 189, 193, 198, 201, 243, 270; deprived of an ultimate referent, 269; differentiated and conflictual, 266–67; division of, 130; egalitarian, 86; free, egalitarian, 216; French, 86; generative principles of, 49; governed, 230; harmonious, 133, 256; and heterogeneity, 271; and history, 102, 102; and homogeneity, 136, 259, 267; including a State, 216; industrial, 202, 267; learned, 74; liberal, 24; modern, xlii, 43, 88, 267; modern Western, 213; mode of, 211; in movement, 49; "mutilated," 130; nature of, 86; organiza-

tion and history of, 100; outside or above, 93; particular, 181, 193; as political society, 215; present-day, 47, 53; probing of, 94; "progressive," 212; rational, 182, 189; real, 83; religious, 163; secret, 74; shattered, 269; soviet, 254, 267; -space, 155; "stagnant," 212; statist, 218, 227; *sui generis* reality of, 40; as torn, 86; totalitarian, 217, 260; tribal, 192; type of, 42, 190, 215, 225, 239; understanding of, 122; unprecedented type of, 190; well-ordered, 28, 68; western, 31, 261–62, 264, 267; without division, 259–60; without history, 211–12; without norms, 201; without power, 215; without the State, 217, 227; without government, 230; with unsurpassable horizons, 260; world, 193. *See also* Civilization: and civil society; Form: of society; Historical society; "New society"; Political society; Primitive society; Savage: societies

Society against the State (Clastres), 208–9, 216

Sociologism, 39, 227

Sociologists, xl, 35, 195, 236, 245, 269; and sociology, 20, 53, 119, 143, 155, 210, 216, 260, 266

Socrates, 72, 237–38, 243; death sentence of, 173, 178

Soderini, Piero di Tommaso, 114–15, 120

Sodomy, 72, 77, 79

Soldiers, 51, 94, 162, 273; citizen-, 136

Solzhenitsyn, Alexander, 256, 258, 278

Souls, 153, 164, 166, 171n 45, 252; hierarchy within, 122; human, 86; immortality of, 36; softness of, 128

Souvarine, Boris, 264

Sovereigns, 148–49, 152, 155, 157; as immortal, 97

Sovereignty, 104, 145, 148, 155, 194; absolute, 104, 153; de facto, 102; de jure, 94, 100–2; divine, 101–2; of the group, 221; of justice, reason, and law, 98, 107; of number, 98, 104–5; of the people, 21, 38, 86, 98–99, 101, 104–6, 186; placed in the land, 101; seat of, 194; of States, 153, 201; theory of, 147

Soviet Union, 200, 215, 252–59, 261, 263, 267, 273–74, 276–77, 279. *See also* Russia, Russians

Space, 13, 70, 155, 215, 223, 272; and the body, 222; Cartesian, 82; concrete, 212; finite, 156; limited, 21; living, 227, 271; neutral, 262; nonseparate, 222; shared, 269; and time, xlii, 17, 23, 92, 147, 165, 212. *See also* Public space

Spain, 126, 145, 176. *See also* Inquisition

Sparta, Spartans, 111, 128, 130, 135, 178, 218

Spartacus, 240, 244

Specialists, specialization, 1, 187, 202; "without spirit," 183, 185

Spectacles, 12, 18, 24, 28, 51, 70, 113, 116, 163, 165, 209, 240, 250, 254, 273, 278; new, 161; political, 254

Speech, xli, 26, 30–32, 75, 78, 114, 174, 210, 224–25, 243–44, 249–50, 254–55, 258, 260; efficacy of, 254; of the excluded, 27; and hearing, 31, 199; incessant flow of, 69; of an individual, 35; interrogating, 224; mystical, 33; mythic, 225; of the other, 208; prophetic, 228; public, 265; religious, 225; status of, in the USSR, 254; unexpected, 31. *See also* Free inquiry: and free speech

Spengler, Oswald, 191

Spies, 11–12; police-, 85

Spinoza, Benedict de, 172, 196, 200, 244; strategy of, 178

Spirit, 67, 95, 143, 212; democratic, 266

Spirituality, 29, 32, 38, 260; and the material, 97, 99, 155; and the real, 117

Sports, 183–84, 199

Stability, 86, 111, 115, 120, 138, 183, 212

Stalin, Joseph, 139, 259, 263

Stalinism, 1, 139, 256, 259, 264, 278; neo-, 273. *See also* De-Stalinization

State, the, States, 56–58, 80, 109, 148–56, 216–20, 222, 227–30, 245, 255, 265, 270–72, 276; absence of, 230, 233; advent of, 214; ancient and modern, 114; building up of, 227; in conflict, 148; democratic, 23; essence, 217; evolution of, 218; existence of, 217; expansion of, 217, 270; formation of, 217–18; founding of, 128; fusion of, 153; growth of, 49; liberal, 24; modern, 89; monarchical, 217; natural independence of, 154; nature of, 218; neutral, 269; new, 215; particular, 201; socialist, 267; soviet, 259; theocratic, 23; totalitarian, 252–53,

259; transformation of, 218; tutelary, 45, 270; universal, 193; "universal and homogeneous" (Kojève), 180–81, 200–1; universal essence of, 228; will for peace of, 151; world, 201

State of nature, 77, 148, 150, 154–55; exit from, 152

Statesman (Plato), 101

Steady-state, 212

Storie, 110

Strata: dominant, 119, 135, 256

Strauss, Leo, xli–xlii, 111, 114, 121–24, 128, 139, 172–206, 244, 247; argument of, 193; and his attraction to Nietzsche, Machiavelli (and Spinoza), 190, 196; and his critique of historicism, 202; and his critique of modernity, 201; design of, 184; didactic writings of, 179; disciples of, 185, 196; exoteric teaching of, 172, 179–80, 190; language of, 180; method of, 173; political philosophy of, 180; reading method of, 183; and his reading of Machiavelli, 173; sampling process of, 180; silences of, 180; thought of, 178, 184–85, 190, 197

Strayer, Joseph, 147

Structuralism, 211, 213, 224, 227; inadequacies of, 213

Struggles, 119, 157; against dictatorship, 261; against the State, 217, 233; for the State, 233

Studia humanitatis, 118

Subject, the, 26, 27, 44, 138, 142–43, 152, 241; and object, 94, 249

Subjection, 132, 150, 167, 226

Subjects, 20, 62, 63, 96, 104, 109, 129, 133, 155, 219; good, 122; Kantian, 142

Submission, 219, 270, 278; loving, to the prince, 219

Subsistence, 211, 214

Subversion, 27, 67, 178

Suffering, 226, 242, 266

Suffrage: popular, 194; universal, 98, 105–6, 263

Superiority, 189, 192, 267; legitimate, 187; "superior qualities," 95, 98, 106–7

Supernatural, the, 33, 44, 165, 223, 226, 238; socio-, 212

Superstructure and infrastructure, 267

Surface and depth, 96–97

Surprise, 29–30, 40–41, 52, 56, 61, 63, 70, 264

Suspicion, 57, 134, 277

Symbolic, the, 44, 102, 155, 210, 215, 227, 231–33, 245, 254, 263, 270, 278; and symbolic space, 155

Symbolism, 27; Christian, 168; and symbols, 143, 168

Tabula rasa, 46

Tactics and tacticians, 255, 274

"Take advantage of the passage of time," 115, 125

Tasks, xxxix, 53, 57, 70–71, 91, 95, 98, 100, 106, 111, 118, 125, 142, 144, 149, 165, 168, 179, 188, 191, 193–95, 214, 230, 232, 246, 253, 266; "impossible," 243; infinite, 169

Taste: bad, 178; forbidden, 266; uniformity of, 272

Taxation, 59, 61, 94

Teachers, 69, 181–82, 189; true, 182

Teachings, 69, 110, 177, 179, 236, 238, 250; of the Bible, 122–23, 145; of Christianity, 39; classical, 198, 203; of classical political philosophy, 122, 179; of the classics, 68; counter-, 115; exoteric, 172; of history, 151; of Hobbes, 195; of Machiavelli, 121, 124, 195; of Plato, 173; of religion, 123, 173, 237; of the Tradition, 111

Techniques and technology, 122, 173, 198, 213, 225, 253, 264–65, 269–72; development/expansion of, 143, 149, 201

Technocrats, technocracy, 254, 261

Temporal, the, 37, 95, 145, 147, 238

Territory, 157; defense of, 136; extension of, 136

Terror, 15, 139, 221, 252, 256, 260, 265; and foundation, 201; French (1793), 51, 55, 105, 139, 166, 168

Tests, 37, 77, 113, 144, 179, 185, 190, 203, 205n 52, 221, 245; of alterity, 225, 269; of complexity, 126; of the enigma of the institution, 229; of events and tumults, 112; of fortune, 113; of freedom, 189; of the human condition, 226; of instability, 137; of the interminable, 36; of an internal contradiction, 243; of internal division, 48; of the irreversible, 203; of knowledge,

6; of the political, xlix; of principles, 74; of reality, 260; risky, xli; rough, 127; of sense and non-sense, 143; of truth, 273, 279; of uncertainty, 29

Texts, xl, 110, 175, 178, 195; and images, 224; of the law on the body, 221; restoration of, 183

Theocracy, 23

Theology, theologians, 121, 145, 239, 247

Theological-political sphere, the, 96, 202, 240

Theory, theorists, xl–xli, 3, 4, 120, 142, 144, 147, 152, 163, 194–95, 203, 209–10, 218, 226, 229, 246, 259; of eroticism, 82; Marxist, 215; modern, of history, 213; and practice, 69–70, 142. *See also* Doctrine: and theories

Theseus, 126

Thierry, Augustin, 88

Things, 28–29, 272; human and nonhuman, 192; political, 172, 196–97; relationship to, 23; sensitivity to, 265; themselves, xlix, xlii, 49

Thinkable and unthinkable, 39, 67, 203, 224, 253

Thinker(s): of Antiquity, xli; Arab, xlii; classical, 122; early nineteenth-century, 243; of the Enlightenment, 71; heroic, 244; Jewish, xlii; liberal, 94; Michelet as a, 246; new, 163; nineteenth-century French, 246; political, xl, 186; as writers, xl, xlii

Thody, Philip, 2, 4

Thought, thinking, xlix–xl, 2, 12, 17–18, 35–36, 38, 40, 58, 67, 73, 139, 155, 171n 45, 174, 176, 178–79, 203, 208, 224–25, 239, 241, 245–48; and action, 143, 268–69; in actuality, 97; and being, 124; centers of, 263; Christian, 114; of Clastres, 216, 220; and drives, 78; essence of, 244; Florentine, 116; political, of Guizot, 89; heretical, 2; of History, 229; of Hobbes, 179; incorporation of, 82; independent, xlii, 174; of La Boétie, 218–19; liberal, 178; of Machiavelli, 179; modern, 142, 195; modes of, 271; omnipotence of, 134; political, 89, 109; "pure," xl, 248; of Quinet, 242; risk of, 243; of Rushdie, 23, 26; of Sade, 68; seeking itself through writing, 248; sharing of,

Words, 2, 26, 32, 73; abstract, 36; and deeds, 29; "useless," 1

Workers, 86; wool (*ciompi*), 119

Works, 24, 173, 196, 243–48; of Antiquity/the Ancients, xli, 177; call of, 249; classical, 179, 238; of Clastres, 210; individual, xl; of La Boétie, 242; literary, xlix, 24, 29; of Machiavelli, 77, 121, 215, 244–45; of Marx, 245; of Merleau-Ponty, 249; of Michelet, 240; of the past, xlix, 244; philosophical, 179; philosophical-political, 179; political, xlix, 246–47; of political philosophy, 179; premodern, 179; of Quinet, 240; of Rushdie, 23, 25, 29, 32; of Sade, 82; of secularism, 30; "of thought," 245

World, the, 23, 26, 28, 53, 193, 201, 223, 225, 245, 249, 253, 263, 269–70; American, 39; ancient, 39, 109, 113; common, 155; finite, 156; of literature, 246; modern, 28, 37, 42, 215; moral and intellectual, 43; natural, 224; new, 165, 260–62; one, 231; orderly and hierarchized, 262; other, 226–27; present-day, 201; primitive, 213; private, 27; single, 203; social, 94, 224, 227; supernatural, 33; terrestrial, 120; this, 113, 118, 186, 226–27; totalitarian, 253–54; as wrought by science, 197. *See also* New World

World war, 142; First, 191–92, 197; Second, 154, 191, 197

Writers, xl, xlii, 1, 11, 15, 22–23, 26–27, 30–32, 49, 77, 82, 87, 114, 160, 163, 202, 208, 243, 245, 248–50, 269; ancient, 119; classical, 111, 248; French, 244; genuine, 71; great, 1, 15, 175; modern, 36; philosophical, 173, 249; prudent, 178; public, 174; revolutionary, 80; thought of, 245

Writing, xl–xli, 4–5, 23, 35, 71, 82, 110, 124, 145, 178–79; between the lines, 173, 175, 192, 245–48; on the body, 221–24, 226; didactic, 179; exoteric, 179–80; mode of, xlix; for no one, 114; of philosophers, 173; philosophical, 178, 247; and philosophy, 250; polemical, 179; political, 67; and political philosophy, xli; primitive, 224; rage for, 69; revolutionary, 67; of the work, 245

Xenophon, 179, 195

Yeltsin, Boris, 273–74

Young people, 125–26, 174–75, 221, 250

Zinoviev, Alexander, 253, 256

CLAUDE LEFORT, cofounder of the group Socialisme ou
Barbarie, is a retired Director of Studies at the École des
Hautes Études en Sciences Sociales and is currently affiliated
with the Centre de Recherches Politiques Raymond Aron. He
is the author of *La complication. Retour sur le communisme*
(1999); *Écrire: À l'épreuve du politique* (1992); *The Political
Forms of Modern Society: Bureaucracy, Democracy, Totalitarianism* (1986); *Essais sur le politique* (XIXᵉ-XXᵉ *siècles*)
(1986, translated as *Democracy and Political Theory* [1988]);
L'invention démocratique: Les limites de la domination totalitaire
(1981); *Les formes de l'histoire: Essais d'anthropologie politique*
(1978); *"Sur une colonne absente": Écrits autour de Merleau-
Ponty* (1978); *Un Homme en trop: Réflexions sur "L'Archipel du
Goulag"* (1976); *Le travail de l'œuvre. Machiavel* (1972);
Éléments d'une critique de la bureaucratie (1971, 1979); *Mai
1968: La brèche. Premières réflexions sur les événemements* (1968,
1988, with Edgar Marin and Jean-Marc Coudray [Cornelius
Castoriadis]).

DAVID AMES CURTIS is a translator, editor, writer, and citizen
activist who has worked as a multiracial community organizer
in the Carolinas and a feminist union organizer at Yale
University, where he also directed research for Henry Louis
Gates Jr.'s black periodical fiction project. With Gates he
established the authorship of *Our Nig* (1859), the first novel
published by an African American woman. Curtis's own
writings and his translations of Cornelius Castoriadis, Fabio
Ciaramelli, Claude Lefort, Jean-Pierre Vernant, Pierre Vidal-
Naquet and others have appeared in American, European, and
Australian journals and books.

Library of Congress Cataloging-in-Publication Data
Lefort, Claude.
[Ecrire, à l'épreuve du politique. English]
Writing, the political test / Claude Lefort ; translated by
David Ames Curtis.
p.   cm. — (Post-contemporary interventions)
Includes index.
ISBN 0-8223-2484-9 (alk. paper)
ISBN 0-8223-2520-9 (pkb. : alk. paper)
1. Politics and literature.   2. Authors—Political and social views.
3. Authorship—Political aspects.   4. Politics in literature.
I. Title.   II. Series.
PN51.L37513   2000   809'.93358—dc21   99-051699